THEATRES OF STRUGGLE AND
THE END OF APARTHEID

New African Histories

Jean Allman and Allen Isaacman
General Editors

David William Cohen and E. S. Atieno Odhiambo
Risks of Knowledge
Investigations into the Death of the Hon. Minister
John Robert Ouko in Kenya, 1990

Belinda Bozzoli
Theatres of Struggle and the End of Apartheid

THEATRES OF STRUGGLE AND THE END OF APARTHEID

BELINDA BOZZOLI

OHIO UNIVERSITY PRESS
Athens, Ohio

To the memory of my mother and father

© Belinda Bozzoli, 2004

Ohio University Press
Scott Quadrangle
Athens
Ohio 45701
www.ohiou.edu/oupress

First published in the UK by
Edinurgh University Press
as part of the International African
Library Series

Typeset in Plantin
by Koinonia, Bury, and
printed and bound in Great Britain
by The Cromwell Press, Trowbridge, Wilts

Ohio University Press CIP data is available
upon request from the Library of Congress.

ISBN 0-8214-1599-9

CONTENTS

LIST OF TABLES

PREFACE AND ACKNOWLEDGEMENTS

Numerous people have helped and advised me during the long gestation of this book. I would like to thank, first of all, the extraordinary team of lawyers who led the Mayekiso defence – especially Advocate David Soggott, and attorneys Norman Manoim and Amanda Armstrong. Without their meticulous work and their construction of a sociologically and historically sensitive defence case, the story of the Alexandra rebellion would never have been told. I was privileged, also, to have been allowed to interview most of the Mayekiso accused during the course of their trial (and afterwards) and would like to thank them for their openness towards me and for the inspiring example they set. The firm Cheadle, Thompson and Haysom was generous with its time and providing me access to all of their documentation. I would also like to thank attorneys Priscilla Jana and Associates for their help in giving me access to materials relating to the Zwane trial, Advocate Norman Kades for discussing the trial with me, and Ashwell Zwane in particular for his time and memories. Members of the Truth Commission, particularly Hugh Lewin and Faizal Randera, kindly invited me to listen to the Alexandra hearings and they and the other commissioners at work in Alexandra were sources of great insight. The late Mr S. S. Modise helped me to understand more about early Alexandra.

Various sources of funding and time were made available to me through the Oxford-based Ernest Oppenheimer Fund and the University of the Witwatersrand. Lincoln College hosted me for two spells in Oxford, where a great deal of writing was achieved. I would also like to thank the now-vanished Institute for Advanced Social Research at Wits for providing me with writing space and research and intellectual support at my home university.

I obtained research and other assistance from a variety of people, all of whom I thank for their meticulousness and dedication – especially Kate Couzens, Nathaniel Ndala, Celeste Mann, Gareth van Onselen, Jessica van Onselen and Etienne Naude. Many friends and colleagues helped, supported and encouraged me, and gave of their time to comment on parts of this manuscript as it evolved. I would like to thank Charles Crothers and Darlene Miller for their thoughtful views; Colin Murray for the time he has spent on the manuscript; Keith Beavon, Phil Bonner, Jim Campbell, Jacklyn Cock, Tim Couzens, Peter Delius, Leah Gilbert, Deborah James, Tom Lodge,

Patrick Pearson, Deborah Posel, Liz Walker and Eddie Webster for their consistent interest, helpfulness and insight; Gavin Williams for his socio-logical imagination and generosity of spirit; Barbara Trapido for the lodestar of creativity that she provides; and Stanley Trapido for his friendship and intellectual brilliance.

Without the help and inspiration of my immediate and extended family, I could not have written this book. Few of them believed it would ever be finished, but they carried on encouraging me anyway. Gareth, Jessica and Matthew have had to grow into adulthood alongside an often distracted and sometimes absent parent and have each in their own way provided me with love and laughter. My husband, Charles van Onselen – a man of unwavering integrity – has sustained me throughout. This book is dedicated to my parents, whose love and wisdom knew no equal.

'Alexandra' by Wally Serote, in Michael Chapman (ed.), *A Century of South African Poetry* (Johannesburg: Ad Donker, 1981), is reproduced by permission of the publishers.

GLOSSARY

amabunu	whites
Blackjacks	Municipal Police
Boers	whites/Afrikaner whites
bond	row of houses in a yard
Buffel	army vehicle
Casspir	army vehicle
Coloured	of mixed race
comtsotsi	criminal masquerading as a comrade
doek	scarf
donga	ditch
Green Beans	National Police
Hippo	army vehicle
impimpi	informer
Knobkerrie (knopkerrie)	truncheon-like stick
kgotla/lekgotla/makgotla	traditional court
lobola	brideprice
location	segregated black township or rural area
Kabasas/Makabasas	police masquerading as violent activists
makhukhu	corrugated iron shack
matric	highest school-leaving (matriculation) qualification
Mellow Yellow	police car
mrabaraba	traditional game
SAP	South African Police
sjambok	whip
skipper	T-shirt
stand	plot of land
standholder	registered owner of a stand
stokvel	savings society
toyi-toyi	victory or protest dance
tsotsitaal	township patois
Umkhonto we Sizwe (MK)	ANC armed wing

ABBREVIATIONS

AAC	Alexandra Action Committee
ACA	Alexandra Civic Association
AME	African Methodist Episcopal Church
ANC	African National Congress
ARA	Alexandra Residents' Association
ASCO	Alexandra Students' Congress
AWO	Alexandra Women's Organisation
AYCO	Alexandra Youth Congress
AZAPO	Azanian People's Organisation
BCM	Black Consciousness Movement
COSAS	Congress of South African Students
COSATU	Congress of South African Trade Unions
CRIC	Community Resource Information Centre
FOSATU	Federation of South African Trade Unions
IFP	Inkatha Freedom Party
JMC	Joint Management Centre
JODAC	Johannesburg Democratic Action Committee
MAWU	Metal and Allied Workers' Union
MK	Umkhonto we Sizwe
PAC	Pan Africanist Congress
PUTCO	Public Utility Transport Corporation
PWV	Pretoria –Witwatersrand - Vereeniging area
SACC	South African Council of Churches
SACP	South African Communist Party
SADF	South African Defence Force
SAP	South African Police
SOYCO	Soweto Youth Congress
SRC	Students' Representative Council
TRASCO	Transvaal Students' Congress
TRC	Truth and Reconciliation Commission
UDF	United Democratic Front

Plate 1: Aerial photograph of Alexandra Township and the surrounding areas, taken in 1987. Alexandra is the very dense, square area in the middle of the photograph. Within Alexandra the three large hostels appear as white hexagonal figures. Partly surrounding the dense township area is the slightly less dense 'buffer zone' of factories and businesses, while further out are the much more generously laid-out white suburbs.

Source: Sky Eye Ltd, Bryanston, Johannesburg, 1987

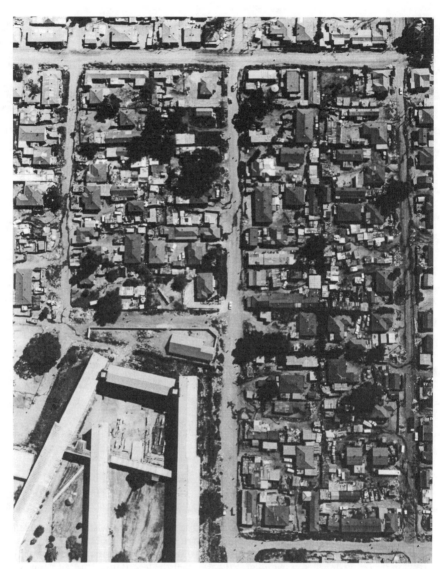

Plate 2: Aerial photograph of a portion of Alexandra Township taken in 1989. The photograph shows the formation of each 'Block' into several 'Yards', and the way in which the 'Yard' system leads to an arrangement of dwellings that is not linear but grouped. Smaller dwellings tend to be clustered around fewer, larger ones. In the lower left of the photograph is part of one of the huge hostels.
Source: Sky Eye Ltd, Bryanston, Johannesburg, 1989

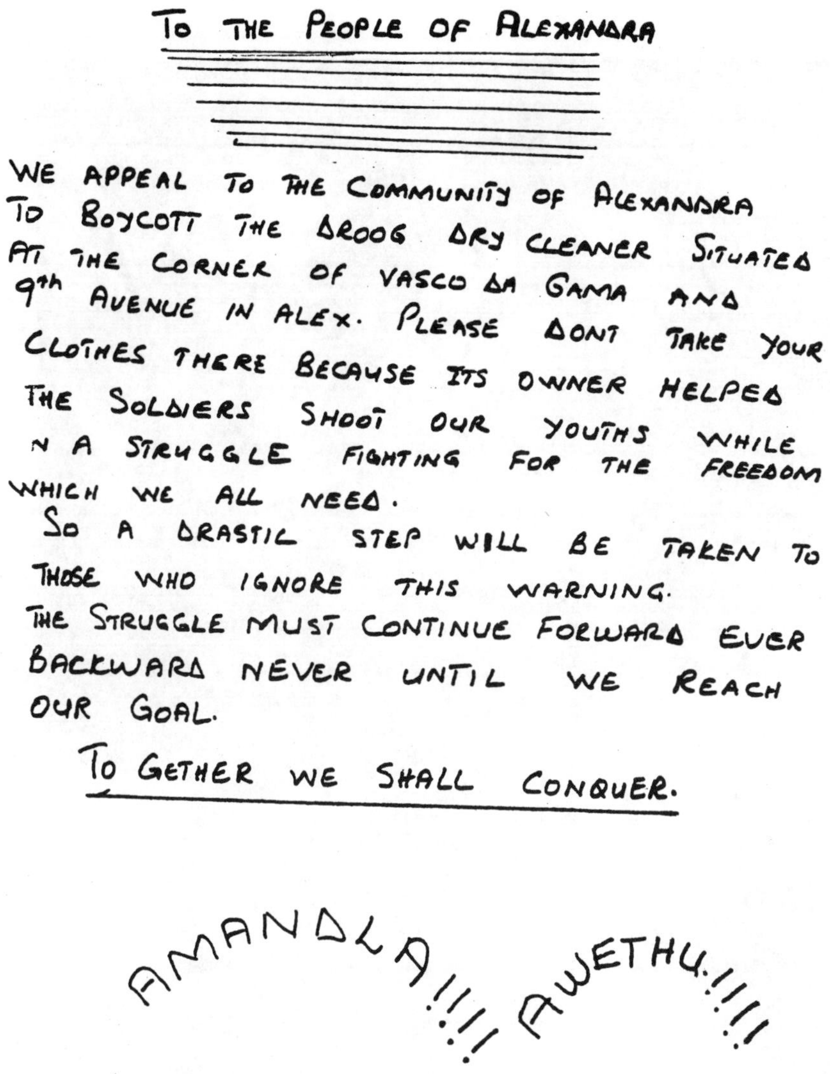

To the People of Alexandra

WE APPEAL TO THE COMMUNITY OF ALEXANDRA
TO BOYCOTT THE DROOG DRY CLEANER SITUATED
AT THE CORNER OF VASCO DA GAMA AND
9th AVENUE IN ALEX. PLEASE DONT TAKE YOUR
CLOTHES THERE BECAUSE ITS OWNER HELPED
THE SOLDIERS SHOOT OUR YOUTHS WHILE
N A STRUGGLE FIGHTING FOR THE FREEDOM
WHICH WE ALL NEED.
SO A DRASTIC STEP WILL BE TAKEN TO
THOSE WHO IGNORE THIS WARNING.
THE STRUGGLE MUST CONTINUE FORWARD EVER
BACKWARD NEVER UNTIL WE REACH
OUR GOAL.

TO GETHER WE SHALL CONQUER.

AMANDLA!!! AWETHU!!!!

Plate 3: Handwritten pamphlet circulated by 'the Comrades' during the Consumer Boycott of 1986, making clear their reasons for the boycotting of this particular business – and threatening those who did not heed the call.
Source: CTH Archives

Plate 4: A 'People's Park', Alexandra, 1986.
Source: University of the Witwatersrand Photographic Archives, photographer unknown

Plate 5: House in 11th Avenue, Alexandra Township, 1986. 'Libya Block' is an example of the re-naming of blocks after revolutionary icons; 'Joe Modise Section' is an example of the division of the township into sections, each controlled by a different Youth Group, and their naming after revolutionary icons – in this case Joe Modise, an ANC leader in exile. Streets were also renamed.

Plate 6: Mass Public Funeral, Alexandra 1986. The poster 'Away with Mothibe and your wife Theresa, we don't need you!' refers to a notorious local policeman and his wife. Theresa was later accused of being an informer and necklaced by a mob.
Source: PJ Archives, collection of photographs used in the Zwane Trial; photographer unknown

1

INTRODUCTION

When there's roll-call of our heroes,
I wonder if my name will be on that roll,
I wonder what it will be like
When we sit with Tambo,
And tell him about the fall of the Boers.
(Youth song of the mid-1980s, quoted in Frederickse 1986: 184)

Alexandra has always been one of the most impoverished of the many black townships in South Africa. It was grossly neglected during the period of 'segregation', which ran from the early years of this century until after the Second World War; and it continued to be 'Nobody's Baby', as it was called by some of its 120,000 despairing inhabitants, for much of the period after the beginnings of apartheid in 1948.[1] First promulgated as a 'non-European' or 'native' 'township' area in 1912, it is located in the north-eastern suburbs of the city of Johannesburg. Not surprisingly it was home to a long and proud tradition of resistance throughout the twentieth century. Prominent leaders of several protest movements had grown up there. Boycotts of the transport provided to those who worked in town, or of schools; squatter movements; resistance against removals; and protest marches, were legion. These were all patterns of collective action found elsewhere in South Africa, but Alexandrans have always – quite rightly, as we shall see – insisted on the special nature of their contribution to the rich heritage of opposition to racism and exploitation. This tradition culminated in a startlingly coherent rebellion against apartheid in 1986, which is the subject of this book.

I lived in Johannesburg during the 1980s and experienced the upheavals of the time. When I first came to look at the Alexandra rebellion of 1986, I was profoundly moved by it. This was a revolt which symbolised the conflict between good and evil. The inhabitants of a small, poverty-stricken, brutalised and racially segregated township had with great courage and considerable imagination rebelled against their dreadful circumstances. But it is the unfortunate fate of South African contemporary history to be considered mainly as a template for measuring morality. When, as a witness for the defence in the 'Mayekiso' treason trial, in which five of the leading figures in the revolt were charged with sedition and treason, I was introduced to the details of the revolt through trial records and discussions with the lawyers who ran the defence case, my stereotyped view of things was soon dented. While the revolt was a compelling morality tale, I found that it had features which went beyond and outside the traditionally binary way of looking at anti-apartheid struggles. Amongst these were the facts that the rebellion was undeniably merciless at times; it involved elements of social creativity which went beyond the idea of 'good versus evil'; it was internally divided; and it concerned itself with the daily lives of township dwellers, rather than simply with opposition to the state. Most strikingly, the rebellion took a spatial and highly theatrical form.

Young people – 'the youth'[2] – not only sustained and led this township revolt; they projected a transformative moral vision which shaped the discourses of the township in general, and which challenged the moral authority of older residents in particular. As we shall see, it was to some extent the geographical space of the township itself that produced a stratum of people with a revolutionary spirit.[3] These revolutionaries developed a strong sense of their own moral righteousness; but this at times slid into a less defensible ethical and moral position, where sometimes vaguely defined ends justified barbarous means. The world of the residents was 'turned upside down'.[4] Ordinary people in Alexandra Township not only came to visualise an alternative world, a Utopia: for a while they actually brought it into being. Their Utopia was not a particularly beautiful one – the kind of idyllic new world dreamed of by middle-class intellectuals (Crossley 2000). Instead it was harsh, even cruel, closer to the Cultural Revolution than the communes of California.

It visualised a future, which was imminent, in which society would be purified. There would, at least some of the youth believed, be no crime, decay or alcohol, no oppression, no suffering. The power of whites would almost miraculously diminish to nothing. There were occasions on which these changes were thought to be coming by a particular day, such as an anniversary of the Soweto revolt on 16 June. In fact by June 1986 the infectiously millenarian spirit had spread to the white community as well, to the point where whites began to build new fences around their children's schools specifically for the coming of 16 June. Many older black township residents too believed that 'it' – the revolution, the overturning of the order – would come on that day.

What happened in Alexandra may also be considered as emblematic, if not rigidly representative, of the broader patterns of urban struggle in South Africa in the eighties. It is at the interface between its typicality and its exceptionalism that the particular case study is at its most revealing of general patterns, and this is how the Alexandra case is treated here. Exploring its extraordinariness allows us to reflect upon its deviations from other revolts and thus throws a comparative light upon the forces and patterns at work in a whole range of local settings. However, conversely, discovering what it had in common with other places reveals the larger processes from whose moulding and shaping force the individual township could not escape.

The wisdom of common sense is not always sufficient to help us explain why, how and when people resist their oppressors. Severe oppression, social dysfunction and poverty were experienced by most South African township-dwellers. But it is not enough to refer to the immutable laws of history (repression must inevitably lead to resistance), to the presence of revolutionary organisations such as the ANC in exile (the vanguard party will inevitably lead the masses to resistance), to simple economic determinism (deprivation must lead to resistance), or to sociological functionalism ('social breakdown' leads to rebelliousness) in seeking to explain the spirit and the rebellions of this period. This is because quite clearly *not* all oppressed, deprived populations in situations of social breakdown rebel, even where revolutionary organisations are present; and *not* all rebellious populations are notably and consistently oppressed, or suffer from economic deprivation and social breakdown.

The problem of explanation could also be turned on its head. If apartheid was so powerful and oppressive, how was it that revolts such as these occurred at all? As one writer has said: 'It is no simple matter to convince timid people that the indignities of everyday life are not written in the stars – that they can be attributed to some agent and that the actions they take collectively can change that condition' (Tarrow 1998: 111). If the African National Congress had been attempting to initiate revolution in South Africa for twenty years, what was it about the 1980s that helped it partly succeed? Other questions are raised if we stop assuming that rebellion in South Africa was a natural or obvious consequence of apartheid. If class and/or race were so clearly the bases for oppression in South Africa, why is it that township revolt was more concerned with the spatial than the racial, with the problem of order rather than that of exploitation? And why is it that such deep cleavages occurred *within* the township population concerning how to bring about a new order?

How and why did relatively small, localised rebellions such as this emerge? Were they simply a result of the revolutionary climate of the time? Or were they a response to the exiled African National Congress's 'call to the nation' to rise up against apartheid, and its many other activities, and to the revolutionary ideas being promulgated by other underground organisations as well? What was the nature and meaning of the utopian visions that emerged? In examining them, can we avoid the romanticism that plagues discussions of South African struggles for liberation?

The comparative study of social movements reveals that resistance to oppression and suffering is by no means predictable and automatic but requires complex and multilayered explanation. Several vital features have been drawn into the explanations offered by the many studies on the subject, some of which are used to gain insight into the Alexandran case. They include the relative strength or weakness of the state; the existence of political opportunities; the availability of movement 'entrepreneurs' and finally the ability of actors to mobilise actual and ideological resources. They also include the notion that movements tend to come in waves or cycles, and are constructed within 'frames' of ideas which identify them both to participants and observers and provide a focus for the mobilisation of identities. Comparative studies identify the 'old social movements', born of the enlightenment, of the discovery of group interests, the spread of literacy and the stark divisions of society that accompany the transition to capitalism, which tend to accompany the rise of modernity. They distinguish them from the 'new social movements', born of the new predominance given to identity, the creation of post-industrialism, and the rise of a new information-based middle class, which have accompanied the emergence of post-modernity. A myriad of different types of movement within these broad, often loose, and contested groupings has been identified, and Africanists have a special interest in nationalism, utopianism, millenarianism, ethnic movements and populism, amongst others.

However in spite of the usefulness of all of these ideas – and most of them are woven into the texture of this study – severe analytical awkwardnesses not catered for in these explanatory frameworks arise from the special situation prevalent in African settings – where what we might think of as *stalled* modernity and *frustrated* capitalism are evident. We cannot simply subsume societies experiencing these processes under the particular analytical umbrella offered by most social movement analysis – and nor can we make African examples 'fit' into pre-defined categories. Where the fit is awkward, as it inevitably will be, African examples of rebellions and movements risk becoming mere 'illustrations' of tendencies elsewhere, exceptions that 'prove the rule', or 'extreme examples'.

Advances in African Studies have been too important for us to allow this to happen. A variety of distinctive social features, all of direct relevance to understanding social movements, is clustered together in societies where modernisation has begun but not ever been completed, where capitalism is present, but distorted or stalled, where states are improperly formed, and where post-modernity has added a new layer of complexity upon already-labyrinthine social relationships. None of these features is on its own unique to African or third world settings. And yet together they provide a context for the rise of collective action which demands a specific analytical response from us.

Here we find states whose chief features are not simply their strength or weakness – although most of them are extremely weak or even non-existent

– but which take paternalistic, patrimonial or clientelist forms, which in turn depend on the peculiar alliances between classes and strata which characterise the third world (Bayart 1993; Bayart et al. 1999). This leads to the emergence of fault-lines in these societies between beneficiaries of these state forms and the less fortunate, who grapple with the partial modernity imposed upon them. Those societies with colonial pasts have been bequeathed forms of rule that use spatial control over their populations in particular vivid ways, predisposing social groups to mobilising spatial replies to their oppression. States, moreover, have their origins in specific forms of conquest and cruelty, rendering struggles over the creation and stability of legitimate and hegemonic ideologies, and over the role of such agencies of legitimacy as the law, particularly passionate. Africans are cast as the 'other', giving them – or at least the middle classes among them – more than the usual incentive to adopt a version of identity politics. Many people barely or recently urbanised, with an incomplete exposure to modernity, retain some incompletely altered or destroyed pre-industrial world views and social habits. They continue partly to inhabit a world in which witchcraft is prevalent; old hierarchies survive, magic has not declined. But these are not just left-overs. They are blended with those aspects of modernity (or sometimes post-modernity – as in the 'identity politics' example) suited to their interests. As a result, their actions in the social arena draw upon a complex mix of repertoires, frames and resources – ranging from witchcraft to the modern media – with many radical differences and effects from those used by contemporary social movements, or even by pre-industrial or early modern movements, in the West.

If the colonial, 'protocolonial', or post-colonial world is not just an 'exception', or an 'extreme example' of tendencies revealed in the literature then does it have its own character in relation to social movements? Can rebellions in the third world be considered simply to be versions of what happened in Europe two centuries ago? At first this seems to be the case. It is authors such as Hobsbawm (1971), Rudé (1959, 1964), E. P. Thompson (1968, 1971) and the historical Tilly (1975) whose work resonates most with African resistance styles. Earlier European movements do provide suggestive comparisons. But not all of the features outlined briefly above are present in pre-nineteenth-century Europe or the US. The participants in the South Africa of the eighties – contemporary uprisings in a third world setting – were not in a straightforward way involved in 'parochial, bifurcated and particular' activities (Tilly 1995, cited in Tarrow 1996). This is how Tilly identifies the older, pre-modern repertoire of contention – which included such events as food riots, charivaris, sacking and tearing down of houses, tax riots and many others – regarding it as 'another world', different from that of the more fully developed modernity and universalism of the movements of the nineteenth century and onwards:

It was *parochial* because most often the interests and interaction involved were concentrated in a single community. It was *bifurcated* because when ordinary people addressed local issues and nearby objects they took impressively direct action to achieve their ends, but when it came to national issues and objects they recurrently addressed their demands to a local patron or authority … [and it] was *particular* because the detailed routines of action varied greatly from group to group, issue to issue, locality to locality. (Tilly 1995: 45)

At first glance such phenomena as the 'necklace', the burning of police homes, the rootedness of township rebellions in popular culture and a moral economy, and many others do indeed appear to resemble those of, say, France in 1780. And indeed the three main features Tilly describes were present to some degree. Ordinary people were indeed involved in direct action and did indeed have patrons to take wider issues further – but here it will be argued that although the parochial and the national appeared bifurcated, nationalism also had roots in the local community which could not be explained away by simple reference to patronage. And while by looking at one small rebellion this study obviously focuses on the particularity of the case, and indeed many particularistic features appear to be present, in fact many of the genres of opposition it used were also widespread. So the revolt does not appear to be clearly pre-modern.

At the same time it is not clearly modern either, or even transitional. The township rebels used methods similar to the emerging nineteenth-century modern European and North American repertoire of boycotting, striking, the use of petitions, urban insurrection, barricades and ultimately the formation of national, and universalistic movements. But it is not clear that the new repertoire was about to transcend or replace the old. The two existed together in a highly creative and volatile mix. Rebellions in the societies with which we are concerned combine a series of features which give them a special character. Pre-modern features are not going to disappear. They will be present in third world movements for a long time to come. There is, in fact, no reason innate in the kinds of social orders which the third world contains, for them to be completely supplanted. And apparently 'modern' features are often only superficially the same as the equivalent features in fully modernised/post-modernised societies. A good example of this would be the nature of the township itself, particularly in the period until the 1980s. While on the one hand it appeared to resemble the 'impacted' and post-industrial American black ghetto, to which the spatially confined 'underclass', with its female-headed households, almost permanent unemployment, absence of proper education and high crime levels, was confined (Lash and Urry 1994: 145ff), on the other its very social and cultural creativity and richness, its extensive moral economy, its surviving particularism and patterns of proto-traditional identity rendered it almost entirely different from these places of despair. The movements emerging from townships – ghettoes and yet not quite ghettoes in the post-industrial sense – displayed a similar combination of elements.

The word 'syncretic' is perhaps closest to providing a description of such movements, just as it has been broadly accepted as an appropriate word for capturing the character of culture in the cities and countryside of Africa (and much of Asia or Latin America). What is a 'syncretic' movement and how does it behave on the ground? The body of this study attempts to answer this question.

SPACE, DRAMA AND REVOLT

There are some settings in which physical space, and the technologies which accompany it, are particularly central to the control of subordinate or distinct populations. Of course the *broad* system of power of rulers is secured because of such factors as the poverty, belief systems and ignorance of the ruled, as well as special configurations of the law, government and economy. But most rulers with a disproportionate amount of power over their subjects – such as those in societies in which dominance is colonial, or racially or ethnically shaped – will *also* use space to assist in controlling them in a highly instrumental fashion (Fanon 1967, 1968, 1970; Cell 1982; Wieworka 1991). Populations are often physically enclosed and controlled, and subjected to obvious and less obvious forms of surveillance; while elites of the dominated group who are also physically close to the subordinate are often used to provide legitimacy and assist in control. Thus space is important, although power cannot be reduced to it. Rather, space is the physical terrain and symbolic expanse over which contestations of power take place.[5] What is the effect of this upon the nature of social movements and collective action in situations of colonial power, or ethnic or racial distinctiveness and separateness?[6] Some analysts question the likelihood of public resistance at all in situations of extreme spatial power (Goffman 1961). To Foucault, for example, the meaning of space in modernised societies is almost entirely to do with its capacity to control us rather than our ability to resist such control. The 'panoptikon' is, in his view, almost unchallengeable (Foucault 1977). Others argue that highly controlled social groups in such settings, while they find it difficult to visualise broad-ranging alternatives, act more informally within private spaces rather than the public domain (Habermas 1989; Genovese 1976; Scott 1976, 1985, 1990; van Onselen 1976; Cohen 1980). On one level this seems common sense. When our daily lives are imbued with spatially structured forms of power, with their obvious physical immovability, and have been for many years, we do not rise to a consciousness of their meaning automatically. We are not *normally* inclined to form *public* rebellions and broad social movements against the spatial technologies which control us, especially when these confine our lives and actions in strict terms. We may define 'normality' in ways which include *private* or 'hidden' transgressions and deviations, small manipulations and little movements, but these do not always and inevitably evolve into larger organised protests. But the 'unthinkable' can be and sometimes is contemplated. 'Enclosed' rebellions do take place. How and why does this happen?

Earlier literatures on working-class communities and/or ghettoes were deeply conscious of the part played by formally or informally enclosed spaces in creating particular and characteristic social and cultural orders (Lockwood 1966; Young and Willmott 1962; Dennis, Henriques and Slaughter 1956; Hunter 1974; Frankenberg 1966; Schlemmer 1968; Gutman 1982; Rossi 1970; Geschwender 1971; Katznelson 1981). These works examined the capacity of physical design to generate networks, which themselves nurtured community solidarity. Those working from the perspective of cultural Marxism built upon these ideas by exploring the layered historical effects of 'experience' in such contexts, and the relationships between spaces and the formation of identity with particular reference to the move from class 'in itself' to class 'for itself' (Thompson 1968; Stedman Jones 1974). There are, they suggested, situations in which this move does not or cannot take place, partly for spatial reasons. Thus to Marx the 'sack of potatoes' which was the peasantry was distinct from the more militant proletariat *partly* by virtue of its relative spatial dispersion (Marx 1963: 124). Workers were 'concentrated in greater masses' within the city and the factory (Marx and Engels 1972: 480) and so their consciousness would be different from those who hardly ever met to form networks, or exchange views and experiences, let alone organise into a coherent mass (Cumbler 1979; Stedman Jones 1974; Bozzoli 1987b). In other contexts those who are controlled exhibit a continual bubbling up of 'informal' but often more private resistance within the spatial realm. In some settings public resistance may become private, and vice versa, when the nature of spatial control itself changes. Stedman Jones demonstrates how the London working class developed different patterns of consciousness when moved from inner city to suburban housing, a change echoed in the substantial work on the French urban poor during the nineteenth century, whose collective identities and capacities for and types of political mobilisation altered with Haussmann's redesign of Paris and a variety of other factors, which had introduced significant changes in their spatial situation (Stedman Jones 1974; Gould 1995; Harvey 1985; Castells 1983). Gould suggests, indeed, that Haussmann's efforts provide a key explanatory factor in considering the different styles taken by the 1848 and 1871 rebellions, because the older Paris bred 'social networks founded on spatial proximity' and these provided 'fertile ground for the emergence of plausible collective identities', while by contrast Haussmann's restructuring of the city meant that social ties were no longer based on joint residence but on diverse interests – a situation in which 'people are likely to see their associates' social networks as distinct from their own' (Gould 1995: 192–4).

By contrast, contemporary social movement theorists tend to avoid giving 'space' a *central* part to play in their explanations of situations where such rebellions do take place and to treat it rather as one factor among many. Nevertheless, features of movement mobilisation such as the development of spatially enabled networks, the operation of localist and centralist politics, the use of spatial technologies and tactics such as barricades, the myriad ways in which crowds occupy, use and manipulate spaces, and the struggles over territory involved in such movements as nationalism, are always present in their discussions (Tarrow 1998; McAdam, McCarthy and Zald 1996; Traugott 1995; Canetti 1962; le Bon 1977).

Thus to many contemporary writers the terrain does matter – not only to the nature of rule, or to the formation of identity, but to the absence, presence and nature of the types of consciousness which facilitate and accompany resistance. The underside of spatial control appears at times to be resistance which, amongst other things, might use space in different ways from those intended, and which is shaped by the identities formed and contextualised within the new spaces thus created. However the significance of spatially shaped resistance cannot be restricted to the matter of identity, or that of networks, formed within, but also limited by, the spatial prescriptions of the ruling group.

Radical geographers and sociologists have produced some of the most insightful work on the relationship between space and community resistance. Some have given detailed attention to the ways in which identity-formation is tied up with spatial meanings (Keith and Pile 1993; Lash and Urry 1994; Fortier 1999) but do not make the leap from identity-formation to resistance. Where this leap is made, as in the work of Pile and Keith, the dualism implicit in these formulations is rejected. The last argue against the idea that 'domination and resistance are locked in some perpetual death dance of control, a dance where domination and resistance hold each other's hands each struggling to master the steps of the dance, each anticipating and mirroring the moves of the other, but neither able to let go' (Pile and Keith 1997: 2). This dualism might limit our grasp of the ambiguities, contingencies, and awkwardnesses of the patterns taken by resistance, which 'needs to be considered in its own terms' and not simply as the 'underside of domination'. Resisters seek areas in which power relations are 'incomplete, fluid, liable to rupture, inconsistent, awkward and ambiguous' so that 'spaces of resistance can be seen as not only partially connected to, but also partially dislocated from, spaces of domination' (Pile and Keith 1997: 15). If space is treated in this more complex manner, it will allow us to understand other aspects of its relationship to resistance – aspects such as the politics of *location* – in which the definition of where one is in the world as well as the grounds on which the struggle is to be fought are created and fought over; the creation and tearing down of *boundaries*; the *movement* through large and small spaces during struggle; and the transformation of space into *territory* (Pile and Keith 1997: 27ff). This is both a refinement of the dualistic approach and also an expansion of our vision of what it might mean to examine resistance in the context of space.

Pile and Keith's refinement and expansion, while it risks leading us to avoid confronting questions of control and domination altogether, is of particular value in discussions of the particularities of apartheid and resistance to it. This is because we tend to take space for granted, or regard it in a dualistic fashion, in this system above all others. The observation that apartheid was a spatially powerful system is not new (Wolpe 1974; Christopher 1994; Mabin 1989, 1991; Robinson 1996; Smith 1992), and is to some extent tautological. Black life in South Africa had, particularly since its establishment as a national entity in 1910, been ruled through political, legal and social means which, in addition to the myriad laws which dispossessed, disenfranchised and dehumanised black South Africans, embraced a 'spatialised' system of control and surveillance. Indeed, both segregation and apartheid represented extreme examples of domination where space was used as an adjunct to power.

A system that defines itself in terms of 'separateness' – segregation, apartness – is bound to have a spatial dimension, and when space and race and even class overlap so closely, as they did under apartheid, and when these overlapping forces add up to create a morally reprehensible and divided system, physical separation seems so overdetermined as to appear to render quite obvious its social effects. The multi-faceted domination that was apartheid must and would lead to resistance against it.

Whether because or in spite of this (a question addressed in the body of this study), the issue of space became extraordinarily central to the nature of the rebellions of the 1980s – and particularly the one in Alexandra – too. Spaces were used to construct public spectacles and events, as well as to develop more private alternative institutions such as 'Youth Groups' and 'people's' courts. Space became a multi-faceted feature of the rebellion. It was a means of control by the authorities, a 'target' for attack by rebels, and also a 'resource' to be used to establish 'alternative' ways of doing things as the rebellion advanced.

The rebels in Alexandra used the spaces available to them by treating them as social and political 'theatres', places within which the varying dramas they sought to mount could be enacted and thus become the means to claiming greater power. This was a vital ingredient of the revolt, which involved not one 'drama' but several. These dramas acted as devices to magnify the revolt and thus to enlarge its claims upon the polity.

Few people have used the notion of 'theatre' to study social movements or collective action. But it is an approach which allows us to move beyond discussions of how and why movements are formed and what their ideological and other resources are (issues which this book does address), into the discussion of the power a movement can acquire in the course of its growth and development. Because 'power is not only what you have but what the enemy thinks you have' (Saul Alinsky, quoted in Benford and Hunt 1992), those involved in collective action have to 'socially construct and communicate their conceptions of power', actually deploy the resources they have mobilised to the end of achieving greater power, inspire their followers to believe and to act, and present their claims to power as legitimate, consistent and viable. Theories of 'dramaturgy' suggest that movements do this through scripting, staging, performing and interpreting their definitions of power as a counter to the dominant ones, and through a myriad of other techniques within each of these broad groupings.

In the Alexandra case the theatricality of the revolt was obvious, ubiquitous and multi-layered (see Goffman 1959; Benford and Hunt 1992). Several different 'theatres' of struggle emerged during the rebellion and subsequent to it. The entire geographical space of the township within which the revolt occurred became a highly theatrical arena, observed by outsiders and insiders. The smaller dramatic spectacles of witch-burnings or necklacings were gruesome tragic performances, some witnessed on international television screens. The more official dramas of large public funerals and their associated marches were the most widely witnessed of all. And the more private but highly theatrical 'people's courts' displayed the drama, and at times the melodrama, of crime and punishment. Memory too was constructed in a proto-theatrical form, through two large and long-running trials and finally, through the Truth and Reconciliation Commission hearings on these events. This study asks how these metaphorical 'theatres' of society worked, whose scripts were followed, who were the players and who the audiences. It suggests that by deploying theatricality, the rebels were able to advance their cause; but that the theatrical form taken by many of the events of the time had significant effects upon popular consciousness and memory as well.

Each so-called 'theatre' provided its own dramatic space, often an enclosed one. But spaces differed from one another in terms of the degree and type of enclosedness they displayed. Enclosedness was both a strength and a weakness for those attempting to use theatricality as a means to moral power. For example the township was enclosed by law, memory, culture and physical boundaries, as well as by the bodily boundaries of racial identification. The stadium – a theatre in all but name anyway – was enclosed tightly by physical boundaries. Both of these bounded theatres of struggle came to be used by the rebels as well as their enemies – the army or police – in contested ways. The people's courts were enclosed by the privacy attached to the home-like places within which they were created, and by the secretiveness surrounding them, as well the militarism of the youths who ran and hence protected them. But the secrecy with which they ran meant that their dramaturgical power was limited, to outsiders at least, although it also made them more greatly feared. The type of audience being played to within each space also varied considerably. Some audiences were mainly the local people; others included outsiders; a third type a combination of both. The chief audience of post-modern social movements, the media and the world to whom their messages are conveyed, were only sporadically present in this rebellion. State control over the media was powerful if uneven. These variations in audience resulted in mixed effects upon the dramaturgical power the rebellion could muster.

The verbal and symbolic script followed in each proto-theatrical performance during the rebellion – a riot, a funeral, a necklacing, a people's court trial – revealed the varying power of signs. This rested in the ways in which old and new genres were used, developed, or mixed together, the processes of 'script-writing' and its relationship to powerful players in the rebellion, the availability of symbolic resources and the effectiveness of the props used to ensure that the space itself acquired symbolic meaning. Appropriate *dramatis personae* evolved in the different arenas. Roles emerged for players, with greater or lesser degrees of power contained in their scripts and capacity to enact what was expected of them. Social mechanisms emerged to secure the proper overall direction of the script and to protect the accompanying means used to ensure what Goffman calls 'dramaturgical loyalty'. 'Backstage' directions could also be discerned, while at times the performances of the movement were disrupted, or in some cases parodied, by 'enemy' infiltrators.[7]

COLLECTIVE ACTION IN A SYNCRETIC CULTURE

This study, therefore, will outline the structural underpinnings of the Alexandra rebellion, showing how they lay in relations of state power, class, generation, space, race, experience and the excluded or 'uncaptured' nature of large areas of township society. It will also examine the forms of mobilisation used in the rebellion, including its use of vividly theatrical and dramatic mechanisms, its highly gendered character, and its network-based, multi-layered, syncretic, generational, spatial, oral and written methods. One of the themes the study will pursue will be to portray some of the resources used by the rebels. These include the spatial configuration in which they found themselves, available white and black intellectuals, oral and written mechanisms, township social systems and popular memory. The study will also set out the most prominent ideological features of the rebellion, identifying three co-existing and usually competing frames of reference: the utopian, the 'rationalist' and the nationalist. It will survey the main cultural features of the rebellion, including the syncretism through which it embraced modernist ideas of, say, trade unionism or lobbying techniques, at the same time as it used older notions of, say, witchcraft, traditional justice, age- or gender-based relationships.

The study will set out to expose the relationships between the rebellion, and broader systems of social power and the state, showing how it occurred under an unstable, weakening and ambiguous state. It also examines the mechanisms of narrative and memory through which rebellions such as this are constituted in the official, public and 'private' minds, looking at the patterning and dramatisation of memory, and the distortions and silences that prevail.

The revolt straddled a broad process of transition – from a failing state whose lack of legitimacy and authority was perhaps its most profound weakness, to a more successful state whose hegemonic ambitions were rapidly being realised. Examining it exposes the ways in which urban revolt in South Africa further weakened state authority in the economically and politically vital cities, drove a wedge between reformers and authoritarians within the state, and between the state and capital, and lent legitimacy and power to the emerging national opposition.

The failures of the modernisation attempted by the racial state and the connected frustrations of capitalist expansion thus underlay and were in turn reinforced by the development of this movement, which exemplifies not only the series of movements of which Alexandra was a key example in the South Africa of the 1980s, but also other movements in third world settings. The movement was above all syncretic; its core character as a generationally divided movement, as well as the range of cultural and political resources it mobilised were drawn from both traditional and modern genres of belief and behaviour.

But it also displayed other features of interest to students of third world movements. The confining of populations of the poor to restricted and socially and politically excluded spaces is not a unique feature of apartheid's racist control of black South Africans – although the form it took there was undoubtedly extreme. The rebellion revealed the kinds of opportunities for mobilisation such confinement unintentionally provides. These lie not only in the physical environment, but also in the very social exclusion which accompanies physical seclusion. The well-developed 'private' world of the township had a wealth of social and cultural resources which not only could be drawn on by those seeking to rebel, but which were extremely difficult for the state to penetrate.

Domination through space in this case did not inevitably lead to spatial resistance. And the form taken by spatial power did not in a simple way determine the form taken by spatial opposition when it did occur. The very fact that two distinct conceptions of 'revolutionary space' emerged – one adult and one youth-based – indicates that a series of specific processes underlay the transformation from spatial power to spatial resistance.

Spatial control is paradoxical. A small, compact, densely populated space may hold the key to social control, but it also has the unintended consequence of permitting many of the ingredients for revolt to develop. These include the presence of social networks and physical landmarks, the sense of social exclusion and physical boundedness, and the development of a certain local knowledge and sedimented memory of space and place which can be turned into a resource. Some spaces encourage these things more than others do.

Spatial control is also political. It is tied up with the historical configuration of systems and ideologies of legitimacy. Legitimation must always take something of a spatial form – government must be physically located somewhere; power needs to be seen; authority needs to be felt. Resistance to political power may and perhaps should take a spatial form.

Some spaces have the capacity to breed crowd-formation and power, and others tend to discourage it. The long wide boulevards of Paris might facilitate control; the rutted and often narrow streets, small alleyways and enclosed yards of Alex do not. But crowds, in order to exert their power, also need *some* spaces that they can occupy *as* crowds – wider streets, squares, stadiums, and churches. Alex possesses these features as well.

Social networks allow spaces to act as resources. If social networks are strong, physical spaces are huddled and close; and the sense of social exclusion and physical boundedness is marked; a lively 'hidden transcript' of meaning evolves which is oppositional in its essence. In these cases, visible 'legitimate' authority becomes vulnerable.

Resistance that operates highly spatially tends to use the technique of inversion. If spaces exist where crowds can form, and in which they can and wish to act, and if this is combined with the presence of some of the more commonly analysed attributes of collective action – a stratum of intellectuals, the presence of a tradition and memory of resistance, some sort of 'crisis' – then the spaces which are used to control the population may become spaces used to attack this control. In these cases, major inversions may take place.

In this case, we explore how inversion takes place in the Alexandra rebellion in an extremely complex dual manner, embracing the inversion of the domination of the state as well as the inversion of domination of adults over the young. This double inversion emerges from the differentiated ways in which social networks were used to organise; the complex manner in which local knowledge came to be turned against outsider ignorance or used, in the case of adults, to evade youths; the transformation of social exclusion and boundedness into a dual sense of internal cohesion and double-sided rejection of the outsider; the competing manners in which physical landmarks came be redefined; the layered mobilisation of the meanings and uses of the spatial marks of poverty – rutted streets, huddled 'yards' – which were difficult for outsiders to control or penetrate. The spaces occupied by 'legitimate' authority became targets, and the boundaries, which rendered this authority so simple to exert, now became the borders over which the authorities were thrust. The purging of state authority created the vacuum within which generational struggles took place. Each type of inversion had its own strengths and weaknesses, and each drew a different reply from those whose power had been usurped.

An important element of the Alexandra revolt, however, is that very little of this was possible without the preceding and decisive shattering of 'normality' – in this case by the brutality of the Six-Day War. However much potential there was for the meaning of 'space' to be reversed, this potential could not be realised in the normal course of events. Fear and retreat are the first responses of 'ordinary people' to attacks on the meaning of their spaces, and a great deal seems to be necessary for these responses to be overcome, if, indeed, they ever are even in extreme cases such as this one. We should not underestimate both the power of hegemony over the identity of those inhabiting a dominated space, and the extraordinary efforts involved in challenging it.

The details of spatial manipulation and attack are important to the capacity of rebels to penetrate hegemony. Staccato violence was used in the Six-Day War – the use of shock, fire, assassination and murder. Time became slow and 'magical'. Private spaces became places to hide, regroup. Public spaces were refigured and reimagined. Familiarity was transformed into fear. The whole township was cast in a utopian light, which entailed a spatial recasting of the contours of power. The space was also brutally exorcised of the resident figures of authority, only to be recolonised by a far more spatially aggressive militarism. Finally, even the state resorted to a vicious retaliation in terms dictated by the reshaped, captured space, in addition to their more predictable militaristic occupation.

The disjointedness between the 'private' world of the township, with its intricate spatial meanings, and the broader public domain proved to be an important underlying feature of the movement, with paradoxical consequences. It strengthened the resources of the rebels but it also weakened their capacity to translate their deeper agendas into a more broadly appealing ideology. Three 'frames' of mobilisation emerged here, displaying unequal levels of social power, with a sharp disjuncture emerging between the more private frames of utopianism and rationalism, and the public frame of nationalism. It was the latter which, through a complex series of processes, finally prevailed. This too is a feature not uncommon in third world settings where nationalism and populism, perhaps with their power to capture on a broader public terrain the syncretism which prevails in the private world, so frequently overshadow other social movements.

THE ARCHITECTURE OF THE BOOK

In order to address the many questions raised here, the book is designed in a threefold manner. First, it takes a roughly narrative form, so that the reader may enter into and grasp the sequence of events of the rebellion as it proceeded. Second, it weaves into the 'story' a panoply of conceptual and interpretive frameworks, so that the nature of the rebellion may be understood in a comparative and theoretical light. Thirdly, the actual design of the book takes a broadly 'cinematic' form. It takes the reader through the narrative of the rebellion. But at the same time it 'zooms in' on it in the first half of the book, moving from a more superficial 'external' view of the township and the rebellion to a depth of intimacy and meaning not sought in the earlier chapters. And it then 'zooms out' from it as the book proceeds towards the end, so that the reader once more withdraws from the very private aspects of the rebellion to the more public and 'external' view. The very heart of the book, the chapter on 'The Private Utopia', takes us right inside the people's courts, the institutions which epitomised the rebellion, and views them from the point of view of those who experienced them.

The book starts with a detailed and multi-layered, and fairly descriptive, depiction of Alexandra ('Alex') itself, and of the beginning of the revolt, and the startling new agendas, styles and repertoires it set in place. Against the background of the changing state, it then explores the evolution of the revolt over the subsequent few months, breaking up the analysis into the relatively distinctive 'frames' within which the rebellion took place – the 'youth utopian', the 'adult democratic' and the 'public nationalist' – exploring the origins and content, the genres and repertoires and the power and the direction of each, and examining the differences in the capacity of each to institutionalise its vision. These 'ideologies of emancipation' – or 'frames' (Tarrow 1998: 20–1), or 'mentalités' (Rudé 1980) – while co-existing and overlapping, are shown to have competed for dominance with consequences both for the course of the rebellion and for its aftermath.

The book then moves to the question of the ending of the rebellion, turning back to re-examine the nature of the state, its capacity for repression over the period of the rebellion and its final crushing of revolt in ways which illustrated both its grasp and its misconception of the 'theatres of rebellion', their power and meaning, and suggesting that this pyrrhic local victory disguised a deeper failure.

Finally, the book examines the issues of narrative and of memory. As already mentioned, within the book great prominence is given to the narrative of the rebellion itself. But that is my narrative! What narratives have the participants and other societal institutions produced? The body of the book discusses and uses academic, autobiographical, legal and finally Truth Commission discussions of the events of the rebellion. The study gives a particular emphasis to the last, the 'official' repository of the public memory of apartheid, and develops an analysis of the way this forum – yet another 'dramaturgical space' – constructed a particular interpretation of the rebellion. It gives attention to the great silences the Truth Commission version contains, examining it in terms of the 'public' and 'private' worlds already established in the study, the three 'frames' within which the rebellion was cast, and the unfortunate ways in which private memories remain sequestered even after their 'public' recall at the Truth Commission's hearing.

A brief conclusion takes the reader to the present, and illustrates that the more things change, the more they stay the same, in the living places of the poor at any rate. Alexandra in post-apartheid South Africa remains a place of violence, crime, dirt, overcrowding, family dysfunction, wayward and disconnected male youth, and even vigilantism. Ambitious new restructuring and development programmes may have been mooted for the township in the new century. But whom will they benefit – and have the courage, wilfulness, creativity, suffering and callousness of the thousands who took part in this increasingly forgotten period been wasted?

During the narrative, thus, the book asks questions of the rebellion informed by the insights of contemporary social movement theory, attempting to reveal the structural underpinnings of the movement and the opportunities for mobilisation presented by the crisis in the state of the 1970s (McAdam, McCarthy and Zald 1996; Tarrow 1998; Aminzade et al. 2001), the forms of mobilisation and resources used, its ideological 'framing'; its main cultural characteristics; the relationships between the rebellion and broader systems of social power and the state as apartheid came to an end; and finally the mechanisms of narrative and memory through which rebellions such as this are constituted.

A NOTE ON METHOD

Theatres of Struggle uses as its chief sources the extremely rich trial records of the Mayekiso and Zwane treason accused.[8] In addition to the normal sources for such events, there were 10,000 pages of trial evidence, from the Mayekiso trial and the other large sedition trial of the period, the Zwane trial, and a further 10,000 pages of supplementary evidence scrupulously collected by lawyers and their researchers including otherwise inaccessible police records, witness statements and other data. These are unusual sources, rich in a particular kind of evidence not usually available to students of collective action and social movements. This was by far the most well-documented revolt of all those of the period. This latter fact has not passed other researchers by.[9] Several studies (again mainly unpublished) have already been made of the events of 1986 in Alexandra, and the trials that followed them.

My own modest involvement in the Mayekiso trial predisposed me towards placing trial records at the very centre of the book, and towards treating them as imperfect but invaluable narratives of the time. To these marvellous records, a tribute to the teams of lawyers who mounted the cases for the defence of the accused, are added press cuttings, police records, detailed records of the Truth Commission hearings on Alexandra, unpublished theses and dissertations and of course secondary sources. Very few interviews are used in this study. Those that were attempted proved unsatisfactory, as by the 1990s the post-liberation teleological myth of the rebellion had come to prevail in the minds of many of those who took part in it, as the section on the Truth Commission shows. I prefer to rely on the stories told at the time, while acknowledging that they, too, are flawed.

The chief claim to methodological novelty here is in the detailed treatment these sources are given. While detail is not in itself a virtue, the poetic, quixotic, noble, passionate, brave, daft, terrifying, angry, bewildered, bewildering, imaginative and stubborn qualities of those who engage in and experience rebellions cannot be understood or conveyed without it. And yet it is not often that we find detail such as this recorded – particularly so soon after, or even during, the event.

To what extent could this trial material be used to examine the actual processes involved in the revolt rather than simply the legal discourses which were constructed in the trials? Of course trials, newspaper records, and police records are as much in need of sceptical reading as are all other forms of source material and no attempt has been made to treat anybody's claims about 'what really happened' as absolute. Apartheid had not ended when the trials took place. Prosecution witnesses' evidence to the trials is used with particular caution, given the brute power which could be exerted over state witnesses at the time; while of course the defendants' stances were often self-justifying and they were silent on crucial issues. Police versions of events combined bewilderment with disingenuousness, while the press, South African to the end, veered between wild optimism and deepest despair. Interviewees in later years proved more selective in their memories than any.

But approximations to the truth can be achieved, especially when there are multiple records of the same event – as is the case in key occurrences during the Six-Day War, the operation of the people's courts, and the vigilante attack, for example; and especially given the wide range of analytical tools at our disposal for deconstructing the evidence we do have, and thus for assisting us to interpret it in more objective ways. Clearly artificially 'constructed' ex post facto versions of these same truths can in fact be recognised for what they are – as was the case with the Truth Commission – and separated out from disingenuous or self-interested or naïve contemporary versions.

Thus, sceptical as social scientists have become about objectivity, to have treated this rebellion *only* as a half-remembered series of constructions, as *only* the composed pattern of a range of discourses, would have been a travesty, and an abrogation of my responsibility to record as well as try to understand the past and hence the present.

The study of collective action tests the capacity of sociology and history, of structure and narrative, of system and agency, to co-exist within single works. The eminent social movement theorist Sidney Tarrow writes of those who document lovingly every detail of the protest they have chosen to study, and contrasts this with the social scientist who is drawn towards the analysis of structure (Tarrow 1998). But sometimes the presentation of detail is born of more than devotion! It may spring from the realisation that the meaning of a particular collective act lies in the very detail. Collective action and social movements are strongly narrative in form. Things happen. They happen in a certain time and place, and in a certain order, all of which are vital to understanding them. They are events, in which detail and sequence are important. And they involve passions and emotions not exposed elsewhere in our social world.

Some of the most perceptive studies of rebellions have been of the sequences of events which constitute them ('event analysis') or of the crowds at their heart (Canetti 1962; Rudé 1959, 1964; LeBon 1977). Experiencing crowd behaviour directly, in all of its (seeming?) irrationality, ferocity and power, as I and most South Africans did during the 1980s, brings this home. The mystery of the formation, explosiveness and attractiveness of the crowd has never quite been explained at a general conceptual level. Social psychologists continue to insist on the importance of the inner psychology of the participant. Others believe in the crowd's essential 'rationality'. But Canetti's more poetic interpretation captures something missing in these views. He sees the crowd as an organic form – almost a living creature in its own right – with its own physics, chemistry and biology. It moves, grows, attacks, kills, spreads, shrinks, sighs, moans and dies. The passionless, theory-driven sociologist is at a loss in the face of this.

The 'view from below' can act as an effective means of revealing these and other hidden truths. To do so it must involve the use of narration, poetry, imagery and metaphor, to convey the meaning, rather than simply the structure, of the event. Thus this study, however much it engages with conceptual questions, is embedded within narrative wherever possible. The thickly layered descriptions used here expose to view what is normally regarded as the 'private' realm – the space inhabited by the poor and oppressed out of sight of the rest of society. By staging a revolt people purposely bring their private world into public view. This hidden world, and its translation into an extraordinary public and theatrical statement, is above all what this book seeks to understand.

2

PLACE, SPACE AND FRAME

> Alexandra was fit only for the green flies in its toilets, the scavenging
> dogs roaming its streets, and the urbanised goats and cattle that
> preferred cheese, yoghurt and meat pie to green grass and fodder.
> (Mogotsi n.d.)

Sometimes the places in which the poor and oppressed live resemble
bounded and prison-like stalags. Nobody approaching Alexandra Township
for the first time could fail to be amazed by its obviously circumscribed
character and its stark imagery of entrapment. Travellers by car turn into
the township from the smart double-highway out of central Johannesburg,
through an industrial estate, past the appallingly conceived 'buffer zone' or
'no-man's land', into a tableau of deprivation and decay. Modernist urban
brightness gives way to a scene coloured in brown and grey. Untarred,
treeless, dusty streets, rutted and undulating, take one past run-down,
rusty-roofed old brick homes, some of them built as early as the 1910s and
20s, which give the impression of being insufficient for the numbers who
need to occupy them. Tin, cardboard and wooden shacks are interspersed
between the houses. The streets in normal times belong to everyone. People
sit in doorways, meander along the streets, congregate on the corners, hawk
fruit and vegetables on what pass for pavements, and pass the time together.
Many are visibly poor. Clothing is ragged. Goats, cows and hens wander the
streets. Dust is not easy to avoid. The collection of rubbish is clearly not part
of life. It blows around. It piles up and stinks, as does raw sewage,
uncollected by any system of piping, and in rainy times, undrained dirty
water and great puddles of mud in the heavily eroded streets. Piles of rubble
mark homes that have been demolished but never rebuilt. Nobody in
Alexandra has their own water supply, and only a handful have any electricity. In 1979, before the rebellion, its approximately 75,000 people lived
upon 358 hectares, in about 4,000 houses, innumerable shacks, some flats
and three 'hostels' – barracks-like single-sex housing. It was, said one
resident of the 1980s, 'a place where pigs would live' (Moses Mayekiso,
M2661).

One of the defining features of the black experience of apartheid was
indeed that of living within the legally, politically and socially restricted

boundaries – the 'bounded space' – of a township just such as Alexandra. A series of combined and overlapping economic, physical, social, political and ideological systems worked together 'from above' as it were, to make these into separate, racial ghettos, defined physically, morally, legally and politically. Each had its own internal sub-systems of spatial organisation and control as well as clear relationships to the city and country around it. Borders around townships excluded black urban-dwellers from white living areas, privatised the life of the poor, separating it from the public sphere, sustained the cheapness of labour, and acted as racial 'sanitisers'.

By enclosing black everyday life within segregated townships such as this one, the authorities intended to confine dissent, and make it invisible to all but those within. Their intention was that these sequestered worlds would turn in upon themselves and that the private realm of the township-dweller would never intrude upon the public realm of the state. Township space, they believed, would not become public theatre. This strategy worked for much of the twentieth century. South African cities could not, by and large, accommodate popular political theatricality of any kind, be it the ritualised theatricality of the state or the more spontaneous political street theatre of the people. There are no equivalents of those great venues for political drama – Tiananmen Square or the Champs Elysées – in the grid-like street design of Johannesburg. Under high apartheid it was anyway virtually impossible for ordinary black citizens to gain access to the few public venues suitable for staging popular events, marches or protests. Even the Cape Town 'Coon Carnival' was confined to a stadium within which its potentially dangerous carnivalesque could be controlled, while the infrequent occasions on which protest marches captured large public spaces, such as the 1956 Anti Pass Campaign march by thousands of women of all races to the Pretoria-based seat of government, the Union Buildings, faded to nothing during the high repression after 1960.

But there are times when rebellious inhabitants seek to transform these stalag-like systems into spaces of their own upon which their meanings are imprinted and whose boundaries become the defiant barricades which keep the authorities out, rather than the symbolic walls which keep the persecuted in. Dramatic social, moral and personal changes have to take place in order for the oppressed to pose fundamental questions about the real and symbolic spatial arrangements within which they live. We need to ask how it is that people think the 'unthinkable'?

In order to do this, we need to explore first the nature of the identities nurtured by the spaces which structured daily life in a place such as Alexandra, the experiences they generated, the ideological 'frames' they gave rise to, and the cultural expectations they encouraged. We must explore the structural underpinnings of spatial power whose weakening must surely precede or accompany any challenges to it. We need to know how authority was actually experienced in the South African context and what contingencies, processes, resources and alliances relevant to collective action were nurtured or discouraged.

EXPERIENCING A BOUNDED SPACE

Within the township, community was felt not only as something 'imagined' (Anderson 1991) or 'symbolically constructed' (A. Cohen 1985), but as something which a much-hated ruling class driven increasingly by a desire to segregate and control had physically constructed. 'They' drew the boundaries that confined the people; 'they' laid out streets within; 'they' designed most houses, flats and hostels; and the physical connections of this huddled community to all the major amenities of life were determined by 'them'. Space was thus both a physical *and* an experiential reality which daily reminded its inhabitants of their subordination (Donham 1993; Wolf 1969).

However, another, less passively reflexive, life was created in the township world. In spite of the enormously restrictive power of the South African state, the experience of living in townships was far from having been shaped by authority alone. Townships were also complex sub-societies in their own right, where residents challenged, worked around, and manipulated the givens of their lives.[1] Entering the township, crossing the boundary, whether as visitor or resident returning, entailed discarding modernity's fancies, adapting one's visual and social discernment, and accepting the logic of the world within. Living in the township meant becoming (or seeking to become) an insider, one who knew the terrain, who could attach memories to places, whose neighbours had been schoolmates, or fellow-churchgoers, or football team-mates; whose aunts and uncles had lived a block or two away; whose grandparents had been buried in the cemetery, whose mother ran the local shebeen in a tin shack, or whose parents had suffered the indignity of having their homes demolished, their liquor stock confiscated or their residence permits demanded at 3 a.m. by the overzealous policeman who may even have lived next door. It meant knowing a great deal, too much, about illness, murder and death; about joblessness and scraping a living; about theft, prison and the venality of petty officials; about wayward and violent men, retributive wives, drunken brawls, decaying schools and just sheer poverty. Although this world was secluded from outside scrutiny, it was a private world without privacy. Most homes were so tiny that living took place on the street, or in the yard's open space, or within earshot of either.

Of course, the township world is generally a widely known feature of South African society. It has been well documented by historians, anthropologists, and other Africanists; by poets, novelists, and playwrights. It is characterised by a variety of patterns of living, in shebeens, schools, gangs, families, sports, and distinctive cultural forms. It has found expression in religion, memory, music, architecture, poetry, literature, social movements and oral traditions. Alexandra Township epitomised – even caricatured – these patterns, combining the notoriety of the crime-ridden slum with the renown of the resilient and resistant community (Mayekiso 1996; Carter 1991a; Pillay 1984; Sarakinsky 1984; Tourikis 1981; Mathabane 1986, Nauright 1998).

However, Alex did have some unusual features of its own, some of which were to prove vital to the formation of identities and consequently to the course taken by the rebellion. Many of these concerned space – its design, its impositions upon residents, and its limits and possibilities. Crucial amongst them was the nature of its system of housing, which was based upon the 'yard': a square space holding one major house, occupied in the old days by the owner of the stand, and several smaller, often one-roomed, dwellings – some of them joined together in a row to make a 'bond'. Far more than one family shared each yard. Thus, while as late as 1979, after home ownership had been severely attacked by the apartheid state, as many as 7 per cent of respondents in a survey of households still said they owned their homes (Lamont et al. n.d.: 20), this did not imply that life in Alexandra was shaped by the individualism that often accompanies home ownership. In many cases nearly all the rooms in the main house and the adjacent 'bonds' would be extensively sublet, so that every room was occupied, often by an entire family. Each yard was so oversubscribed that it became almost a small community on its own. How different this was from the housing in other townships such as Soweto, where rows and rows of identical match-box homes were built separately or in semi-detached form, each with its own tiny bit of land (Morris 1981; Calderwood 1953; Floyd 1951). In Alex, one's address was one's yard, not one's house.

Isaac Mogotsi's semi-autobiographical novel of the early 1960s portrays the room of his aunt Jeannette inside a redbrick 'main' house shared by four families on Ninth Avenue:

> Green grass grew in front of the house, just next to the corrugated iron sheets serving as a fence. To the right there was a pool of dirty water that had formed near the communal tap. ... Several kids were playing in the pool of dirty water, splashing each other in merriment. Their parents, seated on the veranda, watched them playing without any concern.

He was led through:

> There was a large wooden box filled with coal on the veranda in front of Aunt Jeannette's room. The veranda was polished red ....A black doormat showed a hare squatting on its hind legs, a broad smile stretching its lips, its right front leg pointing upwards in the direction of the door. A large inscription read: 'Do not open the door before your knock is answered'. Aunt Jeannette unlocked the door and

showed me into a large room. This was Aunt Jeannette's home, which she shared with a friend ... It was partitioned into two by lace-curtains which were pulled apart, allowing a view of two beds parallel to each other and covered in blue bedspreads. A pillow in a white case was placed on each carefully made bed. There was a large dressing table between the beds. Its mirror had a big crack dividing it into two from top to bottom. A few articles, mostly old looking cosmetics, were placed on the dressing table. There was also a stove, a table and four chairs. The picture was one of rigorous austerity. (Mogotsi n.d.: 20–1)

The experience of living in the yards was one of privation. Most yards would house roughly ten to fifteen families in a marginally greater number of rooms. Nearly sixty per cent of respondents in one 1979 survey of the township said they and their family occupied one room; a further 21 per cent had two rooms. Families averaged nearly six people in size (Lamont et al. n.d.: 9). These ten to fifteen families would share a single washing line, a single tap and three 'buckets', not collected often enough, for sewage. Said one resident, 'At times ... when you go to the toilet you find it is overflowing and you are unable to make use of it. Then people would have to go as far as Jukskei [a river] to relieve themselves' (Moses Mayekiso, M3650). The hated bucket system of sewage collection was extraordinarily primitive, not only in comparison to the rich whites-only suburbs which surrounded Alex, but in comparison to the newer townships of Soweto and elsewhere, in which many Alexandrans' relatives and friends lived. For decades it had been a source of bitterness to residents, as Mogotsi's fictional character Koos, in a scene set in the 1960s, said:

> Uncle Koos reserved his most scathing criticism for the bucket system in operation in Alexandra. Patiently, but with much pain, he told his audience what they already knew: the frustration of having to use a bucket toilet over-flowing with human excrement, of having to squat uncomfortably on the toilet seat in order not to soil one's buttocks. For him the sight of young kids playing games with hardened human excrement was the most powerful indictment of the social conditions of Alexandra. In his opinion, whatever the shortcomings of Soweto, it was definitely an improvement on Alexandra. (Mogotsi n.d.)

Disputes over the meagre resources were common.

Relations within yards were not egalitarian by any means, but shaped by the patronage of the standholder or major tenant over the lesser occupants. Still, this created a more organic set of relations than the individualistic ones encouraged by matchbox housing – and social relations could be less alienated than in the 'matchboxes' because of the shared space of the yard.

Added to this peculiarity of housing (the yard system is discussed further in Chapter 3), was the fact that Alexandra, unusually for black townships in

those drastically segregated times, was located within the suburbs of
Johannesburg, an enclosed black enclave within white suburbia, a Sophiatown that had not been removed. This, plus its comparatively small size, its
relative longevity as a township, and its grid street pattern meant that people
had a strong sense of place and of attachment in Alexandra. The 1979
survey found that over 70 per cent of a random sample of householders had
lived in the township for sixteen years or more – and 42 per cent had been
there for over thirty years. Furthermore family roots and attachments were
deep in the township. Sixty per cent of respondents had a relative who had
lived there for forty years or more, and over 75 per cent had relatives who
were buried in the township – many of them grandparents or parents
(Lamont et al. n.d.: 12–14). Nearly 90 per cent said they would like to live
in Alexandra for the rest of their lives; and when asked what kept them there
the vast majority of them gave as one of their primary reasons the fact that
they loved living there because of its proximity to work, shops and schools,
the low rents, the lack of ethnic divisions, and the availability of public
transport.[2] These factors, they said, partly compensated for the poor housing
and overcrowding, the squalid conditions, the prevalence of crime, the lack
of schools or recreational facilities, maladministration, police harassment
and the prevalence of shebeens – although it was clear that most people
wanted better housing and living conditions.

Alex was home. Its residents knew the streets and even individual yards
by number and location. They could easily name all roads, corners and the
few squares –especially those near to where they lived. Spatial consciousness
was consciousness of district, node and landmark, each of which was given
its own local name, often a nickname drawn from experiences there, as well
as a more official name.[3] While in some respects living there was like living
in the 'classic slum' this was a racial slum and not one defined by class –
indeed, it was a ghetto. The small elite of teachers, town councillors,
policemen, doctors and nurses – proportions are shown in the table below –
lived side by side, in the same yard, house or bond, with the unemployed,
domestic servants, factory workers and beggars. The significance of this
elite is discussed in far more detail in later chapters.

Mean household income was a meagre R568 per month for between five
and six people, in 1984 (Pillay 1984: 21–2). Given this it was unsurprising
that involvement in the informal sector was huge: nearly 30 per cent of
households in 1984 reported members undertaking some work as, for
example, hawkers, hairdressers, dressmakers, herbalists, shebeen operators,
childminders, witchdoctors, tailors, cobblers, painters or golf caddies. Even
children worked as hawkers, newspaper vendors and golf caddies. Some
grew vegetables at home, and others kept their own chickens.

A variety of common spaces – such as squares, a stadium, churches, club
premises and schools – had become, over the years, repositories for

Table 1: Occupation of head and spouse[4]

Occupation	Head of household (20% of whom were women)	Spouse
Housewife	2.4	49.3
Unemployed	5.1	5.4
Not economically active	8.4	1.1
Professional	4.1	4.0
Clerical	4.6	2.5
Skilled labour	37.9	14.0
Unskilled labour	28.6	21.6
Other	8.9	2.2
Total	100	100

collective memories, monuments to common experiences, both everyday and more notable. The stadium, for example, was a soccer ground, a place where in normal times many of the youths, later to become revolutionaries, would play, gather or meet. Over time, residents had built up a moral relationship to the spaces they lived in, moved around, travelled to and from, or stayed within while others travelled away.

Neither work nor markets were located within the township's boundaries. Thus, of significance to residents of this township – and all others – was the nature, experience, ease and cost of its geographical connection – through roads, buses and taxis – to the Johannesburg community within which it was located. Although some jobs were available in factories bordering Alexandra, the draconian labour bureau and other laws under high apartheid meant that residents were often forced to find work many miles away. Therefore, mutual experiences of protests such as bus boycotts held a range of meanings for those encapsulated in this square mile of poverty.

CULTURAL FRAMES

Identities were often constructed through a vibrant syncretism. Creole-like mixtures had emerged in speech, for example. 'It is very seldom that a pure language [or dialect] is still spoken in an urban household ... [and] mixed [street] languages are being used in the home more and more' particularly amongst the younger generation, writes one commentator on township speech patterns (Calteaux 1994: 183). A distinctive black urban vernacular was common, drawing from multiple languages including English and Afrikaans as well as African languages, and operated as a lingua franca. The use of the hybrid language of the streetwise, slick, urbanised and often-criminal young males, *tsotsitaal*, was widespread.[5]

Those who use tsotsi-taal do so with a kind of mocking enjoyment. They do not show respect for Afrikaans, they flood it with vernac,

subvert it with English, load it with words only the speakers understand ... Tsotsi-taal is a warped language. It exists on the frontier
between two groups where language cannot be pure. (*Izwi Lase
Township*, April/May 1983)

Besides this linguistic syncretism, working class youths in Alex displayed
their own multiple sub-cultural forms. 'Ma-Hippies try to "look like middle
class people"', wearing glasses, speaking English 'in the manner of American
blacks', are non-aggressive and 'they don't treat girls roughly', wrote one
observer. Pantsulas by contrast, for example, wore:

trousers that seem deliberately shapeless – I refer to those so-called
voops – which don't fit under the crotch, they are loose around the
waist, so that the belt hangs down as if the buckle were too heavy; then
the trouser legs are rolled up, or they have turn-ups [ashtrays] that flop
over the shoes, and seem to scrape in the dust and get caught under
the heel. (*Izwi Lase Township*, April/May 1983)

Outfits such as these were outrageously expensive, and included the typical
'Christian Dior shirt with sleeves worn too long and his spotlessly clean
takkies with tongues hanging out "like two tired dogs"'. The *Pantsula*
borrowed from the *tsotsi* and from ideas of extravagance and ambition.
Pantsula dance too, was hybrid:

A Pantsula does not only move, he wieties with his body, he produces
visible praises. His dance describes the suede patches on the jersey he
likes, his success with mshozas; describes women looking in the mirror
or hanging clothes on the line. Even if it is capitalists' music, imported
from America ... the Pantsula converts it to his own life's experience.
He makes it ferment in his own bin. (*Izwi Lase Township*, May/June
1983)

It was not only amongst the youth that cultural forms were hybrid. More
generally, township music, churchgoing, dance, marriage patterns and the
arts were all created from elements drawn from a variety of cultural sources.
In spite of later complaints by some that 'cultural imperialism' in the form of
youth clubs and other influences had introduced to Alex 'foreign customs',
such as ballroom dancing, or pseudo-'traditional' dances and plays (*Izwi
Lase Township*, May/June 1983), nothing entered the township without
being given local meaning. This hybridity embraced most but not all who
lived or worked in the township and permitted a sense of 'insider' and
'outsider' to be constructed. (Thus 'Coloureds' were thought of as 'insiders'[6]
but Zulu-speaking hostel dwellers, or Portuguese shop owners, were
'outsiders' – definitions which were to shape future rebellious acts.)

In addition, a variety of genres of non-conformity had attempted to re-
inscribe new meanings upon spaces, or even redesign them. Important to

the rebellion would be the particular memories created by the successive groups of gangsters who, for decades past, had roamed the streets terrorising the population. Gangsterism was a form of popular culture that shaped youth behaviour profoundly. Between the 1940s and 1960s, several effective and territorial gangs worked the township,[7] and indeed Alexandra was notoriously violent from the 1940s onwards. Its locale and geography assisted in this:

> Alexandra is a metropolis of crime ... as an organising centre, recruiting area and clearing house of crime it is probably without rival ... From it radiate roads and paths, some marked on the map and some not, carrying the agents, spoils and instruments of crime to and from regions as far apart as the Cape, Angola and Kenya. Alexandra is the acknowledged headquarters of the dagga traffic and South Africa's safest hiding place for wanted men of African and Eurafrican race. (*Libertas*, August 1942, quoted in Glaser 1990a)

The gangs included the 'vicious and heartless thugs', the 'Spoilers': 'for over five years, the mere mention of that name struck mortal fear into the hearts of the people of Alexandra'. The township was called by some '*slagpaal*' (abattoir) because of its 'brazen show of violence and killings' (*The African Drum*, quoted in Glaser 1990a).

Territoriality – to become a major part of the 1986 rebellion – was part of the modus operandi of these gangs, or *tsotsis*, from an early stage. In 1951 it was said: 'Now they [the "Tsotsies"] are so numerous that they divide locations into slices with a gang in each' (*The African Drum*, quoted in Tourikis 1981: 80ff).

Gangs had their own favourite settings for crimes. 'Every location has its Murder Street', it was said (*The African Drum*, 1951). By 1953, the prevalence of so many gangs in the township had led to sustained gang warfare. Six major gangs emerged – the Spoilers, the Young Americans, the Berlins, the Stone Breakers, the Black Koreans and the Mau-Maus. They proceeded to divide Alexandra into armed camps. At first two such camps existed – the Upper Town, controlled by the Young Americans and Berlins; and the Lower Town, controlled by the Black Koreans. Zones such as these were to emerge under the control of politicised youths in the 1980s.

Protectionism, armed robbery and muggings were only some of the crimes each gang had engaged in. By the late 1950s, residents attempted to counter these depredations by forming a 'Vigilance Committee'. This, however, split into more and less law-abiding sections, with the latter forming a further major gang, the 'Msomis' which ultimately defeated the Spoilers, and came to rule the township with 'their own brand of brutality', calling themselves the 'Kings of Alexandra'. They imposed an extraordinarily organised system of rule, with protection money transformed into 'levies' paid to them by all businesses; and victims of crime given a 'special pass' to prove they had been robbed, and thus exempting them from further attacks.

The origins in vigilantism of the Msomis gave them a bizarrely legalistic and bureaucratic form presaging the 'people's courts' that were to emerge during the rebellion. One Shadrack Matthews, the leader of the gang:

> ... ran the 'Msomi office' in Twelfth Avenue under the thin façade of a rent collection agency; here people came to pay their protection fees, and gang members held their regular meetings, received instructions and weapons and brought back the spoils. (Arnold Benjamin, quoted in Tourikis 1981: 80ff)

This extended to holding their own, highly theatrical, court:

> ... which met in Alexandra and held the power of life and death over the residents. The 'judge' wore a scarlet robe. This 'court' did not hesitate to pronounce sentence of death over its victims. Residents say that when the 'court' met at midnight it was a sign that the death 'sentence' would be pronounced. Death sentences were carried out by a murder squad ... in lesser cases, a fine would be imposed. This had to be paid by the following day – 'or else'. The court acted as a debt collector, taking its rake-off from the money collected. On payment of a couple of guineas, a resident could get the court to 'collect' the money owing to him. (*The World*, quoted in Tourikis 1981: 90)

These forms of gangsterism faded in significance in subsequent years, but were revived with a vengeance in the 1970s:

> During the early 1970s, whilst peri-urban police were in action we saw a lot of the newly born gangsters. To name a few there were the gangs named Dirty Heroes, Young Ones, Mongols, The Hazels, Vale of Tears, 5000 Hellions, Flying Squads, Dead or Alive, Top 7 and many more I cannot name. Many people lost their lives and many women were raped. People used to find dead bodies in the streets.[8]

By the 1980s crime in Alex was rife, but nothing quite so organised remained. However, the patterns of territoriality, violence, vigilantism, youth collective behaviour, bureaucratisation and legalism they set were to be echoed during the revolt.

RESISTANCE, RESOURCES AND REPERTOIRES

The criminals had discovered that one of the ironies of such rigid spatial control of the lives of the poor was that the very enclosedness of the 'ghetto' in fact lent itself to a certain type of spectacular theatricality. The physical 'theatre' of the township had a built-in, highly visible, street-smart and mobile audience for collective acts. While this opportunity for drama was initially seized upon by gangsters, in time protesters of various types used the remarkable venue provided by this township enclave for staging their acts of resistance. In many cases, township resistance took a covert and attitudinal rather than overt and physical form. Nevertheless, genres of overt protest and non-conformity had been well established too – for Alex had not suffered the wrench of total removal affecting other similarly old and rooted communities. Although many thousands of people had been removed from Alex and resettled in Soweto during the 1960s, the township had been reprieved, and lived to resist once more. Traditions of protest and styles of dissension, and all of the networks and memories that sustained them over time, had not been destroyed but had become a patterned part of memory and behaviour. In fact, some of these traditions even survived the removals and were resurrected in those parts of Soweto such as Diepkloof to which Alexandrans had been taken.

The earliest repertoire of resistance in Alexandra (and many other townships) was almost entirely non-violent. It could broadly be character-ised as a type of reformist African nationalism. It was directed towards the alleviation of particular hardships – to do with bus-fares, rents, crime and overcrowding – rather than generalised towards a rejection of the township or the state itself. It could not but be spatial in orientation given the predominance of space as a means of social control throughout the history of the township.

Thus, the squatters who occupied land after the Second World War laid claim to spaces that the state sought to control (Stadler 1979). Bus boycotts focused upon the essential geographical connection between the secluded and excluded space of the township and the wider city which sought to draw upon its labour but refused to embrace its people. The famous Alexandra Bus Boycott of 1957, one of several such protests,[9] had lasted for three months, a time during which nobody took the bus and thousands walked nine miles a day to work and nine miles home again, day in and day out, singing a boycott song, (subsequently banned by the South African Broadcasting Corporation) and shouting slogans such as '*Azikwelwa*' (we will not ride), '*Ha Bongoela*' (we don't drink any more), '*Gein Ukudla*' (keep food for rainy days) and '*Asinamali*' (we have no money) (Lodge 1983: 269). The boycotters in this and several similar episodes who walked miles to and from work rather than give in to price increases trailed along the streets of the suburbs and the city, making visible the spatial realities of segregation and bringing a little of their hidden world to the attention of the 'outside' audience (Lodge 1983; Dikobe 1979). 'For a while,' writes one commentator, 'the black people of Alexandra had become visible to the northern suburbs' (Lodge 1983: 269). This example of street theatre embraced sympathetic whites as well as local Alexandrans, and spilled out of the township into the city itself.

These early acts soon became part of township lore, of the 'sedimented memory' of resistance. As high apartheid made its more brutal assaults upon the township further layers were added – people remember the half-successful resistance to the dramatic bulldozing of hundreds of homes, the removal of tens of thousands of families to Soweto, and the building of the three looming hostels between 1963 and 1979.[10] In the first ten years of this scheme, 65,000 people had been removed from the township to Soweto and other places; 396 houses had been demolished; 2,100 awaited destruction; and 950 remained in residents' hands. Those remaining when the removals slowed and were finally halted as a result of widespread protests, were bereft of a major portion of their community and left with a half-destroyed township, a rubble-strewn space which did not permit them to forget how families had been split. Their homes, in turn, which many of them had owned for decades, were subsequently either demolished over a slow and agonising sixteen year period or appropriated by the state and their owners turned into tenants (Sarakinsky 1984; Jochelson 1988b).

The township's squares – such as 'Number Two Square', in the centre of the township and later called 'Freedom Square' – were places with their own public oppositional meanings, where crowds had gathered in the past in mass meetings of thousands; where *'Nkosi Sikelel' iAfrika'* and other songs with deep oppositional and nationalist meaning had been sung with fervour; and speeches to mobilise support for protests of various sorts had been made by the township's leading, sometimes divided and fractious, politicians. 'No Man's Land', the buffer zone between Alexandra and the rest of the world; 'Don Hall' in Second Avenue, where tenants would meet to discuss their rent problems; the cemetery, where the squatters of 1946 first settled and created a little sub-community with its own social order, songs, leaflets and speeches – these were all places with a history.[11]

Besides the innate theatricality of their inner world, township protestors were often able to mobilise other resources to add to the impact of their acts. For example, the seclusion of the township from the rest of the city meant that it acquired an air of mystery and menace, which bred a second audience outside of Alexandra's moral and physical borders. This consisted mostly of whites caught up in the twistedness of the segregationist strategy many of them advocated. To this audience – which did not include all whites – Alexandra represented the heart of darkness, the unknown, the unclean. Whatever Alex residents did to protest against their adversity, or at least whatever it became known that they did, would be magnified by their fears.

However, another stratum of the white community had a different relationship to the township. Here Alex's spatial location was an advantage. As an enclave within the city, its citizens had always been able to draw upon the resources of white groupings opposed, like Alexandrans, to the government of the day, or moved by the plight of the poor. As we shall see in the next chapter, a wide range of white liberals, communists, social democrats, trade unionists, doctors, intellectuals, religious figures and philanthropists had always been active in township life, many of them in township protest, and some of them in township politics on the ground. They provided numerous resources for resistance, including organisational networks, finance, legal assistance, charity and influence. Not only were they present during bus boycotts, but they often played a role in school protests, squatter movements, anti-removals protests, anti-crime crusades and many others. They had built the only clinic,[12] many of the schools,[13] the stadium and most of the churches. They promoted youth leadership training, football, and other sports. The liberal press reported more frequently upon Alexandra than any other township, although the inner workings of town-ship life remained a mystery to most. Thus some whites within easy range of Alexandra were part of the resources upon which Alexandrans were well placed to draw should they wish to mobilise protest; they had even become a customary feature of township political and cultural life. As we shall see, the weakening of the relationship between these whites and black township inhabitants in this, and all townships, by the extreme segregationism of the Nationalist government after the 1970s had serious political and social consequences.

In sum, spatial arrangements played a vital part in the construction of experience. While the social and cultural order within townships such as this one was not *caused* by the spatial arrangements within them, and did not reflect them in a mechanical way, the chief spatial features characteristic of Alex nurtured some memories, networks and relationships and inhibited others. Whereas to the outsider, the township was simply a hidden, dirty and secluded slum, to the insider it had evolved a moral set of boundaries to accompany or even challenge and manipulate the physical ones. Cultural meanings were attributed to specific parts of that space. The township spaces may have been originally designed as a means of control by the powerful – but they also provided a terrain that over time became imbued with meaning to the powerless. The contours of this meaning were shaped by the decay of the area; the design of yards, housing and streets; its boundaries, its smallness and crowdedness; the role of emptier, common, spaces; the connection between the township and the outside world; or the gaps left by those whose houses had been bulldozed. Good spaces, like sports fields or 'squares' contrasted with bad spaces, like police stations.

In spite of attempts by the apartheid state to impose transience upon the resident urban community, a certain 'settling in' to these spaces had taken place over the years. It was especially the older generation who felt they were the ones who 'belonged', even if this belonging had been won through negotiation within spaces created by others. They had built up a moral relationship to Alex (Lamont et al. n.d.). This generational feature of life in

Alex is one that plays a considerable part in the form taken by the rebellion, as we shall see.

Use was made of the space, the theatre, to apprehend, tolerate or transcend the experience of living in Alexandra. Patterns of protest and deference were imprinted upon people's minds long before any possibility of revolt developed. Spaces and the knowledge, memories and expectations that people carried with them and attached to those spaces were part of the cultural and social capital of township residents. The meanings generated by these ideological, symbolic and experiential referents meant that a sense of attachment emerged. Alexandra came to acquire a romantic meaning to its modest intelligentsia. Serote's well-known poem 'Alexandra', published in the 1970s, captures something of the harshness of, the reluctant acceptance of, and the attribution of romantic and nationalist meaning to this imposed home:

> Were it possible to say,
> Mother, I have seen more beautiful mothers,
> A most loving mother,
> And tell her there I will go,
> Alexandra, I would have long gone from you.
>
> But we have only one mother, none can replace,
> Just as we have no choice to be born,
> We can't choose mothers;
> We fall out of them like we fall out of life to death.
>
> And Alexandra,
> My beginning was knotted to you,
> Just like you knot my destiny.
> You throb in my inside silences
> You are silent in my heartbeat that's loud to me.
> Alexandra often I've cried.
> When I was thirsty my tongue tasted dust,
> Dust burdening your nipples.
> I cry Alexandra when I am thirsty.
> Your breasts ooze the dirty waters of your dongas,
> Waters diluted with the blood of my brothers, your children,
> Who once chose dongas for deathbeds.
> Do you love me Alexandra, or what are you doing to me?
>
> You frighten me, Mama,
> You wear expressions like you would be nasty to me,
> You frighten me, Mama,
> When I lie on your breast to rest, something tells me,
> You are bloody cruel.

Alexandra, hell,
What have you done to me?
I have seen people but I feel like I'm not one,
Alexandra what are you doing to me?
I feel I have sunk to such meekness!
I lie flat while others walk on me to far places.
I have gone from you, many times,
I come back.
Alexandra, I love you;
I know
When all these worlds became funny to me,
I silently waded back to you
And amid the rubble I lay,
Simple and black. (Serote 1981a)

A moral economy of space had developed. What struggles did occur tended to be what one might call 'intra-hegemonic', if one uses the notion of hegemony to refer, not to a static 'thing' but to a 'moving equilibrium' – a situation of subordination which is constantly contested but which ultimately survives.[14] Alexandra had acquired a certain 'veneer' by the 1980s which individual protests had attempted to crack or manipulate. Each protest, instead of destroying or substantially altering the veneer, came to be remembered as part of the 'surface' of memory concerning the township. Space was apprehended through historical experience and the consequent accretion of meaning.

To some extent the township resembled the 'classic' African-American ghetto of the 1950s, which Wacquant describes as having been 'communal'. It was, he says, 'compact, sharply bounded and comprising a full complement of black classes bound together by a unified collective consciousness, a near-complete social division of labour, and broad-based communitarian agencies of mobilization and representation.' He contrasts this with the 'hyper ghetto' of the 1990s:

> whose spatial configuration, institutional and demographic make-up, structural position and function in urban society are quite novel. Ghettoes are no longer autonomous social entities that contain within themselves the principle of their own reproduction and change. (Wacquant 1994)

As in the older ghettoes, Alexandra could establish a folk culture/ideology of its own, was richly endowed with local cultural forms, and had certain resources for its own social reproduction – although these were extremely modest by the standards of American ghettoes of the fifties (Wacquant mentions banks, hotels, movie houses, taverns, ballrooms, shops and so on). However in Alexandra and in most townships, aspects of the 'new ghetto' were also present – such as the 'prevalence of physical danger and the acute sense of insecurity that pervade its streets'; or the 'abandoned buildings, vacant lots strewn with debris and garbage, broken sidewalks, boarded up store front churches and the charred remains of shops'.

3

THE FAILURE OF THE STATE

The government does not have the political will to give black communities enough money and probably even if it wanted to, the present
way that our economy is run would prevent this. Therefore, anyone
who tries to govern a community, no matter how good their intentions, will have serious problems. (Moses Mayekiso, M3049, quoting
from a FOSATU document)

In 1976 a new genre of protest and a new generation of protesters – youths
– emerged and began to challenge the existing repertoires of peaceful
resistance. On 17 June, the day after the watershed Soweto revolt, violence
erupted in Alexandra, led by youths who attacked government buildings,
liquor outlets, buses and cars. The youths were deeply influenced by the
locally evolved, if American-derived, ideas of Black Consciousness which
had emerged under the aegis of a new stratum of black local thinkers and
activists; by the recent rise in trade union action shaped and powerfully
influenced by a new stratum of white intellectuals; and by the recent
independence of Mozambique. They quickly adopted new styles of opposition. They began to treat the township as an entirely separate and enclosed
ghetto, and a dramaturgical space, rather than an umbilically linked
'dormitory' of the city. They erected barricades and attacked policemen.
They attacked schools and rejected their schooling system, the infamous
Bantu Education. The uprising was ruthlessly suppressed. One estimate has
it that thirty-six people died in the township over a ten-week period
(Sarakinsky 1984; Jochelson 1988a).

In subsequent months and years the country simmered, the youth continued to organise themselves, and the government embarked on a reform
strategy designed to pre-empt the revolution they feared. The township
quietened, and by the very early 1980s, it was relatively calm by comparison
with other places. Some said – wrongly as it turned out – that this was because
the removals had got rid of all those with a history and understanding of the
past tradition of resistance.

However, during 1983 to 1985 township protest, here and elsewhere,
began to take on even greater stridency. Indeed, by 1984 it was said that:

The four or five year old playing in the streets of Soweto played games involving the struggle, singing about Mandela, about Tambo, chanting slogans. They were coming up to imitate their brothers and sisters, being politicised by the situation itself. I would ask them – these very young fellows – what is the struggle? And they would say the struggle *ke ntwa*. The struggle is fighting. It is shocking the extent to which children turned into daredevils. Soldier meant only teargas to them, policeman only enemy target [sic]. (Interview with youth leader, Dan Montsisi, cited in Johnson n.d.: 33–4)

The United Democratic Front (UDF), a local and legal front for the ANC, was launched nationwide in 1983 upon the crest of this new wave of township resistance. In Alex, schools, shops, buses and rents were all boycotted at different times and for different periods during 1984 and 1985. Old styles of resistance were blended with the newer, youth-led methods.

New conditions had emerged throughout the land, which facilitated the rise and spread of this new repertoire in many areas, rural as well as urban. During 1984 guerrilla tactics such as petrol bombing, ambushes, road-blocks and underground communication had been extensively used in the Vaal Uprising (Johnson n.d.: 36–7; Murray 1987). School boycotts were legion and a state of emergency was declared in mid-1985 to curb them. The young Mzwanele Mayekiso, arriving in Alex from his rural home during this period – and of whom much more will be heard in the course of this book – felt that the new urban repertoire did not differ fundamentally from the rural types of activism he had already experienced:

Transformation from being a rural student leader to an urban com-munity activist was easy only because of the conditions that existed at both national and local levels at that very time. These include the rent boycotts, detentions, States of Emergency and the like ... it was actually not hard to adapt to these conditions. The experiences organising in the Border and Transkei helped enormously, because of the combina-tion of political independence – which let me assess for myself the situation there, and what role I would play – and organisational discipline. I knew how to operate at levels ranging from belowground, sensitive organising to aboveground polemics against the regime. (Mayekiso n.d., Part Two: 2)

Alexandrans followed national or regional UDF campaigns, and four 'official' protests characterised this period in Alex, all of them boycotts. Schools, shops, buses and rents were all boycotted at different times and for different periods during 1984 and 1985. Old and new styles of resistance were blended when a boycott of buses, started when fares went up in January 1984, lasted for a month, and incorporated the old slogans and songs, mass meetings and pamphlets to mobilise people. As in the older boycotts, women were prominent in supporting the boycott. Nevertheless, the newer, youth-led methods were there as well. Buses were stoned and firebombed. Tensions and deep divisions between youths and adults emerged. Youths boarded buses and shouted at those who were continuing to ride. One survey reported that the majority of adult respondents interviewed felt that the boycott had been forced upon them by these youths (Gobey, Guslandi and Waspe 1984).

Adult participation was higher when a rise in rents announced in March 1984 was followed by a rent boycott which won partial and short-term victories a few weeks later, but which continued sporadically for many months, and which indeed continued in parts of Alexandra for many years to follow. Militant school pupils wanted their representative councils recognised and boycotted schools for this and other reasons in May, August and October of 1984, as well as April and May of 1985. Finally, towards the end of 1985, a consumer boycott was called. Residents were asked to boycott shops deemed undesirable collaborators with apartheid, or with non-black owners. A 'black Christmas' was called as part of a national campaign, co-ordinated by the UDF.

By comparison with later times, this period reflected how powerful the repertoire of non-violence still was as a form of protest in African politics. Decisions were made at relatively orderly meetings or gatherings. Petitions were got up. Leaders were formally requested to act upon the problems of the people. The Alexandra Youth Congress (AYCO), an ANC-influenced force within the township at this time, was emerging as an impressively organised and disciplined movement, particularly given the tendency to indiscipline amongst its young constituency.[1] But two things indicated that it would be the new rather than the old type of protest that would mark this period: the prevalence of the youth as the leaders and shock troops of protest; and the challenges to the non-violent mode by periodic violent but short-lived 'eruptions', almost entirely led by the youth.

In each of the boycotts, thus, the peaceful spilled over into the violent. Buses were stoned, set alight, or petrol bombed; the bus company withdrew its services from the township for large parts of the period. Classrooms were burnt to the ground. Marches and meetings were accompanied by looting and stoning. There were reports of 'enraged crowds', or 'mobs'. Moreover, it was not long before the boycotts came to be ferociously enforced by violent youths impatient with the non-compliance of their elders.

The resort to a more violent repertoire was, when considered over a period of two years, sporadic, although through the month of April 1985 a sustained period of stoning, marching, looting and mass meetings took place, mainly over the issue of schooling, but entering into a new area of protest which was to have considerable significance for the later rebellion. This included attacks on the houses and families of the black, Alex-resident

Town Councillors – Sam Buti, Arthur Magermann and others – who increasingly ineffectually 'governed' the township at the time.

In this manner, youths gradually came to prevail as the leaders of resistance. However, they were not a single group by any means, and the pressures upon them and tensions within them were considerable, as they faced the response of the state and their own elders; and as they split between the 'true comrades' and the more lumpen elements (Carter 1991a; Jochelson 1988a). Responses by the state ranged from formal arrests and charges, through detentions of key youths, house searches, tear-gassing and sjambokking of crowds, to, towards the end of this period, the shooting and killing of activists. However, while the harshness of the police promoted an atmosphere of solidarity within the township, Alexandra's adults were ambivalent about what was happening. While supportive of their children's courage and sympathetic to their suffering, they were not entirely at ease: 'The youth are out of control' said those who complained of being intimidated, in the consumer and bus boycotts, by those young enough to be their own children. In a society where age hierarchies were of great importance, this was of particular concern to older people. Politically sophisticated youths were also worried and began to think of ways in which the explosive energy of the masses of unemployed young people could be channelled. Spatial consciousness provided an answer.

The beginnings of a symbolic and physical possession of the streets by youths entailed a change from passivity to activity in relation to space. As early as 1984, this had taken the form of the renaming of certain streets, and by 1985, the consciousness of space had grown significantly. Youths organised themselves into embryonic 'Youth Groups', which were to provide the seeds of a greater spatial challenge later in the rebellion, each of which had headquarters at a well-known address, and a 'territory' over which to preside. A notion that the 'space' of Alexandra could and should be 'different' from what it was had developed to relatively sophisticated levels.

However, if the 'received' spaces of the township were to acquire different meanings, a change in the moral order established over the years was required. In this case, the potential for a moral overturning lay in the unprecedented assertiveness of the youth over their elders – whether they be parents, teachers, or community leaders. A romantic vision began to emerge. Alexandra would be better, cleaner, less crime-ridden. People would behave better towards one another – particularly the adults, whose ways of living were the subject of harsh implicit criticism. Husbands would no longer stray from or beat up their wives; adults would no longer abandon or harshly discipline their children; drunkenness would be eliminated. A new 'clean-up' campaign sought to clean the streets and redesign the parks. Youths responded with enthusiasm to this project and a range of rather humble 'people's parks' was created, landscaped and named (Moses Mayekiso, M2908).

This was echoed in many other townships during this period, where youths reclaimed waste sites: 'They planted grass and flowerbeds, fashioning "sculptures", benches, fences and goalposts from wrecked cars and township flotsam. Each park was given a name, prominently displayed. "Mandela Park" was the most popular' (Johnson n.d.: 49).

Other names included 'Freedom Park', the most well-known Alexandra park, 'Kissing Park', 'Club Maseru' or even 'Our Park' (Johnson n.d.: 49). One observer saw these as indicators of a new type of emerging consciousness:

> The parks ... were intended to demonstrate to black adults as well as the state that the comrades had a vision of the future and a role in improving township life ... They were an assertion of self (a slogan in one Soweto park read 'People with their own STYLE'). (Johnson n.d.: 49)

The 'anti-crime' campaign – launched in November 1985 – sought to clear Alexandra of criminals by mobilising youths to disarm gangsters. Any possible confusion between 'lumpen' and 'political' youths was to be clarified. Criminal behaviour was not acceptable in the new vision, and the role of youths would be to inculcate new values in those who strayed. The question of discipline and judgement upon criminal behaviour would – like the question of social misbehaviour (husbands straying, wives drinking) – be handled through 'people's courts'.

During this pre-rebellious phase, the vision was never fully realised. The emergence of the 'crowd' in different forms (gangs; youth groupings; processions; funeral gatherings) was important, as were the beginnings of the physical possession of the streets by these new forces, the conscious replacement of the old by the new, and the rejection of state, even in its rather tame local form. These events did eat away at the social fabric of the township, although they did not destroy it. Rather than a place that had been revolutionised, Alex was thought, by the end of 1985, to be a place with 'revolutionary potential' (AAC minutes, 2 February 1986. Exhibit at Mayekiso trial, CTH archives). However, the atmosphere was still extremely tense, and some thought of the township as an 'unexploded bomb' waiting to go off.[2]

Alexandra was awash with organisations and movements. The bitterness of activists had grown with the harsh and sometimes murderous destructiveness of police responses, and critical though older people might have been of what they saw as youth excess, their hatred of the government, state, police and white rule in general had increased. The year 1985 ended with a great sense of an emerging crisis in the township.

What happened in Alexandra after 1976 was echoed everywhere in South African townships from the mid-1970s onwards. Old forms of struggle were being replaced by new ones, in some cases suddenly and in others more gradually. In many places the revolts turned into more institutionalised forms of protest – they became imbricated in civil society. The system of apartheid had been in place since 1948 and segregation more generally was as old as the cities themselves. The suffering of township residents was of long standing. A tradition of the resistance repertoire including styles of boycott and squatter movements mainly under an African nationalist umbrella had already taken root. How do we explain the emergence of new styles of action, new strata of activists, a new propensity to engage with capturing and reshaping civil society, and a new militancy, at this particular time?[3] In order to answer these questions we turn to the state.

GOVERNANCE AND GOVERNABILITY

Unless we know how strong or weak particular systems of authority are at particular times, we are unable to do more than describe the acts of resistance we seek to explain. Because no society can survive for any length of time upon brute force alone, there are always, even in the most undemocratic of systems, cultural, ideological and political threads that bind the ruled to their rulers. Those wishing to resist highly controlling systems such as that which prevailed in South Africa from its inception cannot mobilise large numbers of supporters unless the web of authority, belief and legitimacy that sustains the system can be penetrated (Moore 1978). Can those wishing to resist find weaknesses in the web, and are there gaps within it, which can be entered and widened (Tarrow 1998)?

This chapter now explores the 'webs of authority' which sustained governance over townships in South Africa in the earlier part of the twentieth century; and the complex ways in which those webs were broken as the apartheid state sought to modernise. It suggests that while after 1948 apartheid destroyed, or at least seriously weakened, the old systems of authority set up by segregationists in the preceding thirty-eight years, it signally failed to replace them, thus opening up a range of opportunities for rebellious action.

There were two broadly different institutional types of governance – both based on race – within townships over the eighty years of white rule after the formation of the Union of South Africa. The early township was born of what I have called 'welfare paternalism'; and the later one of what I label 'racial modernism'. An examination of the first type permits us to see why it was that townships in the first part of their existence were relatively 'governable'. What were the moral and ideological, as well as the economic, underpinnings of this 'governability'?

The visionaries of urban racial paternalism first created townships. In this system, the self-appointed guardians of the 'native' in town presided over a complex system of control which created 'buffer' social strata between the rulers and the ruled, and which encouraged the development of patronage systems. A variety of ideologies accompanied this system during its first decades, with serious consequences for the nature of African culture. In Glaser's words, before the 1960s, hierarchical order in the townships was surprisingly efficiently maintained 'through the cultural elements of hegemony'. These included, he suggests:

> adherence to the law (albeit often reluctantly and with striking exceptions in the cases of pass and beer brewing laws); respect for private property; rejection of violence; acceptance of the work ethic; respect for schooling and education; patriarchal family arrangements; respect for elders; prudent living for the future; adherence to religion. (Glaser 1990b: 5, 78; see also Charney 1994)

By definition, a township was a segregated area, designated for residential use by those who were not white.[4] Townships were capitalism's racial dormitories. In a coincidence of racial symbolism and caste-like images of purity, it was sometimes said to be necessary to build such townships because of the dire problems of health and disease caused by inner city slum growth – the 'sanitation syndrome' as it has been called (Swanson 1977). However, it was not always possible for the paternalists of these decades to perfect a segregationist ideal. People of all colours and backgrounds thrust their way into places where they were not supposed to be, creating communities that lacked the racial and ethnic uniformity imposed by the state in later years.

What moral and physical order accompanied the 'governability' of townships in this era? Abstracting from the details of history and using ideal-typical and synchronic analysis, the following major features may be identified (Morris 1981).

The clearly spatial dimension of control and design in the construction of townships is one common feature, as we have already seen in the case of Alexandra. In fact, a variety of spatial forms characterised the era of welfare paternalism, ranging from the early city slum-yards, to the first state-constructed 'locations' – which were larger, segregated, but not always very distant – to the first squatter-built shantytowns, to the beginnings of the modern 'model township'.

These spatial forms evolved – partly by design – in ways to suit paternalism. The early slum-yards were soon cleared – they were spatially too complex to control, consisting of crowded homes and rooms arranged around a central yard; they developed a range of family forms as well as sub-cultures which were unattractive to the white middle classes; they presented 'health' problems; and they were too near white areas. They were also racially mixed, and presented few possibilities for systematic administration (Koch 1983; Hellman 1948). When the first planned 'locations' were declared, by contrast, these were spatially more organised, further from town, and well

ordered in ways that permitted both administration and control.[5] The locations were designed to accommodate, and perhaps create, more 'ordered'
nuclear families housed in separate houses, set out in logical fashion along
straight or gently curving streets.[6] The typical location was provided with
the minimum necessities of a social and cultural life. A Panoptikon-like
system of control was set up, with:

> a large square in the middle of the location at the meeting point of all
> roads which cut across the location diagonally. This square com-
> manded a view of the location in all directions from which location
> officials could survey the entire area. (Sapire 1988: 86)

In addition, locations often had watch posts outside to control entry and
exit. Later, many locations were actually fenced (Sapire 1988: 129).

As the thrusting and inexorable logic of urbanisation continued to
undermine the state's Canute-like efforts, location life again lost its order-
liness. Tenants and sub-tenants crowded into these areas. Shanties emerged,
clustered in squatter settlements. These were unruly and ungovernable,
with distinctive social movements attached, and were not readily tolerated.
However, most squatters in the 1940s – the first period of mass urbanisation
– began to be rehoused in 'orderly' fashion soon after the Second World
War (French 1983; Bonner 1985; Stadler 1979). At the same time newer
township forms, much further from the cities, much more 'scientifically'
planned, and much bigger, were built to replace the locations. At the height
of 'racial modernism', complete and drastic urban segregation was achieved
in most areas. These architectural and spatial decisions ensured that control
could be exerted, and that black life would remain isolated.

A small number of townships developed along slightly different lines
from those described above. Alexandra's yard system, which has already
been sketched out from an experiential point of view, was one of these
exceptions. Yards were originally the relatively generously sized stands
allocated with the development of an urban landholding elite in mind.
Although the view that Africans could own land in town eventually gave way
to the idea that no Africans should be permitted so great a stake in the city
– so that the later 'locations' were all based upon rentals – the presence and
persistence of a stratum of landholding urban-dwellers should not be
ignored. Famous freehold townships included, besides Alexandra itself, the
even better known township of Sophiatown. In Alexandra, a standholding
elite emerged soon after the township was established in 1912.[7] However
not every standholder started well.

Many of those who came to town did so from a position of weakness (the
removal of landholding rights in the rural areas because of the 1913 Land
Act) (Sapire 1988: 16ff) rather than strength. Stands were cheap, though,
and some quite modestly paid urban workers managed to buy them in the

first decades of the century (Bozzoli 1991). But even standholders with lowlier origins became, by the very fact of their having bought stands, part of a new urban elite, separate from those who flooded into the cities in later years when no more land was available for Africans to purchase.

Standholders in Alex soon came to believe they had a genuine stake in the city:

> Since 1912, the inhabitants of Alexandra Township have been invest-ing their meagre and hard-earned wages in this Township because they believed that at last they had secured a home from which no White man should drive them away. (Alexandra Standholders' Committee, quoted in Tourikis 1981: 9)

wrote the standholders' own organisation in 1916. This belief was to sur-vive, sometimes tenuously, for several decades.

However, all locations, as mini-societies in their own right, boasted a small elite – whether or not they had standholding rights (Sapire 1988: 16ff). These were the people with better jobs and a better education than most. Basil Davidson observed in the early 1950s that 'many interesting people' lived in Alexandra, including schoolmasters, students, writers, painters, ANC members, and potential leaders (Davidson 1952). There were also hundreds of small businessmen and women, including the better-off and more entrepreneurial shebeen owners, shopkeepers,[8] bus-fleet owners, taxi or taxi-fleet owners, professionals such as doctors, lawyers and teachers, and sportsmen. The elite included a handful of even more substantial entrepreneurs who had accumulated several shops, stands and/ or houses and lived off rents paid to them by poorer residents, or shebeen owners who as early as the 1950s bought their husbands large American cars and gave their children a good education (Tourikis 1981: 27, quoting *African Drum* Magazine in 1952).

'Respectability' was the defining ethos of those who had obtained the elite status that increasingly divided them from the mass of poorer workers, tenants (whose landlords they often were) and the unemployed. Some saw themselves as a sort of urban aristocracy – a 'civilised', 'educated', 'respect-able' (Sapire 1988: 133) group of people, who lived within a cultural world which included active church membership and a strong belief in education, as well as a profound commitment to upholding law and order in the face of burgeoning criminal activities.[9] Belonging to choirs, playing tennis, holding tea parties; and organising charitable activities were common cultural patterns (Sapire 1988; Bunche, in Edgar 1992). The elite sought home ownership and participation in local government. Some of them were a sort of super-elite – they were 'the names', the 'very cream of the elite'. 'As in the case of any old aristocracy, these few did not need to show their status, for people knew their names' (Brandel-Syrier 1971: 19).

Because the elite had a stake in the city, they provided a moral, economic and political basis for the paternalistic order of the time.[10] Their good mission education, for example, provided them with cultural resources that they used to effect. However, the elite was bound up with the other location dwellers in numerous ways. Standholders depended upon and nurtured their kin; they cultivated their own capacity as city patrons by offering to their siblings, cousins, children and home folk access to living space and to important networks. They became an ethnic as well as an urban elite. Furthermore, in many townships they began before long to become land-lords in a more directly commercial sense, subletting tiny portions of their already small plots to newly-arrived migrants who were not all kin. As urbanisation accelerated over the years, land shortages drove up the price of stands in Alexandra and standholders rapidly built rows of rooms on their land, letting each tiny room to a whole family. The stand became the 'yard', and the standholder became the landlord and the patron to dozens of poor newcomers to town. Standholders therefore provided an economic, social and cultural route deep into the community.

A further feature of this pre-apartheid era was the way in which govern-ment itself perceived and constructed its role in the 'locations'. The system of township administration itself was paternalistic rather than strictly bureaucratic. In Soweto, each sub-township had its own Superintendent as well as one or more Assistant Superintendents – all white state or municipal appointees. Administrators were expected to steep themselves in the town-ship and, according to one memoir, govern by 'exception' rather than by strict reference to the rules, a system the writer calls 'English' by contrast to the 'Afrikaans' system of hierarchical rule-dependence (Grinaker 1986) – although whether he is referring to alleged administrative flexibility, or straight corruption,[11] is unclear. In Brakpan, township administration was hands-on: 'The location superintendent's house was constructed within the location grounds, amidst a cluster of location offices in order to facilitate close contact between this official and the location inhabitants' (Sapire 1988: 86). Such closeness of government, which embraced a consideration of the 'arts' of government, was commonplace.[12]

This system was well meshed with the established standholding and/or cultural elite, whose systems of patronage lent stability – and sometimes a weak form of legitimacy – to township governance. In some cases, township administrators were wise enough to keep their connections with stand-holders well oiled and to the economic and social elite was added a small, but equally significant, political elite. This meshing occurred mainly through the establishment of Advisory Boards, which would 'divert ... petty bourgeois political frustrations into safer channels' and provide for 'some development in the art of self-government' (Sapire 1988: 26). Advisory Boards were composed of black people, whose overt function was no more than their name suggested. However, their latent function was similar to that of the standholders. They acted as patrons, held networks together, and dispensed favours.

Alongside the system of administration went, in many places, a whole range of formal and informal arrangements between township residents and institutions, on the one hand, and white liberal individuals and institutions on the other.[13] Liberals – the middle- and upper middle-class descendants of a long tradition of attempting to mediate harsh colonial relationships – acted as patrons, intermediaries, dispensers of charity, and facilitators of a whole range of cultural and social institutions. Liberals were active in matters of health,[14] child care (Haggie 1994), legal aid, education, sport, music, charity, social work, and many others (Cobley 1997; Jeffrey 1991; Badenhorst and Rogerson 1986; Couzens 1983; Kramer n.d.; Manoim 1983). Through philanthropy here, as elsewhere in early capitalism, the formation of important social institutions was 'policed' (Donzelot 1979). Liberals displayed an increasing awareness over time of the pitfalls of paternalism. Ralph Bunche, in his travels through the South Africa of this period recounts a hilarious interview with a Dr Sachs, who believed that what he thought of as unacceptable paternalism was complemented by a deeply rooted African maternalism – for he held that unregulated breast feeding made 'the native' believe that the government should be benevolent (Edgar 1992: 186).

The effects of liberal initiatives upon the construction of township life were complex. Numerous social and cultural institutions were established which undoubtedly improved the quality of life of many township residents.[15] Many interventions were motivated by a concern for the very poor rather than the upper stratum. But a good number of their interventions did help to institutionalise paternalism by boosting the patronage networks which both the systems of standholding and those of Advisory Boards had already created – helping to nurture the development of 'big men' such as those in the fields of soccer, boxing and music, for example.[16]

Alexandra was an unusual township because of its non-adoption by a local white municipality such as Johannesburg, and therefore its status as 'Nobody's Baby'.[17] However, it, too, experienced a form of paternalism. For the first years of its existence it was more or less under the patronage of Lilian Mary Campbell, who would dispense land and headed the 'Health Committee' which ran the place (the very name a manifestation of the connection between townships and disease in the mind of the time) comprising eminent, and often liberal and left-wing, whites and elite blacks. The township's modest elite played an administrative, cultural and even political role, which from the early days of the township was significant. As early as 1921 the grossly under-funded Alexandra Health Committee consisted of eight black and coloured representatives, elected by the standholders of the township, and three appointed whites, although this surprisingly democratic system was later abandoned and all members were government appointed – with reduced numbers of blacks and coloureds – in subsequent years (Modise 1996).

In the networks established in the township between the black elite (including such figures as Jesse Mahabuke Makhothe, Walter Tshabalala, Jeremiah Mrupe, S. S. Modise, A. B. Xuma, Dan Gumede, and many others), white liberals and communists (such as J. D. Rheinallt Jones, O. D. Schreiner, A. Lynn Saffery, Ruth Hayman, Bram Fischer and A. T. Hoernle), and township residents, a number of voluntary associations were formed. Health, childcare, sport, youth, music and many other spheres, all generated clubs and societies, each with its own bureaucratic habits and status symbols. Liberal connections through charity operated as well.

In this and other locations, the role of the church was complex and crucial. Not only did mission education create and reproduce the elite, church culture, schooling and ideology provided a core around which the 'respectables' constructed their worlds and the poor defined their varying degrees of acceptance of, or resentment against, their poverty.[18] Most schools in Alexandra had their origins in mission efforts. Methodists, Anglicans, Catholics, Zionists, Presbyterians, Dutch Reformed, Swiss Mission, Reformed Jews, the Church of Assemblies of God and Lutherans had between them built the most famous (and later, after they had been taken over by the Nationalist government, notorious) schools in the township (Ramagaga 1988).

Compared with later times, the bureaucratic imposition upon township residents during the segregationist period was not overwhelming and in many cases the reception of bureaucracy by inhabitants was not hostile, a symptom, perhaps, of the presence of patron–client networks which provided a way through it. The leviathan had not yet been born. The pass laws were in place, but they could always be fiddled, and members of the elite made sure they themselves were, whether formally or informally, treated leniently.[19]

However, paternalism was not the only feature of governance in this period. It was accompanied by an element of welfarism that ensured that the township poor could survive – if only just. In townships where the responsibility for housing was taken on by the white-run city councils, government provided finance through the provision of a subsidy from central city councils; through providing beer-halls whose entire profit was channelled into township costs; and later through the operation of a levy on employers. Rents were thus kept stable and low; and facilities of a basic sort were available. This system specifically excluded 'freehold' townships such as Alexandra and Sophiatown, however – these tended to be far more dependent upon landlord–tenant systems of patronage, and liberal-elite networks.

However, on the broader scale, the importance of the modest welfarism that prevailed in most townships should not be underestimated. Townships were at the heart of one of the major contradictions in the South African social order of the time – the contradiction between the need to keep wages low, and the need to make sure the costs of sustaining and ensuring the future of the working class, called by some the 'reproduction costs', were covered. The early literature on this subject suggested that the state sought to resolve this contradiction through the system of keeping the Reserves as places where the old, sick and unemployed remained, reducing the costs of 'reproducing' a single worker in the city to a bare minimum (Wolpe 1974). But others soon pointed to the fact that this displacement of reproduction costs only took place for some – every government in South Africa has had to accept and confront the reality of an urban working class in its full sense of the term (Hindson 1987). The question then became – how could this low-paid working class survive in town? The answer of paternalistic welfarism was: through cross-subsidisation. The answer of the freehold townships was through rental and client relationships with landlords and liberal institutions. The later answer of the Nationalists was, in both cases, to be entirely different.

What classes or strata, besides the already-mentioned elite, were embodied and generated by the paternalistic era? Some have identified clear additional strata. Most important of these was the 'respectable working class'. Isaac Mogotsi's fictional grandmother could have been one of these: 'A workaholic, she was quick to stress that loyalty to whatever work God deemed fit for you should be the paramount principle of life' (Mogotsi n.d.). Contrasted with this worthy stratum were the 'unemployed' and even the 'lumpenproletariat' (Tourikis 1981). But in spite of the presence of identifiable social and economic groupings within townships, other social and economic forces – such as age, networks, ethnic contacts, patronage and rapid mobility – always softened what stratification did exist. Classes were always reconstructed in syncretic ways that embraced rural social identities as well as newer urban ones. Thus township life until the 1940s – especially in townships without landowning rights – was not stratified in any rigid sense. And where land could be owned, the standholding elite's networks of patronage rendered cultural and community bonds quite strong; while the very poor coming into the township were often drawn into local networks, so that stratification was masked by a 'web of authority'. In patterns reminiscent of those characterising the English working class of the late nineteenth century, modernist and Christian values were uppermost in many situations – families were constructed and sustained in difficult economic circumstances; parents wished their children to be schooled; sought respectability through the kinds of jobs and homes they created; and aspired to social and economic mobility. Independent women held homes together through liquor brewing and washing but were driven by strong visions of their own capacity to bind communities together (Bozzoli 1991). These 'softened' stratifications were still of vital importance to the governance of the system and the National Party was later to destroy them at considerable cost.

The politics of this period reflected these features of class, status and governance. Politics tended to be associational and bureaucratised (Tourikis 1981), with clearly defined roles for elite leaders, and sometimes an embracing of the paternalistic idea that associations amongst blacks could and would lead to 'communication' with the state. The politics of influence prevailed. The upper strata had little or no capacity to 'represent' those at the lower levels (Sapire 1988: 181ff) – you do not represent those who are your clients. The political language of the time more often took the form of constructing pleas, rather than making demands, for example. The strength of the early and relatively moderate forms of Nationalism in this period was a corollary of the strength of the evolving family and community structures in townships.

Paternalism constructed its own version of black citizenship. While no blacks were full citizens, the elite saw themselves as potential or actual citizens. They associated home ownership with citizenship;[20] they were not 'foreigners'; they had some land rights; they were accorded some dignity; and they had an acknowledged political role to play. Because their connections with their own co-residents were based so clearly upon patronage, these attributes of citizenship played an important part in the township as a whole, distinguishing the conception of citizenship in this period from that to be constructed under apartheid.

The townships of the time did generate a variety of sub-cultural forms. To observers of the time youth sub-cultures – mild by today's standards – seemed dangerously alternative (Hellman 1940; Glaser 1994). Gangsterism, gambling, alcoholism, truancy, crime, were all thought of as threatening to the social fabric. New restrictions on visitors and residents were introduced in the thirties to attempt to curb the 'moral degeneration' of locations (Sapire 1988: 131); but perceptions of the threat reflected more upon the relatively intact nature of the 'social fabric' than upon the capacity of sub-cultures to erode it. The 'surface of normality' which characterised Alexandran life was present in most townships. A feature of the period is the presence of a sense of the law – to many, a respected and often used system to protect rights and enforce the performance of duties. In Brakpan, the 'Location Vigilance Association', for example, was an organisation of the township's elite, which 'systematically challenged the validity of (location) regulations in the courts' (Sapire 1988: 121, 135). Perhaps this was linked to the relatively strong ideas of morality amongst the population, as well as to the perceived manageability of the bureaucracy.

The paternalistic order gave rise to a range of types of identity around which relationships of power and authority were built, including that of the elite, the elders, the school-goers, the 'respectables', the standholders, 'law abiding natives' (Sapire 1988: 135), 'big' men, and independent women. It may be that Africans derived their ideas from rural racial ideologies in which whites continued to be conceptualised as a differentiated rather than a single category (Bozzoli 1991) – there were Afrikaners, Jews, English-speakers and 'friends of the native' – and that this complexity could have at times alleviated the harshness of the objectively racial nature of the state, by comparison, at least, with the racial monoliths of later years.

It may therefore not be surprising that ideologies of resistance in this period frequently did not reject liberalism but sought to modify it, to remove its more paternalistic elements; to 'modernise' it or redefine it, or soften it if it became too harsh.[21] Here, the rise of the 'stay-away' is an interesting development upon the use of the bus-boycott, as it no longer simply attacks the umbilical cord between town and township, it raises ramparts around the township itself, a presage of the even more closed forms of protest of later years (Sapire 1987, 1988). The kinds of uprisings in which the entire moral order was questioned, reversed, destroyed, were not generally a feature of this period. Instead, paternalism provided a way of coping with poverty that simultaneously addressed the issue and reinforced the position of the elite. In many cases of protest the elite itself, even when relatively distanced from its poorer co-residents, would eventually respond to popular militancy and channel it in non-destructive directions.

This portrayal of a system that was governable – in which forms of hegemony actually existed – needs some qualification. In the late 1930s and the 1940s, urbanisation increased so rapidly that it called into question the stability of township life. Huge numbers of 'squatters' flooded the towns, and the 'amarespectables' – those who prided themselves on their urban sophistication – made sure they distanced themselves from those with less money, less status, fewer contacts and less class. Squatter camps emerged where, much like today, populist and syncretic ideologies prevailed over the more clearly Nationalist and urban ideas of the older strata. Gang and criminal sub-cultures took on a more threatening form, and something akin to class warfare was waged in the townships of the time. It was the presence of the squatters, in part, that created the conditions for the National Party victory in 1948. Until that happened the paternalists were forced to seek ways of accepting the squatters into the urban order.

PATERNALISM UNDER SIEGE

The change of government in 1948 ushered in an era of twenty to twenty-five years during which welfare paternalism was modified and made harsher, but not completely eradicated. These were years of highly uneven, complex and often multi-layered change, and of tensions between central and local governance. The beginnings of Nationalist 'ultra modernisation' were to be found in this period – but such was the complexity of the ambitions and capacities of the National Party that true 'racial modernism', it is suggested here, was only consolidated *in the cities* in the 1970s.[22]

The National Party spent the first years of its rule building upon the systems set by paternalism in the townships, and even introducing them in some areas. It expanded schooling dramatically (Hyslop 1999); and housing too. In many of the cities at least, welfarist and paternalist elements remained. Key to this was the fact that the costs of providing housing were not fully, as in later years, passed on to the consumer (unsuccessfully, as we shall see),[23] but continued to be financed from outside – through levying employers of African labour,[24] and through loans from central and local government. The first years of National Party rule saw the unprecedented expansion in the provision of housing. Between 1946 and 1960, the number of houses for urban Africans increased from 10,000 to 60,000.

Segregationism was entrenched thereby. Outside each town, a 'location' was to be established 'at an adequate distance from the white town'. It should 'preferably be separated from the white area by an industrial buffer where industries exist or are being planned; it should have provision for an adequate hinterland for expansion stretching away from the white area; it should be within easy distance of the town or city for transport purposes, by rail rather than road' and 'it should be a considerable distance from main and more particularly national roads, the use of which as local transport routes for the township should be totally discouraged' (Morris 1981: 50). Between 1960 and 1965, in Johannesburg (which at that stage included Soweto), the increase in capital expenditure on housing was just under R13m – while rents increased merely by just over R700,000 over the same period (Hellman 1978).

Governance also stayed locked into paternalism. Alexandra remained saddled with its paternalistic but under-funded and inadequate Health Committee for the first thirteen years of National Party rule; elsewhere Advisory Boards were kept for a number of years, in spite of attempts to replace them with new Urban Bantu Councils. The full closing down of the Advisory Boards only took place in the 1970s. Local (white) City Councils, as in the case of Soweto, continued to run townships through, for example, their Non-European Affairs Departments. The Johannesburg Department had, by the mid-1960s, a staff of 700 and a budget of R1m per annum and it provided and maintained three stadia, eighty-six sports fields, a sheltered employment workshop, a vocational training school, youth employment centres, recreational centres, a technical high school, and assistance to the aged, disabled and destitute. All of this continued to be financed, in part, from the sales of 'Bantu beer', and, from 1962 onwards, 'European liquor' (Hellman 1978; Lewis 1972), as well as through employer levies and subsidies from the City Councils themselves (meaning, presumably, that some very limited redistribution was taking place within cities, thus reinforcing economically the paternalistic system). Rent subsidies were granted to those eligible (Hellman 1978: 4).

Where it could – and this tended to be in areas that had not been firmly locked into local government, for example in Alexandra and 'Diepmeadow' – the state eventually took over direct control of township government. Alex's relative independence ended and it was placed under the infamous Peri-Urban Health Board in 1958, with mixed consequences for the lives of its inhabitants. At first, the government brought the township into the welfarist systems that prevailed elsewhere. By 1960 it had set up systems through which beer-hall profits would be allocated to welfare, library services were improved, clubs established, sport and recreation organised, some drainage and street lighting introduced, ambulances and electricity improved, meals provided to TB patients. Crime was reduced (Sarakinsky 1984: 26).

The new government still required and desired separate places where the urban black working class was to be housed. Urban dwellers had to be acknowledged and included if capitalism more broadly was to survive. Like those in the governments before them, the 'pragmatists' within the National Party made certain that ideas of complete removal of the black urban population, which had been mooted by more purist segregationist elements, were never implemented. However, gradually the status of townships within the moral, political and cultural order established earlier under paternalism began to change. The seeds of the destruction of paternalism were to be found even now – the first decade of National Party rule featured a more vigorous and bureaucratised modernism than that which had characterised the earlier period.

The Nationalists had, as we have seen, attempted to solve the housing crisis of the 1940s through the building of more townships or locations (Sapire 1988; Mabin 1993). These were to be more clearly segregated and distanced from cities, and more perfectly and 'scientifically' planned (Maasdorp and Humphreys 1975; Posel 1984) – or 'cleaned up', to use the phrase applied to Alexandra. The element of surveillance and spatial control was extended far beyond that which had existed previously. 'By the late 1950s, Benoni, Springs and Germiston could boast large, "scientifically" planned townships quarantined within "buffer zones" on the outer fringes of the towns' (Sapire 1988). Indeed many locations were removed to the new outer townships, adding to the population of former squatters housed there.

In Alexandra the Peri-Urban Board acted to fulfil its brief: to 'remove residents who worked in any suburb other than a northern Johannesburg suburb, to end lawlessness, to impose influx control, to purchase properties, impose higher taxes and, in the end, to reduce the population to 30,000' (Black Sash n.d.). As in many such townships, the response to this was split along class lines. While standholders were resistant to losing their property, shack dwellers moved willingly; many to far better accommodation in the South West. Still 'there were many instances of people being stopped in the streets, their papers taken, endorsed and their owners then being told to move'. By March 1963, the population had been reduced from 98,000 to 52,000 (Sarakinsky 1984: 6, 27) and the board had taken over 472 properties.[25] This was nothing compared with what was to follow in the next phase of the evolution of apartheid's modernism however (Jochelson 1988a: 17).

'Efficient' housing provision held sway over the 'disorderliness' that had come to characterise the locations. Moreover, in a new twist, which added complexity to the consolidation of the modernist vision, these townships were designed to be internally segregated on ethnic lines. Then, there was the rise to prominence of a far more bureaucratic form of governance. A proliferation of rules, laws and regulations indicated that government by bureaucratic decree – issued from the central state rather than local government, in an attempt to control at a distance the operation of local government – was to be the order of the day. Ninety-six Acts which affected the administration of urban Africans were passed between 1945 and 1965 (Hellman 1978). Influx control and pass laws were more strictly enforced; permission to reside in the city became ever more difficult to secure. By the mid-sixties, both man and wife had to qualify for urban domicile if they were to remain in town – wives who did not qualify in their own right were sent back to the rural areas. In Alexandra, these and other laws affected residents' lives both directly and harshly. Every resident was now required to obtain a 'residence permit'. The running of shebeens was illegal (as it had always been) as were certain types of hawking. In addition, unemployment was a crime.[26]

In Alex, the new Peri-Urban Board soon established its own police force, which set out to implement these ever-expanding laws. With their casual arrogance, frequent callousness and a deep venality they soon gained notoriety.

> Instead of maintaining law and order, they harassed the residents in the township. They used to hang at the back of the bumpers of grey Jeppe's vehicles and drive around the township to arrest the people for pass offences (influx control), searching for weapons, dagga, people selling liquor, vendors and permits. (Statement by Paul Tshabalala, CTH archives)

From being a neglected township, Alex became one that was over-policed. 'People from other areas were afraid to visit their relatives in Alexandra because they might be arrested for not having permits', said Paul Tshabalala.

> They, the peri-urban police, used to raid in the morning from 3 o'clock, knocking with their boots at the doors and shouting 'pass,

pass, and permits, permits'. For this reason people had to wake up at about two o'clock in the morning and flee to a veld named Mojeri and make fire to warm themselves. (Statement by Paul Tshabalala, CTH archives)

If you bribed or offered sex to these policemen you would be exempted from imprisonment for permit offences; similarly shebeen owners or hawkers, who were technically earning their living through illegal means, had to bribe the police regularly, or their liquor was destroyed and they were taken to jail. Most of these policemen lived in the township itself. Their names were well known to all residents. The part played in the suffering of residents by such local policemen as Sibeko, Thobejane, Gasela, Sendani and Nxumalo was not forgotten during the 1980s uprising.

The extraordinary expansion and overburdening imposition of a cruel and Kafkaesque bureaucracy – whose operation we understand very little, and tend to study even less – was a feature of the period (Hellman 1978: 2).

A difference in administrative 'tone' also emerged. Ellen Hellman noted in the mid-1960s an 'increasing stringency and rigidity' in the application of the law (Hellman 1978: 12). Thus even in this early phase, the experience of the citizens was radically altered: 'The human tragedies caused by these regulations can be seen and heard daily at the superintendents' offices in Soweto and at the central office of the Johannesburg Non-European Affairs Department.'

The move from 'location' to 'township' also affected the ways in which the township elite was incorporated into governance. In one case, for example, the Advisory Board changed, upon the move, from 'a civic institution of township notables to a political pressure group of township "bosses", and, instead of a channel of communication, it became a barrier between administration and administered' (Brandel-Syrier 1971: 11). The township administrator in this case – a paragon of paternalism in the years of the 'location' – had 'retreated behind an army of European and African officials' (Brandel-Syrier 1971: 12). And the old elite itself found that its patron–client networks were broken with the move from location to township; and that its sources of income (landlordism in many cases) were gone. A new elite began to take its place:

> One by one, the bearers of the big names were dropping out of business life. They went bankrupt; they had to 'sell' their dying shops; they just could not adjust to the change. …And so the veterans had to watch another wave of newcomers settle down … These were the doctors and lawyers, the public servants, the graduates and the trained … They introduced entirely new social customs and manners, and they now set the tone of the social life of the community. (Brandel-Syrier 1971: 20)

However, no political niche, or granting of status by society outside of the confines of the township, was offered to this new elite.

RACIAL MODERNISM AND REBELLION

In essence, this phase saw a more complete overturning of the old system of welfare paternalism. First, the frustration of the central government with municipal rule ended in 1972–3, when control of African townships was finally removed from local authorities. Twenty-two Bantu Affairs Administration Boards (BAABs) were set up over the next few years. The state could at last directly govern the townships.

At a stroke, the economic basis of welfare paternalism was removed, for these boards were expected to be fully self-financing. The services and infrastructure previously subsidised by local authorities were now to be fully paid for by township residents themselves – through rents, continuing sales of beer and 'European liquor', and a variety of levies. While a combination of factors was at play in this shift, including a decline in the consumption of the profitable 'Bantu Beer', it was the removal of two important 'welfarist' components of the financing system – the freezing in 1977 of the levy on employers and the removal of the subsidy by the City and Town Councils – that rendered local administration unprofitable. Not unnaturally, the first line of attack upon this deficit was a massive increase in rents, which doubled between 1970 and 1977, but this was insufficient. BAABs had been placed in an untenable situation by the way in which government had removed the welfare elements in township financing without offering any clear alternative other than the increase in rents (Seekings 1990). This was to prove lethal to the stability of governance.

With the passing of time, the role of the bureaucracy became even more imposing and alienating. It became a leviathan, run by people who spoke Afrikaans – less familiar to blacks in many areas – rather than English; who resorted to the rulebook when insecure about their inexperience in administering; and whose requirements became increasingly burdensome and unjust over time. They came more and more to control personal areas of life in the townships, extending their rule not only into the family, but into the home, the place of work, transport, the body, and the mind. This over-administration of townships by decree encouraged disrespect for the law itself – the excessive legalism of apartheid corrupted the law, rather than protected it.

This era also entailed the transformation of township residents – with the obvious exception of the hostel-dwellers – from a moderately stratified population with varying relationships to land, into a mass of tenants, with uniform relationships to the land and the state (tempered, perhaps, by their different types of housing – 'housing classes' appear to have been created in some areas). Overall, using spatial and architectural means, the new social engineers of modernity devised ways of bludgeoning away incipient or past differences of economic status and blurring previously relatively clear-cut class differences. The state could allocate a home to a doctor next door to that of a street sweeper, with nothing to distinguish them.

A general feature of National Party rule, particularly in the later period, was its attitude towards the black elite, and the patronage structures that were in place. Some might think of the National Party as a parody of post-colonialism – with its pseudo 'independence' for black homelands, for example. However, in one respect, they were far from taking even a mockery of the route of the many post-colonial governments that reinforced existing elites; they took a completely different path – to destroy and dispossess them. The new order left little avenue for elite incorporation.[27]

Thus all standholders were dispossessed in this period, either in situ, through the simple legal mechanism of declaring them no longer to be owners of their own land or through removal to other areas. Both of these methods were used in Alexandra. The epic removals of landowners from Sophiatown, District Six and many others have found expression in literary and poetic form – and the passion with which this loss is mourned suggests that more than landholdings were being lost. These removals were bound up with the forced downward mobility of the black location elite, including standholders, whose position was crucial to the relative stability of the older paternalistic order.

They undermined many other features of the older order. They imposed new restrictions upon African trade, accumulation and mobility. They destroyed the educational and religious channels through which elite status had been sought and obtained. The new system of schooling, Bantu Education, was inimical to the older paternalistic ways. While it expanded the access to schools of the mass of township dwellers, it undercut the process of the production of an elite through the closing down of all mission schools.

Furthermore, the capacity of older people to exercise authority over younger, already weakened anyway by the normal processes of urbanisation and the modernisation of the family, was further undermined through the imposition of grossly humiliating restrictions upon adults. Seared upon the minds of the young were the experiences of seeing parents standing in queues for hours, even days, only to be told to 'come back next week', with more unobtainable documents; or observing the fear and panic in the eyes of their elders when they were vulnerable to pass restrictions. High apartheid made new inroads into the selfhood and dignity of the older generation, whose expectations of paternalistic behaviour were no longer to be met. The rise of the new ideology of Black Consciousness, with its emphasis on selfhood and dignity, was in part a response to this.

The Nationalists also undercut the old elite by removing the Advisory Boards and replacing them with a succession of new systems of local representation. This idea was first promulgated as early as 1961; but it took until 1977 for as many as twenty-four new Urban Bantu Councils (also known as 'Useless Boys Clubs') to be put in place. However, the attitude of the state towards these councils was far less paternalistic than had been the case with the Advisory Boards.

Although the council of the 1960s and 1970s did continue to play a mediating role with some success, as time went on, in many areas the weakened black elite could not muster even a basic legitimacy for them.[28] Phenomena such as brutal *makgotla* and the rise of corruption emerged (Seekings 1990: 71ff, 79ff). Consequently, what modest interest there had been amongst township populations in their own governance declined significantly. By 1974, only 14 per cent of the Soweto (registered) electorate voted in UBC elections, a decline of over half in eight years. When a few years later the government attempted to revive black participation in township government through the creation of 'Community Councils', they were no more successful (Bloch 1982); and their final attempt at achieving the legitimacy of black local government – through the Black Local Authorities Act of 1982 – was even more of a failure, leading directly into the revolts of the mid-1980s.[29] By 1985 only three Black Town Councils were operating.

Tenants too were transformed – for their landlord now became the highly bureaucratic, modernising and racist state rather than the standholder or the paternalistic City Council, placing them in an entirely different structural position within the social order. If the lines of oppression do at least in part dictate the lines of resistance, then this new situation put township residents into a potentially directly oppositional relationship with the state itself, with no intermediaries to buffer it.

In the case of areas that were not removed (Alexandra, in the end, being one), these transformations occurred in situ. This probably made things worse for the residents, for layers of sedimented memory of a different past, reinforced by the architectural and spatial features of the township, were left in place – ready to be activated by new ideologies and turned into powerful mythical forces when social mobilisation began. In the case of the many areas that were removed, the operation of memory took a different form: removals to the newly created townships on the peripheries of white cities entailed the removals of memories as well – and the new areas were imbued with ideas about a number of pasts. New suburbs, such as Diepkloof or Meadowlands, carried with them the bitterness of dispossession. But the censorship and control of ideas forced memories in all of these areas into a forbidden and secret underworld, where again they remained until a new stratum of popular intellectuals sought to mobilise them.

A further transformation that occurred under high apartheid was the re-engineering of the family. All new township houses were designed on the assumption that they would be occupied by something approximating a nuclear family. Furthermore, the way the laws of residence worked meant that family stability depended upon job stability and gender. Far from consolidating the family, these regulations worked to fragment it – to create the conditions for bitter and harmful disputes over the matter of home-occupancy between kin; to force women into marriages of convenience; and to drive those without the right documentation into fraud or flight.

Even greater manipulation of the family took place through the ways the pass laws were translated by the new rulers of the township – to turn all those who worked in town but who lacked urban rights into a family-less, homeless working population of single men and women. To this end, the new regime embarked upon the mass construction of 'hostels'. The Nationalists believed, just as the segregationist politician and planner Stallard had proclaimed fifty years earlier, that the families of workers in the town were 'non-productive', and could live 'just as well, in fact cheaper, in the homelands' (Jochelson 1988a: 20).

They excepted those who had been grudgingly granted 'permanent' status under Section 10 (1) (a) of the Urban Areas Act, which permitted those born and bred in the townships, who had homes there, to remain, albeit subject to the humiliating requirement that the burden of proof as to their own status rested upon them. However, a new and 'ultra modernist' conception of how everybody else – defined as 'single' urban workers – would be handled was conceptualised and implemented in a variety of places. The earliest example of an attempt actually to implement these ideas took place in Alexandra itself. As early as 1963 the idea emerged that the whole of Alexandra township, at the time home to the 50,000 people who remained there after the removals of the period 1958–63, would become a 'hostel city'. No families would remain: 'The whole town will consist only of such hostels. There will be no houses and also no families' (Jochelson 1988a: 21). Against a background of mass opposition to apartheid's expanding vision, and of specific standholder, resident, business, political and liberal opposition to the envisaged destruction of the old Alexandra a further 'cleaning up' took place between 1963 and 1972.[30]

By 1972 a further 19,000 (in addition to the 46,000 already removed) people had been 'removed from Alexandra at a rate of 250 families a month, and these were families in which both husband and wife had Section 10 rights.[31] Families in which either of the parents had no Section 10 rights were sent to the homelands. Those with Section 10 rights were rehoused in the single-sex hostels' (Black Sash n.d.). Children were sent away from their mothers, and married couples separated. Standholders who had not yet been removed were told they were no longer landowners, but that they were now required to pay rent to the Peri-Urban Board (Sarakinsky 1984: 52–3). Meagre compensation was paid and dirty tactics used to get those who resisted out. They passionately opposed this but lost. (Even today, these families continue to fight their dispossession in court.) Against the back-ground of the '76 riots, the removals continued right through the 1970s, until near the end of this mad scheme in 1977 the population of the township had dropped to 35,000, from the 98,000 fourteen years earlier, and taking into account some growth (Sarakinsky 1984: 56–7).[32]

The plan was to incarcerate 'inmates' in prison-like structures:

> Each hostel would house 2,500 people but be divided into sections of 100 to 150 people separated by electrically operated steel doors to prevent unrest spreading and 'for the protection of the inmates them-selves'. Rooms would be provided with a bed, mattress and cupboard, but no central heating or electricity outlets. Inhabitants would share 112 washing tubs and 32 electricity points, one bath for every 25 residents, one shower for every 35, one hand basin and toilet for every 20 and, in the kitchen, one gas burner for every five people. (*Izwi Lase Township*, April/May 1983)

This plan was never fully implemented. Resistance to the plan was mobilised in the township in the seventies, slowing and eventually stopping the process of 'hostelisation'. Standholders continued to be bought out and more residents removed. Nevertheless, ten years later only three hostels had been built – one for women and two for men. They were huge thrusting concrete monuments in the midst of the huddled disorder of what remained of the township; monuments to a mad form of modernity, in which iron gates which could be lowered at any moment were indeed built to separate corridors from one another in case riots erupted; in which communal facilities allowed little dignity or privacy; and in which the construction of 'singleness' was imposed relentlessly upon all. They epitomise the period of extreme racial modernism, both in their grossness and in the fact that they represent a plan uncompleted.

What happened to the liberals – the paternalists who had played so central a part in both the capacity for the governance of the townships, and the development of certain institutions of social and cultural life? In the new order, these kinds of activities no longer had the stamp of state approval. Charity, church, welfare and cultural activities were curbed and made more difficult to undertake through the introduction of harsh measures; relation-ships between the shattered black elite and the white liberal elite were all but destroyed through stricter enforcement of segregation (Haggie 1994: 80). Missionaries were no longer permitted to live in townships. Mission schools were closed or taken over by the state to become Bantu Education schools. Permits to enter the townships became harder to obtain. In 1966 the government decreed that no white organisation could have any rights in Soweto, forcing the City Council to take over (and subsidise) the activities of charities (Haggie 1994: 80) until it, too, was removed from township life.

> The European welfare worker and health inspector, the European minister and teacher, the European sports and music organiser, became rarities in township life where before they had entered the lives and homes of the people. (Brandel Syrier 1971: 13)

Many liberals redirected themselves away from activities which entailed playing some part in the networks and relationships within the townships, and towards acting as defenders of human rights, as in the Alexandra removals, or as intermediaries between the new, far harsher regime itself (at the state level) and the black population. The Black Sash Advice Office, for example, assisted people in finding their way through the new bureaucracy and fought for their rights; and Haggie describes how:

> For years, at eight one morning every week, Pam Reid was at the Polly Street pass office to do battle on behalf of women desperate for work who did not have the magic 'section 10(1)(a) of the Urban Areas Act' stamp in their passes or registration books. The stamp was granted only if the women complied with a series of stringent requirements, and Pam, who is a gentle lady, would stand over the clerks, at times coming near to using physical force to prevent them from applying the hated 'endorsed out' stamp – which would have meant no hope for employment ever again in Johannesburg for the luckless pass-holder. (Haggie 1994: 105)

This was still an intermediate role for liberals – but a very different one from that which had prevailed under paternalism.

Thus, these years consolidated a major shift in the way in which black citizenship was constructed by the state – a shift that had begun in the 1950s. Legal provisions made it clearer than ever before to residents that they were in town as a privilege rather than as a right. Long-standing residents of townships had to prove their residency, their places of birth and a myriad of other things (all difficult for working-class people) before they were given the status to remain. They became immigrants within their own country. In addition, social and personal life was dislocated, networks were weakened, the law was corrupted and dignity was eroded. There was an uncoupling of any, even modest, concept of citizenship from the actual township itself.

This state of affairs was to change in the late 1970s. Alexandra was reprieved from the removals policy in 1979 – the same year that the Riekert Commission report on urban reform was implemented. This was a product of the era of reform that characterised apartheid after the coming to power, in 1978, of P. W. Botha. The state had found itself under increasing pressure to move away from 'high apartheid' – pressure from the growing resistance in townships and workplaces; the emerging weaknesses in the economy; splits within the National Party, and increasing international pressure. It was against this background that Alexandra was to be 'replanned' for 'family housing', to 'become a fully fledged municipality. A model township ... the first of its kind. One that South Africans could proudly show their foreign visitors'.[33]

In Alexandra a 'Liaison Committee' was installed after having been elected as the new local governing body. Building on the credibility obtained in the struggle against removals by the Reverend Sam Buti and the 'Save Alexandra Party', it was supposed to act as a new buffer between the state and the mass of ordinary Alexandrans. Moves such as these, and the Riekert decisions more broadly, may have offered the urban dwellers a much less grudging acknowledgement of their permanence – but the new vision proposed nothing comprehensive to replace either the paternalistic system of social control (Riekert's new dispensation still placed the burden of proof of the new 'citizenship' upon the township dweller, a recipe for resentment), or the welfarist system of economic sustenance. There were no financial underpinnings to the new system, rendering it politically dead in the water:

> Alexandra was the first council to become a black local authority and in many discussions, debates that I had with Sam Buti my own personal feeling was that he should not take local authority status for the simple reason that the funds just were not available ... *That is responsibility without resources?* Responsibility without resources, and to a large extent because Sam had that problem, he had all these ideas and couldn't achieve them and that was a tremendous cause of anger. I mean he had all the sign-boards, you know, rebirth of Alexandra and nothing could be done. (Ricky Valente, M4182)

Buti's attempt to administer the township failed dismally, rapidly deteriorating into a predictable call for higher rents, a series of disastrous housing decisions,[34] the highly unpopular formation of an additional local police force,[35] and the inevitable accusations of corruption and incompetence, until its final demise as a body of 'power hungry mad puppets' deserving to be crushed (A. Zwane, quoting from an AYCO document, Z3903), in the period leading up to and during the rebellion.

Similarly, the rush on the part of reformist nationalism to recreate a township elite in the late 1970s and early 1980s came too late to look anything but cynical – and was accompanied by the segregation and removal of the elite to posh areas on the borders of townships, rather than any serious attempt at the moral, social and cultural reconstruction of the connections between the elites and their co-residents. None of Riekert's ideas worked in the same way as the older elite systems had worked under paternalism. The new order had turned townships into something sociologically different: what had been societies shaped by class, kin and status, became more clearly racial or ethnic ones, in which the possibilities for negotiation were minimised by the imposition of huge and harsh bureaucratic machinery. Their capacity to find a place in, and remain in town had depended in the early regime upon blacks' access to a multitude of networks, resources and culture, including those offered by whites. Now blacks, and only blacks, had the burden of proof of their citizenship placed upon them; and they were subjected to humiliating and nightmarish bureaucratic procedures for the proof to be acknowledged by the state.

An important result of these many processes was the reconstruction of identity within township communities along racial lines. As early as the 1960s, white participants in a mixed-race charity were noting that there had been a 'change in race relations during the last two or three years. There appears to be a definite deterioration in black–white relationships ... which can only be attributed to an increased state of mistrust, uncertainty and possibly antagonism' (Haggie 1994: 70–1). The ideologies accompanying these new identities were not only strongly racially conscious, they were also clearly anti-liberal, in sharp contrast to the earlier tendency towards compatibility between African nationalism and liberalism. Liberals, like the black elite, came to be tainted by the changed legitimacy of their role.

The move from welfare paternalism to racial modernism entailed a loss of citizenship, class, status, cultural security, authority and power, by a range of township-based groups – a removal, in fact, of the resources available to create a certain sort of stability. These things had all existed in particular configurations under the segregationist/paternalistic order, and had underpinned its relative sense of order – blacks were 'governable'. Their loss was more than of economic significance to the elite and their children. It entailed humiliation, downward mobility and shame. It left a vacuum of authority that the new bureaucracy failed utterly to fill, and into which the youth were quick to step.

Ironically, it was the rulers, rather than the ruled, who dislodged this working hegemony. Their reasons for dislodging it may in part have lain in the challenges to paternalism, which were inherent in the mass urbanisation of the 1940s; but this is not entirely the case. Afrikaner nationalism undertook social engineering on a grand scale, thus dismantling a working system of hegemony, and replacing it with a modernism that could perhaps have made a more workable system of urban administration if it had been accompanied by the creation of a new 'buffer' stratum within the townships, but which was doomed to disaster when the modernist order chose to use bureaucracy as its means of rule rather than patronage and clientelism.

The loss of the old order rendered the dispossessed older generation of township dwellers, as well as the stabilising elite, helpless; they lacked the ideological and other resources to pose any alternatives to racial modernism. How could an older style of African nationalism, based as it was upon deal-making and networks, cope with a white ruling class bent upon creating a leviathan-like form of local administration. In addition to their shame the older generation experienced an unprecedented form of political weakness, opening them up to the humiliating taunts of their own children, and to the many indignities inflicted upon them by an unbelieving population of young people, appalled at what they perceived as the failures to resist on the part of their parents. In a telling study of Durban youth, Campbell quotes one who said:

> The old people are scared of the white man. They see him as somebody like God they had never seen before. They never saw that what the white person said might have been wrong or right, bad or good. It didn't even occur to them to question anything. The older generation have been prepared to accept everything the hardest way, they have had to struggle for everything they have got. But the young people don't wait for hard times. They are always active. (Campbell 1994: 102)

Or another:

> Parents appear as fools to their children, people who just say useless things, whose minds have simply ceased to think wisely. This results in growing disobedience, because children do not see any reason to respect them. (Campbell 1994: 2)

And a third:

> At work black people are not given enough money, yet they work hard. In the old days blacks did not complain about this. In these days they do ... there is nothing the old people can teach the young now ... the young must learn from the other kids who know better ... Parents feel bad about this. I know this because I have seen my mother crying. (Campbell 1994: 54)

When the racial modernist order undercut the economic basis of welfare paternalism, it generated opportunities for the younger generation to mobilise, around the crises of rents, schooling and local government – while the emergence of new ideologies provided them with the means. The rebellions of the eighties, therefore, took up immediate and urgent issues of survival for the poor – but against a background, unlike earlier periods, of a pre-existing, and long developing vacuum of authority on the part of their rulers, which gave their rebellions impetus.

It is not surprising, then, that the youths' mobilisation did not express a longing for the old, paternalistic order. The old order depended, indeed, upon styles of patriarchal and age-based authority inimical to the young. So there was no nostalgic nationalism, seeking to restore a lost past. Something different emerged – a strongly utopian element to their thought and behaviour. They rejected both paternalism and liberalism – and in doing so they rejected their own parents – upon whom the earlier hierarchy of control had depended, and whom they perceived as having failed. They sought in fact to 'turn the world upside down'.

The Afrikaner Nationalists were in fact revolutionaries of a sort. In the case of township governance, far from simply 'consolidating' and 'perfecting' the old, segregationist order, as has been argued in innumerable works seeking to emphasise the racism of the pre-1948 period, they in fact undermined it, and installed a new, modernist version of racism. Nevertheless, they were unsuccessful as a ruling class. The new order legislated away the moral, economic, cultural and social securities of welfare paternalism and failed at any point to replace them with a viable alternative. The peculiar morality of paternalism was gone, and a substitute was not offered by the Nationalist government itself.

It was partly in pursuing a doomed urban project of extreme, race-based and almost fascist modernisation to replace the older paternalism that had prevailed, that the 'old state' – the apartheid state – foundered in the 1980s. Its failure was accelerated by profound weaknesses in the capitalism which had long underpinned the racial order. The state had, since the late 1970s, been divided against itself, and increasingly alienated from its capitalist base. The urban black population had always been the proving ground for the compromises and deals between state and capital, and weaknesses in the capacity of the state consistently to produce a stable working class undermined industry both politically and economically. The state began to tread an uneven path between the tentative reformism of some sections and the desire by others to adhere to the pitiless repression of earlier times.

The effects of its at times bizarre and never-to-be-fulfilled commitment to modernism, as well as the ongoing failures of industrialisation, were wide-ranging within the micro-economy and mini-society of each of the many townships that housed the black urban population. Within their clearly defined spaces extremely elaborate and intricate systems of class, status, power, authority and expectation, a well-developed range of syncretic cultural forms, and even a substantial repertoire of resistance styles, had been created over the years.

The modernising imperatives of the state had, by the 1980s, reinforced and exaggerated the spatial significance of township society on a number of levels. Segregation had itself been highly spatial, socially excluding and controlling, but always somewhat at a distance, using paternalistic intermediaries. But now the ambitious state was bidding for greater power, and it sought to enter into and further control the private world of the ghetto. And one of the defining features of apartheid was that space came to be used in extreme ways as a means of ordering society. But while space may be a useful source of power, it is an unstable basis for authority. This paradox of space was revealed by subsequent events. While even newly extended spatial control did to some extent acquire a 'veneer of normality' which lent it some legitimacy, it was but a poor substitute for the older paternalistic systems of authority which had been undercut. The National Party established local power brokers within townships to try to recreate the stability of earlier times, but activists saw that these were weak and vulnerable, lacking an economic base from which to dispense anything that might change power into authority.

4

BOUNDED REVOLT

The youths in the townships are in an unstoppable mood of anger and have seeming disregard for their lives. (*The Sowetan*, 28 February 1986, quoted in Johnson n.d.)

We've got a new breed of children. They believe that they are going to die ... and the frightening thing is that they actually don't care. (Bishop Tutu, quoted in *The Star*, 18 April 1986, quoted in Johnson n.d.)

The failing state was confronted in early 1986 by a new and spectacular attack by rebellious residents upon the already weakened township. This was the beginning of the six-month long Alexandra Rebellion. In it, the newly emerging repertoire of resistance gained ascendancy, and old-style African Nationalism faded. A new kind of violence emerged. The crowd became an active part of the events, and public space came to be crucial to mobilisation and communication. In the first six days of the rebellion – the 'Six-Day War' – the young rebels reimagined Alexandra in bold and inventive ways, turning it into a space within which they could enact their drama of resistance. They began to write a new script. They reinvented 'good' and 'bad' spaces. They occupied and redefined the streets. They introduced more formal patterns of new usage of spaces through ritualised processions and confrontation. They reclaimed and reshaped key public arenas. They delineated a new relationship between private places such as homes and public areas such as streets. They recast the meaning of official boundaries.

Through these means, the apprehended world was symbolically turned upside down, setting 'that in the bottom which others make the top of the building' and setting 'that upon the roof which others lay for a foundation' (Hill 1972: 13).

Such processes of the disruption of space and time are, of course, what rebellions in ghetto-like situations are all about. What follows is not a discussion of the Six-Day War in military or strategic terms, which would, with certain local variations, not be entirely unpredictable. Rather it is an attempt to map this transformation 'from below', as it were – to sketch how the shattering and recasting of 'normality' appeared *at the time* in the minds of ordinary people, whose familiar and taken-for-granted spaces came to acquire different and sometimes shocking meanings. I attempt to capture the spatially widespread and temporally and aurally relentless staccato of mobs, guns, bombs, burnings and deaths that bombarded the township for the next few days – in the hope that some sort of 'virtual' sense of the rebellion's attack upon space and time, and consequently its considerable theatricality, is recreated. I use lists of events, specific addresses and give details of names and places in an attempt to capture a sense of place, immediacy and relentlessness and to show how in reply to, and often preempting the rebels' attempts to recast space and time, the authorities played their own grim games of retribution, occupation, patrol, ambush, invasion, strategic withdrawal and attack.

Those who have not participated in such transformative events might remember their own ordeals, experienced say, when personal and private spaces are invaded, destroyed or altered, perhaps by thieves or a household fire. When such experiences occur on a larger, social scale, involving gross and relentless violence, death, burning or mutilation, their effects upon consciousness and identity, too, are enlarged and rapidly become social rather than personal. Time slows. Relationships intensify. Authority dissolves, mutates, decays. Crowds grow, move, attack, retreat. The experience of the shattering of expected spatial normality *in itself* may come to contribute to the evolution of new forms of mobilisation.

THE 'MAGICAL TIME': THE RUPTURING OF SPACE AND TIME IN THE SIX-DAY WAR

Events, suggests Sewell when writing of the taking of the Bastille, 'should be conceived of as sequences of occurrences that result in transformations of structures. Such sequences begin with a rupture of some kind – that is, a surprising break with routine practices.' The rupture 'spirals' into a transformative event when a sequence of interrelated ruptures 'disarticulates the previous structural network, makes repair difficult, and makes a novel rearticulation possible' (Sewell 1996: 843–4). A 'rupture', it will be argued, took place in Alexandra when the Six-Day War took place.

The rupture originated in the four new styles of collective action that emerged in early 1986: the eruption of a new kind of violence; the concomitant emergence of the crowd; the articulation of new visions, by local adult thinkers and leaders, of the way in which the township could be organised and transformed (these differed from the existing visions of the youth); and the emergence of public space as a crucial part of mobilisation and communication. Together these represented a further change in the repertoire of resistance, and built upon the changes that had already taken place in the early 1980s. The Six-Day War entailed both a violent challenge to the state and a remarkable degree of stylistic inventiveness. New forms of collective action and violence were added to the repertoire of the township every day.

On the eve of New Year the well-known young activist Richard Padi was shot dead by Municipal Police.[1] Alexandra was a small enough place for his name and fate to be widely known. There had been other deaths – but this came to be thought of as one of the first indications that ordinary spaces (streets, homes, shops) were no longer the repositories of the simple meanings of daily life, but were to become the venues for brutality and horror. Padi's death became a community affair, and was followed by the night vigil, funeral and stand-off between crowd and police that had come to characterise such politically defined deaths in Alexandra and elsewhere. The first sign that a new form of response might evolve as a result of this occurred when, on 12 January, the house of Piet Marodi, a local councillor, was attacked. This reflected a different kind of political consciousness.

At the end of January Michael Diradeng, also a well-known young activist, was shot dead by a security guard amidst controversial circumstances. The sense of a shattering of normality that ensued is reflected in the dramatic words used to describe the period by Alexandrans themselves. 'From 15 February, the people of Alexandra began to revolt in a manner unprecedented in our history,' said one activist. It was 'a crucial period of awakening' (Mayekiso 1996: 61–3). The *Sunday Star* said Michael Diradeng's death was the event that had 'sparked off the violence'. 'Almost all agree that even if Mr Diradingwe (sic) had not been shot, sooner or later something else would have touched off the explosion that rocked Alexandra' (*Sunday Star*, 23 February 1986). Ashwell Zwane, also an activist at the time, was poetic about the beginnings of a new phase, saying that the death of Diradeng was 'the last straw'; it was followed by what he called a 'magical time', full of 'unity and extraordinary cooperation' (interview, December 1993).

Day One: Claiming the Terrain

Space is one thing, territory another. While adults organised the Diradeng night vigil for the evening of Friday 14 February, youths began to define the streets as their terrain, mobilising (a word which sometimes hid a thousand less than noble acts) residents by going 'from yard to yard' (Richard Mdakane, M2405). They started to formalise their control over space by appointing marshalls to direct people – who arrived in numbers not really seen before in Alexandra – to and from the vigil. A tent was erected in the Diradeng yard in Third Avenue (Lillian Nkuna, M451).

This bid for terrain was in a sense hostile to the conceptions ordinary residents held of the township. Moreover, of course, it threatened the state. After an hour or two of song and prayer, the vigil was tear-gassed and the crowd dispersed by police. The most militant youths – the 'comrades' – regrouped and staked their claim over territory once more. The first evidence of the widespread use of a new protest style was the way in which, from midnight onwards, groups of youths rampaged through the township, claiming both time – the private times of the long nights now became public – and space as theirs, and using shock tactics, fire and destruction as some of their means of appropriating both. Three shops were damaged just after midnight. Jazz Stores, where Diradeng had died, was petrol bombed and virtually destroyed at 2.10 a.m. Cars were stoned and further supermarkets bombed as the night ended.

The Six-Day War rapidly became a contest between residents, particularly the youth on the one hand, and the two police forces responsible for the area, and the local councillors claiming to represent it, on the other. By 5 a.m. that first day, the police had fully mobilised. A Lieutenant Zeelie remembered it well:

> On my arrival at Alexandra police station, I was informed that Jazz Stores had been set alight. It was observed that groups of youths in Alexandra township had formed groups, and were running up and down the streets, and that they had begun to set more houses alight.

The burning of houses had begun in earnest – and this time, he said, the houses were those of the black South African policemen themselves (M. M. Zeelie, M519–20). The mobs continued, stoning the beer hall, burning more shops and their delivery vehicles and stoning cars and buildings.

The crowd's activities reached a gruesome climax when at eight in the morning they stabbed a policeman and set him alight in Third Avenue. This was the first case of the mob burning of a human being that had occurred in Alexandra. Minutes later, at 8.20, a second policeman was found burnt to death in Thirteenth Avenue.[2] Then, not long afterwards, one Samson Ndaba, former ANC activist but now a willing witness in state cases against his former comrades, was surrounded by a crowd of 200–300 and threatened with petrol bombs and sjamboks. The crowd threw petrol bombs at him as he rushed into his house, one of which exploded and burnt him (S. Ndaba, Z535). This was the beginning of a war between residents and local and national policemen, with significant cross-currents between strata of the residents as well, such as adults and youth, people wishing to live their daily lives and those wishing to alter the space into a battleground.

Day Two: Bounded Space Contested

Bounded spaces are more about power than street design. On Day Two of the Six-Day War the territory and boundaries of Alexandra began to change in meaning and significance. Confronted with borders designed to separate and confine – to keep black people in – the rebels transformed the township's boundaries into metaphorical and at times actual barricades designed to keep outsiders out. At the same time, they extended their existing claims over the streets to the whole territory. Control over the territory and borders of the township was as a result hotly contested through the use of violence, symbolism and other elements of the repertoire of collective action by rebels and their allies in the township population; and defended by the police and eventually the army. Ordinary residents expressed complex emotions about these occurrences, a mixture of bewilderment at the transformation of their venues for daily living, horror at the deaths and violence that came to pervade their world, and a profound loyalty to their own children and kin whose lives were being taken by a despised regime.

The day began with Michael Diradeng's funeral, which drew upon a staple of the repertoire of resistance all over South Africa in the 1980s – the political funeral – but came to acquire its own meanings for Alexandrans because of what had preceded it. A tense atmosphere had spilt over from the events of the previous night. Police and youths were sporadically fighting. The funeral procession left for the stadium. Thousands of people had been mobilised – by the events of the night before, by the zealous marshals and by their sense that something of great import was happening. Before the funeral got off the ground, however, further eruptions occurred.

Policemen, their offices and homes were attacked again. Another policeman was burnt. Lieutenant Gert Petrus Zeelie, of the SAP, described the event:

> The black detective (Mashile) had to report for duty at 8 am. On the way to the Alexandra police station he was attacked by a group of youths. The black detective fled to a shop … but was told he must leave the shop or it would be burnt. He left the shop. About 20 or 30 metres from the shop, he was attacked by the black youths, and set alight. He was taken to hospital with very serious burn wounds … I visited him in hospital soon afterwards. He was in a very bad state of shock … his whole body was full of burn wounds. (M. M. Zeelie, M520–1)

He was taken to the Hillbrow hospital where he remained for two or three months, after which he died of his wounds. An ex-Town Council policeman remembered that more widespread attacks on policemen also occurred:

> They were throwing stones, as well as petrol bombs, saying the police must get away from there … Those who were in front of the group were children of about 10 to 15 years of age, but at the back there were adults – between 20 and 30 years old. (M. Nxumalo, M180–1)

He continued:

> The police were on duty that day, frightened off these people by shooting in front of them. They were shooting plastic pellets in front of them. This caused dust and stones were sent flying. When this happened, one of the people in the crowd said: 'We are not fighting …' I then said in reply, 'If you are not fighting, you can go past in peace. We are also not fighting you. We are only protecting our police.'

He described further looting and attacks, which began to take a racial form – the defining of insiders and outsiders began to consolidate:

> They went past and went to the Indian shopping centre, where they broke one of the shops and removed everything from inside the shop. From there they proceeded to the corner of Selborne and First Avenue, got to another shop, broke it down, took some of the items from the shop and burnt the rest.

Further attacks on police homes took place:

> Again, on the same morning of the 15th, some members of the group came to my house and attacked my house with stones and petrol bombs. The police scared them off. The municipality police scared them off with plastic pellets. (M. M. Nxumalo, M1801)

At least three further police homes were attacked.[3] The police used bullets in reply. Nono Lucy Ledwaba, a young girl – almost a child – had been standing at the gate of her home when a bullet hit her and she died immediately. Another young man died that afternoon after being shot while throwing a petrol bomb.

The War on Day Two

10 a.m.	a car was stoned at 134 Fifteenth Avenue
10 a.m.	police shot dead N. Ledwaba, a young girl standing at the gate of her home
10 a.m.	a fire engine had to be escorted to a fire in Second Avenue.
10.30 a.m.	a Casspir had been petrol bombed, and a policeman injured
11.15 a.m.	another petrol bomb was thrown at the corner of Selborne and Third Avenues
1.05 p.m.	a private car was stoned, at the corner of Selborne and Thirteenth Avenues
2 p.m.	a petrol bomb was thrown at a car on the corner of Selborne and Eighth Avenue

Sources: Wynberg Police Station Incident Book, no MR258.2.86; Ops Book February 1986; Zwane trial, Exhibit TTT, Priscilla Jana archives (henceforth PJ archives)

Later in the afternoon, the Municipal Police offices at 95 Second Avenue were attacked; an 'unknown black male' was shot dead by police after throwing a petrol bomb; and Municipal Policeman Warrant Officer Edward Moikanyane's house was attacked (M. M. Nxumalo, M182).

In the meantime, about 10,000 people had gathered to attend Michael Diradeng's funeral. It was held in the central and familiar Alexandra stadium which was, said activist Albert Sebola, regarded in the township as a place 'of importance' (Ashwell Zwane, Z2543). This central social space, already imbued with memory and meaning, now became something different – a dramatic venue that embodied the rapidly growing sense of a newly imagined township community, and of the Nationalism and utopianism of the period. It was to play a significant role in making possible the ongoing theatricality of the revolt over the next few months.

With Moses Mayekiso, the emerging leader of the 'adult' wing of the resistance, as Master of Ceremonies, the funeral was an emotional affair. The symbols of resistance, in the form of flags, songs and slogans, were omnipresent. Youth activists took the opportunity to propagate their ideas for how to solve the problems of the township. Following the lead of the newly formed adult-based organisation, the Alexandra Action Committee, they distributed a pamphlet advocating the formation of a widely based system of Yard, Block and Street Committees as a means of solving Alexandra's problems – the first complete visualisation of a new order for the township:

Reproduction of Diradeng Funeral Pamphlet

Street Committees: PEOPLE! WE HAVE GOT TWO PROBLEMS IN ALEXANDRA: DISUNITY AND PROBLEMS NOT SOLVED. TO SOLVE THESE PROBLEMS THE ALEX PEOPLE HAVE DECIDE TO FORM STRUC-TURES THAT WILL ENCOURAGE UNITY, COMRADESHIP AND ACTION – STREET COMMITTEES (AVENUE COMMITTEES). WE WANT PEOPLE TO HAVE GENERAL MEETINGS IN THEIR YARDS TO ELECT YARD COMMITTEES TO UNITE PEOPLE IN THE YARD. THE YARD COMMITTEE THROUGH ITS GENERAL MEETING SHOULD ELECT THE CHAIRMAN, SECRETARY AND TWO REPRESENTATIVES TO THE BLOCK COMMITTEE. THE TWO OFFICE BEARERS AND TWO REPS COMPIRSE THE YARD COMMITTE. THERE SHALL BE WEEKLY GENERAL MEETING FO YARDS.SOLVED AMTTERS/ PROBLEMS WILL BE REFERED TO BLOCK COMMITTEES.	THE 'STREET COMMITTEES' WILL BE FORMED OUT OF REPRESENTATIVES FROM BLOCK COMMITTEES, TWO STREET COMMITTEE REPRESENTATIVES TO ALEX ACTION COUNCIL AND OFFICE BEARERS CHAIRMAN AND SECRETARY THERE WILL BE MONTHLY GENERAL MEETINGS TO DISCUSS AND SOLVE THE PEOPLES' PROBLEMS ALL UNSOLVED PROBLEMS HERE ARE SENT TO ALEXANDRA ACTION COUNCIL.THE ALEXANDRA ACTION COUNCIL WILL COMPRISE OF TWO REPRESEN-TATIVES FROM ALL ALEXANDRA STREETS (AVENUES) FROM 1st TO 22nd AVENUE. WILL ELECT ITS CHAIRMAN AND SECRETARY. WILL HAVENUENUE ITS GENERAL MEETING QUARTELY AND ALEXANDRA ACTION COUNCIL MONTHLY MEETINGS TO DEAL WITH MATTERS/PROBLEMS FROM STREET COMMITTEES AND TO ENCOURAGE COMRADESHIP. THIS COUNCIL SHALL HAVE LINKS WITH THE NATIONAL STRUGGLE GENERALLY IN SOUTH AFRICA.
THE BLOCK COMMITTEES MUST BE FORMED OUT OF TWO REPS FROM YARDS IN THAT BLOCK B\PLUS FOUR REPRESENTATIVES ELELCTED FROM THE BLOCK COMMITE TO REPRESENT THOSE PEOPLE TO THE STREET COMM. THERE SHALL BE FORTNIGHTLY GENERAL MEETINGS TO DISCUSS UNITY AND TO SOLVE PROBLEMS. UNSOLVED MATTERS OR PROBLEMS WILL BE REFERED TO THE ALEX STREETS COMMITTEES.	STUDENT-WORKER ALLIANCE FOR PEOPLES POWER
	UNBAN COSAS
	BAN APARTHEID EDUCATION
	TRASCO

After the Six-Day War was over, many of these ideas were in fact implemented, as we shall see.

After all the speakers had finished, a hearse drove the coffin to the Jukskei Cemetery on the edge of the township, and, engaging in another theatrical ritual – the community march from stadium to cemetery – mourners followed on foot. No police or army presence was apparent. There the burial took place with prayers from a priest (A. Sebola, Z2546). Afterwards, yet another ritual took place in the streets – a procession assembled to walk back to the Diradeng house for the traditional washing of the hands. So firm was the control of the funeral organisers over the streets that buckets of water had been placed on corners for the vast crowd of peaceful residents and the more militant youths, to wash their hands, as was customary after a burial (Black Lawyers' Association 1986: 4).

It was at this point that the state reinserted itself – the ceremony was illegal under the State of Emergency – by throwing teargas at the crowds. The war restarted. About 6,000 youths 'gathered in large groups in the streets'. When they got to Fifth Avenue, two Casspirs and several other vehicles blocked their way. The ordered and ritualised way in which the streets had been used ended abruptly as 'people then ran in all directions as they tried to escape the billowing smoke'. Not for the first time, homes became hideouts. Police fired on the crowd with birdshot. Many were injured – one participant estimated about fifteen (*Sunday Times*, 23 February 1986). Some started throwing stones in retaliation.

Attacks on police and councillor homes continued.[4] By the afternoon, those police who lived in Alexandra felt the attack on them was so severe and the threat to their lives and families so great that they abandoned the township and their homes en masse. Some moved to a safe area within Alexandra. Others moved to be accommodated in cells at the Wynberg Police Station or the Technical Depot in the neighbouring suburb of Kew. The army and riot police sent in supporting vehicles and men; but for the next few months police were forced to operate from the borders of the township. This was another major step in the transformation of the township.

One 'Jane Mabala', a 'mother with four daughters aged 20, 18, 16 and 8', described her experiences of that afternoon, one during which normality had been replaced by an eerie horror, in which the spaces and places of everyday life became threatening and difficult to negotiate:

> When I returned home [from work] at about 3.30 p.m., I saw heavy smoke and teargas all over the township and people were screaming. I saw several cars burning and youths and adults bleeding. Police and army vehicles were patrolling the streets. I had to find a safe way home, but it was virtually impossible to avoid the situation as youths had regrouped themselves in several corners of the township(s) [sic] and police were everywhere. I was soon caught up in the chaos, coughing

and crying like the rest of the youths and adults who were in the street. Just then I saw a group of youths armed with stones, approach a police Casspir. There were several shots from the Casspir and I saw two youths collapse and those around them run for their lives. This happened 20 m from me and I thought I would be caught in the shooting. The two boys who were lying in a pool of blood were aged between 12 and 14 years.

'Jane Mabala' was terrified:

I feared for my life as I was not very far from the line of fire. I do not remember how many times I prayed to God to prevent the bullets from hitting me. All I wanted was to reach my children at home ... I saw several bodies and much blood all over the streets. Youths in particular seemed more militant. Groups were picking up stones and hurling them at the Casspirs. But each time they tried that, more were shot.

Her home had been used as a refuge. She discovered that this had, in fact, been part of the battle plan of the youths:

I finally reached home and was surprised to find the door open. Earlier I had seen all the doors in the township opened and I wondered why. Only when I got home did I find out the reason. My daughters told me they had been told by other 'comrades' ... not to close the door as they could be used for shelter when police gave chase. Residents should open their doors as the youths were fighting for their liberation. (*Sunday Times*, 23 February 1986)

The natural 'spatial' response of residents to the mayhem outside – to close doors and hide – was reversed, and by drawing adult spaces into the struggle, the youths created a sense of complicity which horrified adults were otherwise reluctant to give.

Between about 3 p.m. and 10 p.m. a second series of eruptions took place:

The War on Day Two (continued)

3.05 p.m.	two motor vehicles were stoned at 108 First Avenue
4 p.m.	a human being was set alight by a petrol bomb, at 45 Fourteenth Avenue
4.20 p.m.	a petrol bomb was thrown in Second Avenue
4.30 p.m.	there was a stoning at 106 Phase One
5.39 p.m.	a Casspir was attacked in Second Avenue
5.45 p.m.	incidences of public violence were reported in Selborne Street
6 p.m.	a car was stoned along First Avenue
6 p.m.	a petrol bomb was thrown in Third Avenue
6 p.m.	Reuben Mosaka was shot dead by police '*tydens oproer*' (during unrest).
6.30 p.m.	a car was stoned along First Avenue
6.45 p.m.	a motor vehicle was petrol bombed corner London and Cumming Street
6.45 p.m.	a police vehicle was stoned corner London Street and Second Avenue
7 p.m.	house was petrol bombed at 16 Sixth Avenue
7.05 p.m.	a motor vehicle was petrol bombed corner Selborne and Third Avenues
10 p.m.	a car was hijacked along Vasco da Gama Street

Source: Zwane trial, Exhibit TTT, PJ archives

A police bus travelling down Seventh Street was attacked with stones and petrol bombs as it crossed Fourth Avenue. 'The driver momentarily lost control of the bus as a petrol bomb hit it on the side and set part of the vehicle alight' (*Sunday Star*, 16 February 1986). The bus careered down the street under a hail of stones. Fighting spread across all of the township's twenty-two avenues. Roaming mobs each attacked a whole series of targets, while security forces replied with increasing force. 'A five hour running battle between mourners and the police' was how one paper described the main action of the day (*The Star*, 17 February 1986).

The War on Day Two (continued)

- A crowd attacked a bottle store. The West Rand Development Board's security men ran for cover as they saw the crowd. They looted it while others stood guard outside. One woman was killed.
- An information centre was set alight.
- Groups of people clashed, and estimates varied widely as to how many were actually killed. Some said at least four, others possibly as many as eleven.
- A three-year-old was wounded in the head by a stray bullet when a truck driver fired into a crowd closing on him at Fourth Avenue.
- Police used teargas to disperse the mob, but failed.
- The mob gathered stones and moved towards the Town Councillor Reverend Sam Buti's house, which they did not attack – indeed it was guarded by scores of council policemen for twenty-four hours a day.
- 'Terrified' Indian shopkeepers closed their businesses and gathered in a group.
- Police vehicles were petrol bombed, and company vehicles were set alight.
- Rioters turned parts of Alexandra into a 'battle zone', erecting barricades of burning tyres and overturned cars. Wearing handkerchiefs to cover their faces, youths, wielding stones and petrol bombs, barricaded streets and taunted the police to come after them.
- The entrance to the township was blocked by two burning cars.
- Twelve further people were injured, including five policemen.

Sources: *Sunday Times*, 16 February 1986; *The Star*, 17 February 1986; the *Sunday Star*, 16 February 1986; *The Sowetan*, 7 March 1986

Clouds of dark smoke were to be seen from afar. 'Alexandra was besieged by so many policemen and flown over by so many helicopters that some people thought the end of the world had come' (*The Sowetan*, 7 March 1986). Police reacted by bringing in more Casspirs; firing more teargas and rubber and live bullets; and ordering reporters to leave the township.

The police were insufficient to the task of territorial defence, and the state considered this a military emergency. In the evening, the army arrived. Troops lined the perimeter roads of Alex, creating a barrier between the township and the white suburbs. War had been declared, effectively, between police and residents, with the army as the buffer between the township and the surrounding areas.

Parts of the township looked like a battle zone as police Casspirs nosed through barricades of burning tyres and cars turned over by rioters ...

> Security forces and police had difficulty getting past the blockade of burning cars and tyres. (*Sunday Times*, 16 February 1986)

By the end of this, the second day of the war, four residents had been shot dead by police (Mayekiso trial, Record of Deaths during six day war, CTH archives), seven had been injured and twelve arrested. One policeman was to die from burns inflicted by rebels, and several police homes had been destroyed. In Mzwanele Mayekiso's words:

> The anger bubbled to the surface. In fear, the police left the township, and instead guarded the outskirts. Every weapon at the community's disposal was gathered. Trenches were dug to prevent police infiltration. A war had truly begun. (Mayekiso n.d.)

Day Three: Public Turmoil, Private Retreat

By now, many of the streets and public spaces had become almost entirely occupied and controlled by rebels, or had become 'no-go' areas because of the violence there. 'Jane Mabala' returned from Soweto at 6 a.m.

> I was surprised to hear freedom songs from the stadium. It turned out to be the youths, including girls [sic], who had stayed at the stadium all night singing freedom songs and reciting poetry. There was an eerie hush over the township that day as people licked their wounds and counted their dead … All my children were safe. Other parents were not so lucky. By this time, some families had run out of food. Shops were closed. The situation was terrible. (*Sunday Times*, 23 February 1986)

Rumours began to spread. Some claimed that about twenty-seven people had died. Like Jane, people tried to continue with normal life, but found this difficult. Paul Tshabalala, a well-known soccer referee – later to be accused of treason in the Mayekiso trial – arranged a party for that night, inviting all his friends in the sport. Albert Sebola, a soccer player, and later an accused in one of the treason trials, arrived for his Sunday game at the stadium at midday, but it was disrupted by 'unknown' young people. Later, when he returned to the stadium he found broken bottles on the field, from a nearby liquor store, 'Square One Bottle Store', owned by the Town Council – which was being looted. There were many drunken people about. On his way back from the stadium to his clubhouse, he saw a bus, probably hijacked, being driven by a 'young boy'. Later a Casspir appeared, and fired a teargas canister at him and his soccer friends. He hid in the clubhouse the whole day and only ventured home at 7 p.m. He heard gunshots, was aware of heavy police presence and indeed feared for his life were he to venture out. People walking the streets would see hijackings, police firing teargas and youth violence. Many hid for fear of their lives. The attacks by rebels and police grew more vicious and widespread:

The War on Day Three

11 a.m.	a house was attacked at 25 Fourteenth Avenue
12 noon	a Toyota Hiace was stoned on the corner of Tenth Road and Third Avenue
12 noon	a bus was stoned between Thirteenth and Fourteenth Avenues
12 noon	a Putco bus was stoned along Fifteenth Avenue
12.20 p.m.	another Putco bus was stoned on Fifteenth Avenue
12.30 p.m.	another Putco bus was stoned on the corner of Fifteenth Avenue and Selborne Road
12.30 p.m.	there was stoning on First St Marlborough, the adjacent suburb
12.30 p.m.	a petrol bomb was thrown in Fifteenth Avenue
1.30 p.m.	a Volkswagen Combi was threatened on the corner of Sixth Avenue and Vasco da Gama Street
1.45 p.m.	there was stoning on Fourteenth Avenue
2 p.m.	a house was petrol bombed at 1018 Second Street Marlborough
2 p.m.	a motor vehicle was hijacked along Sixth Avenue
2.45 p.m.	a factory was petrol bombed at 1121 Second Avenue Marlborough
3 p.m.	there was stoning on the corner of Hofmeyr and Second Avenue
3.30 p.m.	a petrol bomb was thrown on the corner of Selborne and Third Avenue
3.40 p.m.	there was an 'incident' on the corner of Ninth Avenue and Selborne Street
4 p.m.	an 'unknown black male' died of bullet wounds on the corner of Twelfth Avenue and Roosevelt.
4 p.m.	a motor vehicle was burnt at 1067 First Avenue Marlborough
4.15 p.m.	a Datsun was stoned on the corner of London Road and Thirteenth Avenue
4.30 p.m.	a motor vehicle was stoned on the corner of Thireenth Avenue and Wynberg Road
4.35 p.m.	a Casspir was stoned in Fifteenth Avenue
4.35 p.m.	a 'black female' was burned on Fifteenth Avenue
?	a firebomb was thrown on the corner of First Avenue and Hofmeyr Road
5 p.m.	a motor vehicle was stoned along Eleventh Avenue
5.20 p.m.	a motor vehicle was stoned along London Road
5.30 p.m.	a motor vehicle was stoned on the corner of London Road and Fourth Avenue
5.30 p.m.	damage was done to the building of 'Marlborough Panel Beaters'.
6.30 p.m.	youths were found making petrol bombs along First Avenue
7.25 p.m.	a policeman's house was petrol bombed at 16 Sixth Avenue.
?	a building and cars were stoned at 'Marlborough Panel Beaters', 21 First Street
7.30 p.m.	a motor vehicle was stoned in Phase 1
8 p.m.	a motor vehicle was stoned on Fourth Avenue
8 p.m.	windows were broken and a petrol bomb thrown on the corner of Second Avenue and Second Street
8 p.m.	a construction company building was petrol bombed at 80 Wynberg Road
8 p.m.	a petrol bomb was thrown on the corner of Selborne Street and Twelfth Avenue
8.30 p.m.	Erphraim Mambono took the corpse of an 'unknown black male' who had been shot, to the clinic
10.25 p.m.	a building was petrol bombed on the corner of Second Avenue and Sixth Street
10.25 p.m.	police shot an 'unknown black male' on the corner of Vasco da Gama Street and Fifteenth Avenue
10.25 p.m.	a second 'unknown black male' was shot by police on the corner of Vasco da Gama Street and Fifteenth Avenue
11.30 p.m.	a motor vehicle was stoned near the Alexandra Flats, Phase 1

Several further shops and a bus were petrol-bombed during the night.[5]

Sources: Wynberg Police Records, Alexandra: MR 255.2.86 GO 31.86; *Sunday Times*, 23 February 1986; Mayekiso trial defence documents, CTH archives

The targeting of spaces ranged throughout the area, leaving few residents unaware of what was happening, and few places out of earshot or full view of specific incidents. Even old paternalists were being attacked. One garage, owned by a particularly paternalistic Italian was targeted during these six days.[6] 'About 300 or 400 Blacks came, stormed and attacked the garage and smashed everything to pieces and threw petrol pumps and broken the office door open and started to loot the place'. He had shot at the rioters and when he came to be boycotted later, the event took on a vengeful tone.

The police had stepped up their retaliation and youths had continued to burn, stone and even necklace. According to Mzwanele Mayekiso, 'The killings became frequent, as the police began making raids into Alex. Their R1 rifles peeked out of hippo portholes. People were armed only with stones' (Mayekiso n.d.). Residents retreated into their private spaces. 'People kept indoors and were scared of walking the streets' (Paul Tshabalala, M3272).

By now at least five residents had been shot dead by police and an unknown number injured.[7] A woman suspected of being a 'witch' was burnt when set alight by rebels after petrol had been thrown all over her in Fifteenth Avenue. Her friend had had a tyre placed around her neck but escaped when police came to her rescue (*The Sowetan*, 17 February 1986). In addition, late that night, Paul Tshabalala's friend Stephen Sithole left a party and was not seen alive again. About an hour afterwards, said Paul:

> I was made to understand that he had been shot at Fourteenth Avenue. People came and asked me transport him to the clinic. I went out to go and see. I found there were other people who had been shot there. Some were lying down.
> *Did Stephen Sithole subsequently die from his shotgun injury?*
> Yes, he ended up dead.
> *Who did you understand had shot him?*
> It was said it was the police. (Paul Tshabalala, M3272–4)

Paul went on:

> His story frightened the people, because he was a child who was not involved in the unrest activities, as well as any organisation ... We were all shocked to hear that he had been shot without provocation.

That day, that weekend, said Paul, 'there was no freedom in the location' – people 'came together and realised that these people wanted to kill them'. By the afternoon 'people kept indoors and were scared of walking the streets' (Paul Tshabalala, M3272–4).

Day Four: Authority Bestowed

Day Four represented the high point of the Six-Day War. Not only did violence reach a peak, but also a clear transposition of moral authority over the township space took place. At first, Day Four seemed simply a continuation of the conflict between youth and police. Soon after midnight, the first petrol bomb of the day was thrown. The attacks continued. Shops and factories were an early target:

The war on Day Four

12.07 a.m.	'Rosi's Wholesale Store' was burnt out on the corner of Fourth Avenue and John Brand Street
12.49 a.m.	'Ace Fast Foods' was petrol bombed on the corner of London Road and Third Avenue
5 a.m.	a factory was petrol bombed at 1129 Second Street, Marlborough
5.15 a.m.	two were injured for disobeying a roadblock on the corner of London Road and First Avenue
5.45 a.m.	a Casspir was petrol bombed on Thirteenth Avenue

The fear with which residents regarded the most violent comrades was mingled with respect for their courage in having challenged the township's moral order. However, the militants were not heroes in everybody's eyes. It took courage to attempt to curb youth excess, and assert a less violently millenarian vision of how the Alexandran space should be imagined:

> One morning at the height of the Six-Day War, I ran into a crowd of young comrades. Singing revolutionary songs about how the police are sell-outs, they were leading a black policeman who was clearly about to be necklaced. A tyre was being prepared with petrol, to hang around his neck ... I requested that the comrades consider asking the policeman whether he was prepared to resign from this job. They did, and he responded enthusiastically: yes, as from now I am resigning. The comrades replied: if you have resigned, we want all of your police kit, including gun and uniform. The policeman readily agreed ... everything that was connected to the police was turned over to the comrades ... They ... wanted to exorcise the police part of the ex-policeman, so they took the uniform and kit, doused them with petrol, set a bonfire and began to toyi-toyi.

'The comrades celebrated the winning of one of the police over to their side', continued Mayekiso, but, not surprisingly, the policeman thanked him profusely, and he never saw him again (Mayekiso n.d.).

Ordinary working people also found themselves at odds with militant comrades. The contrast between their mundane lives and the stirring actions of the rebels was extreme, and they were sometimes bewildered by what their living spaces had come to represent. Paul Tshabalala said that 'people decided' to hold a stay-away from work that day. 'They were scared that should they go to work on Monday, those that will remain and the children at home, they might find them dead.' This talk of a stay-away spread, and when Monday dawned, many people did not go to work (Paul Tshabalala, M3724). However, the 'people' who had decided did not include everyone. 'Jane Mabala', like many less politically involved residents, did not know of the stay-away:

> I thought the rioting would come to an end as people returned to

work. But I was wrong. I left the house at 6 am looking for the usual taxi or bus, but there were none. Instead I saw several youths carrying sjamboks and shouting that no one was going to work. I thought of my job and the problems facing me. I ran as fast as I could towards the outskirts of the township. The less fortunate ones were sjambokked by youths and turned back home. I was lucky to get a lift to work. (*Sunday Times*, 23 February 1986)

While she was gone, the attacks on cars, factories and houses, and the retaliatory and sometimes pre-emptive shootings of activists and others went on:

The War on Day Four (continued)

6.13 a.m.	the police fired ten teargas canisters at a group on the corner of Selborne Road and Tenth Avenue
6.45 a.m.	a motor vehicle was hijacked on the corner of Twelfth Avenue and London Road
7 a.m.	a motor vehicle was stoned along First Avenue
7 a.m.	there was a stoning on the corner of Pretoria Road and Vasco da Gama Street
7 a.m.	WRA police houses were attacked at 42 Fourteenth Avenue
7 a.m.	one Meisie Tshabalala was shot dead by West Rand Development Board police, who had, it was said, been attacked with petrol bombs
7.15 a.m.	a motor vehicle was stoned on the corner of London Road and Eleventh Avenue
7.30 a.m.	a factory was petrol bombed on Old Pretoria Road, Wynberg
7.30 a.m.	an 'incident' took place on the corner of Main Pretoria Road and First Avenue
7.30 a.m.	a building was stoned and looted on the corner of First Avenue and Vasco da Gama Street
?	a house was burnt out, 19 Tenth Avenue
7.45 a.m.	a stoning took place on Louis Botha Avenue
8 a.m.	a single room was petrol bombed at 195 Phase 2
8 a.m.	a Casspir on Seventh Avenue was surrounded and petrol bombed – the police shot back
9 a.m.	a motor vehicle hit by a bottle on the corner of Fourth Avenue and London Road
?	a 'forearm' (firearm?) was found in 16 Eighth Avenue
9 a.m.	a petrol bomb thrown at the corner of Fourteenth Ave and London Road
9.20 a.m.	an 'unknown black male' died corner Vasco da Gama Street and Second Avenue
9.45 a.m.	a person was found in possession of a petrol bomb on Fourteenth Ave
10 a.m.	a motor vehicle was stoned in Selborne Street
10 a.m.	a Constable Mamabolo was 'involved in a shooting incident' in Thirteenth Avenue
10.20 a.m.	a government vehicle was attacked on John Brand Street
10.30 a.m.	a Councillor Mashile was shot in the stomach at 132 Nineteenth Avenue
10.30 a.m.	a business was stoned at 57 First Street
10.30 a.m.	a factory was stoned at 9 First Avenue
10.45 a.m.	a motor vehicle was stoned on Wynberg Road
10.45 a.m.	a motor vehicle was burnt at 43 Eighth Avenue
?	a shop was burnt (place unspecified)
?	a bottle store was broken into on Second Avenue
10.55 a.m.	a person was found in possession of a petrol bomb on Fourteenth Avenue
11 a.m.	a Constable Senoamadi's house attacked at 43 Eighth Avenue – he shot back (one person was wounded)
11 a.m.	A house burnt down at 57 Fourteenth Avenue
11 a.m.	a house was petrol bombed at 53 Ninth Avenue
11.15 a.m.	a 'riot bus' was petrol bombed and stoned on John Brand Street
11.15 a.m.	a policeman was attacked and an 'unknown black man' was shot and killed on the corner of John Brand Street and Fifth Avenue
12 noon	a petrol bomb was thrown at 57 Fourteenth Avenue

12 noon   a Sergeant Tsipa was found burnt to death at 50 Thirteenth Avenue
12.15 p.m.   a petrol bomb was found on the corner of First Avenue and Hofmeyr Road
12.30 p.m.   a bus was stoned and burnt on the corner of Fifteenth Avenue and Selborne Road
12.30 p.m.   stoning took place on the corner of Selborne Road and First Avenue
12.30 p.m.   a petrol bomb was thrown in 13th Avenue
12.30 p.m.   another petrol bomb was thrown in Thirteenth Avenue

Albert Sebola was still, somewhat poignantly, trying to get a football game going. He went to his clubhouse at 8 a.m. On the way he saw a house burning down – the house of a policeman. Forty-five minutes later, he heard shots. He went out and saw that police were firing on a group of people watching the house burning (M. M. Zeelie, M2555). The police 'were on their Casspirs'. This may be what Constable Zeelie was referring to when he talked of his experiences on this Monday with Detective-Sergeant Tsipa: 'We received a message to go out to his [the policeman's] home in Alexandra Township, because his home was being burnt and during the burning of the house, he was being killed by black youths ... I personally went to the scene' (M. M. Zeelie, M523).[8]

The situation struck adults as urgent. Sometime that morning, three of them went to the South African Council of Churches in Johannesburg. They told their story, and five eminent churchmen were elected to attempt to put a stop to the war.[9] However, as 'Jane Mabala's' experience of the fourth day revealed, the adult view was far from prevalent. On her way home from work she filled her handbag with food for her family – carrying plastic bags from the shops would not be acceptable to the comrades. However, she began to fear that even this would incur their wrath when she saw that:

> On my arrival at Alex, I found several groups of youths with sjamboks beating up those who had gone to work. These adults had defied the threats of the morning. I saw elderly men run for their lives with children sjambokking them as they ran. The youths invariably ran faster than their elders – many of whom were soundly flogged before being allowed to go their way. I sneaked into my eldest daughter's house near the entrance of the township. There I cooled off for a few hours in the hope that the youths would be tired, but instead they were getting more vicious. I knew my children were very hungry and were waiting anxiously for my return.

Attacks in the township as a whole were legion:

The War on Day Four (continued)

1.30 p.m.   a petrol bomb was thrown (unspecified where)
1.30 p.m.   a Sergeant Andries Ngange was shot in Fourth Avenue
1.30 p.m.   a Councillor Magerman's house in Phase 2 was attacked
1.35 p.m.   there was a 'public violence incident' on the corner of Third Avenue and Hofmeyr Road
1.35 p.m.   a petrol bomb was thrown from a blue car at a police vehicle on patrol on the

	corner of Hofmeyr and Third Avenue and police fired back – one 'black male' was killed
1.43 p.m.	a Sergeant Mohale's house was burnt down at 63 Ninth Avenue
1.55 p.m.	a motor vehicle was stoned in Wynberg Road
2 p.m.	a house was attacked and shooting followed at 43 Ninth Avenue

At 2 p.m. Paul Tshabalala saw the burning of Johanna Hlubi, who was accused of being a witch.[10] Hlubi's burning by a mob appeared to fit seamlessly in to the violence of the day:

> *The allegation of witchcraft: is that a serious allegation or is it of no importance?* ... In 1986, it was very serious, especially with the youth. I remembered they burnt a certain old lady who stayed at Thirteenth Avenue, by the name of Johanna Hlobo [Hlubi] ... If one talks about witchcraft, those children just go straight there. It was the first time I saw a person being burnt in Alexandra. Now, the allegation of witchcraft is very serious.
> *Did you actually see the burning of this lady?* I saw it. (Paul Tshabalala, M3773; *The Star*, 27 October 1987)

Hlubi was eighty years old. She was doused with petrol and set alight outside her house. One of the five youths who had burnt her said

> he had been walking with some friends past Mrs Hlubi's house one night in January 1986 when they had seen her jump out of a window, and run down the street completely naked. On another night, the teenager was with some friends when they started talking about Mrs Hlubi. Someone suggested that they kill her and shortly thereafter she was attacked.

She died later in hospital. Five teenagers were subsequently found guilty of her murder (Paul Tshabalala, M3773; *The Star*, 27 October 1987).

The War on Day Four (continued)

2.30 p.m.	a petrol bomb was thrown (unspecified where)
2.30 p.m.	Sergeant Ngange was reported again as having been attacked on Ninth Avenue
2.34 p.m.	police again reported to be shooting at Magerman's place: twenty rounds
2.46 p.m.	police reported to be shooting at the corner of Second Avenue and Hofmeyr Road
3 p.m.	stoning took place in Louis Botha Avenue
3 p.m.	a house was set alight at 74 Fifteenth Avenue
3.05 p.m.	Municipal Police at Sam Buti's house were fired on by an AK-47
3.30 p.m.	a firearm was taken from a truck at 40 Twelfth Avenue
3.45 p.m.	a car was shot at (by police?) at the corner of Fourth Avenue and Hofmeyr Road – one man died and two others were injured
4 p.m.	a motor vehicle was stoned along Hofmeyr
4 p.m.	an incident of public violence took place on Second Avenue
4 p.m.	a Neil Williams was shot dead by a black policeman in the street outside 21 Second Avenue
4.40 p.m.	a bus was stoned on the corner of First Avenue and Louis Botha Avenue
4.50 p.m.	an Alfred Motemba was shot at 31 Seventh Avenue

4.50 p.m.	an Alfred Hadebe was shot in the stomach at 50 Seventh Avenue and died
4.55 p.m.	two were wounded in an attack on a police vehicle at 48 Seventh Avenue
5 p.m.	a vehicle was petrol bombed on the corner of First Avenue and Second Street
5.45 p.m.	a petrol bomb was thrown at Seventh Avenue
?	a motor vehicle was stoned in Pretoria Main Road
6.35 p.m.	an 'unknown black male' was shot and wounded on the corner of Hofmeyr Road and Fourth Avenue
7 p.m.	a butchery was plundered on the corner of Second Avenue and Vasco da Gama Road and police fired shots – one 'unknown Black Male' was shot, and a Sina Mopane of 9 Fourteenth Avenue was shot in the hip
7.30 p.m.	a house was petrol bombed at 114 Sixteenth Avenue
9 p.m.	a car was hijacked on the corner of Thirteenth Avenue

Sources: Wynberg Police Records, Alex MR 286/26, CTH archives

'Jane Mabala' had to survive, and used her knowledge of hidden spaces and places to do so:

> Finally, I devised a scheme, which, thank God, worked. My daughter lent me a blanket in which I placed the food. I put this on my back in the manner that most black women carry their babies, and picked a route home. I was petrified that the food would fall out the back of the blanket and my ruse would be discovered. In the township, the youths had manned several roadblocks and they searched whoever passed them. Fortunately, I found routes where no roadblocks had been set up. Finally, I reached home and that is how we managed to have our first decent meal in three days. Other families had nothing but water. In the evening, I could still hear gunfire. The youths warned everyone not to report for work the next day.

All policemen resident in Alexandra were withdrawn at the end of that day. In spite of their severe and growing losses, the rebels felt they had won a major victory. Deaths had peaked on this day. Eight residents had been shot dead, and again an unknown number injured.[11] The rebels had burned three people, two of them to death, and shot one policeman.

The events of the first four days of the war had shocked residents. Albert Sebola's mother did not go to work because 'she could not walk clearly on the streets because due to the presence of police' (A. Sebola, Z2557). In fact, everyone stayed at home. The shops were closed, and some families were now hungry (*Sunday Times*, 23 February 1986). Moreover, the events shook the government and the South African public at large to the core. These brutal events were not taking place in a remote rural backwater, but in the heart of the largest city in the country. Alongside some of the weal-thier suburbs of white South Africa was a township in flames, under siege, surrounded by the army, and patrolled by Casspirs.

A double challenge to authority had taken place. The state's immediate and situational authority over the township's space was forced to become militarised, leaving a vacuum of legitimacy that could be filled by the authority of the comrades. At the same time, the young were beginning to usurp the traditional authority that the older generation had held over them within the township's space – and the Alexandra Action Committee (AAC) tried to counter this. While the army and police repressed them and their families, the youth had begun to turn themselves into the arbiters of justice and moral and political rectitude in this circumscribed area.

Day Five: Ritual and Repression

Comrade ascendance did not mean state acquiescence – unsurprisingly, it provoked quite the opposite, a concerted state attempt to recapture the spaces lost. 'At midnight on the night of 17 February a convoy of security police came to 27 Seventh Avenue, the Mayekiso household. They searched the place and took some books ... they led Moss [Moses] away for a three week lockup'(Mayekiso n.d.). The authorities (subscribing to the 'great man' theory of revolution) believed that he was behind the revolt. Eighty-five further arrests were made throughout the day. Nevertheless, comrade authority was displayed through the fact that a protest stay-away they called was successful. Moreover, throughout this day, too, attacks continued:

The War on Day Five

6.45 a.m.	a car was hijacked on First Avenue
7 a.m.	a house was stoned at 129 Fourth Avenue
7 a.m.	there was a 'public violence incident' on the corner of Eleventh Avenue and Hofmeyr Road
7.30 a.m.	a shop was looted at 1 Second Avenue
7.30 a.m.	there was a 'public violence incident' on the corner of Twelfth Avenue and Hofmeyr Road
7.30 a.m.	police said they were attacked with a petrol bomb – Elias Nkosi was shot dead
7.30 a.m.	police said they were attacked with a petrol bomb on the corner of Hofmeyr Road and Seventeenth Avenue – Jabulani Mkele was shot dead and two others were shot and injured
8 a.m.	a petrol bomb was thrown at the corner of Nineteenth Avenue and London Road
8 a.m.	Owen Hlopolosa was shot by police at the corner of Nineteenth Avenue and London Road
8.30 a.m.	Elias Mahlaba was shot by police at the corner of Eleventh Avenue and Hofmeyr Road
9 a.m.	a motor vehicle was stoned in Wynberg Road
9.15 a.m.	a motor vehicle was stoned on the corner of First Avenue and London Road
10.15 a.m.	a motor vehicle was stoned on the corner of First Avenue and London Road
2.40 p.m.	a motor vehicle was stoned and then taken at the corner of Tenth Avenue and London Road
4.30 p.m.	a motor vehicle was stoned corner Eleventh Avenue and Wynberg Road

Source: Wynberg Police Records, Alex MR 286/26, CTH archives

Senior residents attempted to avert further chaos by channelling the war into ritual. They approached clerics such as Bishops Tutu and Buthelezi to address a mass meeting of the township. The youth backed the idea strongly.

They saw such ritual as a means whereby the distance between themselves and residents could be closed. They spent the early part of the day mobilising residents with varying degrees of menace. Cars with loudhailers went up and down the streets, calling the people of Alexandra to gather at the stadium. Paul Tshabalala was disturbed at home:

> there came boys with sjamboks ... They told me that there is a big meeting at the stadium and all people are required at the stadium. I told them that I would follow but I was afraid ... as I went out the gate I saw the police, there were many police outside. I got a fright to get to the stadium and thought we might be shot at the stadium, but as I saw the people going towards the stadium, I decided it is better for me to go. There will be many of us to die. I then went to the stadium. (Tshabalala, M3703)

Within a few hours, tens of thousands of people had gathered at the stadium, by now the customary symbolic space for community self-expression. Albert Sebola was there with his mother and three younger sisters. When he arrived there were 'plenty' people there – between 40,000 and 45,000, according to Paul Tshabalala. However, because the township was sealed off, and surrounded by the army, it was proving difficult to get the church leaders in to address the crowds. A local liberal politician, Ricky Valente, negotiated their entry. When the meeting was over, the huge crowd left the stadium and marched through the township towards the police station. The seizing of the performance space of the township by this new, public mass is discussed in more detail in a later chapter.

Soon afterwards, the army moved from the perimeter of the township right inside. That night several attacks occurred; and six people were shot at the corner of Twelfth Avenue and Hofmeyr Road at 8 p.m. Three died (*The Sowetan*, 7 March 1986). There were six arrests during the night.

By the end of 18 February, there had been eighty-five arrests and twenty-one detentions. Later records show that five people had been shot dead on that day. Two additional deaths had occurred since the Friday, but no inquest records were ever found, and no date of death firmly established (Mayekiso file on Six-Day War, CTH archives).

Day Six and after: Ground Regained

Severe repression and army occupation recovered some of the ground the state had lost to the rebels, while black authority figures within the church and the AAC had begun to recapture some of the moral authority adults had lost to the young. By Sunday 23 February 1986, the war was over. At least twenty-four, perhaps as many as twenty-seven people, had died at the hands of police. Several had been killed by the youth. In the next few days, a church delegation met the Deputy Minister of Law and Order and Defence,

Mr Adriaan Vlok (Mayekiso file on Six-Day War, CTH archives) to whom they presented the 'specific grievances of the people of Alexandra'. On 21 February a 'report back' was held. Bishop Tutu told the assembled crowd that he had made a little progress with the government, and urged calm. In a clear indication that the war was in fact far from over, however, this normally highly respected figure was then booed by the youth. Comrade authority was by no means crushed. It was to re-emerge shortly, in a different form.

Conclusion

This had been 'a week of living hell', said one journalist, 'Alexandra would not be the same again' (*Sunday Tribune*, 23 March 1986). The atmosphere was one you could 'cut with a knife' (*Sunday Star*, 23 February 1986). In this short period, one can detect the main motifs of revolt and reaction that were to characterise the rest of the six-month period of rebellion in the township. The uprising provided the necessary 'rupture', shattering the veneer of normality in Alexandra. Old repertoires of collective action were finally transcended. The previously predictable street life of residents was transformed into the disturbingly unpredictable, unforgettable period to which all would refer back to as the Six-Day War.

How was it that this brief period succeeded in creating so profound a rift? Clearly, the attack upon space was its most striking achievement. Old definitions of space were radically disrupted by hundreds of random acts of violence throughout the six days, day and night, by both youths and their chief opponents, the police. Small and large groups of youths had moved up and down the streets using fire, bombs, occasionally guns, stones, whistles and crowd energy. Violent and invasive acts had spread to every street, so that all physical space came to be thought of by residents as vulnerable and therefore unpredictable. Police shot many to death, whether adults, youths or children, sometimes randomly and sometimes more deliberately. As mobilisation increased, the nature of the fatalities had changed – whereas of the sixteen killed in the 1984 disturbances ten to twelve had been students, it was increasingly non-students and older people who were killed two years later. Uncontrollable mobs of youths and sometimes adults and children directed a murderous destructiveness against police, local councillors and suspected informers and witches. Most police fled, thus directly weakening the tangible sources of power in the township. The outside borders of the township were sealed, with police and army controlling exits and entrances. Inside, some trenches and barricades were used, but at this stage of the revolt youths seemed mainly to rely on randomness and their own physical assertiveness in the streets. In addition, private space began to alter – homes became places of meeting and of retreat where active rebels could gather, or be harboured by adults.

Besides this recasting of their venue for revolt, the rebels posed challenges to the rhythms of time (Adam 1990: 133; Giddens 1987; Levi Strauss 1978; Thompson 1967).[12] What we think of as 'normality' appears to be so because it entails the presence of 'cyclical' time. In advancing their bid for power, they imposed changes in this. The repetitiveness of everyday life – the 'duree' – whether short or long – was challenged. Different, often unpredictable, temporal rhythms were imposed. The one square mile of huddled housing and familiar streets was subjected to a new regularity – that of attack. The distinction between day and night was blurred. One young comrade remembered how different things had seemed when she looked back at the six days almost nostalgically. 'During the Six-Day War you would only sleep between 9 and 10 p.m.,' she said, and then, 'people would come to where you are staying ... they would shout 'vuka maulele' – wake up. I would jump and get into my trousers, maybe with just my nightshirt, and join the war again' (Carter 1991a: 268). Furthermore, 'cyclical' time was challenged by comrade visions of 'transcendence' which would occur through the realisation of their utopian alternatives to the present order.

The tenuous legitimacy of administrative rule within the township was shattered. The state's immediate response was to subject Alexandra to what amounted to occupation by the military – a force far more experienced in combining control with persuasion than were the police. It developed a longer-term response only after the township had experienced further profound changes. This military occupation, plus the reassertion of their presence by the police, and the experiences of the Six-Day War itself brought into question the moral universe that had previously seemed normal to residents. The population of Alexandra as a whole, and not simply the younger generation, came to see things in new ways and make themselves available to new ideas. The Six-Day War reversed the meaning of the township's space. Old styles of existence – even of protest – were disrupted. The effect of this short, harsh period upon the minds of the inhabitants of Alexandra was profound. The way was opened for the development of a revolutionary climate within the township. The whole of Alexandra came to be redefined as a theatre for new genres of collective action.

GENERATIONS, RESOURCES AND IDEAS

My mind comes to a standstill when I think about the young ones. I am always confused ... the way they respond to us adults looks to us as if they are possessed and I have a fear that there is nothing to be done to stop them ...(Durban parent, quoted in Campbell 1994: 96)

I grew up understanding the word 'father' as meaning he is the only head of the house with the final word and decision making power. This is no longer the case. They are all disobedience and contempt towards the elders. (Durban parent, quoted in Campbell 1994: 98)

What exactly led to this unprecedented *mobilisation* of the township masses? We have argued that the state's weakness, ineptness and authoritarianism combined to create new strata in the township 'uncaptured' by old social and cultural systems of authority and open to new repertoires of action. However, all this means is that people in the townships were probably predisposed to act in new ways – it does not explain the fact that they did act or that some of their actions were highly politicised and even revolutionary. Their resentment and alienation could, hypothetically, have been expressed through new types of criminal behaviour, high suicide rates, migration, sub-cultures, religious or ethnic movements or a variety of other manifestations of discontent. Was it, then, the exiled and influential ANC that had generated mass mobilisation? Certainly, this is one perception of the events of this period. The ANC was present, it was vocal and it was active. How influential was it, precisely, over the form and trajectory of the rebellion itself?

ANC ideas had, by the time of the rebellion, thoroughly penetrated the township. The ANC in exile ran a clandestine radio station based in Zambia which was widely listened to; and its popular publications – *Mayibuye*, the *African Communist*, and *Sechaba* – were all known in the townships.

My father used to listen to Radio Zimbabwe (sic). He was interested in the history of his country. He would say why there's fighting there. He would tell us (his children) the whole story, and end up with the ANC in South Africa.' (JB, Alexandra activist, Carter 1991a: 130)

Furthermore, the 1976 generation of youths who had fled into exile provided a much enlarged source of cadres who could be sent back inside – as early as 1978 an underground network of ANC cells was operating in Soweto, Alexandra, Rustenburg, Pietersburg, Sekhukhuneland and Lebowa (Carter 1991a: 130). The death by his own hand-grenade of the well-known Alexandran youth and cadre infiltrated from Zambia, Vincent Tshabalala, in 1985, sent a clear message to residents there: 'It was with Vincent's death … that I knew that there are cadres inside the country,' said one activist (JB, Alexandra activist, quoted in Carter 1991a: 130).

Mozambique's independence struggle and victory had become known through radio and television and was an inspirational event to young black radicals. And the ANC itself had begun to support insurrection rather than war, calling for and encouraging the kinds of actions already being undertaken in townships.

In March 1984 *Sechaba*, the official organ of the ANC, carried the ANC president Oliver Tambo's New Year message, in which he had stated: 'To march forward must mean that we advance against the regime's organs of state-power, creating conditions in which the country becomes increasingly ungovernable.'

Throughout 1985, and up to and during the revolt these kinds of calls continued.[1] After the Six-Day War the ANC explicitly endorsed what was happening in Alex itself: 'Recently, the people of Alexandra have demonstrated for an end to police repression, and the whole town became a no-go zone in March for the funeral of those shot by police' (*Sechaba*, April 1986).

By May 1986 the ANC's pamphlet: 'Call to the people: from ungovernability to people's power', was being widely distributed inside the country, carrying an appeal which could and would be heeded. It ran:

> The surge of people's resistance and active defiance have reached new heights. The face of our country is changing before our very eyes.
> - In the black ghettos of the urban areas the legitimacy of authority of all types is not just under attack, it has been largely destroyed. Most of those who served white rule in so-called urban councils have suffered the wrath of the people. But many have respected the demands of the people by resigning …
> - The people, by their actions, are teaching black police and soldiers that there is no place in our communities for those who wear the uniforms of apartheid and who carry out orders to kill, maim and torture their brothers and sisters.
> - We call on our communities in the black ghettos to replace the collapsing government stooge councils with people's committees in every block which could become the embryos of people's power.
> - We call on our people, and more especially our fighting youth in every black community, school and university, to find ways of organising themselves into small mobile units which will protect the people against anti-social elements and act in an organised way in

both white and black areas against the enemy and its agents. Every
black area must become a 'no-go' area for any isolated individuals
or pockets of the enemy's police or armed personnel.
• Make apartheid unworkable! Make the country ungovernable!
  Forward to people's power! Long live the ANC the vanguard of our
  revolution. (Barrell 1991: 7)[2]

Sechaba later ran an article on the 'People's War' of this period, which
mentioned what it called the:

> emerging embryonic forms of self government and popular power,
> and the creation of peoples committees. In most of the areas torn by
> the upsurge, government instituted community councils have been
> destroyed and those who man them have either been killed or forced
> to resign. Black police and informers have been forced, through mass
> revolutionary violence, to quit most of the townships. We have 'no-go'
> areas, they claim. Apartheid is becoming unworkable. The country is
> rapidly degenerating into a state of complete ungovernability ... [there
> are] organs of self-government and popular power: challenging the
> apartheid authorities for control of these areas. These should be trans-
> formed into mass revolutionary bases, through which we can realise
> our strategy of people's war.

The publication recommended that in these areas local 'revolutionary
peoples committees' should be created, whose tasks would be

> organising the masses and transforming the no-go areas into strong
> mass revolutionary bases to provide the ground for growth of a
> people's army; to serve as organs of insurrection and self government;
> to ensure that the expelled and rejected organs of apartheid power do
> not return; escalating the campaign of making apartheid unworkable.

At first, it appears as if the revolt that erupted in Alexandra was a simple
reflection of these kinds of demands. Mzwanele Mayekiso wrote later that
he and many others had been strongly influenced by this. He said that 'from
the beginning' the ANC's 'Charterist' ideas held powerful sway in the
township: 'The tradition of ANC ideology was overwhelming,' he said.
'Through the United Democratic Front (UDF) the Charterist ideology
ruled then and still does today.'
  But even in the organisation's own documents there are suggestions that
the ANC was trying to co-opt an emerging and existing struggle rather than
to create one. Their switch from infiltration to insurrection tactics had been
forced upon them by the Nkomati Accord, which had cut off their guerrilla
infiltration route, and forced expulsions of ANC members from Lesotho,
Swaziland and Botswana (Barrell 1991). They knew that the townships had

generated their own forms of struggle and sought to turn this to their own use. They believed that from the raw revolutionary material that had emerged, they could constitute a 'young revolutionary cadre of the peoples revolutionary movement', which would then 'earn the honour of being called the Young Lions': 'That army of stone-throwers has to be transformed into an army with weapons. Our people have the mood and spirit; every stone thrower wants a gun; we have to put guns in their hands,' wrote ANC military strategist Ronnie Kasrils (*Sechaba*, May 1986), who was struck by the emergence of what he called 'the people's improvised tactics'. The entire repertoire of urban street fighting – the barricades, trenches, barbed wire, tactical street fighting, people using the labyrinth of township lanes and streets to lure the enemy into ambush, petrol bombs, knives, using the enemy's own weapons or 'rough justice' against community councillors and informers (all genres of protest which were emerging in cities throughout the country) – was endemic and indigenous rather than imported and imposed. While a myriad of ANC-forged ideas had flowed into South Africa during this period, nearly all of them were illegal and dangerous, and highly censored by the law, and access to them was punishable by the state's brutal security forces. This gave them an air of romance and a certain power amongst black township dwellers. But their very illicitness also weakened the capacity of such ideas to operate as mobilising devices on a broad scale.

The rebellion could only work because of a developing alliance between these ideas and the local cultural and ideological networks of rebelliousness within the country and the township. As we have seen, since the early 1970s, both township dwellers and workers throughout the country had evolved forms of protest that by no means simply reflected the strategy of the liberation movement. Indeed, some might argue that it was the other way around – the strategies and repertoires came from the people and the ANC capitalised upon them. Even Davis (1987), who is mainly concerned with the ANC's perspective, points to the ways in which local rebelliousness throughout the country took the ANC by surprise and often overwhelmed its modest initiatives with an almost uncontrollable intensity and spread. New repertoires of action had been born; new types of activists had been mobilised; and new ideologies of emancipation had rapidly developed. But over time those with rebellion in mind came to heed the call of exile movements for revolution or, in the case of the ANC, 'ungovernability', and an explosive mix of local politics and exile power developed. Youths and adults alike knew that they were also forging something of their own. They expressed strong criticism of the centralising traditions of Nationalism and preferred their own ideas about leadership (Mayekiso 1996: 14).

During the actual rebellion this resistance to the simple importation of outside ideas led to the development of two different strategies following the

Six-Day War. Each entailed the construction of its own visions of Utopia. Both confined themselves to the area within the township's borders. On the one hand, the militant, revolutionary youths – what Kasrils called 'the Young Lions of Alexandra' – sought an overturning of all authority and the creation of a better world. On the other, alongside their romantic millennium there emerged a competing adult-based genre of opposition, which tried to create a 'popular democracy' within the township, and to calm the rising violence of the young. Both were composed of a subtle mixture of inward-flowing and illicit ideas and the indigenously forged ideas of township intellectuals and their followers. Both were overlaid by a third strand of ideas and behaviour – what I have called 'public nationalism' – which was the legalised face of the ANC.

This chapter is devoted to exploring some of the prime social constituents of the township – and by extension of other townships – which generated the different types of mobilisation that were to appear, asking who the rebels actually were and what resources, networks and world-views existed in their social worlds. If the rebellion was staged in a societal theatre, then these were the *dramatis personae*. What scripts were likely to emerge from them? What parts did they choose to play? And why did they play them?

THE EMERGENCE OF SOCIAL GENERATIONS

Generational conflict is a common feature of rebellion, although, compared to thirty years ago, it has fallen from favour as an object of study in the West (Altbach and Laufer 1972). In Africa the history of generational struggles is moderately well documented, partly because generational differences are a particularly significant aspect of social reality, as they are sanctioned by a strongly surviving traditionalism in many places. In most African pre-industrial systems, both production and power depended partly in age hierarchies for their effectiveness,[3] although they are, unsurprisingly, everywhere undermined by a variety of forces associated with modernity in different ways. How did the generational theme play itself out in Alexandra?

It is a mistake to assume that all biological generations become socially distinct entities. 'Generation' is defined here in the sense of what Abrams calls a 'social' or 'sociological generation' rather than a biological one, that is: 'that span of time within which identity is assembled on the basis of an unchanged system of meanings and possibilities. A sociological generation can thus encompass many biological generations' (Abrams 1982: 256).

In this particular township, like many others, the generations were divided in this broader sense. The older social generation did not constitute a different class from their children, but certainly had features which marked them as having been differently socially located:

> Any given location … excludes a large number of possible modes of thought, experience, feeling, and action, and restricts the range of self-

expression open to the individual to certain circumscribed possibilities ... Inherent in every location is [also] a tendency pointing towards certain definite modes of behaviour, feeling and thought. (Mannheim 1972: 106)

The youths and adults constituted social rather than biological generations.

If a new sociological generation is to emerge, a new configuration of social action, the attempt of individuals to construct identity must coincide with major and palpable historical experiences in relation to which new meanings can be assembled ... Life history and world history coalesce to transform each other. Identity is made within that double construction of time. (Abrams 1982: 255–6)

It was as a result of a variety of historical and political processes that specific cultural and ideological resources – social and cultural capital – became available to each generation. Each of the two generations had experienced particular kinds of identity formation; and each had recourse to distinct sets of intellectuals, ideas, popular support and resources. It was on this basis that each attempted to implement its own plans for the revolutionary metamorphosis of Alexandra.

It has been suggested above that a marked transition in style and form of governance within townships had accompanied the consolidation in the urban areas of what some have called 'high apartheid' in the late 1960s and 1970s. When the older system of township rule – 'welfare paternalism' – was replaced by a new system – that of 'racial modernism' – the seeds of generationally different resistance styles were germinated. Because in each era, the creation and sustaining of townships was not only about accumulation, but was also about power, space, authority and class (from the dominant group's point of view) as well as about meaning, kinship, family, social stratum and survival (from the point of view of township inhabitants), the move from welfare paternalism to racial modernism entailed a loss of citizenship, class, status, cultural security, authority and power, by a range of township-based groups, mainly those of the older generation – a removal, in fact, of the resources available to create a certain sort of stability. These things had all existed in particular configurations under the segregationist/ paternalistic order, and had underpinned its relative sense of order – blacks were 'governable'. Their loss entailed humiliation, downward mobility and shame. It left a vacuum of authority that the new bureaucracy failed utterly to fill, and into which the youth were quick to step.

Apartheid had at last created its own nemesis in the townships. By socially re-engineering urban life with an arrogant modernism, the government had broken the ties that bound generations and communities together, destroyed the black elite's claims to legitimate authority, and removed but not replaced the cushion provided to the black urban poor by paternalistic welfare. By doing all of these things with blind, over-bureaucratised tyranny, against a background of economic stagnation and educational debasement, they had no one to blame but themselves when the governable became ungovernable.

A 'free-floating' stratum of young people had been created by the 1980s. Slow economic growth failed to draw this stratum into employment, and the networks which had drawn most earlier youths into township society – through schooling, age hierarchies, family influence, patronage systems and cultural forms – were substantially weakened. The humiliations and degradations their parents and elders experienced as a result of apartheid's laws, which themselves were invasive of the previously private realm, added to the weakening of adult legitimacy in the eyes of the young.

The processes at work here reflected the syncretism of the times. The cleavage between the generations had been a defining feature of traditional African societies, but it had been regulated by a variety of social mechanisms. It now became exaggerated and highly politicised. The social disruptiveness of the modernising thrust of the state was typical of early capitalism. The state moved rapidly and uncompromisingly, oblivious of the complexities of the social worlds it sought to transform and the unintended consequences it was likely to generate.

Thus when the racial modernist order undercut the economic basis of welfare paternalism, it generated opportunities for the younger generation to mobilise, around the crises of rents, schooling and local government – while the emergence of new ideologies provided them with the means. The rebellions of the eighties, therefore, took up immediate and urgent issues of survival for the poor – but against a background, unlike earlier periods, of a pre-existing, and long-developing vacuum of authority on the part of their rulers, which gave their rebellions impetus.

THE COMRADE GENERATION

This revolution, it is a child.[4]

It was not uncommon for child-activists to live in bands without adult supervision, substituting the security of political hierarchies for those of the family.[5]

The core of the rebellion rested in the hands of the 'comrades', a series of groupings of young men and some women who had adopted a revolutionary world-view. These children of workers or the unemployed were the visionaries of the time. Themselves unemployed, they were products of a disrupted and radicalised schooling in desperately inadequate and skewed Bantu Education schools. Of poor, violent and often single parent families, they had transformed their consciousness from that of the helpless and marginalised in the unwanted ghettoes, to that of resourceful and determined idealists, willing martyrs, and unforgiving opponents of the social order they had inherited.

'Comrades' and 'youth' were synonymous in many people's perceptions – although to insiders there were crucial differences. To the observer of the township, the youth were constructed in the mind of the time in different, contradictory ways. In the apocalyptic view, the young people of the townships of the 1980s were 'menacing', 'violent', 'marginalised', 'idle', 'savage', irresponsible and irrational anti-social rebels. By contrast, the liberatory view saw them as 'young lions', 'heroes', purposeful, altruistic, brave, enthusiastic and militant (Seekings 1993: 7–8). The two stereotypes overlapped in that both saw 'the youth' as curious and rebellious, militant and impatient, impulsive and impressionable.

But 'the youth' consisted, in fact, of a variety of social types and political groupings, including the often distinctive category of the 'comrades': a grouping which embraced a certain percentage of idealists; the less altruistic *comtsotsis* (whose violent pseudo-political behaviour was often debased); those who were apolitical; and many others. Thus not all youths were comrades; and not all 'comrades' were idealists.

The term 'comrade' first emerged in the early 1980s, and had become part of common currency by about 1985. To observers of township revolt it was a generic, ill-defined term; it came to be used to refer to practically any black youngsters engaged in resistance. The 'comrades' became a catch-all phrase for young militants such as leading activist Dan Montsisi, who felt they were:

> at the forefront of the confrontation between the state and the people … for planning and execution it was the young people who put up posters, organized meetings, went from house to house. In the formation of street committees, defence committees, they were in the forefront and most visible. They were also the first to be detained, the first to be shot. (Johnson 1988: 41–2)

But in fact to insiders 'comrade' status was much more specific. It referred to those whose political commitment was known, who belonged to particular groupings, and whose style and presence were instantly recognisable. One of the 'comrades' accused in the youths' treason trial, Albert Sebola, was questioned on this issue:

> The comrades refers to any person who belongs to an organisation and a person who identifies himself with the problems of the people, and of course the social meaning of the word is a friend … *The evidence is that groups of youth, young people who were seen moving about this township and also other townships, but this township more particularly were identified as comrades* … I do not agree to that. As I have said a comrade is a person who belongs to an organisation and who identifies himself with the problems of the people. (A. Sebola, Z2679)

Here we do not attempt to discuss the 'youth' as a whole, but rather to focus on some of those who were activists in this particular rebellion. The social character of the 'comrades' varied from region to region. But the Alexandran case does provide us with insight into the social, political and cultural origins of the various kinds of young people involved in rebellion, and helps us to understand the complexities of what it meant to be 'a youth' or 'a comrade', as well as to address the ways in which the image of young people was constructed by outsiders.

NETWORKS, MALENESS AND SOCIAL CAPITAL

Mobilising resources for revolt was difficult for the poorest and youngest of the rebels. Still, their social networks, their willingness to see the space of the township as a resource, their access to an increasingly significant stratum of leaders and the brief availability of radical and appealingly illicit ideas came together in the early eighties and provided essential under-pinnings for their capacity to mobilise.

Growing up in the yards of Alexandra during the 1970s was tough. Besides the grinding poverty, the mainly working-class families of the township had to cope with the various ways in which the police, the law and the bureaucracy constantly undermined their efforts to establish stability and security. Life at home for youngsters was not easy. Family discipline was harsh especially, but not only, for boys. Most parents used sjamboks to discipline their sons, and teachers chastised their pupils in the same way. Some children regarded this as normal and perfectly defensible. As Chicks Phalongwane said at his trial for sedition after the rebellion: 'I say my lord that if you punish person with a sjambok this does not mean to say that you hate that person. My parent does it on me also, that does not mean to say my parent hate me' (P. C. Phalongwane, Z4876). Nearly all of the accused in the Zwane trial reported having experienced such violence at home or in school. Some, for example Albert Sebola, were far from sanguine: 'Most of our parents as a traditional thing they feel that in the township by beating a child you will get him straight but he has had no education my lord' (A. Sebola, Z3304).

These were revolutionaries created not only by hardship and an easy familiarity with violence, but also by the many unintended consequences of the policies of their patrons and rulers. One of these was the frustration many young people felt as a result of their unrealised ambitions. Many, if not most, younger people in Alexandra in the 1980s went to high school there and, unlike their parents, most reached Standard 8, or even matri-culated, only to find themselves trapped within a working-class dormitory with a stagnant economy and a racist social order. While some accepted the few working-class occupations that came their way, quite a number of them had higher ambitions. An irony of high apartheid was that it had expanded access to schooling – albeit of deliberately appalling quality – for youths such as these,[6] creating a generation that wanted more than their racially separate world could offer them. Becoming leaders within youth politics gave them a way of expressing their capabilities and pursuing their dreams.

The highly structured little society of the township provided a number of environments in which a social and cultural life for young people was created. The streets were the most obvious. At home, rooms were so small and crowded that most people – especially youths who were out of school and unemployed – spent most of their time in Alexandra's street corner society, where neighbourhood and peer, mainly male, networks were rendered strong (Bundy 1987). The social world of the comrades in Alexandra was not necessarily the same as that of its notorious gangsters who also forged their sub-cultures on the streets. Politicised youths were always just slightly better-educated, more socially aware and morally driven than were straight 'tsotsis' – although the boundaries were shaky and often the gangster and the comrade were teenage brothers or cousins; or the same boy would move from one world to the other. This combination of a tough street life, familiarity and contact with gang behaviour, unemployment, family hardship and violence, and social and educational decay and disruption bred a commonalty of young people able and willing to turn their social and political resentments into militancy. Almost entirely consisting of impatient and impetuous young men, guided by their transcendent but flawed capacity to imagine another world, their hopes were for immediate salvation from oppression and for a tangible transformation of their surroundings.

By 1984 'comrade' forms of contention had emerged. 'Youth groups' had already formed; and the 'faction', 'gang' or 'posse' was visible. One school boycott, at the contentious Minerva High School, entailed running battles between boycotters and prefects. The latter appear to have become more than simply monitors of trivial behavioural deviations, and rather, a political force for the control and discipline of the politically conscious. Boycotters and prefects each formed their own clearly gang-like grouping (making it politically impossible for anything resembling a prefect system to continue in black schools after liberation). Two thousand enraged pupils, accusing the principal of stealing the money given to the school for buying material, stormed the school building, causing the head, a Mr Baloyi, and eight prefects to barricade themselves in a staff office (*The Star*, 16 October 1984). The boycotters burned down classrooms, stoned the principal, the prefects and the buildings, burnt cars, and attacked the principal's wife and children (*The Citizen*, 14 August 1984). Many pupils were arrested, and even when the school was reopened some time later, the rest would not attend classes again or write exams until they were released (*The Sowetan*, 25 October 1984).

Mob or gang-like contention also appeared in 1985 such as when attacks on local councillors began, or when 'junior councillors' (another gang-like deformation of what had been intended as a form of civic socialisation) abducted a member of the Alexandra Residents' Association, and locked him in a Council police cell. These radical actions were reinforced by the presence of trained ANC insurgents on some occasions.

Underpinning the emergence of these tightly-knit forms of youth action were the extremely dense networks that bound young people, and particularly young men, together in a series of overlapping social worlds each with its own powerful pull upon loyalty and commitment. Campbell shows how in a similar setting in Durban, vivid differences in identity construction and networking patterns existed between young men and young women (Campbell 1994). Whilst young men questioned about their social priorities associated themselves with sport, drinking, gang activity and gambling above family, comrades and education, young women in the same survey gave their highest priority as family, followed by lovers and education. Male loyalties were powerful, often finding expression in a profound and sometimes patronising sexism.[7] Wife beating is and was common in township families.[8] Youngsters in the Natal study believed that the complex traditional institution of *lobola* was simply the equivalent of payment by the husband for the wife's services (Campbell 1994). It is not surprising that while many young women were deeply involved in township politics, they came to play a secondary role when violence erupted. As one young woman said: 'In fact its mostly boys who go to meetings, and not girls. I do not go to meetings … because it would take me away from home' (Campbell 1994: 107).

Leadership in the Alexandran case was predominantly male, but supporters were about one third women in several places where figures are available. They were younger than the men, and they were often excluded from higher positions, or from violence, on grounds of their actual or perceived female responsibilities and interests. 'Boys are not afraid to make things happen, also they don't have the job of cooking and cleaning,' said one participant; and as another comrade in a similar township said:

> Women are ashamed to hit someone or to kill them. When someone has been murdered women feel ashamed to see the body. Whereas men have no shame in these matters – and will just go to that place to look straight down at the corpse … there are no girls who do the attacking, only men. And we go out as men to meet these men. We are men. How can we tolerate being attacked by men. Boys have got the desire not to be shamed in this way. (Campbell 1994: 107)

Youth groups, too, were male dominated. As one female comrade put it:

> Such things in the township are done by boys. Girls just usually follow them. *What do you mean by this?* For example if the boys are following after someone who has been stealing, the girls will follow the boys and

throw stones, but the boys will lead the procession. *Why is this?* This is because girls are afraid and boys are bold. (Campbell 1994: 107)

Street life provided one of the bases for male networks; and the ties and commitments that accompanied the world of the young soccer player appear to have been even stronger. Nearly every male comrade played or followed soccer in Alexandra, and an extraordinary number of the soccer players and fans – and hence comrades – knew one other. The world of soccer was not only extremely tightly knit and a powerful bonding force, it was also a school for acquiring skills essential to political mobilisation. It was here that young men learnt how to lead, how to organise, how to regulate group behaviour, even to take minutes, run committees and hold meetings.

But a huge range of other social networks also existed, not surprisingly, given the resilience and richness of the syncretic popular culture of the township – there were some Rastafarians, some churchgoers and some choir-members amongst the comrades. Youth clubs, schools, gangs and churches all acted to provide networking and mobilising systems, which underpinned social and political activism. A prominent local churchman, Father Cairns, noted that the Catholic Church had about 20,000 members in Alex, and that 'Churches provided networks and resources, not only for individual youths, but for things like meetings – church halls and so on' (Father Cairns, M4355). At times the same young man would attend, and indeed lash wrongdoers at, his local people's court in the day and go to choir practice at his local church in the evening.

Some comrades were youth club members, many were neighbours in small localities, and of course all had gone through the politically searing and mutually socially binding experience of attending school in the late 1970s and early 1980s. Long-standing traditional rural African expectations that young men would move in 'age cohorts' had not died completely in townships, while more urban traditions of gangsterism had provided examples where male cohorts also became strongly neighbourhood-based. These too added to the bondedness of these groupings.

The threesome of Albert Sebola, Ashwell Zwane and Piet Mogano, three of the eight accused in the Zwane treason trial, formed a social, political and friendship network which illustrates something of the kinds of young people involved in comrade activities.

Albert Sebola, who was perhaps the archetypal 'comrade', was born in 1965 in Alexandra and had lived there his whole life (A. Sebola, Z2535). His father had died when he was younger and he had three younger school-going sisters. The whole family lived, cooked and slept in one rented room, part of a 'bond', with one bed, one wardrobe, one table, four chairs, and a stove. Sixty families shared his yard, he said, sharing one tap and four toilets. He was far better educated than his parents were. His father had been an unemployed motor mechanic who had worked at home. His mother was at first a lowly hospital cleaner, but when she had at one stage lost her job, she had been subjected to that grossest of apartheid indignities, being 'endorsed out' to remote Louis Trichardt and forbidden from seeking further work. Her appeal took two years after which she worked as a domestic servant in the suburbs, leaving home at 6 a.m. every day and returning at 6 p.m. They had at that time moved to another room which had no water-borne sewerage and no drains, said Albert. Everyone just threw their water into the streets. It was, argued his defence in his trial after the rebellion, medieval.

Albert went to two of the schools which were crucibles of Alexandran radicalism – Boveti Junior and then Alexandra High until it was closed during the boycotts of 1985. His ambition then was to study electronics, and he had always fixed cars and radios. Besides being ambitious he was also a leader amongst his peers. He was a member of the Student Christian Movement. He was a keen soccer player and captained his team, Alexandra Santos. Sebola's modest puritanism and sense of a need to control 'way-wardness' amongst his fellow-youths, was a common feature of comrade identity, as was his more general moral toughness (A. Sebola, Z2535).

Sebola gives a portrayal of the life of the football player which suggests a degree of belonging, bonding and loyalty which went beyond simple team membership. During the Six-Day War and after highly politicised funerals the clubhouse became an overnight refuge for him and his friends:

> I stayed there because my team mates were there and I used to stay there ... and that in view that there were policemen my lord ... I am used ... to stay in the clubhouse and I do not spend much of my time at home ... I would say that by staying there I am creating a spirit of trust ... within my team mates so that togetherness is victory ... in our team ... there is nothing else that we can do besides playing cards and listening to music ... As members of one team we have decided to live such a way as that we are a community, belonging to Alexandra Santos. (A. Sebola, Z2575)

Albert believed in the virtues of education and had in fact always opposed the boycotting of schools as a political tactic. When his school had been closed in 1985 he had studied at home alone.

Ashwell Zwane was a year younger than Albert, and in another typical pattern had been born in the Soweto suburb of Meadowlands, a place with which many Alex residents had strong family ties because of the removals to Soweto from Alex in the 1960s and 1970s. He, like many young African children of the time, went to live with his grandmother at the age of six. She had remained in Alexandra and he went to school there for a few years, returned to Soweto for a while, and then went back to Alex as a high school pupil where he attended another politically turbulent school, Minerva High.

Ashwell was a Catholic, an altar boy as a child, and later a Catholic Youth Club member. He belonged to the church choir and remained an active singer throughout the rebellion. He also loved football and for a time had belonged to the same team as Albert, whom he had known since childhood. His ambitions were even higher than those of Albert – he aspired to the middle classes and wanted to study law.[9] He had joined the Alexandra Youth Congress after he left school, together with a group of his friends (A. Zwane, Z3662ff). He espoused their principles in his evidence. He believed, he said, in 'non-racialism' not 'multi-racialism'; non-racialism meant that 'you are going to be taken as a South African before you could be asked whether you are white or black (A. Zwane, Z4104–5).

Piet Mogano, an 'older' comrade, considered himself a youth even though he was in his thirties – 'youths' could be as old as thirty-five, he claimed (P. Mogano, Z4426). Mogano had moved to Alexandra from his birthplace in the countryside in the late 1970s. This was another typical pattern – connections between township and countryside were extremely active and many young people did their schooling in the rural areas and then moved to town where networks were available for them to activate. Piet had first lived in his brother's *makhukhu* but this was destroyed in 1982 by the Municipal Police. He slept in a scrap car on the streets until he found another more permanent place. He had worked in numerous different small companies as a driver, and had far more experience than the other youths of the hardship entailed in earning a living in segregated South Africa. He had three hours of commuting to and from his workplace, and earned a modest wage of R550 per month. He was the only one of this group of comrades with union membership – he belonged to South African Allied Workers Union (P. Mogano, Z4326, Z4387ff).

The three comrades had known each other through various networks. Sebola said he virtually 'grew up with' Zwane. They had played soccer together in 'Alexandra Santos', until Zwane left to join 'Alexandra Real Fighters'. They had lived in adjacent streets. Piet had, in turn, been an avid football fan and supporter of 'Alexandra Real Fighters' and would spend a lot of time with the players of the team, where he met Ashwell – who was known by his 'soccer name' of 'Mugabe',[10] a name which came to acquire more sinister overtones when Ashwell began to take part in a people's court. All three belonged to the Fifteenth Avenue 'Youth Group', which operated its own anti-crime campaign and people's court, of which far more will be said in the next chapter.

THE CULTURE OF COMRADESHIP

Comrades in general, but particularly those at the grassroots, were young people with a strong sense of their own separateness from their parents whom they saw as 'rejecting the struggle' while their own 'children had to

die fighting for their rights'. They regarded the heroes of the armed struggle
with awe. The post-1976 exodus of youths from South Africa to guerrilla
training camps in Zambia had included many from Alex, some of whom
were now, as the struggle developed, returning home (Davis 1987). These
returnees, with their sophisticated knowledge of armed conflict, were
greatly admired for their bravery and often their martyrdom.[11] In a poem
written by one comrade we read of the 'shining unconvinced ray of *umkonto
we sizwe*', of pride in their own preparedness to fight and die because 'the
storm of oppression will be flown by the rain of my blood. I spill my blood
for those who remain behind. I am proud to give my one solitary life':

Mamakutheni[12]

Mamakutheni when children had to
Risk their lives hijacking for freedom
Charter while mothers and farthers hiding
for income tax and increase tax mamamakutha

Mamakutheni when children had to die
Fighting for their rights shouting the
Name of the struggle while parents
Rejecting the struggle mamakutheni

Mamakutheni when children are to be
Killed daily heroes are to be killed
Daily – heroes are born heroes are gone
Ben Moloise was born Ben was killed Vincent
was born Vincent was killed
Jerry was a heroes not because
was gunned down because
of his dids
Let me not remember the voice
Of vincent Tshabalala who shouted
Before he was killed
Mamakutheni
No pelice under apartheid
Forward with the
Peoples power
Longlive the strong ungover-
Nable masses of the AAC
Long live the shining unconvinced
Ray of umkonto we sizwe
Forward with the
Peoples court
Forward with the struggle

They want us to retire
And we won't retire
Because target is also part of
Struggle because we are cripple-
Ing the economy
Im proud of what I did the storm
Of oppression will be flown by
The rain of my blood. I spill my
Blood for those who remain
Behind. Im proud to give my one
Solitary life. Mama go and tell whole
World Africa shall be overcome

From
Comrade
Andrew B. A. Matarget.[13]

One meeting in March 1986 of 300 youth and student activists in St Michael's church hall in Alexandra epitomised the comrade political culture: it was highly colourful, 'punctuated by songs and many "vivas" – mostly for the UDF and ANC'. 'Lord, Lord what have we done to these Afrikaners. Give us strength,' they sang. They wore T-shirts, carried banners or placards with such slogans as: 'Organise or starve'; 'Submit or fight'; 'UDF unites, apartheid divides', singing 'Join, Join the struggle', 'Farewell, farewell, spirit of the nation' (the lament sung at funerals) and 'Welcome, Welcome and down with oppressors'. A poet – probably one Jingles Makhothi, who was known as Alexandra's own 'people's poet' and who was later to be killed by vigil-antes – led the crowd in a strongly Africanist poem which cast the struggle as destined for inevitable victory – 'it is coming today, it is coming tomorrow':

I am that I am

I am who I am.
Call me the man of the soil, oppressed.
Call me, greet me, I am Africa.
Respect me, protect me. Call me Uhuru. I am somebody.
Do not believe them when they say it is far.
It is coming today, it is coming tomorrow.
This drought will be broken.
For us it will be that the rains have come.
Do not believe them when they say we do not know why we are
    dancing. Lapha, a man has to sweat in order to succeed.
Cry Africa, because there is no one to cry for you.
Cry until the rains come.
Cry until the dawn when water disappears in a mist

The comrades replied: 'Botha will you fight for it? We will fight for it.' (*Sunday Star*, 16 March 1986).
 What did comradeship mean?

> It means a lot. It means that a person is even more than a brother, is even more than a friend. By saying to a person 'comrade' you don't just mean that person is a friend or a brother, he is both. It is beyond that ... I would trust a comrade more than my own brother because it means a lot to me. (Carter 1991a: 232)

Belonging to the comrades 'was a significant factor in providing ... a sense of mastery and control' in one township, providing the model of a 'strong and powerful being, forging ahead under impossibly difficult circumstances and taking control of life under conditions of uncertainty and deprivation':

> When you are a comrade you know where you are going, compared to others in the community who are billowed around by strong winds. (Campbell 1994: 101–2)

> Being a comrade permitted young people – young men in particular – to 'define themselves in opposition to what they saw as the bumbling older generation who in their view had bequeathed to the young an unbearably oppressive social reality' (Campbell 1994: 101–2).

Many at the grassroots – by contrast with those in leadership positions – did not have a political education and were 'just doing it for fun',[14] attracted by a culture of 'militaristic camaraderie'. On one level this was a culture of the *toyi-toyi* and of freedom songs, a highly stylised youth form of belonging. On another level it was one based on collective action, which was both social and political, rooted in the political ideology of the Freedom Charter on the one hand, and the confrontational messages of Radio Freedom and the reality of street violence on the other. So the daily experiences of comrades were redolent with the collective actions and symbols of the struggle. Violence was a part of the culture (Sitas 1992: 48). This meant that criminals were attracted to the comrade milieu (*Weekly Mail*, 8 February 1990).
 It was not long before the more utopian comrades became a relatively distinct grouping, separate from those with criminal intent – the '*comtsotsis*':

> I get confused about comrade because a comrade is a kind of a universal term that is given to every youth but there are comrades who are serious about upgrading the township and about unity and peace and law and order in the township and there are what we call tsotsi comrades. (Father Cairns, M4379)

While 'comrade' originally meant 'a member of a politically oriented organisation', it now changed meaning, and became split into two: 'comrades

comrades disciplined comtsotsi not disciplined

meant those who were disciplined members of organisations' 'comtsotsis was used to denote those who were undisciplined'.[15]

The core initiative for, leadership of, and control of comrade activities rested with young men. Indeed some have argued that masculinity, violence and 'comradeness' were in fact a mutually reinforcing nexus of beliefs and actions that characterised these groupings (Campbell 1992; Sitas 1992). Certainly the comrades themselves experienced it as such and, against the background of the new left culture, even began to wonder at its acceptability. At one stage, for example, one comrade grouping's minutes recorded the felt need to 'recruit female members' and the difficulty in doing so: 'Members should have patience in recruiting female comrades' they wrote.[16]

The comrades would congregate in large crowds at their youth headquarters and observers never failed to mention the overwhelming presence of men at these gatherings.[17] They would march up and down the streets in smaller groupings, armed with sticks and sjamboks, and once more, most of them were men. A surprise raid on one people's court towards the end of the rebellion resulted in twenty-seven arrests. Only three of these were women, and all of them were probably attending the court as witnesses or complainants – the latter a far more common role taken on by women in relation to the people's courts – rather than comrades.

One female comrade, DP, was perhaps an exception which proved the rule. Her camp, the Eighth Avenue Youth Group, was predominantly male (thirty out of thirty-five core activists were men) and she said girls of her age were 'afraid of the fighting or harassment by police and detention. They'd said "I'd like to be involved". We'd say "are you aware of the bucket system and conditions of the township?" They'd say "yes, but I'm scared of the police" (Carter 1991a: 268). DP herself seems to have been treated as something of a latecomer and apprentice to the life of the comrade. She espoused a feminist and critical perspective on her cohort of young women. She said many of them 'would dress up especially to go to a meeting' or would simply 'second motions in meetings' without articulating their own positions. She also criticised her own previously low self-image: 'The problem is with us; I say, no man, just chuck that inferiority,' she said. This she did, with a vengeance. Dressed in trousers, an uncommon form of dress for girls in those times, she would join in every battle from the Six-Day War onwards while the girls in skirts, she said, would get caught jumping over fences.

MORALITY AND PURITY

The comrades should be serious, disciplined, determined and confident. There should also be self-respect among the comrades, there
should be smooth relationship between the youth and the parents. (A.
Sebola, quoting Ashwell Zwane, Z2646)

The comrades were moralistic and even ascetic. They sought to distinguish
themselves from their imperfect parents, but also, in theory at least, to make
peace with them. As one said in his subsequent trial: 'What type of fathers in
the future are we going to make if we are starting at an early age drinking?'
He had lashed a young girl for drinking which he

saw ... as a nice thing so that we in future would not have drunkard
type of mothers, but we should have respectable mothers in the future.
We are going to be the fathers of the future and if we are not getting
things right now we are going to grow bad situations. (V. A. Ngwenya,
Z5377–8)

This puritanism was projected, thus, onto an envisaged future, which would
come soon and suddenly. It would avenge the past. Ashwell Zwane wrote a
poem expressing this:

Luyeza Usuku

Luyeza Usuku, Luyeza usuku
The day is coming
When the Boers will
Be made to pay for innocent
African blood which is wasted
Day by day.[18]

In explaining the meaning of the poem, Ashwell said that he felt revenge was
necessary:

*Did you foresee the day when the Boers will be made to pay for what they
were doing in Alexandra or didn't you?* ... I just thought that day will
come ... That was just in my mind that this which is done by *amabunu*
to people are going one day to pay for it ... a person who does
something bad will ultimately pay for that. (A. Zwane, Z4104–5)

As the prosecutor here observed, such notions of revenge were not
compatible with ideas of love and comradeship – but in fact the comrades
did espouse these latter ideas within their own world, and saw themselves as
embodying good. 'We want to create a spirit of trust, responsibility, understanding, love amongst the people,' said Albert Sebola (A. Sebola, Z2705).
Maintaining these standards would be difficult given the innate tendency of
Alexandrans to engage in degenerate behaviour! One worried comrade

interviewed in another context commented on how: 'Youth were mainly interested in liquor, and they would fight [in shebeens]. There was a high rate of crime. Only a few youth were actively participating in the youth organization' (DP, quoted in Carter 1991a: 211ff).

'Purification' of the comrades – the development of 'perfect people' – would be necessary to make sure that this degeneracy did not infect the comrades themselves:

> There will be those people in a struggle who will bring confusion of any kind, and it is our duty as organisers to make it a point that the survival of our revolution needs those purified comrades who will guard against such people, at all costs. Because you are one stream you see. You start like a rivulet in the struggle. And then as you grow, you will be contaminated by all kinds of people. And then to maintain them and all those kinds of things is not easy. To develop them into perfect people again is not an easy thing, so it depends on those few, who are very well, to maintain this thing, which is very demanding really. (NP, quoted in Carter 1991a: 272)

Comrades should set a high standard of morality in their behaviour during the struggle. 'Undisciplined' youths should be kept in line by those in positions of responsibility (A. Sebola, Z2637–8). Comrades who strayed were not to be helped – a line must be drawn between true comrades and those of their own who slid into crime. As one of them said: '*And you regarded yourself as a comrade?* Yes, because I was not a tsotsi.'[19] Just as they wished to improve the behaviour of their parents, so the comrades, said Albert Sebola, wanted to stop the youths 'doing mischievous things' like going on the streets, smoking glue, smoking dagga, drinking liquor and carrying knives. 'That is how gangsters arises there' (A. Sebola, Z2752, Z2756).

Comrades should be active and 'participatory'. 'A member must be active he should not be passive because passiveness is something bad' ran the minutes of one comrade meeting. Action, therefore, should always accompany the concord that must arise amongst the comrades: 'We got to unite and understanding each other. There shall be *Actions* to oppose system.'[20]

Comradeship was codified in sets of formal written rules – in some cases, the constitutions of groups or organisations – and the rules, as well as the documents in which they were printed, should be respected: 'People who are given this constitutions must be well participating, acting, understanding and loving each one, then take care of those books given.'[21] They should offer each other mutual assistance and, of course, solidarity against the police or army:

> *Assistance on harassed comrades.* A question arised in a fashion of if a political activist is harassed in a yard? Will the people help him/her or not. *Suggestions.* The house declared or committed themselves to assist a harassed comrade.

Comrades should fulfil their duties by ensuring participation by all, whether young or old, in the struggle, but without arrogance:

Encouragement of (absent) comrades (mobilising):
The necessity of encouraging is to mobilise our fellow comrades the roots of the struggle. A comrade who is aware of the happenings of the struggle should not recruit in a boasting manner. A manner of approach is the key to or of success. Mobilising is the root and the way to win our liberation. Our parents should be recruited as they are our backbone of our struggle. NB Unity, action and understanding is the way which a comrade should follow.

Comrades should be aware that their parents' interests were not identical with their own, and 'conscientise' them accordingly:

Highlight parents with the role of trade unions here in SA, they cater the problems of the struggle of the workers. NB A youth shall bring his/her parent to the headquarter for further information based on the latter.[22]

Neutral People: Some residents of Alex are neutral, some say that they respond only when forced to do or act during stay-aways. *Suggestions*. Our aim is to sow them the green light or highlight them and preach to them the name of the struggle.[23]

Cleanliness, politeness and decorum were emphasised: thus shops were boycotted because they treated workers and customers badly. Furthermore, shops must be tidy and clean: 'most of the shops in the township were very filthy, they were not tidy. The discussion was that those not boycotted must keep their shops clean.'[24]

Dirt in the yards where people lived was also an important issue. And, surprisingly, regular and dutiful attendance at school – at least during times of calm in those troubled institutions – was recommended. One agenda for a meeting of comrades, for example, contained the following items:

1) Poor attendance of schools (ASCO)
2) Parents should encourage their kids
3) Students should not have keep order at schools.[25]

It was believed that comrades should be disciplined, serious and confident.[26] They needed to be wary of making unfounded witchcraft accusations, and they should not harass adults, take away their goods or hijack their cars.[27] Comrades should heed the fact that 'older people' – in other words the adults of the township – were complaining bitterly that their cars and groceries were being taken by the youth. Only discipline would solve these problems, although sometimes its rationale was less than idealistic:

Tsotsis are hijacking our struggle. We say to them go back to your townships. If we alienate our parents, the authorities will arm our parents to kill us. And we will have to kill them. I can see this situation if we do not change.

But to some, being a comrade was a matter of idealism rather than pragmatism. One young man quoted in a Durban-based study of comrade life said:

> Comrades are people who are sympathetic to others and stand for the truth, even if they might end up dying for it ... They help the community to avoid crime, and help at school where children want to rape the teachers or the other students ... they usually speak for the whole community and not only for themselves, they help people who have problems, and they want people to be more clear about the new South Africa when the time comes. (Campbell 1994: 102)

At the grass roots the comrades were active, independent and resourceful. Much of the background of the youth had been in educational struggles and this had forged their commitment and honed their skills as opponents of those in power. While they still continued to support some educational campaigns, however, they tended to worry about the degree to which the school-goers of the mid-eighties were missing school owing to extensive and frequent school boycotts. The core comrades were in fact committed to education and had themselves, as we have seen, benefited from fairly long years of schooling – although their levels of literacy remained low, as their written documents indicate.

LEADERS AND FOLLOWERS

While the grassroots comrades straddled the legal and illegal worlds and had some access to ideas from outside generated by their own resourcefulness, they also depended for access to ideas upon a stratum of young leaders who were more highly educated and resource-rich than themselves. After the unstoppable politicisation of the young had begun (after a post-1976 lull) in the early 1980s in South African cities, and rapidly established itself in Alexandra, evolving in the closed milieu of the schools, it was not long before a new political class of youths began to be forged and separate itself out from the mass. The grassroots members were separate from, and distinctly more radical, violent and fundamentalist than, their more formally designated leaders (Seekings 1993: 45). If the grassroots comrades represented the 'folk' culture of the youth, a culture drawn almost entirely from within, then the emerging stratum of youth leaders represented the next stage up. These were increasingly people whose political spurs were not earned on the streets but in organisations.

> For the most part this leadership comprised politically articulate activists, motivated by political idealism and a sense of participation in political change. Even when youth organisation was formed amidst violent conflict, eloquence, intellectual sophistication and organisational enthusiasm were widely regarded as qualifications for formal leadership. (Seekings 1993: 43)

Many came from better-off households, and were students or former students. Some had come through 'semi-political youth clubs where they were influenced by older political activists'. Others 'were politicised at home by older family members' (Seekings 1993: 45). Politically self-educated, they read alternative media, banned literature or Marxist texts. Schools were the key shaping institutions for the development of this stratum (Carter 1991a: 34). School campaigns demanding improved student representation, better exam systems and an end to corruption were frequent. They were less exclusively male than were the grassroots comrades.

While 70 per cent of the sample in Table 2 were male and their mean age was 18–21, the mean age of the 30 per cent of the activists who were women was markedly lower, at 16–18, suggesting that a certain subservience was likely in spite of their relatively high numbers.

Leaders were not trapped, as their grassroots supporters were, in the sparsely resourced township milieu: they had access to such social, cultural and political assets as whites, liberals, the ANC, the United Democratic Front (UDF), and many others. Besides the networks of school, soccer and street, other more formal institutions existed that suited the most ambitious of all the comrades, partly owing to the combined efforts of socially concerned Alexandrans and well-meaning whites. Those creating or supporting the soccer teams, youth clubs and church choirs which pervaded the township – social workers, cultural entrepreneurs, the old elite, liberals and philanthropists – had often intended them to act as forces for social cohesiveness

Table 2: Age and gender breakdown of 71 AYCO activists

Age	Total	Male	Female
30+	1	1	0
28–30	3	2	1
25–27	10	9	1
22–24	12	11	1
19–21	20	17	3
16–18	15	8	7
13–15	9	2	7
12–	1	0	1
TOTAL	71	50	21

Source: adapted from Carter (1991a: 123)

and stability through which gangsterism would be reduced. As a result they often consciously attempted to create and nurture a leadership stratum.[28] Refilwe Mashigo describes the formation of Thusong, a youth club which catered for 'youths and drop-outs of a school going age'. 'I had a structure within where there was, we termed that person a Mayor, they were all leaders but they chose a mayor and below that mayor were leaders' (*The Sowetan*, 28 September 1984). The club had a regular clientele who took part in such activities as sewing, developing their communication skills, discussion activities on the general community, and planning 'outreach' campaigns – such as 'cleanups' in the township. The more revolutionary consequences of providing social capital such as this were entirely unintended! Youths such as these soon came to occupy leadership positions in the emerging youth and student movements, to embrace the influences of the UDF, non-racialism, the broader nationalist movement, and even to promote gender equality.

By 1982 a powerful cohort of leaders had completed school and sought, with the exiled ANC's backing, to create a new youth organisation not intended for pupils but for the growing numbers of young people who had left schools, whether because they had completed their studies, failed or dropped out (Bapela n.d.). The resulting Alexandra Youth Congress (AYCO) gave a voice and focus to non-school youth – later to be the dominant force amongst the comrades.[29]

AYCO espoused a far more 'constitutionalist' approach to its own internal organisation than did the grassroots comrades. With its 'executive', its actual constitution, duly drafted and adopted, and its more formalistic protest style, it rather resembled a traditional civil rights movement. Following the ANC's admonition to 'focus the minds of our people beyond local to national issues', for which it was 'necessary that we should achieve the political unity of the masses of our people and their democratic movement' (AYCO NEC report, quoted in Carter 1991a: 88), it soon sought to dominate the township's disparate forces. Its 'charterism' (i.e. adherence to the ANC's Freedom Charter) reflected its ANC sympathies. It moved to defeat a small independent Trotskyist movement which had established itself in the township and sought to make the 'charterist identity hegemonic' (Carter 1991a: 87).[30] AYCO leaders sought to differentiate themselves from what they called 'workerism', from 'ultra-leftism' and from Black Consciousness approaches, setting the tone for the emergence of a broader nationalism at the expense of smaller movements.

The AYCO constitution was both literate and politically sophisticated:

> We the youth of Alexandra living in South Africa, regarding ourselves as members of the oppressed and exploited society and realising that the youth is the most creative and energetic part of society, fully commit ourselves to the realisation of non-racial democratic society.

The aims of AYCO were:

1) To unite all the youth in Alexandra.
2) To respond to the demands and aspirations of the youth, whether they be cultural, economic, religious or political.
3) To normalise relationships between parents and the youth.
4) To create a spirit of trust responsibility, understanding and love among the people.
5) To encourage the youth to strive for dynamic systems of education and complete their academic education whether part-time or full-time.
6) To directly involve ourselves in relevant community projects.
7) To represent the youth of Alexandra in all relevant national fronts ...
8) To establish meaningful links with all progressive people/organisations committed to the realisation of a truly non-racial democratic society. (AYCO Constitution 1983–4)[31]

AYCO was well structured, with an executive, a co-ordinating committee and seven sub-committees. It aimed to be disciplined.

> A member may be disciplined by GC (General Council) or any affiliate executive, only after he or she has been afforded opportunity to present his/her case ... All disciplinary action shall be geared towards correcting and not destroying individuals or affiliates. The extreme form of discipline shall be suspension and expulsion ... (AYCO Constitution 1986).[32]

Portfolios and responsibilities were carefully defined. The organisation looked very different from the way in which adults were to conceive of organising the township, or from the utopian vision of the grassroots.

AYCO policy was recognisably Marxist, but it reflected the neo-Marxism which was current in universities, unions and elsewhere at the time, rather than the more Soviet-influenced Marxism which the exiled ANC embraced. And the 'popular frontism' of the UDF came through in its focus on encouraging multiple, often cultural activities, such as drama, poetry, music, gumboot dance, cultural dance and art. Jingles Makgothi, author of 'I am that I am', was recognised as the 'AYCO poet'. The leadership placed greater emphasis on learning than did the grassroots comrades. AYCO for example, had its own educational committee, which hosted weekly political discussions. Works for reference were suggested. A person would read them, prepare a paper, and then present it for discussion:

> We read extracts from Gramsci. We had a discussion on how it fits in with South Africa. We read histories of other struggles, such as the French Revolution, the white miners strike in South Africa, World War II, the question of the Jews and the Arab community. We would ask What Happened? Who waged the struggles? And Why? We also

analysed the slogan 'liberation today, education tomorrow'. (Carter 1991a: 125)

AYCO was relatively small in the period leading up the revolt – 'they were about a hundred and they were not all attending meetings,' said one member. During 1986 the membership grew but 'it was very difficult to get many youths to attend these meetings.' Youths 'feared to be arrested'. Over time, more came along – mobilised through youth organisations,[33] many of them people who had failed matric and 'were frustrated and angry' (O. Bapela, M4026).

The social and political mobility of the leadership was destined to be rapid, and they soon began to move away from pure 'comrade' street and school based politics, and from spontaneity, recklessness and violence, towards a more ordered – and in some cases vanguardist – approach. The resulting differences and tensions between leaders and led were similar to those which occur in many social movements. The leaders sought systematic organisation and guided revolutionary engagement, while the followers, the mass of the now-mobilised youth, had different dreams and understandings. In fact when AYCO itself was launched in 1983, 'there was a poor response from the youth of Alex' (*Voice of AYCO*, November–December 1983) – perhaps it failed to appeal to their more utopian mentality? Some of the more senior comrades were concerned about the millenarian types. AYCO tried to co-opt the more spontaneous youth activities into its own and tried to organise and 'discipline' the youth, to control and regulate the naming of streets, and to bring a halt to the consumer boycott.

Thus the body of the youth felt the need for leadership, and the perceived heroism of many of the leaders was a spur to general mobilisation; and the leaders knew that they had a potentially revolutionary mass of followers at their disposal to whom they could offer guidance and focus. But there were undoubtedly tensions between the leadership and the grassroots. These threatened to become actual divisions at times. When, in 1985, there were widespread arrests of leading activists in the township, those left behind directed their anger and resentment at the imprisoned leaders, and attempted to seize control of the township.[34] It was on its release that the AYCO leadership tried to regain its authority by such tactics as trying to organise the Youth Groups themselves. Still, even to the less organised youth, AYCO was a resource and not one to be sneered at. Two of the more grassroots comrades mentioned above, Albert Sebola and Ashwell Zwane, both sympathised with AYCO (A. Sebola, Z2584). They espoused its non-racialism, its constitution and its unifying and anti-criminal strategy (A. Zwane, Z3669).

The comrades, thus, had some leadership and organisational resources at their disposal, in spite of their poverty and deprivation. But to Mzwanele Mayekiso, who had associated with the comrades, these were in overall terms grossly inadequate. He writes of lack of resources as a 'chronic problem':

> This included our own personnel, many of whom could not read or write. Many comrades were not skilled at running meetings. Many were not able to become independent-thinking activists. There were just too few resources and too little time to address these problems ... the comrades were sometimes not completely aware of their role or of how to interpret important issues. Sometimes the comrades were left to address symptoms of problems, without a clear analysis of the causes. (Mayekiso 1996: 23)

THE ADULT GENERATION

Older Alexandrans, even revolutionary ones, were cut from a different cloth. Their intellectuals, networks, repertoires and ideologies were different from those of younger people in a clear manifestation of generationally stratified politics. 'Adults' were almost entirely poor working people, many with strong roots in Alex and quite deep layers of sedimented memories of the township – their own grandparents and parents had in many cases lived and even been buried there, and their children had been brought up there. Those who had lived there the longest tended to occupy the 'better' homes or flats; others lived in single rooms in the yards while the most recent and poorest lived in shacks. Those who had come more recently to Alex still had rural connections, while because of the removals and the general longevity of their time in the township many had quite dense connections and networks with people in other townships such as Soweto. Identities were thus strongly rooted in the township with tentacles spreading outwards to a broader sense of mainly urban community. Stratification, while present, tended to be blurred by a sense of common historical, spatial and racial experience.

In strong contrast to the macho milieu of even the best educated of the comrades, in the world of adults women were far more prominent. This did not mean township society was not patriarchal. Mothers in townships were:

> still regarded as second-class citizens in a community where patriarchal ideals dominate ... [and] ... are often not accorded the respect and authority that would be accorded to fathers – for example ... the authority necessary to discipline teenage sons, who, without the stern hand of a traditionally feared father figure to keep them in check, often 'run wild' as a result. (Campbell 1994: 55–6)

Since most township households were female headed this had serious consequences for family life. One young man said:

> Mother failed to discipline us as teenage boys on her own. Boys need a father to guide them. If father had lived with us there would have

been a difference. There were many times when we took no notice of mother, unlike the notice we would have taken of a father. (Campbell 1994: 56)

By contrast, in the case of young girls, their brothers would do the disciplining and policing of their lives.

However, this had another side to it. Being the single head of a household also vested a considerable amount of power in adult women. The 'strong woman/weak woman' dichotomy was a feature of the perceptions of adults. Women would be beaten by husbands, or despised by male children. But:

in some ways their concrete experience of their own family lives and the powerful role played by their mothers in the family would serve to contradict the stereotypical 'subservient wife and mother' recipes for living that these very mothers in the family might seek to teach them. (Campbell 1994: 55–6)

Strong women, particularly professional women of all ages, or older township matriarchs, lived side by side with the weaker, often younger, ones. They were socially prominent and politically influential. They used political organisations to assert and express themselves (R. Mdakane, M2595); and they were strongly networked through women's organisations, churches or welfare organisations (R. Mdakane, M2599). Mrs Mahlodi, for example, from 34 Seventh Avenue, provided the venue for quite a few Alexandra Action Committee meetings. She lived, it was said, in a house even bigger than that of one of the stalwarts of the movement, Sarah Mthembu (R. Mdakane, M2616). She was a Yard Committee representative, and a strong supporter of the AAC (R. Mdakane, M2615).

We have seen how older Alexandrans had forged their identities in times when a kind of working-class respectability (Goodhew 1991; Bozzoli 1991) was valued. Some had been to school in the days before Bantu Education, and they were mission-educated, articulate and highly literate; but the proportions that had been to high school were lower, and most older Alexandrans were in fact less well educated than their children. Their lives had been affected profoundly and directly by the increasing harshness of apartheid after the 1950s. If the youth were the victims of frustrated upward social mobility, the adults were often the victims of actual downward mobility, and most had personally experienced the brutality of the state. Their paternalistically structured relationships to the state had been destroyed and the movements to which, in earlier times, they had given their loyalty were banned.

Some adults had been young in the heady days of 1976 and experienced then some of the romanticism that the youth of the 1980s displayed. However, if they had not gone into exile and/or joined the ANC, ten years later they were wary of the 'quick fix'. The limits of spontaneous rebellion in the face of an authoritarian state had been all too clearly revealed to them. Others had passed through youth politics and were now the older cohort – looked up to by youth, but still somewhat separate from them. Still others were even older, and had other traditions to draw on – those of the earlier repertoires of township politics were the most common, including trade unionism, old-style African nationalism, and religion.

These earlier forms of adult politics were sometimes violent and factional.[35] Solutions to factional conflicts were often murderous – 'death to the other faction' had been the usual philosophy. However the power of factionalism as a form of mobilisation was undercut by the emergence of the 'repertoire' of the township mass meeting, at which a sort of popular democracy held sway. Thus during the Bus Boycott of 1957:

> It was decided at one of the first mass meetings held at Number 3 Square, that policy decisions would be taken only at mass meetings; also that press statements would be made only at mass meetings; also that future meetings would be arranged only at mass meetings.[36]

The virtues of stoicism, tolerance and non-racialism were familiar ones in adult political culture. Many had memories of fruitful contact with whites of a left, liberal or paternalistic persuasion and the AAC had substantial access to white resources. As Ricky Valente, a white liberal with a powerful presence during the rebellion, put it: 'Father Cairns and myself in different ways could be regarded as sort of conduits in an organisation or in a discussion process' (R. Valente, M4188). They also had connections with leading black churchmen such as Desmond Tutu, whose role became increasingly important as time went on. Nevertheless, the experiences they had had of high apartheid had also seared upon their consciousness a bitter resignation.

ADULT INTELLECTUALS AND NATIONAL AND GLOBAL IDEAS

Taken on its own, the older generation appeared unlikely to become politically mobilised during the late 1970s and early 1980s. But a set of unusually powerful intellectuals and leaders emerged, at least in Alexandra, to act as a major ideological and political resource for the township residents. Some of these leaders, but not all, were more highly educated than the youth; one had a national and international reputation, and all had organisational experience and access to media and resources outside the borders of the township and in some cases the state. A handful of them are described here.

The adult intellectuals and leaders came from a range of profoundly differing resistance traditions with strong connections to what were then illicit ideas. They included a white Trotskyist, Richard Harvey, who ran a township newspaper through which was introduced a smorgasbord of ideas, drawn from the New Left of the time as much as from classic Trotskyism, and several more conventional African Nationalists. But the central figure in the rebellion, Moses Mayekiso, came from the trade unions and brought with him years of experience of their tradition of participatory democracy. This made him an unusual 'township' activist – not only in Alex but also in township politics in the country as a whole. Most unionists of the time confined their activities to the workplace. Mayekiso rapidly took steps to distinguish himself from them as well as from other township politicians.

He started his adult life as an extremely poor migrant labourer in heavy industry. He lived in the poorest of hostels and 'knew a great deal about the hardship of working class life in Johannesburg' (J. Baskin, quoted in Carter 1991a: 196). By the time of the revolt he had already had seven years' experience in trade unions, first as an unpaid volunteer for the powerful and politically sophisticated Metal and Allied Workers Union, then as its branch secretary for the Transvaal province. He had established shop stewards' councils and was committed to building strong grassroots organisational networks within unions, while also aiming to capture the spontaneous militancy of the workers.

Mayekiso had strong links to white activists and union intellectuals, whose access to oppositional ideas had been easier by virtue of their relative freedom.[37] He had attended courses in Labour Studies run by some of them (Moses Mayekiso, M2733), where he had absorbed their 'workerist' (as opposed to populist or African nationalist) and pragmatic ideas. These ideas embraced a belief in direct democracy and accountability 'so that leaders could not be able to do anything they liked' and a commitment to developing legal methods of acting in opposition. Mayekiso rapidly became a leading figure in one of the key 'workerist' trade unions, where he too promoted a left-pragmatism by recommending that unions register and organise under the new 'reformist' dispensation rather than boycott legal mechanisms and act entirely outside the purview of the state. Worker leaders, went the workerist argument, must be tactical, like guerrilla fighters, but this could not be done without building an organisational base. Otherwise, the argument ran, it was likely 'we will destroy a clear worker identity since workers will be entirely swamped by the powerful traditions of popular politics' (Moses Mayekiso, M2721ff)

These ideas eventually moved into a broader definition of politics. Workers came to be thought of as people with lives outside the factories in which they worked – and workerism could, therefore, logically enter into places where traditional trade unionism did not usually tread, such as townships, which had always been the domain of the 'populists' (Moses Mayekiso, M2731).

By contrast with a 'workerist', a populist was 'a person who wants to be famous, presenting himself as a politician' (Moses Mayekiso, M2731); or 'a person who disregards democracy and does things without consulting the

masses' (Moses Mayekiso, M3112). Populists were a kind of petty bourgeoisie: 'educated people who wanted to use the masses in order to further
their own interests and not to further the interests of the masses' (Moses
Mayekiso, quoted in Carter 1991a: 203). ANC populism was believed to
have had serious limitations because nationalist leaders were likely to
'hijack' the struggle and in the end would 'have no option but to turn against
their worker supporters' (a view not without prescience) (Moses Mayekiso,
M2879).

Mayekiso's trade unionism was also distinct from what he called 'extreme
workerism' such as that displayed by elements within the legal union
movement, as well as in the ideas of Trotskyists such as Richard Harvey:
'Their ideology was that liberation would come solely through organized
workers. They were workerists' (Moses Mayekiso, M2890–1). He was also
guarded with youth, as they were with him at first. They saw how different
his approach was and initially feared that he might 'introduce his politics
into the township' (BM, quoted in Carter 1991a: 209).

To Mayekiso the answerability of leadership was more important than
'great men', which meant that unionists should move into townships to
build politics there rather than allow townships to be controlled by populists.
Township issues such as rents were profoundly working class, as were classic
'populist' township struggles around education, violence and poverty.[38]

> Workers do not want just political change, but political, social and
> economic change. This struggle has taken us three hundred years. We
> would not like to waste time by, and blood chopping the branches of
> the main tree of oppression – capitalism – we have to chop the stem
> once and for all – it will fall down with its branches and we will plant a
> new green tree. (Moses Mayekiso, M2839)

The method of 'collecting opinions from workers' was typical of this type
of unionism and Mayekiso saw it as a form of socialism:[39]

> I regard myself as a person who believes in socialism ... I also believe
> in mass democracy ... By 'mass' I mean I believe in an organisation
> that concerns a mass of people, which has been built by people, either
> in the locations or in the factories. I do not believe that a leader should
> just come and make himself a leader. The leadership must come from
> the masses ... and the issues must also originate from the mass. The
> mass should give mandates to the leadership and that leadership must
> be controlled by the mass. (Moses Mayekiso, M3111–12)

Mayekiso's translation of workerism into a form of grassroots and anti-
nationalist socialism eventually led him to make links with British-based
Trotskyists, and on a fateful trip to England, his connections with their ideas
led him to be viewed by the state as a trafficker in revolution.[40]

If Moses Mayekiso could deliver a perfectly tailored trade union-based ideology of local organisation and popular participation, Obed Bapela could legitimise it by his long experience of township politics, his wide-ranging connections with white and black liberals and the 'new left' outside of Alexandra, his publicity and media experience, and his 'struggle credentials' and consequent legitimacy with the youth. Although from an entirely different tradition, he and Moses Mayekiso both valued such things as leadership and accountability, rationality and being 'sensible'.

Obed Bapela was twenty-eight at the time of the revolt. Born in Alexandra, he was raised by his grandmother in Sekhukhuniland until the age of eight, after which he returned to his mother in Alexandra and went to school there. His school, Alexandra Secondary, was deeply involved in the unrest of 1976, and Bapela's close friend, Philip March was killed at the time. He moved to a Catholic school where again he experienced and took part in boycotts and other protests. He failed Standard 8, and around the same time his stepfather was imprisoned for theft. He had to leave school to look for work. He took a variety of small jobs and at the same time joined the 'Save Alexandra' campaign, which kept him politically active for several years. His political career was wide ranging, and culminated in his central role in the Alexandra Youth Congress (AYCO) from the time of its formation in 1983. He was soon arrested for his activities, and rapidly began to attain the status of a respected older comrade (O. Bapela, M3916).

Bapela was a community-builder. He sought to assist in the creation of facilities for youths in particular, and was a key figure in co-operating with Alexandran and white liberal charitable efforts. In 1979 the Thusong Youth Centre was formed, with funding from white business and charities. Bapela had been one of the central figures. The club organised classes or sessions in drama, ballroom dancing, traditional dancing, drum majorettes, indoor games, outdoor sports and scout meetings. Social workers would attend, and try to assist (O. Bapela, M3907ff). The club was an important social institution which, using the resources of the enlightened Christian training centre at Wilgespruit, introduced ideas about representation and organisation into youth culture. 'We would be trained at Wilgespruit,' he said, in 'how to run an organisation and as to how to chair a meeting and how minutes are recorded and when you have problems in the organisations, how to solve them'. Bapela himself was either the club's 'deputy mayor' or its 'mayor' for several years and saw himself as working for the upliftment of the youth and the healing of family rifts. Bapela acquired additional useful skills and important contacts in the world of white professionals and activists through his job in the left-leaning 'Media and Resources Services' (MARS), where he learnt how to produce pamphlets, posters and T-shirts, how to do layout, paste-up and designing, and how to negotiate the law concerning such activities (O. Bapela, M3918–19).

He won the respect of young people and was highly regarded by them as a leader, a senior, knowledgeable person. His 'struggle credentials' were good, his commitment to education solid, and he had considerable leadership experience. At one point the AYCO youth decided to attempt to influence and perhaps tone down the millenarian elements in the Youth Groups. Bapela was sent along to do the job, and was introduced to the Nineteenth Avenue youth in these terms:

> They introduced me to the youth, because many of them were not known to me amongst the youth. When I was introduced I was intro-duced as Obed Bapela, as a person who was being involved for a long time in the struggle, and he is determined on the struggle, and that he has been arrested a few times, and he is a person who is at Thusong and he is mayor at Thusong, and he is working with the youth, and he is also a member of AYCO presently. (O. Bapela, M3927)

He himself emphasised the need for good behaviour:

> I remember that I accepted their introduction of me to them and what they were doing I appreciate. That seeing that they had seen it better to stop being tsotsis and help in participating by helping the commun-ity. It is something that we also accept. (ibid.)

In fact we know already that grassroots comrades valued education ex-tremely highly and it is not surprising that the youth at Nineteenth Avenue asked Bapela to give them lectures on history.

> Many people there, especially the youth, knew that I was involved in the struggle. Because of that I have knowledge of the South African history. I used to help students who are doing matric and JC, especially in history. (O. Bapela, M3928)

The youngest 'adult' leader, Moses's brother Mzwanele Mayekiso, was also well placed to play a crucial intermediate role between adults and youths. Born in the Transkei, he moved to Alexandra in December 1985 to join his more well-known brother. An impressionable youth, recently out of schools where major boycotts had occurred, he knew and had close contact with other youths in AYCO and its school-based sister organisation, ASCO. He, like Bapela, was able to bring to the youth political culture a degree of social and cultural capital – in the form of knowledge of Eastern Cape struggles and their styles and forms (Mzwanele Mayekiso, M4070.) Highly creative, he dreamt of writing a book about his experiences, and before the revolt had written a partial manuscript.[41] His notes of discussions held in early 1986 reveal the level of refinement achieved. They drew on the neo-Marxism current amongst left-wing white intellectuals in universities at the time, on the non-racialism of the ANC tradition to which he and his group adhered, on the immediate interests of Alexandran people, and on youth and student concerns:

My Voice

My aim in writing this book is to outline how capitalism entrenched itself amongst the African people more especially in South Africa ... My dear Africans, capitalism is rotten from the core, because of its evils it has created chaos within the African community in which this type of capitalism is a new fashion. In speaking out my voice I would like students to take a sharp look at this monster which has created class distinctions amongst Africans, they are the future elders of this, our continent. Even to those who fell victims of the evil creature, there is still time to turn back and be part of the community. As Africans we are not used to capitalism because in it there is exploitation, cruelty and that even results in murder of those who are the voice of the voiceless with the claim that they are endangering the existence of capitalism by making the working class aware.

Author: M. A. AFRICA.[42]

He evolved a sort of workerist Africanism, which suggested that South African society was an example of class inequality and division. It was divided into two major, mutually antagonistic classes. The sub-text was almost always that the ruling class was white and the oppressed black, but conceptual room was always left for it to be imagined that black people could become oppressors, and white people could be part of the poor and deprived classes. The ruling class retained its power through cultural hegemony – the control of religion, education, culture, sport and the media – on the one hand; and repression on the other. Each of these forms of control had a specific manifestation in black life. Religion had 'been used by the oppressor to keep the oppressed people loyal, inferior and subservient'. Education, through Bantu Education, had 'denied the black majority opportunities enjoyed by the minority white group ... [and] served in promoting tribalism and racism in the urban areas'. Cultural control had operated through the replacement of 'our culture' of 'songs, poems, music, dance and art', with 'the kind of culture that promotes their values and ideas'. Sport had operated through the suppression of African sports such as hunting, fishing, stick fighting, *mrabaraba* and so on, and their replacement by an ethos of competition and wealth accumulation through sport-as-business, such as soccer, which was being 'used by the ruling class and its government in turning people to be self-centred and individualistic'. The media had been 'used to promote and develop values and ideas of the ruling class ... that make people have higher expectations'. Repressive methods included the parliamentary system, which denied blacks the vote; the army and the police, who 'have occupied the townships and they [the army] can be sent to quell labour unrest'; the courts 'protect the interests of the oppressor'; the law itself – laws 'have been made by the ruling minority class to control and dominate the lives of the oppressed and exploited class'; and prisons, which 'serve as camps where the offenders come out being hardened criminals and more dangerous to the society' rather than as places of re-education and rehabilitation.

The analysis was strategically driven. If it was argued that South Africa was primarily a *class-based* and *capitalist* society, and that apartheid was merely an additional tool in the hands of a basically capitalist ruling class, then the struggles of the oppressed should not be shaped by ideologies such as blackness (as in the Black Consciousness movement and its associated organisations), but by the fact of their class oppression. Rather than constituting the structural underpinnings of the whole system, in this analysis, apartheid was simply a weapon of domination, and racially based resistance ideologies a form of false consciousness. Corollaries were that blacks could become part of the enemy to be resisted, and white people could be allies. Thus the struggle came to be defined as *necessarily* a non-racial one, which should emphasise national unity, social, cultural and political emancipation, and the capture and reform of the state. This accorded with the non-racialism of the ANC rather than the racially driven ideas of Black Consciousness, and gave Mzwanele something in common with the two other key adult leaders.

So, adults drew upon trade union traditions of participatory democracy, youth political traditions, local memories of older resistance movements, revived by the 'people's history' movement then active amongst the white intelligentsia, left-wing non-racialism, as well as the more common organisational forms which adults throughout the country were using at the time – lobbying and mobilising committees, workshops and large peaceful meetings. Their networks were located in churches, trade unions, older youth and political structures, yards themselves, work, shebeens and sport.[43] Their intellectuals, repertoires and ideologies were different from those of younger people in a clear manifestation of generationally stratified politics.

CONCLUSION

Each of the two generations was to posit a new vision of the future, the one more millenarian and romantic than the other. Each generation would articulate a different ideology of emancipation, draw on different resources for mobilisation, and see and use space and time within the township differently. The young were to play one type of role. Predictably, perhaps, this would involve a radical and thoroughgoing recasting of temporal relations. Their parents' generation would also play a part. Unlike many rebellions involving generational difference, this one was mainly, but not entirely, directed against an enemy common to both generations – apartheid

– rather than being solely inter-generational. But the adults' part was to be more nuanced, their 'utopia' less visionary, their disruptiveness markedly muted. The tensions between themselves and the younger generation at times threatened to overwhelm their common project in attacking apartheid.

These divergences emerged from the different trajectories of 'structuration' sketched here. As a result of a variety of historical and political processes, specific cultural and ideological resources – social and cultural capital – became available to both generations. Each of the two generations had experienced specific kinds of identity formation; each had recourse to distinct sets of intellectuals, ideas, popular support and resources; and each was to attempt to implement its own plans for the revolutionary metamorphosis of Alexandra, sometimes in opposition to the other and sometimes alongside or even in co-operation with it.

While generational difference and conflict here had substantial historical roots in traditionalism, shaping each generation's expectations of the other, traditionalism articulated in so many complex ways with the historical evolution of the twentieth-century political economy of the South African township in general and Alexandra in particular, that its 'determining' influence was substantially diminished. The generations were, rather, sociologically reshaped by such factors as the evolution of the political economy of the township over time; the changing role of the state and systems of authority in particular and the differential availability of social capital and mobilising resources. Traditionalism became a resource, which each generation could use (either as something to be sternly advocated, or passionately rejected) to pursue its own more contemporary and mainly utopian ends.

6

COMMANDING THE TERRITORY

Over the next few months the spatial attack on Alexandra became more sophisticated. Just as in the Six-Day War, spaces continued to be violated; and mass meetings not only continued but also grew in size and significance. The war ebbed and flowed. Throughout the period, intellectuals and leaders put forward their visions. Meetings, workshops and planning sessions were held. Ideas for how to further the envisaged revolution flourished. Violence persisted, in periods of concentrated bursts, and in spectacular form at times. The crowd evolved into a vital force. The youth and the adults existed in an uncomfortable alliance, and it is moot which of them prevailed at particular periods of time. Episodes of mass mourning, when deaths had occurred, were followed by periods of consolidation of power in the streets, and then further defeats and attacks as the police, both local and national, and in the end the army, sought reciprocally to seize the streets for themselves. A period of social inventiveness followed, introducing a strangely fantastical quality to the violence and defiance of the time.

The rhythms of time imposed by school in the case of young people and work in the case of the older generation were also disrupted. School boycotts and work stay-aways were called for and implemented – by force in many cases. The days became unstructured, and time more malleable. Hours of the daytime were taken up with mass meetings whose temporal structure was vague and unpredictable. The many who died during the revolt were given mass funerals that lasted all night and most of the following day – in some respects a reimposition of pre-industrial ceremonial rhythms and expectations of time in this partially industrialised setting. Days designated for funerals or mass meetings became the symbolic markers of a different conception of the passing of time. Thus the institutionalised time that had been reified sufficiently to control the lives of many Alexandrans was challenged. The rebels may not have gone as far as proposing such revolutionary devices as a new calendar, but their disruptions served to undermine the existing order in crucial ways.

The long surviving private cultural realm, with all of its social forms, not only provided resources and sustenance for the emerging movements, but continued to prove to be relatively impenetrable even by the increasingly invasive and eventually occupying police or army. The effect of this was not to break down the borders which surrounded the township, rather to reinforce them, but at the same time to reverse their meaning. How did this reclaiming of bordered spaces come into existence?

A complicated logic underlay what the grassroots comrades did. It went something like this: the main oppressors – Afrikaner nationalists and capitalism – were outsiders to the township; their control of black lives had led to poverty, suffering and racism; previous attempts at resistance – led by older generations – had more or less failed; and now the mass of township residents were either too afraid to resist, or were not aware of the desperate need to resist their conditions of life and instead had sunk into despair, immorality or passivity themselves. The horrible conditions in Alexandra were thus the result both of the oppression visited upon it by its rulers, and of the failures of its residents. It would be the task of the comrades, enlightened and brave as they were, to change all of this. They could and would bring hope; they would bring new dreams to the residents and would introduce a new determination amongst Alexandrans to take control of their own lives and destinies. But at the same time they would never forget who their primary enemies were. Everything they did should and must strike a blow at the evils visited upon them by government and/or capital – and preferably a revolutionary blow at that, one that would force the ruling classes onto the defensive and make room for a broader revolutionary strategy to be pursued.

In pursuit of these aims, during and after the Six-Day War the grassroots comrades took the lead. Their militant street-roving groups had broken the spell of normality through their violent appropriation of the space that was Alexandra. Now these same groups set out to reshape the social landscape in ways that were simultaneously threatening to their core enemies.

Several strategies were followed, each drawn from different origins but all given the distinctive stamp of 'comrade' activity. Some were a response to ANC calls for ungovernability; some a development of earlier tactics such as the boycott or strike; some built upon a combination of these. If the 1980s constituted the 'decade of the comrades', it was in their innovations in collective action that they made themselves felt.

The militant, revolutionary youths sought an overturning of all authority and the creation of a better world, while alongside their romantic millennium there emerged a competing adult-based genre of opposition, which tried to create a 'popular democracy' within the township, and to calm the rising violence of the young. A period of several months followed during which 'normality' patently failed to reassert itself in Alexandra and both the youth utopians and the adult popular democrats sought to preserve and/or consolidate the spatial gains and moral inversions first achieved in the Six-Day War by moving from simple mobilisation to more complex forms of institutionalisation – from the spatial to the social. Each group sought to embody its visions in newly created social institutions, which were concerned with the inner life – the habitus – of the township as much as with its experience of control and now invasion from outside. The long surviving private cultural realm, with all of its social forms, not only provided resources and sustenance for the emerging movements, but continued to prove relatively impenetrable even by the occupying police or army.

PATROLLING, LANDMARKING AND NAMING

The Utopia they envisaged needed a new space in which to be constructed, and the abnormality introduced by the Six-Day War into the spaces of Alexandra made it psychically and morally possible for them to be remapped. A common sight in Alexandra during this period was that of groups of young men patrolling the streets, singing freedom songs and laying claim to the spaces around them. Then the comrades had begun to reconceptualise the township space with the early formation of people's parks. This continued and became increasingly elaborate, as the township began to be cast in a new image.

Youth Groups wanted to give each of their areas its own name. Schools and streets too needed new names, something which the Youth Groups had long attended to, albeit in a haphazard manner – many schools had graffiti daubed all over them including new revolutionary names. But at the height of the rebellion the youth leadership, realising that control over the process of naming might rein in the grassroots rebels, made sure that a more systematic approach was adopted. Lists of names of sections, schools and streets were proposed and adopted.

Soon, the whole of Alexandra began to be renamed, based on the pantheon of heroic names and symbols arising from the national and local struggle for freedom, and with suggestions for section names such as Lusaka, Amandla, Amanda Kwadi, Vincent Tshabalala, Steve Biko, Moses Maphita and 'Communist Party' (A. Sebola, Z2729). A campaign was initiated to make sure all streets, schools and landmarks were given the new names agreed upon:

> The names of Streets and schools in Alexandra were last week replaced with those of black political leaders and activists in a massive renaming campaign covering the whole township ... Groups of youths in the township were busy writing the new names on the walls and boards of some of the renamed roads and schools on Tuesday amid intensive SADF patrols ... The main road leading into the township, Selborne Road, has been renamed after the African National Congress, ANC Street. A community school, Ovet [Boveti], has been named after an ANC cadre who was hanged, Solomon Mahlangu. It is now Mahlangu Higher Primary School. Halls, streets and schools have been renamed after black leaders, among them ANC leaders Nelson Mandela, Oliver Tambo, Govin Mbeki, Walter Sisulu and Moses Mabida. An ANC

Cadre who killed himself in a shoot out with police in the township, Vincent Tshabalala has also been honoured by renaming a street after him at the new phase 1 and 2 complex. (*The Sowetan*, 26 May 1986)

A revolutionary grid devised by the comrades replaced the authorities' grid-like pattern of township layout – created in most townships for easy control.

Table 3: Renaming of zones, streets and schools in Alexandra 1986

Zone, street or school	Headquarters of youth group at:	People's Court at:	Renamed as: (spelling as used by comrades)
1st–4th Avenue Zone	86 3rd Avenue	86 3rd Avenue	
3rd Avenue			MK Street
5th–7th Avenue Zone	31 7th Avenue	31 7th Avenue	Mayekiso
5th Avenue			Mandela Street
8th–10th Avenue Zone	8th Avenue		Mdakane Camp
7th Avenue			Dos Santos Street
8th Avenue			Abion Makhaythini,
9th Avenue			Jabulane Mkhele
10th Avenue			Joe Skosana
11th–13th Avenue Zone	10th Avenue and/or 12th Avenue		Joe Modise Section/ Libya Block
11th Avenue			ANC or Lusaka St
12th Avenue			Katrida Street
13th Avenue			Mabhida or Slovo Street
14th–16th Avenue Zone	63 15th Avenue	63 15th Avenue	Vincent Tshabalala/ Lusaka/Amanda Kwadi
14th Avenue			Handgrenade/Mbeki St
15th Avenue			AK47
16th Avenue			Bazooka/ Sobukwe
17th–22nd Avenue Zone	55 19th Avenue	16 and 55 19th Avenue	Freedom Charter
17th Avenue			Amandla; Oliver St
18th Avenue			Moses Kotane
19th Avenue			Arthur Goldricks
21st Avenue			Mother Mphosho
22nd Avenue			Winnie Mandela
Selborne Rd			ANC Street; Vincent St
Rooth St			'Soviet St' or 'P.W. Botha Soviet'
Rooseveldt St			Mark St [Marx?]
'TB Area'			Elijah Barayi
School at cnr John Brand and 12th Ave			Katrida LP School
School at 92 3rd Avenue			Lusaka HP School
Boveti School			Solomon Mahlangu
Ithate School			Oscar Mpetha
Realogile School			Tambo High

Sources: Minutes of AYCO meeting 4 July 1986; and numerous photographs in Mayekiso trial Exhibit Y, CTH archives. Other names were also referred to in the AYCO minutes of 2 June 1986; these included: Steve Biko, Moses Mphita and 'Communist Party'. Mayekiso trial, CTH archives.

These street and other names were actually used at times in comrade documents – the minutes of people's court meetings, for example, give the addresses of the accused as 'Grenade St', 'AK47 Street' and so on.[1]

In a society in which the ruling classes had seen townships as places within which spatial, symbolic and economic control could be exercised, these rezoning and renaming exercises were perceived as remarkably threatening, considering their almost entirely symbolic nature. Re-naming was part of the indictment brought against those tried for treason in later times.

ESTABLISHING NODES OF CONTROL

Over these months it became progressively clearer to all that certain spaces in the township had been 'marked' in ways relevant to the struggle for control. The youth in particular identified certain addresses as landmarks – their already-established Youth Group headquarters. These, in most cases, became gathering spaces for large numbers of youths at crucial points. They called them 'camps':

> Camps were a spontaneous creation as a result of political activity in the township after the Six-Day War ... Groups got bigger and bigger in the course of time. Say five activists in one area would organize, People would come together. (BM, quoted in Carter 1991a: 212)

Like the gangs that had preceded them, the comrades divided the township into sections. There had been earlier attempts at this in late 1985, as we have seen, in the time when the Youth Groups were still independent of any organisations (Ashwell Zwane, Z3673–4). But it now took a much more coherent form. Like gangs, camp groupings would dispute their territorial boundaries. A clearly demarcated dispute between two 'groups' of boys – one led by an evocatively named 'Romeo Cronje' – each of which came from a different vicinity in the township, took place early in the period (P. Tshabalala, M3744). Comrades thought of this as the process of 'demarcation' (A. Sebola, Z2730).

Some saw the formation of camps as a bid for power by the grassroots, an attempt to displace the frequently detained leadership stratum. When during 1985 the AYCO executive had been detained, hostility towards them developed in their absence. They were thought of as the 'old guard', who had been sympathetic to the old 'reformist' resistance styles. Critics of the old guard took it upon themselves to reconstitute the pattern of authority in the township while the executive was detained (Carter 1991a: 44). And when the executive was released from detention, the grassroots bid for power continued:

> When these youth groupings started they were not started by AYCO. AYCO members at the time, most of them were in custody, but the constitution does state that AYCO must have branches. When most of

the executive members came out of custody they found that those youth groupings were already existing. (O. Bapela, M4007)

Bapela believed that the grassroots comrades were unhappy with the leadership's role:

> There was misunderstanding between the youth groupings and the AYCO executive. There were complaints from the youth as to how the executive was conducting things, complaining that monies are being embezzled in the organisation and also complaining that the executive itself is not doing anything for them. Since they came back from custody they only attend parties. That is the cause that made the youth groupings not to like AYCO. (ibid.)

Eventually the section-based 'Youth Groups' were incorporated by the more formal youth organisations. These camps constituted an effective reshaping of the nature of AYCO – by the grassroots rather than the leadership; a 'restructuring ... from below' (Carter 1991a: 213). AYCO even established its own 'camp' in order to consolidate its position – a controversial move, given the volatility of the grassroots comrades:

> The AYCO executive then formulated their own executive, youth grouping, which was at Fifteenth Avenue. When this youth grouping appeared it got into loggerheads with the other youth groupings, because they did not know where it originated. There was an enquiry as to who had formulated it and it was discovered that it was the executive of AYCO that had formulated it. There was that problem between the youth groupings and AYCO. (O. Bapela, M4007)

Gradually 'camps' began to evolve into increasingly powerful centres. Some were relatively organised and even bureaucratised. The oldest one, the Eighth Avenue Youth Group or 'Mdakane Camp' formed a model for the remainder. It elected a committee of eleven people, which acted as a local executive. Each executive member had a portfolio – chairperson, organiser, education officer, treasurers, and so on. The camp itself was divided into blocks, and block representatives met with the executive. The camp held workshops and other meetings on such topics as 'Alexandra and apartheid', 'Apartheid, the national democratic struggle', 'The role of women in the national democratic struggle', 'Trade unions and the national democratic struggle', and 'Discipline'. The last, it was said, 'should include: "loyalty, respect, dedication, devotion, self control and responsibility"' (BM, quoted in Carter 1991a: 216). DP, the woman comrade mentioned in the previous chapter, presented a paper, for example, on what something like 'people's power' meant:

> I presented a paper on 'the people's organs', on the theme of 'the people shall govern'. We took this clause from the Freedom Charter, and asked

how shall people govern? We discussed People's Courts, people's education, ways of creating people's organs, such as street committees ... [people's power] meant changing the whole set up of government – changing it to a non-racial government ... maybe the government itself having the whole people participating – negotiating for studies and the set up of schools – having non-racial power. That would be people's power ... The unity of the people and the formation of democratic structures, building people's organs'. (DP, quoted in Carter 1991a: 216–17)

The Eighth Avenue group would thus discuss 'charterist' ideas. They also tried to 'censure the social behaviour of other township youth' (Carter 1991a: 44). Mzwanele Mayekiso called it:

the general misbehaviour of the youth in the township. At the time, the youth did not have a coherent organisation and leaders of the youth; some of them were in jail, some of the executive members. They were now trying to bring the youth together as well as the executive with which the youth had a problem. (Mzwanele Mayekiso, M4070)[2]

Pre-existing gang and territorial spaces certainly underlay the positioning of at least some of these boundaries and headquarters. On 6 March, the day after the first mass funeral of those killed in the Six-Day War, Obed Bapela describes how he went to 53 Nineteenth Avenue and saw the beginnings of what was to become a key headquarters for the youth:

I found many youths in that yard and they were holding a meeting. *How many approximately?* Between 100 and 150 ... Some were seated and some were standing behind those who were sitting ... there was somebody talking to all of them ... concerning that it is better they left tsotsi-dom and they stopped gambling. Now they have come together as youth, they are comrades and they must also see how they could take part in the struggle. He went on to say that there should be educational and political discussions among them, which would teach them about the struggle, as to how it goes about. (O. Bapela, M3926–7)

This address was, he said, 'a place where the gangsters and youth who wanted to gamble used to gamble there. The gang that was then there at the time was known as the "Speak and Verstaan" gang.' Adults 'as well as women' were also sitting and listening (ibid.).

Ashwell Zwane's version was that a congress of AYCO was meant to happen on 12 April, but on 11 April it was postponed to an unknown date because:

there were youth groupings at the time not belonging to AYCO and they were not consulted in time or told in time about the congress.

COMMANDING THE TERRITORY 131

And the reason why the congress was then postponed was that those groups of youths were interested in being part of the congress, they wanted to partake in the congress. (A. Zwane, Z3673ff)

They were, he said, 'youth groupings with no names', and the AYCO executive 'had to introduce itself now to these other youth groupings so instead of the congress taking place that meeting of introduction then took place'.

Two of these unofficial and independent youth groupings – presumably representing the more grassroots initiative of comrades – came to that meeting and said they would join AYCO. Ayco incorporated at least three groups – the Third, Seventh and Nineteenth Avenue Youth Groupings – as a result, and set out to 'consolidate' the remainder from its 'headquarters' at 63 Fifteenth Avenue.[3]

Thus it seems that the street groupings preceded the consolidation of AYCO and influenced its subsequent shape and form. Later, existing members of AYCO were encouraged to form their own youth groupings in their own areas. So, said Zwane: 'I and the members who were staying in my area came together and we show each other how to go about opening a branch' (ibid.). The expansion of AYCO very likely took place through its successful mobilisation of grassroots structural forms (A. Sebola, Z2821, Z3281).

REVERSING THE MEANING OF BORDERS

The outside borders of Alexandra had always been significant – they had of course marked off the black and poor from the white and well off in a more than usually vivid sense. It was during these months that the rebels attempted to create symbolic markers of their own, which reversed the meaning of the borders, so that they no longer meant that the poor and black were 'kept in' but came to mean that those who were *not* poor and black or who were in other ways not symbolic of 'those belonging to Alex' were to be 'kept out'.

The comrades also patrolled symbolic borders of belonging and exclusion. Belonging to the township meant committing oneself to its struggle. Parents who sent their children out of Alexandra to boarding school, to schools in rural areas, or even to the few private schools that in those times would accept black pupils, were told to bring them back. They must, said one, commit themselves to improving education for everyone, and not simply selfishly improve their own education (A. Sebola, Z2660, Z3716).

This definition of symbolic and actual borders and defences was reinforced by the revival of the 'consumer boycott', which, following a long tradition of African resistance genres (C. Bundy, M4330ff), had originally started with the 'Black Christmas' campaign of the previous December. But the consumer boycott moved far beyond symbolism. It could be pursued from within the township, and in theory at least, struck at the growing significance of the black urban working class for fulfilling the consumption needs of the economy – a change from earlier times when they had tended to be regarded almost entirely as producers, while the wealthier white classes had been targeted as consumers. Here the comrades came up against two obstacles to their utopian vision. The first was that while their power base lay within the township it was also limited to the township, or at the outside limit, to the borders. But segregation had meant that the major shopping centres were far away. This was why the borders of the township became so important – within the comrades' range of influence were the consumers of Alex themselves and the small, independently run shops, some owned by whites, on the immediate periphery of the township.

The boycott in these months set its sights on those shopkeepers of Alex who were physically or metaphorically outsiders. Shops defined as 'not part of Alex', as 'unsympathetic to the struggle', as 'dirty' or 'racist' were boycotted, or in some cases attacked. Local shops, inside Alex, owned or run by residents, were acceptable. On 21 April the boycott was to begin:

> And no business dealings should be entered into with anyone of the following: Ascapo, Goldies, Hazel, Freddie's Spar, Jazz Stores, Johnnies, Mielie's, and Benny Goldberg. No shopping should be made in town. Purchases should be made from local shops. (Mzwanele Mayekiso, M4154–5)

Jazz Stores was on the borders of the township. It had already been burnt down during the Six-Day War because it was there that Michael Diradeng had been shot and was, said Ashwell Zwane, 'not part of Alex' (A. Sebola, Z3679). Numerous Portuguese-owned shops, many of them actually on the physical borders of Alexandra anyway, were deemed to be 'other' – dirty, racist or too expensive (A. Sebola, Z3711).

This turned the comrades' envisaged struggle against the agents of capitalism to an actual struggle against the modest petty bourgeoisie on their doorstep – some of whom were also members of the already besieged local Council; and their customers – some were the policemen they were seeking to drive out, and the adults whom they were seeking to 'conscientise'. The Alex Boycott Committee listed twenty-five shops in and around Alex where shopping was prohibited: shebeens, dry cleaners, hair salons, liquor outlets, filling stations, and councillors' shops (*The Star*, 22 April 1986).

An ethnic dimension also at times entered into this aspect of the revolt, for many of the smaller shopkeepers were Chinese, Indian, Coloured or Portuguese rather than African – and it was often their ethnicity rather than their race that counted to the comrades. The Chinese owner of Ho's Fish and Chips, known as Hazel, knew Alex well, having had a shop there for thirty-five years. She said she was especially selected because the story amongst the comrades was that she used to sell food to the police. After the boycott began in April 1986 she said that:

When the customers came to buy there were a lot of children standing outside and as soon as they walked out, they would take their parcels away from them and tear it up and threaten the customers ... These children would be about from the age of 12 to 15. (*in camera* Witness 2, M26)

The children were, she said, mostly boys. The boycott of her particular shop petered out after six weeks. Portuguese shop-owners were repeatedly said to have maltreated customers – and the experiences of Portuguese shop-owners were broadly similar: Portuguese-owned Estrella's Take-Away and Pan African Meat Centre were both boycotted for as long as three months. Every time a customer of theirs went out with food, a group of young men would 'open the parcel and they would empty everything on the ground' (*in camera* Witness 3, M35ff). The Wynberg Food Centre was boycotted for even longer – five or six months, during which groups of young men would wait outside and stop people going in, or run inside the shop and chase people out. Several other fish and chip shops and other take-aways, food shops and restaurants were similarly treated. A few closed down, and some were attacked, looted and destroyed.

Shops that were not owned by whites and that may also have escaped the 'maltreatment' accusation were attacked for being politically unacceptable, as had been the case with Jazz Stores, the venue of Diradeng's death. Often this was because the shopkeepers were in some way connected to the much hated Town Council – illuminating how it had been mainly the middle class who had chosen to take part in Council politics.[4]

Local shops, inside Alex, owned or run by residents, were mainly deemed to be acceptable and their use was encouraged, although housewives found them very expensive. As early as 1983, 'people's shops' had been identified (*Voice of AYCO*, November–December 1983). But these should not abuse their advantage, said the comrades: there should be 'a ruling price for all the different consumer goods' and 'the non-boycotted shopkeeper should stick to their normal prices'; 'the plan should be devised to consult the shop-keepers'; and 'there should be cleanliness or tidiness of the non-boycotted shops'.[5]

The circumscribed power of the comrades meant that they could not control the consumption of anybody other than their own adult community – their neighbours and parents. These were people who lived on the bread-line anyway and whose purchases from shops tended to be of the most fundamental and limited sort. They were not major consumers, but extremely minor ones, for whom every cent and every purchase counted immensely. And yet the comrades expected them to fall into line. As com-rades told one resident: 'we should not enrich whites – and so should not buy at shops outside Alexandra' (J. Nkuna, M448). In fact residents' parti-cipation in the Consumer Boycott was uneven. Many said they were forced to participate and there are harrowing reports of women being forced to drink cooking oil or other consumables that they had brought into the township, to destroy their groceries and being generally harassed by youths enforcing the ban on shopping 'outside'. If you did not listen, said one resident, 'you would be assaulted and your articles be thrown away and your house would be burnt'. This had happened to him, he said. After shopping in town he was accosted by youths when he came home:

> They took my groceries and a boy of about fifteen years of age walloped me with a sjambok and said I do not want to listen ... They trampled the articles that I had bought, spilt out the cooking oil, as well as soap powder and meat. (Barker et al. 1986)

One trial witness named Thoko gave evidence of how, in May, she was attacked in the street by comrades while she was simply going to the Commissioner to get maintenance from her child's father. She knew going out could be dangerous at a time 'when it was said that people should not go about in the street, but I forced matters to go there and find out whether he had brought the money' (*in camera* Witness 16, Z1342–3). She came across the comrades and said she was not going to work but going to the Commissioner.

> And they said it seems to me that you don't want to listen, that is your habit and then thereafter I was just slapped over my eyes ... They kicked me, I fell down and they snatched the plastic that I was carrying ... They left me lying there.

She never went to the Commissioner (*in camera* Witness 16, Z1342–3).

Not all of these reports are urban legends and it was these kinds of experiences that augured the beginnings of adult disillusionment with youth behaviour, and signalled the emergence of a distinctively adult political stance. Many adults were deeply disturbed by the emergence of this particular boycott, and its *de facto* victimisation of the residents rather than the authorities. Refilwe Mashego's yard committee was against it:

> We had a shop in our street and we felt that is the shop where we should go and buy from and we knew this person, he was one of the people in the street and again this consumer boycott would have turned out to be instances where a lot of upset was caused because whenever people came with their groceries they will be thrown in the streets and fish oils opened and poured out of the bottles and I think that is wrong for people going to buy and having all their money wasted by that. (R. Mashego, M4279)

Activists interviewed later confirmed that comrades had behaved ruthlessly towards adults: 'In Alexandra township ... elderly women returning from white shops in Johannesburg – which had been placed 'out of bounds' by boycott organizers – were forced to drink the cooking oil they had pur-chased' (Johnson n.d.: 88). During this period a complaint was lodged at one of the people's courts: 'There is a bad manner of approach from the youth to the parent when it comes to times of securing the local boycott.' Albert Sebola explained what this meant:

> The discussion again raised from the floor, and that discussion was about the local consumer boycott and the complaint was from an adult who said that there were some youngsters who took his plastics away … Plastic bags, with goods inside … So the discussion was that a person should be approached in a good manner and then reasons given why there is a local consumer boycott and then you must agree with the boycott voluntarily. (A. Sebola, Z2640)

But these 'comrades' were regarded by some 'true' comrades as *abosiya-yinyova*, or thuggish lawless youths (Johnson n.d:. 42).

This particular boycott was driven from below and there were tensions between the youth at the grassroots and their leaders, many of whom did not agree with it at all (O. Bapela, M4014). Mzwanele Mayekiso was clearly hostile and even implied the presence of *agents provocateurs* in promoting the boycott – presumably in order to divide the youths from the adults: 'As I see it … I would say it were underground people who were pushing this con-sumer boycott, because the people behind the consumer boycott were not known' (Mzwanele Mayekiso, M4151).

Young children used to deliver the pamphlets, he said, and when he asked them where they had got them they said from 'other men standing on a certain corner who had asked them to distribute this pamphlet'. But a more likely explanation was that, as one observer put it, 'there seemed to be youth that is not disciplined, which was harassing the people who were buying.' The actions of these freely operating comrades had not been endorsed by organisations such as AYCO. The boycott probably originated with the impatient and relatively independent Youth Groups, who wished to exercise their power within the space of Alex and were prepared to do so at the expense of the adults who would not concur. This willingness to punish their own was to develop further as the revolt evolved.

Adults rejected youth tactics in the consumer boycott:

> Children were misbehaving. When you come from Oks (OK Bazaar) for instance, with your parcels, they would take them and destroy them. I personally bought a 'Sowetan' [newspaper] one time and it was des-troyed in my hand. (P. Tshabalala, M3854)

Adults did not like youth behaviour. 'The youth would tear up their articles and some would even be sjambokked. They were not in agreement with that'(R. Mdakane, M2262).

BANISHMENT AND BURNING

Of course there was still powerful competition for control over the space of the township. Besides the comrades, the police and the army continued to patrol Alexandra, and to attack its residents from time to time – particularly towards the end of the rebellion. The spaces controlled by the rebels could not survive unless they, too, were physically defended. Systems of defence had already emerged in the Six-Day War and continued in this period too. Trenches were built and 'tank traps' dug between February and August (P. B. Botha, Z304). Building upon the spatial war that they had already waged, and using older deep-rooted gang traditions of territorial belonging, they used the youth groupings to control their precisely defined territories, at times patrolling the streets to find and disarm, or beat, criminals, or those carrying weapons. The sense of bizarre abnormality in the streets was reinforced in this period of consolidation by sudden and brutal mob actions. At the core of comrade power lay their newly discovered capacity to rout the policemen who lived in Alex, to identify and purge police spies, informers and witches; and to make life almost as difficult for the local members of the Council which represented the state's failed attempts at reform. These were labelled collaborators and treated accordingly.

The police themselves experienced this as a period during which they were harassed, marginalised and weakened. They could not, said one policeman, even stop in the township to talk to a friend. The police in this period, said one of them (P. Botha, Z301) were termed sell-outs, could not buy goods at shops, use roads in township, and their children could not attend schools. Some activists thought police were, at times, a relatively easy target. They were often drunk, it was said, or high on marijuana. In this kind of case they could be disarmed relatively easily: 'We would disarm them and shoot them with their own gun' (NP, quoted in Carter 1991a: 235).

After the war, they added social ostracism and persecution to the strategies they had already used. A 'non-participation' campaign was launched whose purpose was to 'isolate all collaborators socially'. 'Their children are not welcome at school. Their businesses are being boycotted. They are also isolated at social gatherings. Neighbours no longer talk to them, and their relatives stay away.'[6]

The burnings began with policemen but were not restricted to actual holders of office in the township. Informers – *impimpis* – alleged informers and those accused of being malign witches were also attacked and killed. It was a frightening time, a reign of terror, with comrades patrolling the streets. Of four informers uncovered within AYCO one was 'subjected to intensive interrogation', confessed and was removed from 'sensitive' activities. One was 'isolated' and left the township; one was attacked, assaulted and burnt, but survived. Then, on 12 April, one Theresa Maseko, the same young woman who had led some of the singing at Michael Diradeng's funeral, was dragged from her home and necklaced by a mob of youths who accused her (correctly, as it turned out) of being a police informer (BM, quoted in Carter 1991a: 239).

Necklacing had, by now, become part of the repertoire of township resistance. In Theresa's case, the 'mob' was perhaps more overtly political than it had been in the case of the first victim, Maki Skhosana, but it still included an extraordinary range of people. Theresa had in fact joined the comrades in 1985, and 'went around' with them; but soon after the Six-Day War it began to be suspected that she was an *impimpi* and also that she was in fact the wife of a notorious policeman – Sergeant Mothibe. At one of the funerals of this period there had been a board held by comrades reading: 'Away with Mothibe and his wife Theresa, we don't need you'. Then on the afternoon of 12 April, a group of youths fetched her from her home. They seized an axe and told the family they were going to 'chop her to death' with it. When her 52-year-old mother Mrs Jane Maseko pleaded with the youths to leave the axe, one of the four people who entered the house warned her to 'shut up or else we will chop your head off'. Scores of other youths waited outside the yard. Theresa was put into a van that had been hijacked.

Her sister remembered:

> We were playing cards (at home) whilst Theresa was reading a novel, she was seated on the sofa next to the door. And while we were seated there we heard Theresa screaming. She got up and ran away ... She got out of the dining room into the kitchen and while we were still waiting there there came another man [with Rastafarian hair] ... This man had a sjambok with him. He was followed by some boys and as they got into the house there they said to her 'Theresa come out with your firearm' and at that stage Theresa had already run away. (A. Maseko, Z505–6)

She escaped into another room but was pursued by her attackers. She escaped once more, through the window, when the group stormed the house. Anastasia remembered them vividly:

> Some of these young men ... entered through the kitchen door. Amongst them there was a girl there who was dressed in a pink pair of trousers and she had also a [lemon coloured] skipper on which it was printed UDF and a black jersey and she had a doek on her head, the doek was tightened up to just above her eyes ... And then there was another boy who was dressed in a check shirt, this young man went to the back of the stove and took an axe there and then at that stage my mother then screamed and said oh my child. And shortly thereafter the man with an axe then threatened to chop my mother. And then some of these young men then said 'we have got her, let's go' ... When we got out we saw that they had her ... They went away with her and

then at the next street these young men then stopped a passing car there … a navy van bakkie with a white canopy … She was put in that van and they went away with her. *Can you estimate how many of these young people were there at your home? Inside and outside the house?* They were about more than 150. (ibid.)

The inner door was broken and the telephone wire was cut. The sjambok was black and long. The next time she saw Theresa was at the government mortuary two days later.

A participant in the necklacing remembered it slightly differently, saying that Theresa had actually been tried in a people's court:

She was visiting her mother. One of the neighbours saw her. The whole street was organized by that time. Our intention was just to question her, to see if she was an informer. But we believe in majority rule. Maybe the house would say let's kill her, then we would do that. She was taken to a court. The whole youth decided not to know of that. (Carter 1991a: 241)

She was subsequently paraded naked in the street by a group of several hundred youth – who called this 'modelling', before being assaulted and burnt (Carter 1991a: 242). M. Phosa, a policeman, saw the necklacing happen:

I heard a noise in the street … I saw many people in the street. There was a Renault vehicle in the midst of these people … this car went and stopped in front of number 31 … I saw some people of the car driving a girl out of the car. They went with her into number 31 … after about five minutes, I saw this girl coming out running and she did not have clothes on. While she was fleeing a group chased her and they got hold of her. I heard one of the people of the group talking loud. He was talking about petrol and a tyre. Some of them had tomahawks and pangas. They were striking at her at that time. … I saw one person of the group coming with a tyre and put it over the girl … Later I heard that the girl who was being attacked had been killed … I heard from the screams that they were calling her Theresa … From the way they were scream-ing they were saying that she is a police informer. (M. Phosa, M1765–6)

Phosa feared that he would be next:

Whilst I was looking through the window I closed the door and they continued hitting her. I was afraid that one of the people might see me and notice that I am a policeman and they might have killed me too.

Eventually he drove to the police station to get help, but 'she had already been killed'. The crowd, he said, was about 100 strong. Their ages were mixed. There were, he said, some 'old ladies' in the mob (M1765). The police arrived and fired teargas; she was rushed to hospital where she died.[7]

The family subsequently lived in fear; Anastasia no longer went to school after threats of 'necklace treatment' by other pupils.

One commentator argues that AYCO was worried by necklacing – mainly because it fitted so neatly with what the 'enemy' said activists were doing, and also because the state could turn it against them. There had been at least 263 necklacings in the country as a whole between January and July 1986, including over 100 in the Northern Transvaal, and nearly 100 in the Eastern and Western Cape.[8] Nevertheless another necklacing did take place in Alexandra on 5 June. Shadrack Lebusa, a motor mechanic, was also suspected of being an informer and a tyre was placed around his neck by a group of angry youths. He too was burnt to death (*City Press*, 8 June 1986; *The Sowetan*, 10 June 1986).

These events have not been forgotten by residents of Alexandra. Theresa's death in particular is emblematic of many of the events of 1986 – or at least of those aspects that involved youth political passion and public brutality.

Councillors in the once popular local Council were also subjected to attack. By 1985, life for anyone connected with government had become difficult. Councillors were now regarded as puppets, as this wave of distaste for the reformist institutions of the state, partly initiated and encouraged by the ANC in exile, grew to become a national phenomenon.[9] During the Six-Day War councillors had become, or felt or feared they had become, targets of youth violence. Councillor A. Mashile had been shot in the stomach at his shop in Nineteenth Ave (*The Sowetan*, 18 February 1986) and Councillor Thomas Molepo's 14-year-old son from out of town was shot in the head. He died ten days later in hospital. Although it was likely that the young Molepo had actually been shot by police, his death added to the general feeling of persecution on the part of councillors, and his father eventually resigned from the Council citing:

> pressure from his family and the conflict his membership of the council was causing among his relatives … His children were being isolated and could no longer walk freely in the township because he belonged to the council. (*The Star*, 28 February 1986)

His eldest son said:

> While my father could always count on the protection of the police, his councillorship places our lives in jeopardy because people see us as bad elements in society. It is now even difficult for me to patronise most shebeens or to attend residents meetings because people say I am a spy. (*The Sowetan*, 3 March 1986)

Mr Molepo asked for his son to be buried with the other victims of the Six-Day War. Mike Beea, in response, as chairman of the mass funeral committee, said:

> Mr Molepo has realised that no man can fight a crocodile in the river because he has little chance of winning ... All those who are saying they will fight the system from within have been misled. We urge all our brothers and sisters who are still in such bodies to reconsider their positions and resign. (ibid.)

By March 1986 the attacks, threats and personal and political pressure upon councillors had reached epidemic proportions. By 27 March only four of the original nine councillors remained in office, and there was no longer a quorum (*The Star*, 12 March 1986), with one of them, Darky Rametse, saying: 'My family, relatives and friends have pleaded with me to quit the council post and the Save Alexandra Party. The whole community of Alexandra was one in telling me to quit' (*The Sowetan*, 10 March 1986). After the mass funeral Rametse had driven around the township 'and met the youth groups. The youths apparently told him he would not be assaulted, but asked him to resign from the Council' (*Sunday Star*, 16 March 1986). Another, Reuben Mashile, said that he had realised that the black Town Council system was unacceptable; that he had created enemies for himself and family; and that members of his church, family, relatives and friends had asked him to resign (*The Star*, 27 March 1986). In April the Junior Council – an attempt to include youth in local governance which had already been depleted by resignations of seven of its members in February – also resigned, saying: 'They took us as if we were being sponsored by the government. Because we were serving under a council which was operating under the Local Authorities Act, we were automatically branded agents of the system'; and citing threats by youth organisations, who had said that 'if we don't [resign] they'll burn down our houses and kill our families' (*The Citizen*, 17 April 1986).

Town clerk Arthur Magermann resigned too, because, he said, of the absolute rejection of Town Councils throughout the country; the danger to the life and property of himself and his family; his desire to return to the people and not continue as an outcast; the attitude of some of the councillors towards him which could break into open hostility and create instability and danger; and appeals by friends (*The Star*, 16 April 1986). His son remembered:

> *Would you describe life in Alexandra in 1985 as fairly 'normal'?* No ... There were a heavy presence of police. The people started turning against the council and they were coming on real strong during that period. They were not just talking, but they were acting ... They started stoning our house ... Personally for me 1985 changed, because people started rejecting me. My friends started turning against me. My girl-friends would reject me and I was an outcast. (Errol Magermann, M150)

Sam Buti, the mayor, who had swept to power in local elections on the back of his successful efforts to save Alexandra from demolition, no longer commanded much support. He represented the older generation of the petty bourgeoisie, a churchman whose pragmatism, values of respectability and politics of patronage were discarded by the purifying utopianism of the young. He had been attacked in the recent past and was by now deeply embittered by the fact that the public's opinion of him as a leader and developer of the community had changed to the view that he was no more than a corrupt collaborator.

The councillors, while they had not been elected under a full democracy, had also not been outsiders imposed upon the township. They were members of old Alexandran notable and middle-class families, with roots in core social, economic and cultural institutions such as family, football, patronage politics, church and trade. Their rejection was more than a blow at the apartheid state. It was a blow at the old Alexandra itself. Buti's bitterness stemmed from this.[10] He observed that, although participation in the campaign to oust policemen and councillors had indeed gained public support, it had originated in comrade power, militancy and violence. This, he noted, was all very well, but it would have unintended consequences for stability in township communities which were all based upon a series of social and cultural institutions, and upon generational systems of authority. Other adults were concerned by this: 'It is all right to mobilise the people to boycott but not to the point where authority – parental, school or otherwise – is undermined', said one (*The Star*, 6 April 1986). Of course this gave Buti a reputation for conservative collaborationism. But in fact these observations were increasingly to be echoed by more radical adult leaders over the period of the rebellion.

CONCLUSION

The remapping of the township, combined with the persistence of old conceptions of space and place, lent an extraordinary spatial complexity to the period. The demarcation of zones and the establishment of Youth Group Headquarters were tenuous. The township required constant patrolling – as if to reinforce its abnormality. The patrolling took place internally as well as externally, physically and symbolically.

As the rebellion proceeded the comrades came to be feared and in some cases respected by the township population. Their own leaders found that they had difficulty in keeping up with them. In many cases the leaders would hastily try to follow the example set by those they wished to lead, and attempt to systematise and control the multiple ideas about how to act collectively bubbling up from below. To the comrades the township was theirs to transform – a space upon which they could impose their own vision. After all they were, they believed, the conveyors of a just cause. Their parents and the ordinary township residents were behind the times, or slow, or unable to see what it was that was really oppressing them, or just straight reactionary. They, the youth, would make sure that the adults were freed from their own oppression.

The township space, having been profoundly disrupted, was gradually turned into a proto-theatrical venue in which a range of different performances could take place. The borders which had acted as repressive and controlling forces came to signify emancipation, liberation, control. New geographies and new ideas about belonging were constructed within the township as ordinary streets, schools and homes became invested with different and revolutionary meanings. The Youth Groups divided the township into their own controlled spaces, and invested them with symbolic and actual power. The boycott, the necklace, the persecution of councillors, the punishment of adult and youth transgressions each constructed new audiences, actors and scripts, some of them – particularly the act of necklacing – highly dramatic in form. The dramatic construction of events posing good against evil cast the comrades as liberators and moral protectors. And although not every audience applauded them – and adults in particular, sometimes found themselves unhappily cast on the wrong side – there is no doubt that these dramas furthered the broader possibilities of rebellion. When an unusually widespread 'crime spree' took place in Alexandra in March an 'anti-crime campaign' was begun with roots in the zones identified and named by the Youth Groups, and with clear objectives. Crime was actually reduced at first. The comrades came to regard themselves as the moral protectors of the community. Within the very heart of the new spaces that had been created, the next chapter shows, even more profound new enactments of new moralities took place.

7

THE PRIVATE UTOPIA

I was convinced that by the end of 1986 we shall have taken over, and by the end of 1987 we shall be free. (MM, quoted in Carter 1991a: 181)

We did not want to be governed by them any longer but we wanted to be governed by ourselves. (*in camera* Witness 9, Z1033)

I found a kind of utopia mentality developed amongst certain idealistic youth who thought that they now could have freedom and run Alexandra as a separate entity forgetting about the rest of the world, a very insular kind of mentality. (Father Cairns, M4365)

Triumphalism was in the air. (Johnson n.d.: 46)

During and after the Six-Day War both time and space had been challenged. Now they were 'transcended'. Spaces of oppression became spaces of liberation; 'structurated' time became 'utopian' time. But the Utopia would be a private one. Although they wanted to overthrow the forces of state and capital, the comrades ignored the outside world in their concerns to reshape the social contours of their township. Perhaps this is not surprising, considering Alexandra's enclosed and manageable nature, their youth, and their lack of experience of any other world besides those of family, street, club, church and school. They envisaged a future in which the mundane improvements needed for daily life would accumulate so that a better world would be created for all. This would mean, for example, that basics such as houses, proper streets, sewerage, lighting, school and transport would be provided for all. But their Utopia would also bring into being a population of township residents free of all the sins of crime, drunkenness, child neglect, acrimony and fighting, and would thus reflect the glory of the struggle of the people. They would 'cleanse' the township of its moral decay, including the moral decay of their own elders, at the same time as liberating all from oppression. They would lead and implement a revolution that would combine a callow Marxism, a naive African nationalism and burning youth romanticism.

> We're going to take over, take over
> Take our country in the Mugabe way

Run away, run away, Botha
Umkhonto has arrived
We are the soldiers of Luthuli, led by Mandela
Even if it is bad we are going
Move aside and give us way. (Frederickse 1986: 48)

After the first six days of the rebellion were over, the youths managed to subject adults to their authority to a remarkable extent. A combination of brutality and passion drove them. The vacuum caused by the driving out of police was filled, it was said, by 'a new breed of leader – the comrades, ruthless and efficient'. They combined this with a devotion to a self-administered legality. Without regular law and order, one observer was asked, 'How is it that chaos does not reign?' 'Because the comrades bring all malefactors to book' (*Sunday Tribune*, 2 March 1986).

THE CAMPAIGN AGAINST CRIME

Do people living in violent communities become inured to murder, drunkenness, theft and robbery? It seems not – at least in the case of Alexandra. Nobody liked going to work in the morning, as one resident put it, and seeing 'a person who has been stabbed who has been covered with paper' lying in the street (*in camera* Witness 9, Z1083).[1] However, criminals were not outsiders who came in to rob and kill. They were not the 'other', the simply deviant – even when they could be identified as excluded subgroups. Moral panics would not do as a way to cope with the problems they presented. Most day-to-day crime was committed by the fathers, sons, acquaintances and neighbours of residents themselves – criminals whose lives were intertwined with the social worlds of their victims. Anyway, everybody in Alexandra was in fact already somebody else's 'other' – that of those who ruled the society as a whole – and thus defined as an insider to the circumscribed township.

This placed the doing of immoral deeds by Alexandrans themselves in a peculiar ethical limbo. The outside world could not be relied upon to provide and enforce alternatives – for it was itself immoral and illegitimate. The older respectable classes had always coped with this by holding to and advocating strict ideals of uprightness for those within, and propagating them through churches, schools and associations. Nevertheless, by the 1980s, as we have argued, these elites – and the older generation in general – had been irreparably weakened. In the eyes of the young they were no longer acceptable moral guardians of the community. To the comrades, it seemed that their parents were powerless to construct a moral universe capable of transcending the increasing evil represented by the state, and the growing social decay that surrounded them.

Just before the main rebellion began, the comrades started to turn their attention to rectifying Alexandra's inner social problems; and in doing so to begin to use the methods of collective action they had already evolved for purposes of opposing apartheid, to impose a new ethical order upon the township. The resulting 'anti-crime campaigns' were examples of the preparedness of the comrades to impose their will upon those whom they saw as the immoral, as criminals, or as potential criminals.

Anti-crime campaigns, like street committees, were part of the repertoire of collective action in many townships. Some aspects of the campaigns were benign – youths would sometimes protectively escort young girls home late at night (H. Banda, M1301). But from late 1985 onwards groups of comrades started patrolling the streets actively looking for criminals, *tsotsis*, drunks and those involved in fights, and accosting them. Their aims were simply, at first, to remove weapons or sometimes drugs. When it started in 1985 it was relatively mild:

> a student was stabbed to death in a shebeen ... So that is when I realised the anti-crime campaign because the following day ... Sunday the youth in the township moved around searching for knives ... They went into shebeens and they even stopped young people in the street. Because I remember I was stopped and searched too. (P. Tshabalala, M3855)[2]

Refilwe Mashego saw it like this:

> the youth had organised, there was crime going on in the township and a lot of mugging and fighting in the shebeens and criminal element going on, so in order to reduce that type of behaviour the youth organised themselves in the way that they will patrol the streets. Whenever they see a drunk person in the street they will escort him home and they even go into the shebeens to see that there are no disruptions there and again the delinquents who went about carrying knives were disarmed ... the reaction was that there was scum in the township and those people who knocked off late from work were no more afraid of their pay and lives on their way back home and there were little, the number of people walking up and down at night was greatly reduced. (R. Mashego, M4255–6)

This first anti-crime campaign died down in about January 1986, but it had set a pattern, and after the rebellion proper got under way the aim of ridding the community of crime was revived and an even more systematic and wide-ranging series of campaigns was mounted. An unusually widespread 'crime spree' took place in Alexandra in March and a new anti-crime campaign was begun, a far better organised one, with roots in the zones identified and named by the Youth Groups, and with much clearer objectives. The comrades had come to regard themselves as the moral protectors of the community. As Albert Sebola said, the comrades did not like people who drank, sniffed glue or smoked dagga; or youth congregating on street corners. These things 'caused gangsterism' and must be stopped (A. Sebola, Z2753–6). One Youth Group felt that the campaign was necessary to act 'as a form of security to our residents of Alexandra'.[3] At first the campaign, again, was relatively free of violence:

> In the beginning it was such a well-organised thing because it led me to believe that it was the community orientated youth who were interested in seeing to the smooth running and the reduction of crime in the township … it wasn't youth at random … I don't know whether they had formed an organisation, but it was basically well-organised at the beginning. (R. Mashego, M4272)

Comrades would meet at their youth headquarters and plan their anti-crime campaigns from there. The minutes of one Youth Group indicate that the comrades felt that what they were doing was, indeed, worthy. 'We take whatever danger from the spot. We got people who are very famers [famous] of what they are doing which is danger to our parents example by roofing [robbing], stabbing each other et cetera' (A. Sebola, Z2681).[4] Friday and Saturday evenings were the peak time for township criminals and drunks, and groups of young men would sign up for patrol on one or the other evening.[5] One participant in a patrol described how two people would walk in front of the campaigners and if they saw police they would warn by whistling and then the group would disappear into the yards and hide. Once free to do so, they would walk around the streets and stop and search people for weapons. They were feared and also – at least at first – respected:

> *Did any of the persons searched object at all?* No … They were afraid that we would discipline them … They knew we were comrades because we were walking there in a group … We as Comrades were being feared. (*in camera* Witness 9, Z982–4)

Shebeens, of which there were literally hundreds in the township, were the logical destination for most such patrols. The comrades would march through the streets in groups of up to eighty or 100, sometimes under the leadership of a 'commander' (*in camera* Witness 9, Z977), in 'their' zone, enter shebeens, order the music to be turned down, and then remove all guns, knives and screwdrivers from shebeen patrons (A. Sebola, Z2681–2). Anybody drinking there who was under age would be removed. One owner gave evidence on what happened in his shebeen:

> My wife told me to put off the radio or the music … She said the Comrades have arrived to search people, searching them for dangerous weapons like knives … I put off the music and they did all as they wanted to … Four got into my house … I think they searched them all [his customers]. (*in camera* Witness 10, Z1173–4)[6]

Sebola remembered his experience of actually going on anti-crime campaigns:

> We conducted an anti-crime campaign. *Do you recall how many of you went out?* Plus minus twelve ... In the shebeens we would enter and request the shebeen owner to switch down the music ... And explain why we are here ... The explanation is that we were searching for knives and other weapons ... Thereafter we will then get permission from the shebeen owner to search his patrons ... Then we will search ... on that day we found knives, screwdrivers and a gun ... So the owner of the gun ... is Donald ... He thought maybe we would misbehave with his gun, he did not trust us. So accused 1 (Ashwell Zwane) and myself we took him to the executive committee ... we explained that we found this man with a gun ... we left them there discussing so we got the report that Donald would get his gun tomorrow, and of which it was returned back to him. (A. Sebola, Z2681–2)

He says gun, screwdrivers and knives were all left at the executive office.

That night, he says, they did not carry sjamboks. At 10 p.m. they went home. The whole campaign had lasted two hours. Such campaigns, said one participant, actually had the full support of some older residents, who were concerned about crime.

> The discussion about the anti-crime campaign was that most of the young people visit shebeens and after getting drunk they misbehave and if they are in possessions of knives it results that somebody will be stabbed and he will die. As I have stated that this was discussed generally the parents supported this because they were most concerned that the youth or the young people we are talking about was their very own children. *The parents supported what?* Supported the conducting of anti-crime campaign. And they were not in favour that young children must visit shebeens ... (ibid.)

The campaign rapidly became punitive. Wrongdoers had to be 'disciplined' and whipping was the punishment of choice – 'they used to wallop them. *With a sjambok?* Yes'. This was something of which many young men had some experience, whether in the home, at school or even in prison. As Ashwell Zwane put it, 'Even at school we were being beaten here on a buttocks, we knew that if you want to punish a person you give him lashes on his buttocks' (Ashwell Zwane, Z4091).

The righteousness and confidence unleashed by the rebellion gave the comrades a taste for punishment. A systematic punishment code was worked out by at least one Youth Group. One victim of such a punishment talks of 'cuts' (which is five cuts [lashes]) and 'double cut' which is five and five as punishment for possessing a knife.[7] They had a 'commander' amongst them who would take possession of the knives (*in camera* Witness 9, Z988) (although this was denied by the accused). Any youths found there would be taken out and disciplined. One comrade – a committee member of the 'Eighth Avenue Youth Group' remembers having been punished herself:

> Friends of mine visited from Soweto and they said 'let's go to the shebeen'. I explained to them that there's an anti-crime campaign. They thought I was joking. ... when they found me there comrades said 'you!', because I used to insist on giving a lot more lashes if we found a comrade drinking. They said I must get six myself. They said when I'm bored I decide to take the campaign, and when I'm not bored I decide to go to the shebeen. It was painful. I was so mad! (DP, quoted in Carter 1991a: 258)

Ashwell Zwane – also known as Mugabe – did a lot of lashing:

> We were lashing the youth. *Yes, well, that is what you say. Did you ever lash anybody?* Yes ... in the campaigns quite a number which I have punished, I can't remember how many ... *And five strokes?* Sometimes three, sometimes five. *Depending on what?* The person whom I found in possession of a knife I gave him five, but the youth I used to give three. (A. Zwane, Z4088–9)

The shebeen owner quoted above confirmed Zwane's general description of the kinds of things that would happen:

> A short while after my wife came back to me again and she told me that there were people being assaulted outside, assaulted by the comrades [he went outside where] ... I saw many people walking away at the gate and I managed to call three of them, they came. And I asked them why they were hitting my customers ... And then they told me that those who have been assaulted there are those who are under 25 years of age ... They are not supposed to be at the shebeen, they are supposed to be joining them ... I told them that those very people who have been assaulted are adults, they have got families and I also told them that I don't allow youths to drink at my shebeen. (*in camera* Witness 10, Z1173–4)

He did not report this to the police because 'I was already known that should anyone go and report a matter to the police his house would be burnt' (ibid.).

Other problems within the ranks of these community-minded vigilantes began to arise – some did not search everybody:

> Some members of the campaign were not faithful because when one was supposed to have searched his friends, only to find that, that friend of his might be the one who will commit murder. Such mem-

bers will be punished by the whole youth group irrespective of position in the youth group.[8]

The vaunted adult support for these tactics was certainly not universal. At one point adult leaders were so worried about the violence of the anti-crime campaign that they investigated reports of the case of 26-year-old Lucky Kunene, who, it was said, was of his own accord 'harassing, disciplining and lashing people' in the street because of such misdemeanours as taking other people's cars by force, or quarrelling with shopkeepers (R. Mdakane, M2582).

THE FORMATION OF PEOPLE'S COURTS

The 'Comrades' are people who move around in Alexandra, and if anyone has a complaint against another person, then they take the parties concerned to a court which is called the 'Peoples Court'. There the guilty person is heard by the appointed judge, and punishment is meted out. (Zwane Exhibit OO, PJ archives)

Ignoring the concerns of some adults, and, as we shall see, addressing the concerns of others, comrades set up what they called 'people's courts'. As the anti-crime campaign evolved, the comrades had begun to set themselves up as rivals to the police – who, in spite of their ousting from their homes within the township were still the official point of referral for criminal cases. Residents began to be told that the comrades had forbidden anybody to report crimes to the police. Fear of what might happen to those who did approach the police station was widespread. Furthermore, the police's rancour over what had happened to them soon led them to 'recommend' the courts to anyone who came to complain to them: 'Somebody told me that people no longer go to the police station, because the police would refer you to the comrades', reported one shopkeeper (*in camera* Witness 13, M1142). Such reports were legion, as police vengefulness took the form of a sort of boycott in reverse: 'Go to the comrades,' they would say with laboured irony to victims of robbery, rape or murder, 'they run Alexandra now.'

The combination of comrade threats, police malice and a spreading utopianism gave the people's courts a footing in Alexandra. People's courts represented the highest form of institutionalisation of the utopia (Seekings 1989b; Scharf 1988; M. S. W. Bapela n.d.). They followed logically, within the comrades' vision of things, from the Youth Groups and the anti-crime campaign.

What were the people's courts like? One description of an Alexandra court reveals its proceedings to have been as theatrical as they were pseudo-legalistic. Each court, it seems, provided a space within which a series of small dramas could be enacted.

One Saturday in May journalist Sipho Ngcobo managed to convince those who were behind one of the Alexandra courts to allow him to attend a trial. Ngcobo was one of the few writers of the period to describe the inside workings of such courts (which by then were in existence in a number of townships) in some detail and without attempting a whitewash. Nine men, he said, ranging from youngish to very young, sat around a table in a tiny but 'spotlessly clean room' in one of the yards. The court's set-up and proceedings had some resemblance to that of the *makgotla*. But some striking inversions became apparent. Here it was the young people who were exerting authority, rather than the old. The names given to the various court functionaries were those of Western rather than African custom. Four of the men were 'prosecutors', comrades wearing red, black and white caps bearing the slogan 'A luta continua' ('the struggle continues'). A fifth, sitting alone opposite was the 'magistrate'. The atmosphere was unpleasant: 'The silence is deafening. Uneasy, frightening tension grips the venue,' wrote Ngcobo (*Business Day*, May 1986). The accused, a younger man accused by a far older one of theft, appeared terrified:

> He is shabby and shaking like a leaf. He has on a light v-neck jersey, no vest, and no shirt underneath. His hair is uncombed and his bloodshot eyes are restless. Looking at him, I suddenly wondered whether his shaking had to do with the fear of being about to be tried by the 'comrades' who, in township circles, are associated with 'the necklace' [a burning tyre around the neck] by anyone who offends the oppressed, the nation.

It was the latent power of the prosecutors and magistrate that frightened this young man, an alcoholic and habitual thief. In fact they were at pains to assure him and the rest of those present of their good intentions. The magistrate made an opening statement possibly for the benefit of the journalist-observer as much as for the accused:

> You all know of the misconceptions and ridiculous talk about us, the comrades. We are said, in misinformed quarters, to be the most ruthless, bloodthirsty, uncompromising and always ready to kill or even burn alive without flicking an eye ... I can assure you that all these beliefs are not true. They are all flimsy, malicious rumours spread by the system to discredit us and tarnish the integrity of those committed to fighting the oppressive policies of the country's ruling government.

The magistrate's speech was more romantic than punitive. It revealed something of the utopian ideas that prevailed at the time:

> We are committed to positive and constructive change and not destruction. We want to rebuild Alexandra and engender a spirit of trust among its residents. We want to live as a united and civilised people, free of crime.

Self-help, local problem solving, truthfulness, trust and unity in the face of 'Boer' molestation and murder were the path to building Alexandra and the 'whole nation of South Africa'. When the accused was found guilty of theft he was sentenced accordingly. Far from being sjambokked or necklaced he would be disciplined by his nephews and his accuser into never being allowed to take liquor again; he would be monitored by the Alexandra Action Committee; and his savings, which he had allegedly frittered away on drink, would be controlled as well. It was hoped, said the magistrate, that the accused would be 'rehabilitated and then join the struggle for freedom of the oppressed people and contribute in rebuilding and reorganising Alexandra and the whole of our land'. Indeed, said the magistrate, 'He may be a potential freedom fighter who will one day free you and me from the chains of oppression, but provided he is converted into a sober-minded human being.'

'Are you prepared to live peacefully with the people of Alexandra?' asked the youngest prosecutor. 'Yes! Yes!' replied the accused, presumably with great relief and surely with considerable optimism about his own capacity to conform to these requirements. The third main party to these events, the complainant, accepted the judgement, but not before an outburst in which he asked for something a little more dramatic. '*Thupa ya lukisha*,' he cried, fuming. 'Sjambokking is the best medicine. The boy must be sjambokked.'

In spite of the appeals by the complainant for retribution, the trial that Ngcobo attended was not violent. Perhaps this means it was at one of the mediation courts, such as that in the house at Seventh Avenue discussed in the next chapter. Or perhaps a special display was put on for his benefit. But Ngcobo's description captures some of the other major features of the people's courts trials: they were ordered – even ritualised – and at the same time used theatrical methods to appropriate a degree of power. Various types of symbolism were used, ranging from the legalistic to the fear-inducing.

However this description is of a court in which an 'outsider' became the audience. It is clear that the ceremonial and symbolic allusions in this hearing were partly directed at Ngcobo himself, and the 'public' world to which he would speak. This was not, in fact, how most courts operated. Their actors, 'audience', scripts and symbolism were most commonly confined to those within the township. Most hearings were private, thus, in the sense that outsiders to Alexandra had little idea of what went on within them. This was partly for reasons of security; but perhaps also it was woven into the very construction of the courts – which were largely seen as means of revolutionising daily life. Their theatricality remained, as we shall see, but it took a different form from that which Ngcobo observed.

USURPING RITUAL

The theme of existing literature on the subject is that the people's courts should be seen as arising 'from a long tradition of extra-state township courts in South Africa'. It is true that numerous types of dispute resolution and disciplining mechanisms had grown up in townships over the years. The comrades were adept at drawing on past traditions to help build their strategies in the present. Some authors on the subject, thus, have seen the courts as simply a continuation of older traditions. The 'continuity' thesis was supported by commentators who, often for political and strategic reasons, wished to play down the revolutionary, violent and disruptive character of township resistance, instead portraying it as an expected and explicable outcome of the situation. Rationality, continuity and predictability were emphasised. Bapela, for example, gives a particularly romanticised interpretation of the courts in Mamelodi township, where, he said, as a result of the courts' operations: 'Order and peace reigned ... children were made to respect their parents and the crime rate was reduced considerably. Reconciliation, restitution and rehabilitation were the true goals of the people's courts.' But a few pages earlier he mentions those found guilty of some crimes being sentenced to up to 100 lashes – an almost murderously high number (M. S. W. Bapela n.d.). Mathole Motshekga wrote in similarly romantic vein, again of the courts in Mamelodi, that their 'underlying philosophy' is the 'doctrine of social solidarity or unity and its inherent principle of humanism. The Punishment meted out by these courts are clearly motivated by love for people's unity, high moral (or ethical) standards and cooperative social life' (Motshekga 1987).[9]

The analysis put forward here suggests a more complex relationship between an idealised 'traditionalism' and the reality of revolution. When, after 1985, over 400 townships saw the emergence of 'people's courts' under the aegis of township comrades, it was the young radicals rather than the old conservatives who became the tyrants. They became places where 'youths are solving the adults' problems'. This reversal was what rendered the people's courts of the 1980s capable of subverting the social order in ways which made them both frightening and capricious in the eyes of some – but, significantly, not all – residents. Their contrast with the older courts was almost as vivid as the continuities. Like the protesters at Tiananmen Square in 1989, these would-be revolutionaries had adopted an accepted ritualised form – the traditional court – and turned it into political theatre. This move from ritualistic to theatrical form involves a complex process of transformation of relatively strictly choreographed and hierarchical scripts into a freer dialogue, one which permits a 'capturing' of old stage settings, a reversal of meanings and a granting of permission to performers to deviate, innovate and 'play' with ritualistic prescriptions (Esherick and Wasserstrom 1990).

The old form of disciplinary ritual was the *kgotla*, or traditional court. While naturally such courts had rural roots, there had been many occasions over the years when one or another version of them had emerged in the crime-ridden cities, although few took such a theatrical, political and wide-spread form as the people's courts. Older male residents, frustrated with the law's inadequacies, had run courts, which had sometimes worked for brief periods, but which also had a tendency to merge into vigilantism. The comrades were, according to Ashwell Zwane, aware of such courts and believed they had something to offer them in their attempts to bring order to the township:

> *Makgotla* is a group of men, this happened in Soweto, a group of men who would meet and fight crime and unlawlessness. Like for instance children who stay away from school, they were taken there to *Makgotlas* and the *Makgotla* will discipline the children, give them a hiding, tell the children to go back to school. Children who run away from home, those who go about smoking glue, smoking benzine. A *Makgotla* will deal with such people ... [then] in 1976–7 ... the *Makgotla* stopped operating and from there another person initiated that and he was known as *Madipere* ... The *Makgotlas* were known as *Madipere*. They were known like that in Meadowlands, one is to be sent to a *Makgotla*, they would say I am sending you to *Madipere*. If for instance you are dodging school. He will take you to *Madipere*, or take it for instance if you prowl, you walk at night, you are told that we will take you to *Madipere*. That is why we were scared, they used to tell us that they will take you to *Madipere*. (Zwane, Z4260–1)

Here, councillors played a role very different from the patronage systems of earlier times. In 1976, the role of Soweto councillors in disciplining youngsters and criminals was described by one councillor as follows:

> I believe naughty children should be *sjambokked*. So if children under eighteen are brought to us for disciplining, we sit as a *lekgotla* ... If the kid is found guilty, we let the parents lash him in front of us so the child cannot fight back. People with domestic squabbles come to us and we talk to them ... Robbers, attackers, murderers, rapists, and car thieves, we lash if they are under age, but if they are eighteen we send them to the police who sort them out. (Seekings 1990: 74)

During the early 1980s, the Soweto courts became more and more brutal. Run by well-known councillors, they became 'private and paramilitary rather than civil and judicial institutions' (Seekings 1990: 78). Several people died at the hands of this *lekgotla*, and its initiators were convicted of homicide and assault.

While such courts were more common in Soweto (Hund and Kotu-

Rammopo 1983), some comrades knew that they had existed in the 1970s in Alexandra as well, under the name of their initiator, one Thiza. *'Thiza* would go looking for children who dodged school in the passage by his car, drive in his car looking for those children' (A. Sebola, Z3819–20).

In 1983 one of the Alexandra town councillors, Thomas Molepo, created a 'kangaroo court' in which he held hearings and imposed fines (and by which he was in the end himself prosecuted!) (*City Press*, 1 July 1984). These, then, were cases of the elders attempting to control residents, often including the young, often through violent means and nearly always in ways which induced fear in the population and which often deteriorated into tyranny. As Obed Bapela put it: 'the *Makgotlas* in Soweto ... used to be a problem to the people ... they introduced curfews, arrested people and flogged them in public. That caused that the *makgotlas* had been hated in Soweto.'

Nevertheless, as Seekings argues, the fact is that:

> there existed a range of township courts in the PWV. These were generally not 'traditional' ... although their concerns and (in some cases) patterns of leadership were derived from earlier periods. Older leaders predominated. Their primary concerns involved the maintenance of 'community', and in particular of a specific social order that they thought (rightly or wrongly) bound the 'community' together. (Seekings 1990: 8)

By contrast with these older courts, the people's courts in Alexandra entailed a granting of authority to, as well as a usurpation of authority by, the young, rather than a means whereby to control them. At least six people's courts existed at different periods during the months of the rebellion, three of which we know operated highly effectively. Father Cairns believed they had started as a result of adult anxiety about the absence of an effective police force and because they met a felt need for order: 'And I think there was a need for people to have some law, to have some order, to have some justice, to have some court of appeal' (Father Cairns, M4364).

Not surprisingly, most of the courts were situated at the Youth Group Headquarters, by now powerful bases from which large numbers of youths operated their various campaigns to 'cleanse' the township of moral decay and wrongdoing, including the anti-crime campaign. We know little of three of these. The Eighth Avenue court was developed at the headquarters of the group originally formed out of concern by AYCO leaders at the way in which youth behaviour had deteriorated. The court was in fact at the home of an adult civic leader, and youth based there had been the first to launch an anti-crime campaign. Quite early in the rebellion, police were aware of the court and were telling residents to go there to get their problems solved (R. Mdakane, M2176). It probably played a largely mediating rather than punitive role. The Third Avenue and Twelfth Avenue courts are even less well understood, other than that the Third Avenue one called itself an 'AYCO' court, and that one John van der Merwe was the presiding officer (*in camera* Witness 26, Z612ff). However, extensive and unusually revealing, if flawed, evidence concerning the remaining three courts was given, subpoenaed and/or submitted in the two trials following the revolt, and the remainder of this section is based upon a cautious use of this unique, material.

At number 31 Seventh Avenue, two courts existed in one yard, which was not one of the old Youth Group Headquarters. Both had been started only after the February revolt. One was a 'people's court' in one of the shacks; and the other was what witnesses in the subsequent trials called a 'mediation court', run by the Alexandra Action Committee, of which more will be said below, in one of the homes within the yard. One Wilson Moses said he used to go to report cases there (W. Moses, M400ff). Refilwe Mashego said:

> What I heard was that there was actually two courts in that yard, there was a court in the house which did a lot of counselling where marital problems went and were attended to. And there was a court, which mainly consisted of youth in a shack, we call it *makhukhu* … At the beginning it seemed helpful to the community, but the issue of sjambokking came in and people really disapproved of what was happening in that *makhukhu*. (R. Mashego, M4259)

The *makhukhu* court was run by youths and the house court by adults.

> *Did the adults approve of it* [the people's court]? No, they didn't … It was difficult just to go to an unorganised structure and try to say something and the youths at that time was so militant and you wouldn't know what could happen to you … The youth had already gone into this practice for some time, it was already something which belonged to them and it wouldn't have been easy just to go in and break it. (R. Mashego, M4260)

The central figure in this people's court in the *makhukhu* was a woman – Sarah Mthembu. Her activist son Jerry had died a notoriously horrifying death during the Six-Day War.[10] Mthembu was an ambiguous figure, being both a supporter of the adult AAC,[11] and the instigator of a people's court of ill repute.[12] She came to be seen by the youth in the area between Fifth and Seventh Avenue as a maternal, even matriarchal figure. According to Richard Mdakane: 'the youth started flocking at her place. The youth used to come there to console her as a person who had lost a son. She in turn gave them food and they also loved her' (R. Mdakane, M2176).

The congregation of youths at her home became particularly active after the Six-Day War: 'They used to go out to do what was referred to as the anti-crime campaign. They would come back with weapons that they had found on the people and would bring them at Sarah Mthembu's place' (R. Mdakane, M2177).

It was her decision to open a people's court at her address at number 31, in Jerry's old room – a shack in the yard in which she lived – and her initial motivation seems to have been to stop a type of crime which the police had never taken up – domestic violence. Thus she said women complaining to her that their menfolk had assaulted them, and despairing of any authority that would take them seriously had initially motivated her.[13] But the court was soon flooded with cases:

> After hearing that [the police would not take cases] then the youth, as well as Sarah said, 'We are now going to start taking people's cases because the police are driving us away.' ... Then all the people in Alexandra started going to number 31 to go and lodge their complaints. (Moses Mayekiso, M2972–3)

The Nineteenth Avenue court was run mainly by youths, at the Youth Group Headquarters, which we know had previously acted as the rallying point for gangsters. During the rebellion a shack was built there and became known as the 'comrades' office'.[14] We have seen how Bapela observed the formation of the Nineteenth Avenue Youth Group; and how one of the early meetings included a call for a campaign against crime. Over the next days and weeks, Bapela observed this yard evolve into a more fully institutionalised expression of youth ambitions. He heard that there were certain 'boys in that youth grouping who had started a people's court and there are those who are opposing this people's court. Those who wanted this people's court [wanted it] to be led by David Wessels.'

The youth grouping began to attract youths from a wider circle, and to draw them into its sub-culture. One mother complained that her child, a member of the youth grouping, 'did not sleep at home and has been away without her permission'. She:

> was very angry, saying that they were the cause that the child must go, must leave, because they did not come back to come and find out from her to ask what had happened to her ... the youth grouping ... seemed to have come together just for love affairs and she was now going to stop her child from attending. (O. Bapela, M3931)

Bapela was asked by the mother to intervene and tell the Youth Group not to interfere with parental authority, which he did, requesting them not to 'alienate us, between ourselves and our parents'. Bapela tried to dissuade the group's leader, David Wessels, from starting a people's court, saying that 'it might fall into the hands of wrong people and you find people being burnt' and reminding him of the hatred Sowetans had felt for their *magkotla*. He also told him that:

there can be a lot of flogging taking place at people's courts, because it was already known that it was already occurring at Seventh Avenue, and that what might also happen is that people would be punished in the people's courts and thereafter in objection thereto they might form a vigilante activity and that can cause a turmoil in Alexandra and not peace. (O. Bapela, M3934–5)

David, however, was adamant that the court was necessary: 'He said there is nothing they could do, because people were pestering them that they must help them with their problems. They sometimes come during the night and knock on their doors and then ask for help.' Like Sarah Mthembu, Wessels saw the courts as places where women could be helped: 'They give an example that sometimes a woman would coming running, screaming and knock on the door saying "My husband is beating me."' In addition, Wessels said, people were being driven away from the police station; and the Nineteenth Avenue youths 'would like to help them so that some order may be established among the people' (O. Bapela, M3935).

The Nineteenth Avenue court continued to evolve. A 'shack' was constructed and Bapela himself attended some sessions as a mediator:

> *Why should these adult people look to you in Nineteenth Avenue to help them clear up misunderstandings, solve problems, resolve antagonism ...?* The way I view it is like this: many people regard me as clever. For instance after talking to Mma Dlamini about her problem, that spread in the place and another thing ... my involvement with organisations was well known ... in my area of all the youths I was regarded as the one who was well behaved and my morals were regarded as good too. (O. Bapela, M3940)

But according to some, Bapela in fact presided over the court on many occasions. He listened to 'cases such as the children who do not want to listen to their parents ... Cases when parents disagree, when father and mother quarrelled' (Hendrina Banda, M1301ff). The shack eventually came to act as a people's court, which at its height heard twenty to thirty cases a day.

The Fifteenth Avenue court is the most well documented example of a people's court that we have, and was the headquarters of the Fifteenth Avenue Youth Group, which had formed towards the end of the rebellion, after the other courts had been destroyed by vigilantes, in a devastating attack on the community and the rebellion itself. (This attack is discussed in more detail in Chapter 10.) At first comrades in the Fifteenth Avenue area had formed a 'defence committee' in response to the attack, staying up all night to guard their area, and using whistles to warn residents of new invasions (A. Sebola, Z2630ff). Somebody from the yard volunteered the use of his shack to help co-ordinate Youth Group activities, and frequent meetings were held there, often with adults attending as well as youths. This shack was to become the people's court. Adults 'used to bring their disputes there and they wanted us to solve them or help them'. On 2 June, the issue of forming a people's court was discussed by the Youth Group:

> Item C: The peoples Court: The headquarter shall serve as a place where problems are to be reported not as a place where problems (cases) are to be solved. Two members shall be available to solve a case. NB The two shall be members from the headquarters depending on the case (majority shall be needed).[15]

The court was later described thus:

> the corrugated iron shanty adjoining a brick house which police said formed the people's court. A rickety table served as the presiding officer's desk, a small, sharpened wrought iron pick as the judge's gavel. On the wall hung two motor-car tyres, painted red and white – reminders of the awful 'necklace' death which awaited collaborators with 'the system'. The 'sentences' meted out ranged from beatings to death, sometimes by burning.[16]

Sebola said that inside the court there was 'a bed there and a small table' (A. Sebola, Z3162), and that Ashwell Zwane was the chair at most of its meetings. 'He controlled the proceedings of the meeting whereby he has to see to that the meeting is being run properly, that is how I view that a chairman does and that was what Accused No 1 was doing' (A. Sebola, Z3159). He wrote things down in a black book 'a small book, almost like a Bible'.

The venues for theatricality were thus established. How did the small domestic dramas of township life play out within them?

FROM MORALITY TO BRUTALITY

Each court was different. One commentator distinguished between 'disciplined, organised youth' who helped set up 'accountable organs of people's power' and the 'bands of youth' who formed kangaroo courts.[17] In many parts of the country, courts that had been set up by more long-standing members of youth organisations were often taken over by other youths, who clashed with earlier leaders, and in one case 'punishments in the court became increasingly brutal, procedures became grotesque and the court rapidly lost support' (Scharf and Ngcokoto 1990; Seekings 1989a). Father Cairns believed that the need for justice felt so strongly by Alexandran residents could, in his opinion, be manipulated by the comrades – who were in no position to offer genuine justice: 'and I think maybe just some youth usurped that power ... It was a very bad situation because obviously such courts could not do justice or give harmony or peace to anyone ...' Instead, they brought fear:

in my limited experience of people who spoke to me and asking them what was their attitude towards the peoples court, I think people feared it. They were afraid that they could be falsely accused and dragged before the peoples court and have punishment dished out to them. I think in general there was a fear and because of the fear a very serious suspect and a certain secrecy not to voice their opinion openly. (Father Cairns, M4364)

Most courts rapidly gained a reputation for violence and brutality. At one point Mapule Morare, a senior adult activist, was sent to verify reports of sjambokking at Youth Headquarters at Third and Eighth Avenues. She found that indeed sjambokking was taking place, and 'the people concerned did not want to stop it' (R. Mdakane, M2285) even after additional adult leaders had been there to try to end the violence (R. Mdakane, M2287). The Seventh Avenue *makhukhu* too began to deteriorate after it 'changed faces':

It started as a facility which was utilised generally by people seeing their cases being attended to and solved to their satisfaction and when the sjambokking came in, you could see that there was a change of face and that not the very same people presided at all these cases. (R. Mashego, M4276)

The youth were 'not calm' during this period, after the Six-Day War; 'they came out with a lot of aggression' (R. Mashego, M4263) and lashings were common.[18] Adult leader Paul Tshabalala, who used to preside at the other, less violent, Seventh Avenue court, remembers how at one stage: 'There was a girl with the allegation that there is a certain boy of Thirteenth Avenue who wanted rape her. Shortly thereafter I saw the boys standing up and taking this man out and they lashed him with a sjambok.' At times, he said, 'I used to hear people crying' (P. Tshabalala, M3838).

It soon became known that there was 'the screaming of people which was an indication that people were being assaulted' in the shack (R. Mdakane, M2177–8). 'The youths were always full in the yard and not always inside the shack' (Moses Mayekiso, M3677). Neighbours complained of the noise of the screaming and when Mzwanele Mayekiso visited the shack he reported that 'the youth who were controlling the people's court at Number 31 were very aggressive and they did not like any person who was criticising or condemning the lashing of the people' (R. Mdakane, M2181). It was said they lashed youths and adults alike (R. Mdakane, M2184). When Theresa Maseko was necklaced it was said to have happened outside the Seventh Avenue court, after she had been brought there by car. It was at this court, too, that the youths were said to have detained people in what some called 'Mandela's Jail' (R. Mdakane, M258; Moses Mayekiso, M3669).

At Nineteenth Avenue too, perhaps inevitably, with time, it was reported that the disciplining of offenders began to get 'out of hand'. David Wessels had originally tried to implement rules about lashing. But 'people started to, the picture we have is that people started to complain, this Mandla has taken over and he is just lashing people'. It was said that Mandla was answerable to nobody. Soon the youth grouping began to punish those of its own members who stepped out of line. Obed Bapela was again approached to get him to stop Mandla, and met with the Youth Group, urging them to close the court down (H. Banda, Z1265ff).[19] However, this was at about the time of his arrest by police, and he was unable to proceed. After his release from jail, Bapela had lost touch with Nineteenth Avenue – but heard that Mandla was now in charge of the court and that he continued to be a 'flogger'. This became widely known in the immediate vicinity, and many people complained to Bapela about it. He again tried unsuccessfully to persuade Mandla to stop (O. Bapela, M3942–3).

It was the Fifteenth Avenue court which, above all, epitomised youth millenarianism. Both the accused and the defence lawyers for the subsequent trial of Zwane and some of his comrades conceded that violence had indeed occurred there, and frequently.[20] Ashwell Zwane, the court's 'magistrate', admitted in court to many instances of lashings (A. Zwane, Z4264, Z4270ff, Z4279ff, Z4303ff, Z4315ff). Much more will be said about this court below.

THE STAGING OF CRIMES AND PUNISHMENTS

The people's courts epitomised the youths' vision of the new social order within Alexandra. Adults – particularly and strikingly men – were considered less 'morally acceptable' than the youth would have liked them to be. Cases of child abuse or neglect, of desertion of wives by wayward husbands, of wife beating and of other social and personal transgressions were brought to the courts, in an attempt to bring adults to a more ethical standard. As Moses Mayekiso observed:

> When the youth were looking at the crimes that were committed at the township … they were indicating that there is a reason why there should be lashing, because these people are spoiling in the community, such as the rapists. They wanted to administer this lashing for that reason … Believing that it would stop the people from being wayward … it was (they believed) the only method to put people straight. (Moses Mayekiso, M2976)

Although it was often the comrades themselves who brought cases to court – for example, by accusing people of 'attending shebeens' or discos, of not co-operating with stay-aways, of being informers, working with the system, selling out or refusing to attend meetings – the willingness of residents to seek solutions to their problems through these amateur courts was astounding. Although adult organisations and leaders were concerned about the propensity of people's courts rapidly to decay into 'flogging', and, as we shall see, tried to substitute them with less violent institutions, there were many adults – particularly women – who backed the comrades in their anti-crime campaign as well as the formation of courts. Albert Sebola claimed that many of the suggestions for punishment in the anti-crime campaign actually came from adults – such as the suggestions that the youths carry sjamboks; or that the punishments be ten to fifteen lashes. He described one middle-aged woman who was quite clear in her own mind that this was the number of lashes required in cases of drinking, because 'as a woman that she has children and in view that most of the youngsters drink liquor and they misbehave and they stab one another' (A. Sebola, Z3303). In Sebola's words again: 'most of our parents as a traditional thing they feel that in the township by beating a child you will get him straight' (A. Sebola, Z3304). A township businessman agreed:

> *When some youth misbehaved, would the older people then go to the bands of youth and say: Look this youngster is behaving badly, and ask them to discipline him or her?* Yes they used to go. *And the bands of youth would then deal with the person who was accused of misconduct?* Yes. (A. Bowes, M235)

The matriarchal figure Sarah Mthembu supported the people's courts, as did other women. This created quite a moral panic amongst patriarchal men, who saw the courts as having encouraged women to 'misbehave':

> After the Six-Day War women started taking advantage of their husbands and they were relying that they would go to the youth and the youth would help them. You would find that a woman would not mind whilst the husband is away at work, she would bring the boyfriend into the house, relying that if the husband wallops her she would go to the youth and the youth would come and wallop him. That is what I experienced, that many women, in general they were starting to misbehave. (P. Tshabalala, M3836)

Thus it is not surprising that, according to one adult activist, 'At the beginning the people's court, many people were in favour of it and people who were very much in favour of it were women' (P. Tshabalala, M3766). As Moses Mayekiso said:

> In my opinion and as I heard, that women, the majority of women were in favour of it, because they were the people who had problems with fathers, sometimes with children. Now, People's Court was helping them greatly ... *When you say 'fathers' I take it you mean husbands?* Yes, my lord, naughty men who sleep out. *And what else?* As well as other problems faced by the community, mainly women. (Moses Mayekiso, M2976)

Women liked the people's courts, said Paul Tshabalala, because:

> It is that the women were getting help when their men were no longer giving them money or supporting their children, and that when they sleep out at places where they liked, the women used to go to the people's court and the people they find at the people's court were able to help them. *And the men?* When they are fetched, at times they were to get a little lashing. (P. Tshabalala, M2521)

Women, youths and men alike brought a variety of different cases to the courts. The Seventh Avenue *makhukhu* tended mainly to focus on marital disputes, while the Nineteenth Avenue court handled a broader variety of cases. The Fifteenth Avenue court seems to have tapped into a far more disreputable side of Alexandran life, handling cases such as youth battles, car theft, theft, reckless driving and even murder; but it also handled the staples of marital disputes and parental authority. Some figures for the first two of these courts are available.

The violent crimes that came to these courts included assault – at thirty-five cases in all by far the highest of all complaints – theft and robbery (twenty-three cases) attempted murder, the possession of arms, threats of death and violence, damage to property and three cases of rape or attempted rape.

The high figure of domestic cases reported is also revealing. The comrades appear to have tapped into a well of unhappiness and dysfunctionality. Their proclaimed Utopia was indeed something that resonated with the desires and dreams of ordinary people, adults and the young alike. Achieving it came up against the morass of proletarian life. Families did not, would not, hold together. Wives, children, husbands absconded. Relationships were fraught. Children and young people could not be controlled. It is likely that amongst the high numbers of unspecified assault cases were many which occurred in domestic situations.

Some of the recorded cases directed towards ordinary residents included accusations by mothers, girlfriends, boyfriends, husbands, siblings or

Table 4: Known cases brought to people's courts at 7th and 19th Avenues[21]

Type of case	Number	Percentage
Violent crimes and associated	81	49.4
Domestic/family	43	26.2
Personal relationships	12	7.3
Political/struggle related	9	5.5
Landlord/housing problems	5	3.0
Work-related	5	3.0
Miscellaneous	5	3.0
Complaints re witchcraft and/or tribalism	4	2.4
Total	164	100

neighbours. For example one case accused a 'yard rep' of 'acting cruelly'. A mother accused her son of 'stampeding' a child of three. Others had stolen clothing, or cars, refused to pay *lobola* (brideprice) or child maintenance, or engaged in 'fighting in the yard'. One 'female comrade' came to get a divorce 'seen to'; another 'female comrade' – Sophie – was accused of not bringing 'money at home' to support her children. One woman said she had been 'rendered … pregnant. And now he is not supporting the child.' One wife said her 'husband did not sleep at home'. A disgruntled boyfriend said his girlfriend 'complains' a lot when 'she asks him for money to support their child'. A worker who had been dismissed laid a charge against his foreman. Politically linked charges included those made against two back-yard mechanics who were accused of 'collaborating with the police'; one accused of 'being an *impimpi*' (informer); and the family who 'refused to take part in the struggle'.[22] At least one murder charge was laid in the Fifteenth Avenue court.

Comrades or *comtsotsis* could themselves be charged. One case was brought against an 'undisciplined comrade', and another against 'unknown people who … used the name of the comrades'. A disgruntled shebeen-owner whose shebeen had been emptied during the anti-crime campaign, was told at the people's court that he could complain about the comrades – but he would have to go to what they called the 'Senior Comrades' at Fourteenth Avenue, where he found that residents were present in numbers, all complaining vehemently about the comrades. The complaints were all about form rather than content. The youths, it was said, would not actually search shebeens if they were offered free liquor, or were not sticking to their zones in patrolling (*in camera* Witness 10, Z1177–9).

A court 'style' appears to have emerged within what were known as the 'sjambok courts' (as opposed to the 'mediation courts' to be discussed in the next chapter) during this period. This included several different aspects, each of which mirrored, or perhaps parodied, the style of the formal legal system:

Accusation: accusations were either laid with the comrades by the aggrieved party; or made by the comrades themselves, who may have observed or heard of a particular transgression of their moral code. One woman being attacked was said to have 'screamed for the comrades', who arrived and took the attacker away (*in camera* Witness 8, Z796ff).

Investigation: In some cases the accusation was investigated before any arrest took place – comrades would 'ask around' to see how others viewed the case.

Arrest: Comrades in groups of up to ten or even twenty, often carrying *sjamboks*, would appear at the home of the accused and take him or her away to the court. Sometimes the accused would simply be instructed to appear at a particular time – and only fetched if they did not do so. If they had observed a transgression themselves they would immediately inform the transgressor that he or she had done wrong and instruct them to appear to the court (or haul them away there and then).

Subpoena: A group of comrades would go to the home of those they had identified as witnesses and either take them to the court directly, or issue them with instructions to appear at a particular time – and fetch them if they didn't.

Trial: The trial would be held outside in the yard or inside a building – usually a corrugated iron shack especially set aside for the purpose. The Fifteenth Avenue court had benches and blocks of wood in the yard, which was often busy and filled with comrades. The shack had one door, and all of its windows boarded up, and old car-seats around the walls. As the Ngcobo description indicates, a degree of ritual and formality was sustained during people's court trials. There would be a designated 'judge' or 'magistrate' who sometimes wore identifiable clothes, and who sat facing the assembled people; he often was said to have had a 'black book' – called by one 'the book of the law', or the 'law of the comrades'. The accused would sit on makeshift chairs. The yard or room would be filled with comrades and people waiting for their cases to be heard. In one case candles were burning, and one tale mentioned that *sjamboks* were lying around. Silence was expected.

Confession: The accused was encouraged to confess – and in one case failure to admit guilt led to a vicious assault on the accused by the 'magistrate' and one of the comrades.

Sentence: It appears to have been rare for the accused to be found not guilty and most ended up being sentenced for the crime of which they had been accused. Sometimes the audience and accusers would call out to the magistrate for harsher sentences to be imposed. Some claim that the courts had formal sentencing rules; others that the 'floggers' (such as 'Mandla') would decide on their own sentences.

Punishment: Most of the guilty were sentenced to caning or sjambokking, which would be administered there and then. Many said they were made to lie on a bench with their back or buttocks exposed; some said they were tied down; others that one or two comrades would sit on them to keep them still. Men and women alike were given the same punishments. Claims about the numbers and viciousness of these punishments vary. One woman made the

Table 5: Individual cases heard in people's courts, Alexandra 1986

Name of case	Accuser	Accused	Court	Accusation	Finding and punishment	Upshot
The drunken wife Part One	The wife	The husband	19th Ave.	Not supporting	Guilty, six strokes	
The drunken wife Part Two	Neighbours	The wife	19th Ave.	Not taking care of child	Guilty, 'thrashed'	
The petty thief	'Anna'	'Maria'	19th Ave.	Stealing R15	Guilty; 10 lashes	
The unemployed father	Thoko	Sipho	15th Ave.	Failing to pay maintenance and assault	Guilty; required to pay via comrades	Only one payment made
The car and the panga Part One	'David'	'Mandla'	15th Ave.	Damaging of car	Must repair car and pay compensation	Car was repaired but compensation never paid
The car and the panga Part Two	'Mandla'	'David'	15th Ave.	Hitting with a brick or panga	Guilty of fighting; five strokes each	
The drunken brawl	Isaac	Sethane	15th Ave.	Stabbed after drinking	Guilty; eight lashes with cane	
The stokvel, the affair and the murder Part One	Joseph and Moses	Billy and Josiah	15th Ave.	The murder of John (Joseph and Moses' brother)	No conclusion	
The stokvel, the affair and the murder Part Two	Moses and his comrades	Joseph	15th Ave.	Going to the police to report the murder of John	Guilty: sjambokked	
The stokvel, the affair and the murder Part Three	Moses and his comrades	Josiah	15th Ave.	The murder of John	Assaulted and beaten, possibly threatened with necklacing to make him confess	Probably not guilty
The stokvel, the affair and the murder Part Four	Moses and his comrades and eventually Josiah	Lowlife, Elias and Barney	15th Ave.	The murder of John	Elias and Barney confessed; Moses' case ended by police raid	Inconclusive

fairly unlikely claim that her attacker was given ninety lashes and she saw him faint. Others say they were given five to ten lashes. One man found guilty said that he was tied to a bench, thrashed and then threatened with necklacing. We have photographic evidence that some thrashings did draw blood.

Some sentences were, even in the 'sjambok courts', not corporal – fines were sometimes imposed, or compensation required. Here the comrades came up against a serious limitation to their own capacity – they could not enforce their own sentences beyond the immediate period surrounding the trial.

Record-taking: It appears that minutes or notes were quite often taken in court, and some of these survive. Here names, dates, case details and sentences were recorded. In the case of Fifteenth Avenue, this was in barely literate English.

A number of stories were told in the two treason trials about what happened inside the people's courts in Alexandra. They were mainly, but not entirely, told by witnesses for the prosecution and this at first led me to think they should not be included. Substantial confirmation of the essence, if not the detail, of each story, however, also appears in the defence case in each trial, as well as the actual minutes of the Fifteenth Avenue court. Here tales from the youth-driven 'sjambok' courts are presented, with due attention having been paid to the nature of the evidence put forward, and with the intention of attempting to convey something of the scope, atmosphere, dramatic content and narrative conception of the trials that took place.

TALES FROM THE 'SJAMBOK' COURTS
The drunken wife

One J. Vuyeka, aged 48, told this story (*in camera* Witness 25, Z1553). One day he arrived home to find his wife drunk. She was with their three-year-old daughter. He had had to do the cooking when he got home, he said, much to his chagrin: 'Now who was supposed to make the food for the child? It was the wife,' he said. He was not happy with the situation, but after supper went out to a shebeen, where he chatted to his friends about his wife. Her brother was there and pleaded leniency in the face of this dereliction of duty: 'they said I should not thrash her. I should just leave her like that.' But two weeks later, he got home and found she had gone out. She had left the child alone with her brother, and gone drinking. He confronted her. She reported him to the comrades: 'When I asked her why she did not prepare food for the child she went and reported me in order to have me arrested, to the people that are referred to as comrades ...' He was arrested and immediately punished:

These people came and fetched me. On my arrival there I was given corporal punishment on my back. *Where did you arrive?* At number 55 Nineteenth Avenue. That is where I was thrashed. *Who thrashed you?* There were many people. There was a sort of a gathering in a corrugated iron shack ... *Did they tell you why you were punished or thrashed?* They told me that it is because I am unable to support the child and they will take the child to the welfare people. I told them that they should not take my child, because I am healthy and I work ... My head was dragged down and corporal punishment was administered on my buttocks ... I was lying flat on a *bank* [bench]. There was one sitting on, at the back of my neck ... Six strokes ... With a sjambok.

All this took place in what was known as 'the shack' at Nineteenth Avenue. He had heard of such places, he said. 'Even if they find me along the street walking and you are drunk they take you away to go and thrash you ... They used to take Omo [washing powder], mix it with water and make you drink it so that you would vomit the liquor' (J. Vuyeka, M602–3). About fifty people were there, inside and outside the shack. Three people thrashed him, taking turns. Some were old, he said, and some young.

The case did not end there. Some days later his wife was fetched by the comrades while he was at work, and also brought to the 'shack', where she was also thrashed. 'They were saying why does she not take care of the child,' said the husband.[23]

The petty thief

State witness AT recalled to one of the treason trials how in May 1986 she had had a 16-year-old girl named Maria living with her (*in camera* Witness 28, Z1664). Fifteen Rand went missing from her home. On discovering this she grabbed a stick and hit Maria, who ran away. AT chased her into the street and carried on hitting her. She was seen by a group of comrades, who stopped her and asked why she was hitting the girl. She told them that Maria had taken money. The comrades said that she should know that she should not hit a child in the street and told her to go to the Nineteenth Avenue headquarters.

Leaving nothing to chance, at nine that evening they fetched both her and Maria from their home. They were taken to the Nineteenth Avenue yard, where at least ten comrades were present. At the people's court they questioned them both, not about AT's chasing and beating of the girl, but about the missing cash. They asked Maria where the money was and she admitted to taking it, saying she had used it to buy shoes. One of the comrades said she must be given ten lashes, and another administered them on her buttocks with a sjambok while she lay on a bench.

The unemployed father

At the Fifteenth Avenue court, 28-year-old Thoko laid charges against Sipho, her child's father, for failing to pay maintenance. Sipho, she said, was a bad guy: 'He would come there to my home and he would assault me and he was despising the people at my home' (*in camera* Witness 16, Z1351). After Sipho had stopped paying, she went to the commissioner and they gave her a letter to give to Sipho. But he still did not pay – he said that he was not employed and they told him that 'just when he would start working again he must bring the money'. He did not. She would often 'go and have a look at the Commissioner's … to look for the money for the baby … but I found out that he did not bring the money.'

In this case the comrades decided they, rather than the commissioner, would administer the payments. Sipho himself recalled that one day two young men arrived and said he was wanted at 64 Fifteenth Avenue. He didn't go. After a few days 'Thoko with many Comrades arrived … at my house … One of the young men asked Thoko who is the father of the child here … And then Thoko pointed at me. And then I asked what is going on and they said that they have come in connection with a maintenance case [*indaba*].' They insisted that he pay R20 per week, to them, and they came to collect it on the Sunday. But they never came again. But this single payment was systematically recorded:

> There is a book where they wrote down and there was a slip … they took the slip and the duplicate remained there … They said to me whenever they came to collect I must see to it that I have a book and that they are going to sign on it and that the duplicate will remain and I would see on that duplicate that payment had been made. (*in camera* Witness 15, Z1339–40)

The car and the panga

Toto, a youth, reported having had a fight with two of his friends, Sipho and Gimba, who had taken his car and had an accident. Toto, furious, hit Gimba with a brick – others say it was a panga. Sipho reported this to the comrades, who went to JR's house and told him he should not have got involved in a fight – he should rather have reported his complaint about his car to the people's court.

The next morning another group of four comrades carrying sjamboks arrived and took all three friends to the court, where there were about forty people standing in front of the *makhukhu*, discussing another case. The three friends sat on 'blocks of wood' outside, surrounded by comrades who turned to his case, asking the three of them questions and taking notes in a black book. They all told their stories. This is how the case was minuted: 'The accident was cose becouse Sipho doe'nt know to drive a car well.

Gimba was teaching Sipho to drive a car on the street while Sipho doesn't know how to drive a car perfently.' All three admitted guilt: 'Sipho and his friend they have say that they are guilty ... Toto was guilty because af cutting Sipho with a panga of wich is not allowed.' The case, the minutes concluded, 'was conducted by discipline'. This meant that all three were given five strokes with a sjambok. Toto said that: 'They said to me that I should look away from them and they hit me from behind ... with a sjambok.'

Part of the sentence was that the motor car which had been the cause of the fight should be repaired by Sipho and Gimba; and Gimba, the man who was hurt with the brick/panga, should be paid compensation. This was never paid, but the vehicle was repaired (*in camera* Witness 13, Z1280ff).

The drunken brawl

IM, a young man, told of how one evening he went to a disco, drank some beer, and got into a confrontation with one Sethane, who took out a knife and stabbed and beat him. IM was hospitalised for four weeks.

The day he came out five members of the comrades came to his house with Sethane. One of the comrades asked for an explanation of the brawl, confiscated Sethane's knife and told them both to appear in court the next day at 12 noon.

The court was held inside the single room of a *makhukhu*. Only about five people were there including Sethane. The magistrate wrote details about both IM and Sethane in a black book. IM did not give evidence as 'the case was already known'. It was ruled that Sethane must get eight lashes with a cane. Two comrades took off Sethane's trousers, tied him to a bench and whipped him on the buttocks. 'I saw that his buttocks bled,' said IM. The magistrate told both of them that they must not fight again. They left.[24]

The *stokvel*, the affair and the murder

One Friday in early July an elaborate case began in the Fifteenth Avenue court (*in camera* Witness 5, Z633ff). This one, involving a *stokvel*, a murder, a feud between families, the betrayal of one brother by another, jealousy and an affair, was particularly well-documented, because it was actually still in progress three days later, after several meetings and hearings, when the police raided the court and arrested all those present – including the comrades, the observers, the complainants and the accused. After the arrest, the Fifteenth Avenue *makhukhu* was burnt down, and not long afterwards the rebellion itself came to an end. This, then, was the last people's court case of the revolt.

The complexity of this case is revealing, and was probably not unusual. The people's court found itself entwined in byzantine family politics and mazes of truth and rumour, as it tried to identify a murderer in its own extra-legal and imprecise fashion. It made serious errors of judgement along the way.

The story was told by multiple witnesses. Joseph (*in camera* Witness 5, Zwane trial),[25] an illiterate, rather simple Afrikaans-speaking black man, had three younger brothers: Matthew (who plays no part in the story), John and Moses. John was the murder victim. Moses, at 20, was the youngest brother, and was one of the new generation of youths. He was more highly educated than Joseph, and had 'long been a part of the comrades' – he had particular connections with the Fifteenth Avenue people's court, as we shall see.

That Friday night, John and his friend Billy went to a *stokvel* at the shebeen-home of Josiah (*in camera* Witness 6, Zwane case) and his wife Maria. John was attacked by three men and stabbed. Josiah and Maria found him lying dying outside their back door. Someone took him to the clinic, but it was too late. He died of his wounds.

Billy, Joseph and Moses took a risk. They went and made a statement to the police. They had to do so, they said, in spite of the anti-police rules of the people's courts, because murders were different: the body would not have been released by the clinic unless they had been to make a statement to the police, said Moses. The police opened a dossier. The two brothers fetched John's body and took it to the mortuary.

It was rumoured that the older brother Joseph had heard the murder take place, and in particular that he had heard the voice of one man called Lowlife saying 'the man is dead'. But the case went through numerous convolutions before this rumour was taken seriously. First Moses heard the rumour. He knew Lowlife and asked him what had happened. Lowlife claimed he had indeed been present at the murder, but had simply helped John 'because somebody else was there on top of him stabbing him'. Moses had at first believed Lowlife's story that he had been protecting John: 'because I honoured this man Lowlife, we are of the same Football Club' (*in camera* Witness 9, Z1099). And anyway, Moses suspected someone else – he had long thought that John was in fact having an affair with the *stokvel* owner's wife, Maria, and that there was more to the murder than a simple Friday night brawl. He believed that there had actually been a plot to kill his brother, by Josiah himself, who had been jealous of the affair. Josiah and Maria knew more than they were letting on, he believed. He believed that Billy, too, had not told them the truth – which was that he knew who the murderers were as he had been there all the time.

Moses and Joseph grabbed Billy and took him to the court where they told Ashwell Zwane this theory. Zwane remembered that:

> they were accusing Billy and saying that Billy was with the deceased during this incident and Billy does not want to tell exactly what happened at the time ... [but] according to Billy they were drinking at a stokvel ... then ... he ran away and left this man behind. (A. Zwane, Z3800)

Billy, in turn, tried to deflect attention to Josiah.

In the meantime the comrades were worried about another issue – the fact that John's friend and brothers had been to the police to report his death. The next morning – Saturday – a group of comrades arrived at Moses's home and said his brother was wanted at the people's court for going to the police. Moses went along to the Fifteenth Avenue court himself at about 10 a.m. He said that if he had refused to attend the people's court – of which he was himself a member – he could have been disciplined. 'I know anyone who is against the regulations of the comrades, is being disciplined,' he said (*in camera* Witness 9, Z1138).

When Moses arrived he found that the murder investigation was also moving forward. Following Moses's and Billy's suggestions, Ashwell Zwane, the most prominent figure in the court, had ordered his comrades to detain Josiah, the allegedly jealous owner of the *stokvel*. They took him to the Fifteenth Avenue yard, where they questioned him while they sat on 'chairs' – blocks of wood and some ordinary benches – outside. Josiah claimed he could remember nothing and they let him go, but not before instructing him not to play music at his shebeen that weekend. This was because, they said, somebody had died and the neighbourhood was in mourning (A. Zwane, Z3802). But Josiah interpreted this instruction differently. He believed that they had told him that he and his wife should no longer sell liquor at all, not only out of respect for the deceased but because the comrades 'did not believe in liquor'.

The comrades could not take the case further, and sent the dead man's brothers, Joseph and Moses, away too. But the comrade, Moses, was still certain that Josiah had something to do with it, and carried on with his enquiries over the rest of the weekend. He felt strongly that the police would never get to the bottom of the case, particularly since he believed that Billy knew the truth and would never tell it to the police. The other comrades, too, were not satisfied with how things had ended on the Saturday.

Parallel to the case of John's murder was another charge – the fact that the murder had been reported to the police rather than the people's court. At first Joseph had tried to explain to the comrades why he had gone to the police to report John's death – but the comrades were not convinced, and they decided to arrest him as well. On Sunday afternoon Moses and Billy arrived at his older brother Joseph's house and escorted him to a 'meeting of the comrades' at Fifteenth Avenue (although Moses's own version is that he had not betrayed his brother – he had been told what to do and arrived at the court without knowing the background).

Joseph described his impressions on their arrival. They went into the *makhukhu*. It had one door and several large windows. There were lots of people – more than twenty – in there seated on old car seats against the walls. About eight of these were there to do with other cases – he knew them. The rest were comrades. Candles were burning. There was a table, or perhaps a sideboard, by the door where Ashwell 'Mugabe' Zwane sat facing the people sitting on the car seats. Joseph knew Mugabe from football. There was a book on the table. Joseph remembered that Moses had had a similar book at home, which Joseph thought of as 'the book of the law ... the law of the comrades'.[26] There were two or three sjamboks lying inside the *makhukhu* and others outside. It looked like a court. He sat there listening to other cases for a long time. Silence was expected.

When it came to John's murder, Joseph said that they asked him what he had meant by going to the police. (Zwane later vehemently denied this part of the story.) Moses defended Joseph, saying he had not said anything to the police. The comrades discussed the case amongst themselves and then Zwane said Joseph must be 'disciplined' for this; he was an *impimpi*.

Joseph said that they took him outside and made him hold onto an old white scrap car lying outside while several people sjambokked him several times. (This was denied by Zwane.) He said he saw a five litre plastic container of petrol – he smelt it. 'I asked them what they meant by "discipline".' He was then told to wait because they were going to kill his brother's murderers by burning. After his beating he went painfully and angrily back inside.

Joseph's trial having been completed, the comrades turned to the matter of the murder again. They questioned Josiah again. They showed him a photograph of the murder victim, John, whom Josiah had claimed not to have known. He could not (according to him) or would not (according to Moses) identify him. Josiah said the comrades were extremely angry with him when he failed to identify the man in the photograph. They took him outside and hit him several times with sjamboks on his back. They poured petrol on him and threatened to kill him. They tied wire around his neck and forced him to drink petrol out of a five-litre container that had been lying there. They hit him with their hands and fists, and kicked him.

Zwane acknowledged that he was one of those who assaulted Josiah:

> As we were questioning him [about whether he recognised the photo] he made me fed up and then I gave him some lashes, two actually ... I just said stand with your back towards me. *Well he knows nothing about being hit on the buttocks, he said you hit him several times over the shoulders, on the back.* No I only gave him two on the buttocks.

Zwane's prosecutor persisted with these questions:

> *What do you mean when you say you got fed up, Mr Zwane?* In Zulu I will say *yenganyenga*, that means fed up ... I thought maybe this man was scared by the others, now he thinks I am protecting him, let me also scare him so that he can talk ... As I talk to him he thinks that I am defending him, he is no more now talking straight so he has been

refusing the obvious thing or denying the obvious thing. I thought that he will maybe talk if he sees me also doing some lashing on him. *I see, he might be more scared and he may then give the answers you expect?* Give the right answer ... *It is rather a violent way of investigating the matter.* It is not violent ... *What was their reaction when you started assaulting him? We know they had no reaction when the petrol was used, apparently, did they show any reaction when you assaulted the witness.* When I gave that man one, two lashes Joseph said no stop it, leave him actually. (A. Zwane, Z4316–17)

But the *stokvel* owner said he was assaulted by five of the comrades in the people's court – and Zwane's claims of a 'modest' assault are belied by the photographs of Josiah's upper body which the police had taken after the people's court was raided that very day. These show him with severe cuts all over his back (Exhibit Z, Zwane trial, PJ archives).

But this, said Zwane, was not his doing. It had been the young hot-headed Moses, angry at the murder of his brother, who had, together with his friends, taken things too far. Being 'very emotional' about the death of Moses's brother, 'they assaulted Josiah and poured petrol on him'. Zwane says in fact he was the one who stopped this assault and tried to regularise it. To Zwane, this was how it happened:

I got out and went to where the husband [Josiah] was outside and there I saw Moses having a bottle and I smelt petrol and I concluded that the bottle might be containing petrol. And I noticed liquid on the face of the husband. And then I concluded that there is something that Moses witness was doing, putting petrol on this man. I just recently heard that he is a new member and he is acting in an unwanted manner, I stopped him I said look petrol is not needed here. And it appeared as if the friends to Moses were assaulting the man. I stopped it, I said look even your friends are not members of our organisation, I do not know what they want here, How can they come and act like this here. You are also claiming to be a member but you are acting in an unwanted way. (A. Zwane, Z3809–10)

He recalls then taking Josiah back inside, and it was then that he gave him the lashes he admitted to:

We then sat there with Josiah trying to discuss this problem He also saw the photo there [of the deceased who was supposed to be having an affair with his wife]. He was asked whether he knew that person. His answers were also not satisfying, on top of the allegation which Moses brought. I then also became fed up and I lashed with a sjambok. And that did not help us. We could not get the truth and we could not see where the lies are. (ibid.)

Josiah was then taken back outside where he said his wife was sitting crying with a swollen jaw. (This was strongly denied by Ashwell Zwane, Z4302–3.)

The case took a turn, now, when Joseph came forward, a while after he had been beaten for going to the police. He now recalled that he had heard the name Lowlife being shouted at the time when John was stabbed. This cast doubt on the whole case that Moses and his friends had persuaded Zwane to mount, and that they were pursuing with such passion. Josiah and Maria were told to wait until Lowlife could be found. This took until the evening, and the two stayed and listened to cases including, they said, another murder trial.

Finally, the comrades found Lowlife and brought him into the *makhukhu* with his friends Elias and Barney (A. Zwane, Z3810). Moses knew all of them from football. Long discussions followed, during which Joseph and Moses began to take the position that it had been these three new accused, Lowlife, Elias and Barney, who had murdered their brother. Indeed the treason accused said that Moses knew it had been them all along.[27] In this new situation Josiah now became an accuser rather than an accused – a role which he presumably adopted with alacrity. He joined the comrades in asking Lowlife questions. Lowlife repeated what he had told Moses right at the beginning – he had not killed John, but had intervened to stop him being killed. At first, he tried to throw the blame on Zwelakhe – who was no longer there.

Josiah and Maria were now talking freely. They both gave evidence that two of these three newly accused attackers – Elias and Barney – had in fact been responsible for John's death. Nobody will ever know whether this evidence was given to protect themselves from further accusation, but in fact Elias and Barney finally admitted that they had killed John.

Towards the end of these dramatic proceedings, Moses went out to the cafe for something, and spotted the police coming towards the *makhukhu*. He ran away, and was not present when the hearing, just reaching its climax, was interrupted by police raiding the shack. Albert Sebola recounted that:

> I heard screams saying 'don't move, don't move, this is the police'. So the shack of the door was flung open, then I saw a black policeman whom I knew very well because he used to patrol in the township and so he was having a gun on the other hand and on the other hand he was having a sjambok … And he started beating the people who were inside there'. (A. Sebola, Z2762)

The police assaulted most of the people present, and arrested them all, whatever their reasons for being there. This bizarre gathering of people, so passionately in dispute with one another, were all thrust together as they travelled to the police station in a large yellow truck. Inside Zwane spoke to them all, telling them not to tell the police who the comrades were. Then the police stopped him from talking, and they went the rest of the way in silence.

The roles of all those involved were soon to be reversed. Most of those assaulted and accused in the people's court, including Joseph, gave evidence against the Zwane group of comrades in the subsequent treason trial. And Moses, the hot-headed comrade who had attempted to use the people's court to find justice for his dead brother, became a state witness.

In his trial for treason Zwane said he felt the case of Joseph's murder had been a complex one, which the people's court had not been able to solve (A. Zwane, Z3809–10). The prosecutor said that one thing was for certain, however – in the end it had turned out that the *stokvel* owner had had nothing whatsoever to do with the murder.

CONCLUSION

While the evidence presented here must be treated with due caution, these tales, carefully interpreted, do reveal a great deal at the level of meaning and process. They expose the desperation of those who went to the people's courts. They also act as an indicator of the way in which the idealistic motives of the youths were intricately intertwined with their violence, arrogance and puritanism. They suggest that courts such as these could not cope with mendacious witnesses without resorting to violence; and show the degree to which residents treated the existence and proceedings of the courts as within the bounds of acceptability – albeit driven as many of them were by fear. They also reveal the difficulty the courts had in imposing any sentences other than those which could be instantly carried out.

Each of these courts constructed a newly ordered dramaturgical space, which inverted the age-based authority systems Alexandrans had grown up with. They parodied the 'traditional courts' or *lekgotla*, by placing the youth at the pinnacle of a reformed moral universe. Here the ideals of good behaviour (not drinking; not abandoning one's family; being a good husband, wife, or comrade; not fighting; not committing crimes; paying maintenance to divorced wives) could be induced within – or imposed upon – adults and young people alike.

Not surprisingly, responses to the courts were highly ambivalent. Some emphasised their successes. The courts had worked in some respects. According to one policeman:

> The figures clearly showed that there were fewer cases during this period of unrest … [when] … the so-called 'people's court' was in place. These people or complainants went to the people's court and reported the cases there. (Sergeant Zeelie, Z412) (BB's translation)

Crime reported to the police went down during the period of the rebellion – although we do not know whether this reflects an actual decrease, or whether it was simply a result of the ban on reporting.

Many agreed that crime had indeed dropped during these months, and

Table 6: Crimes reported to Alexandra Police Station, January 1982–June 1987

Month	1982	1983	1984	1985	1986	% drop 1985–86	1987	% change 1985–86
January	219	220	231	259	236	8.9%	217	−16.2%
February	231	263	269	215	164	23.7%	199	−7.4%
March	262	275	229	276	134	51.5%	239	−13.0%
April	245	227	224	240	112	53.3%	241	0.0%
May	297	189	215	199	129	35.0%	286	+43.7%
June	255	227	191	201	112	44.3%	268	+33.3%
July	276	269	224	269	109	59.5%		
August	274	224	258	246	154	38.4%		
September	254	234	278	258	185	29.3%		
October	249	240	283	281	174	38.0%		
November	290	281	270	270	172	36.3%		
December	341	277	267	260	209	19.7%		

Sources: Adapted from Exhibits ZZ and BBB, crime statistics from Alexandra Police Station, 1982–7 and also 'Kodelys van Misdrywe', Department of Statistics, Pretoria, Document No 08/02 (1979), Zwane Trial PJ Archives.

that the success of the people's courts had been both rapid and tangible.

> *Is it correct to say that the effect of their activity was to clean up crime in Alexandra in a way that it has never known?* Yes, during the time they were doing that there used not to be people who were found dead in the streets, because people were scared that those people would come and wallop them. *In other words, the murders and the stabbings more or less came to an end?* I would say so.[28]

Residents defensively tried to play down the violence within the courts, and told the panicking press in April that the function of the courts was to solve family disputes amicably 'and nobody was ever sentenced to death by "necklace"' (a burning tyre). They said the painted tyres hanging on the wall in the Fifteenth Avenue court were 'just decoration and not tyres ready for someone found guilty' (*The Star*, 25 April 1986). Others said that drunkenness and its associated crimes of fighting or stabbing, had clearly been lessened:

> Drunkenness became less, because the people were now scared to be found in the streets. They were mainly scared of the very people who were busy with the anti crime activity. Most shebeens closed. When we come now to the incidents of stabbings, these stabbings in Alexandra usually takes place when people are already drunk during the night. Now this cause the reduction in drunkenness, because they were no longer finding more places where they would drink and get drunk and enjoy stabbing one another. (M. Nxumalo, M197)

Paul Tshabalala, a participant in one of the adult courts discussed in the next chapter, was asked: '*Was the crime rate reduced during this period? ... This period when the youth were in control of everything?*' His answer was unequivocal: 'Crime did reduce ... the dying of the people, that was greatly reduced' (P. Tshabalala, M3837–8).

The people's courts became, briefly, part of the township way of life:

> People had no problems with the people's court. One would find that when a group of people have come together trying to solve something, they would say we are at the people's court. Even in the yards where people were trying to solve their problems, they would say they are in the people's court. You would find children in their play they would say 'we are playing the people's court' ... you would find them sitting and playing and then saying 'This is a people's court', 'You see, this is a people's court'. (P. Tshabalala, M3838)

But this was not the only view. Combined with their sense that the people's courts had something to offer were deep and serious reservations, many of which were extremely difficult to acknowledge to an outside world all too ready and willing to believe the worst stories of African 'savagery'. There is no doubt that many adults rapidly began to develop a sense of the local revolution having swerved out of control. Because the 'rule of the comrades' drew so extensively on repertoires of older, gang behaviour it was not surprising that the ideal 'good comrade' proved a difficult part for militant young men to play consistently. They came to be feared for the ways they patrolled and controlled the streets, wielding sjamboks and destroying the meagre possessions of shoppers who had broken the consumer boycott, or herding the unwilling to meetings. Some took part in spectacular mob burnings and necklacings of those whom they believed were witches and informers; the line between the two forms of accusation was a fine one. Some groups of youths became so distinctively criminal that they came to be labelled *comtsotsis* ('comrade-criminals') perceived as bad elements masquerading as comrades. The presence of a mass of unemployed and socially uncaptured youths perhaps rendered this decay into criminality inevitable. Their abrogated position at the moral pinnacle, as well as their high level of militaristic organisation and ferociousness gave the utopian youth an increasing sense of their rights and power over adults, whose failures they had self-righteously proclaimed. Their highly symbolic as well as militaristic revolution seared itself upon the minds and memories of the adults. The township public found unforgettable the theatrical imagery of the period. Their 'realist' response to this utopianism is the subject of the next chapter.

8

REALISM AND REVOLUTION

There can only be one law, not two kings. These children, they are born of us, found us abiding by the law. It is difficult for us after giving birth to these children, they find us abiding by the law they come with their law and they want to operate on their law. (P. Slolo, M881)

The least theatrical form of mobilisation in Alexandra was that involving adults. Two things underlay the growth of a distinctive adult view on the ongoing upheavals in the township: the 'structurated' generational differences that had emerged in the 1970s and 1980s, already outlined above; and the presence of a 'realist' type of thinking amongst the adult social generation, as opposed to the 'millenarian' or 'utopian' thinking which dominated youth world views.

The notion of realism has multiple meanings, referring to such things as literary or artistic form (realism as distinct from romanticism; socialist realism), philosophical stance (realists as contrasted with nominalists, or realists as materialists) or everyday thinking ('let's be realistic', as opposed to idealistic). Here it will be used in a sense which most reflects the last use – to refer to a mode of thinking amongst ordinary people which stresses the process of 'facing up to things as they really are, and not as we imagine or would like them to be' (Williams 1976). 'Let's be realistic', says Raymond Williams, often refers to accepting the limits of a situation, looking at 'hard facts, often of power or money in their existing and established forms' (Williams 1976).

How does the notion of 'realism' square up with a situation in which the apartheid system was clearly under substantial attack from both adults and youths, an attack which resembled a revolution in some respects? Obviously the adults involved were not 'realists' in the sense of resigning themselves to an acceptance of their subordination to state and economic power – although such a stance had been quite visible during the years of high apartheid. But by the mid-eighties earlier repertoires of resistance, mostly taking a realist, practical and even parochial form (bus-boycotts, squatter movements, rent boycotts) had been recalled through a variety of mechanisms.

Many old forms of urban social capital – particularly those which provided a link between the private and public worlds of the poor – were destroyed or curtailed by high apartheid, including systems which cushioned poverty, which provided access to influence, which produced an educated stratum, and which softened state–citizen interactions. However, the deeper-rooted habits of syncretisation and memory-construction – while damaged – did not die. The 'hidden' world of township life had by no means been destroyed. Even when the modernising regime bulldozed townships and removed many thousands of their residents to other places, recognisable features of old township expectations and behaviours remained. But the link between the 'hidden' and the 'public' worlds was broken. Attempts were made to create new mechanisms that would revive this link during the 1970s.

A striking response to the resulting vacuum in township life with a strong realist component had been the rise of the Black Consciousness Movement (BCM) in the 1970s, one of whose main platforms was the creation of a revitalised urban culture and a series of systems of community activism and self-improvement. While it was unsurprising that the imposition of 'blackness' from above led to its discovery from below, the BCM – unlike many other ethnic fundamentalisms, and in sharp contrast to the tone of black consciousness-influenced discussions today – did not confine itself to matters of identity, but addressed civil society as well. Much of its work in building clinics and schools and encouraging community development projects took place in rural areas; but township-dwellers too were drawn into a vision of social change which 'sought to develop a culture of the oppressed as a means of transforming the whole of society into a new and superior ethical order' (Mangcu 1993: 4; see also Nolotshungu 1982, Gerhart 1978). Towards this end activists 'initiated community-wide organizations in the arts, education, culture, the economy and politics' with an explicit mission further to rid African communities of the white philanthropists whose positions had already been substantially weakened by Afrikaner rule. While all of the Black Consciousness institutions were destroyed in the late 1970s by vicious state repression, it would be a mistake to assume that they left no legacy in people's minds and memories. The community projects the BCM started and ran were an example of progressive institutional development, which drew from the syncretic and memory-saturated culture of African communities and created a visionary emancipatory ideology around which they could be mobilised and organised, while paying specific and quite detailed attention to the inner workings of the projects themselves.

Their destruction only served to exacerbate the latent tensions within the society as a whole, and within places like townships in particular. It is not surprising that new forms of struggle emerged soon afterwards, so that by the 1980s a significant change in orientation had taken place. As Mangcu puts it: 'whereas the black consciousness movement had concentrated on inward-looking strategies of community development in preparation for an idealized non-racial order, the new movements directed the struggle almost exclusively outwardly' – concentrating more on 'the mobilization of the masses than on organization and institution building' (Mangcu 1993: 6). In this some assistance continued to be given by the erstwhile white philanthropists, many of whom had turned, too, to radical politics after their ousting by the state and the BCM.

But realist civic traditions did not die. Although memories of repertoires of resistance do fade, in the eighties a series of processes of reconstruction and memory were engaged in, and in Alexandra these were important in focusing some strata of the rebellious towards grassroots, and realist, rather than utopian solutions. The Trotskyist newspaper *Izwi Lase Township* reminded Alex residents of their own history, and provided a world view in which their everyday township experiences were treated as important dimensions of a larger system. Eschewing the patronising simplifications of some of the worthy literacy papers and magazines of the time, the paper raised issues concerning feminism; sociological interpretations of crime; the virtues of graffiti as a political art form; memories of ANC stalwarts; popular demands for such things as housing; the nature of capitalism as exploitative; sport as a form of social control; populism versus the potential evil of leaders; uncovering 'hidden histories'; how evil the advertising industry is; how the press lies and distorts; African history; the evils of consumerism; and South African history, particularly the history of apartheid.

This fed into the mix, and when in the 1980s a new kind of violence had erupted – a clear assertion of the translation of private social capital into public demands – these demands did not all remain at the level of romantic emancipatory wish lists. The private world of the township was mobilised into a public set of differentiated institutions, which could make claims upon and oppose the state. The experience of Alexandra was of course unique to it, but in most townships some equivalent form of social organisation emerged to accompany the revolutionary fervour of the youth, heralding 'their own organizational ethos as the embryo of a new form of existence' (Adler and Steinberg 2000). But here civic mobilisation was based upon the adult history of practicality, specific patterns of resource mobilisation and ideologies of emancipation.

Older Alexandrans preferred incremental rather than revolutionary solutions. Sam Buti, erstwhile mayor of the township, and ambitious reformer, ran foul of this.[1] He had controversially accepted 'municipal status' for the township and envisaged the 'disappearance of current Alex – crumbling houses, rutted and untarred streets, dogs scratching through litter'. He sought to substitute this with a romantic vision of 'a network of tarred and tree-lined streets winding in curves and crescents down to the Jukskei River through a variety of flats and houses, parks and gardens, sports grounds, shopping centres and libraries', where electricity and sewerage were properly supplied (*The Star*, 25 February 1980). He did build the flats, a youth centre, the stadium and some better class housing. But this put up the backs of the very poor, who could not afford the new homes, and who wanted 'proper big houses' at low rents. Buti soon realised that anyway, in the light of the apartheid state's rejection of welfarism, the redevelopment would ultimately have to be paid for by the residents themselves (*The Star*, 8 September 1980). When he then forcibly removed residents from their homes and placed them in unused buses to 'redevelop' the sewerage scheme (*Rand Daily Mail*, 20 September 1987), Buti suddenly became an oppressor, whose actions provoked resistance under the aegis of the Alexandra Residents' Association (ARA), and ultimately, a successful rent boycott. The ARA, like *Izwi Lase Township*, continued to mobilise for the three years preceding the Six-Day War, expressing worries about Buti's intention to establish his own riot squad; and rumours of his corruption, and his council's threats to demolish shacks, saying in one pamphlet:

> anyone who lays hands on a shack without providing proper alterna-
> tive accommodation, calls down on himself the law of the golden rule:
> DO UNTO OTHERS WHAT YOU WOULD HAVE THEM DO
> UNTO YOU. If the Council demolishes shacks, they will be causing
> trouble for themselves as much as for the residents of Alexandra who
> live in shacks. People must live somewhere, and they will defend
> themselves from being kicked around, by all means at their disposal.
> (ARA pamphlet, 1984)

Presaging the ethos of Mayekiso's AAC, the ARA used spatial and 'popular democratic' means to organise, in which 'Each unit (block, zone etc) shall elect a Chairman and a Secretary, who are members of ARA', and where reporting then would go up from chairman of these units to the Area, and finally to the Central Committee. The main unit would be a 'small area of about 10 yards'. The concerns of the ARA would be practical and material issues such as housing and rents (ARA pamphlet, *c*.1985).

Over time it became clear that the level of mobilisation was unexpectedly high. The ARA even issuing a pamphlet, just before the Six-Day War, warning that:

> Buti's policies, and in particular his creation of a riot squad, would
> cause a violent eruption. He ignored us, and now see what occurred ...
> these houses belong to the people, and they are likely to resist eviction,
> we fear that another eruption could be the result of any aggression
> from the council. The residents demand the resignation of all coun-
> cillors. (ARA pamphlet, 1986)

The ferment amongst working adults was also expressed through the Alexandra Civic Association (ACA), led by Mac Lekota and Mike Beea; a group of Coloured residents led by John Grant, who protested at their racially motivated removal by central government from the township to a 'Coloured' area (Moses Mayekiso, M2905ff); and the Alexandra Commuters Committee, which led 3,000 people in a bus boycott (reviving a major tradition of resistance), against increased fares in January 1984. Their eminently experiential grievances included: 'bumpy Roads, Dust caused by buses is a health hazard; untidy buses, poor services, no toilets in Wynberg. Those in 15th Avenue are badly cared for; rudeness and careless of drivers; no shelters'.[2]

Thus by the mid-eighties adults were aware that youth power and state decline had won space for strategies of change, and that their realism need no longer imply resignation. Instead an extraordinarily high level of hopefulness about what was possible had already appeared. What could be and should be changed was rooted in a difficult 'real world', a world of sense and experience, and it was from this real world that strategies of change should emerge and be developed. Unlike youths, adults saw their local revolution as a revolution of everyday life, rooted in the petty indignities and physical and psychological hardships they knew and experienced themselves, the 'harsh reality' of apartheid.

It would be misleading to ignore the fact that the adults of the township did show some support for the millenarianism that surrounded them. As we have seen there were those amongst the adults – particularly women – who would bring 'cases' to the people's courts, and sometimes request even harsher punishments than those visualised by the youths, as we have seen. Adults would sometimes participate with zeal in burnings or necklacings. But often their support for youth utopianism stemmed, in fact, from a realist perspective. Thus the rent boycott, with its roots in the anti-Buti movement, met with widespread support amongst adults not because it would lead to a Utopia but 'because they were believing that the monies they are paying in rent. They are not getting the services for it in return ... They also believed that money is being misused by the councillors' (Moses Mayekiso, M2987–8). By the time of the Six-Day War adult support for the boycott was so widespread that rent payments dropped drastically. As one resident put it:

> After the six-day war people stopped their rent without anybody having told them to stop. Because the people were mainly complaining that they had been paying rent for a long time in Alexandra and the conditions in Alexandra are worse as compared to in other townships and now the other thing is that Alexandra was in the heart of a posh township between Johannesburg and Sandton, posh town places. Now people living in Alexandra, he walks hardly ten minutes and then he starts seeing the very beautiful places and then that would be painful to him as to, and he would ask what sort of person is he for living in such poor conditions. He pays rent, but he sees no improvement ... To put it in a general way, it is the conditions that caused the people not to pay rent in Alexandra. (Paul Tshabalala, M3854)

Table 7: Rent income in Alexandra from 1985–6

Month	Total rent in Rands
July 1985:	157 000
December 1985	155 000
February 1986:	130 000
March 1986:	51 000

Source: Exhibit AAA, Zwane Trial, PJ Archives.

Similarly, some believed, not without justification, that youth tactics had helped stop crime – an eminently realist concern (R. Mdakane, M2232). Few people minded if criminals were disarmed or beaten. And most were not averse to having a militant and militaristic force of young men within the township when it came to coping with the despised and feared occupying army or police force. Thus, because of this realism and conservatism, and in spite of some surface similarities in their perspectives, the utopianism of the youth was often regarded as insupportable. To many adults, the youth were 'uncontrollable' (R. Mdakane, M2160). In the township at large, said the well-known adult leader Richard Mdakane, 'The youth themselves were unable to control themselves in the community. They were stealing cars and driving them in any manner in the townships in the streets' (R. Mdakane, M2214).

Later, Mdakane was to observe:

> People ... were insisting that all misbehaviour must be stopped. They were referring to all sorts of misbehaviour, killing and all that, such as assaulting people in the streets, demanding for food from shops, to dispossess taxi-owners of their vehicles, going about in peoples shops and forcing them to give food. They were hijacking the taxis. (R. Mdakane, M2528)

The youth wanted, for example, to drive the police out but 'the adults seemed not to be pleased about that. They were afraid to confront the youth, because the youth was dangerous' (P. Tshabalala, M3831). Township opinion was also clearly hostile to the consumer boycott, as we saw earlier; while the 'non-participation campaign' presented problems for day-to-day life:

> especially concerning taxi people as well as with the community, that it would not be feasible if one policeman gets into a bus with seventy other passengers, all seventy must get off and be late for work just because of this one policeman. That was going to interfere with their work. The taxi people were also worried that it would interfere with their business. The business people in the township saw that if they must not sell to the police there could be unnecessary interference there from the youth that were not disciplined. In this whole consumer

boycott and non-participation campaign the feeling in our constituency was that they were not in favour of it. (Moses Mayekiso, M2986)

Adults tended to believe that the youth were wild and prone to drunkenness, uncontrolled behaviour and violence. They appeared to be beyond
reform, worrying immensely the older generation, themselves the product
of deeply hierarchical values. Youth behaviour seemed lawless, wilful,
dangerous, undisciplined and, worst of all, a threat to the older generation's
world view and authority. At an important meeting of township groupings a
prominent speaker, Benjamin Lekalakala, said that:

> the youth in Alexandra township is not well-behaved. They behave
> badly, is uncontrollable ... because they steal cars and bring them to
> the township, which causes the police to follow them up and they start
> shooting and people get injured by the bullets that are being fired by
> the police. These car thiefs take cars and park them in other peoples
> yards without telling the owners of the yard why they park it there.
> When the police come there they harass all the people in the yard ...
> The youth must be disciplined and stop going to people's shops and
> force them to give them food and frighten people. (reported words of
> B. Lekalakala) (R. Mdakane, M2230)

Many were deeply worried about the beatings that were taking place in the
people's courts. The idea of the people's court, on the surface an admirably
'alternative' institution of justice, and one often set up by idealists with a
clear desire to replace the discredited system of law (Modibedi n.d.), was at
heart dangerously invasive of the moral order, placing responsibility for
judging life and death, right and wrong, outside of the realm of accountable
institutions.[3]

THE MOBILISATION OF THE PAROCHIAL

It would not do to offer adults a mobilising 'frame' or world view rooted
entirely in dreams of the future or in a fundamentally inversionary
perspective; adults would act more willingly, it seems, within frames which
posed action as effective, local and immediate, and which did not entail a
threat to their own authority.

Moses Mayekiso had already begun to emerge as a potential unifier and
township leader during 1985, and began to take steps to distinguish himself
from other township politicians (see Carter 1991a: 196ff). When the ACA
approached him to ask him to assist them in ending the school boycotts – to
adults an unacceptable political strategy – Mayekiso's response was suitably
pragmatic:

> I was saying that we should not merely say the children must go back
> to school without stating the manner in which they have to go back. I

then suggested that there should be a committee, a joint committee of the students and the parents who would meet the education authorities or the schools concerned and the problems that the students are complaining about should be put right, so that their going back should be something that would solve a problem and their problems must be dealt with. (Moses Mayekiso, M2889)

These democratic proposals ran against the ACA's prevailing strategies, which were what Mayekiso called 'not democratical' because they were 'just presenting their feelings to the people and then it would end there, and there were also no good structures on which the civic was based'. He also met with the ARA, who were against rent increases, but had criticisms of them too as they were too 'workerist' (albeit within the township):

I realised that they were also not working properly, because they were against the students' organisation, as well as the youth organisations that were present at the time. I saw that as a great mistake. In their method of working they were merely referring to workers. They did not want to talk about other sections of society. Their ideology was that liberation would come through organised workers. Without meeting other sectors of the community such as the students, the youth, I regarded that as what is referred to as workerism. (Moses Mayekiso, M2890–1)

Mayekiso also met with John Grant, the leader of Coloured resistance to removals, and again he advocated inclusiveness, opposing the idea of a separate Coloured organisation as Grant had suggested. Pursuing the theme of unity, by early 1986, while youths were reclaiming the streets, Mayekiso set out to institutionalise adult interests in a new organisation, the Alexandra Action Committee (AAC) (see Carter 1991a: 193ff), the committee which was to generate the 'frames' (Diani 1996; Tarrow 1998; Klandermans 1997; Snow and Benford 1992) through which further attacks upon, and alteration of meaning of, spaces were to be conceptualised. Rejecting the term 'ungovernability', with its anarchistic implications (P. Tshabalala, M3798), the AAC sought rather to create a system through which the township could govern itself; through promulgating a unity of vision it aimed to unite the disparate elements within the space.

Mayekiso saw the organisation as a means through which he could apply his trade union experience of grassroots democracy to the township (*Financial Mail*, 21 March 1986).

In organising for the union, I found workers had many problems that did not originate in the workplace, which could only be solved in the community. You can't divide the issues facing workers and say that Factory organisation should stay separate.

Organising both where people live and where they work was, he believed, the only way to mobilise broadly enough to end apartheid:

> Its not a battle that can be won on the shop floor. If the community is not organised properly, we could lose. That's why the AAC helps community organisation and wants to forge unity between workers and the township youth.

He displayed remarkable leadership and organisational creativity, combining union ideas together with ideas about township organisation and applying both to Alex which had, like all other townships, mainly been the preserve of what he disparagingly called 'populist' nationalists[4] and 'vanguardist' youth.[5] Some of the translation of ideas had been, he said, inspired by his wife Kola's reports about what was happening in townships in their common birthplace, the Eastern Cape (Moses Mayekiso, M2895). On her return from a trip there: 'She put it as a woman would do, that there is no longer fighting of the people, there is no longer killing of the people, as she knew Queenstown before.'

Harmony, she said, had resulted from the formation of street committees, and a good 'civic' organisation, which worked democratically. People would discuss problems and street matters, and these would be put forward to the civic (Moses Mayekiso, M2896). He was inspired. He took 'the idea from Komani [Queenstown] and the idea of the union structures and brought the two together and realised that there was something we could do in Alexandra'. Early in February a concerned group of adults – headed by Mayekiso – planned a series of 'street meetings' within the township to 'launch the Street Committees'. At the rate of one street meeting per night, it was envisaged that between 10 February and 7 March, meetings of residents of all twenty-two Avenues within the township would have taken place. As it happened, the sequence of meetings was interrupted by the Six-Day War, but there had been sufficient indication of interest from the residents of the various streets to bring leaders to the realisation that the mobilisation of adults was a distinct possibility. The first more formal meeting of what was to become the AAC took place as the war itself broke out, the day after Diradeng's death. Moses Mayekiso was elected chairperson of the 'acting executive' of the emerging organisation; John Grant the vice-chairperson; Richard Mdakane the secretary; Kola Mayekiso the treasurer and Mapula Morare the vice-treasurer – the presence of the latter two women emphasising the fact that adult organisation would not be confined to males. At its launching meeting those present said they set out to: 'organise the community into yard, block and street committees'; to 'help the people to solve their own community problems'; to 'represent the community to other organisation and the authority'; and 'to unite people regardless of their race, colour, believe – creed and tribe'.[6]

The response of citizens to the street meetings, it was said, had been to use them as an opportunity to raise numerous problems:

> High rentals specially at new houses, bad houses with no repairs, bad road with dongas, poor electrification, dirty toilet with no sewerage system, poor old houses and overcrowding, bucket system, demolition, of houses and syhacks with no suitable accommodation being provided, high rate of crime, unemployment, caused by retrenchment with no new job creation, prices very high, standard of living very low resulted in starvation, Putco fares and taxi fares very high, Putco buses stopping at Pan Africa with broken windows, poor education causing boycotts, students demand not met, police occupation of school and Township, some teachers and principals not cooperative to the students demands, liaison Committees, Peri-urban police harassing residents, councillors and the impimpis, influx control, hostel system, apartheid and the killings of youth and residents by army and police.[7]

Those present were ambitious. Not only did they wish to organise the entire community in order to address all of these problems, but they also wished to supplant, or at least absorb, the other existing civic organisations – the ARA and the ACA (which 'are not satisfying the community since they have no proper structures') – in the township into one overarching (adult) organisation.

As adults found themselves both inspired and horrified by the events of the Six-Day War, the AAC-in-waiting began to grow, and consolidate. Over the next few weeks and months, notwithstanding numerous short-term detentions of its leaders, it became increasingly powerful, making its symbolic presence clear through printing its own T-shirts and creating a logo and letterheads; ensuring a political place for itself in township life by holding public meetings, or lobbying the police; and giving itself a firm bureaucratic basis through the drafting of an impressive nineteen-page constitution. In so doing it had made good use of the unusual range of resources available to both Bapela and Mayekiso himself (access to printing and design facilities; legal advice and other things), and this distinguished it from almost all of the other emerging groupings in the township.

Three days later, the committee called a general meeting of all Alexandra residents, in Freedom Park, one of the People's Parks. It was the first mass meeting of its kind in the township. Mayekiso drew up the agenda and the record of the meeting. Alexandra was to be divided into manageable zones, and the AAC would devise systematic ways of ensuring that the people participated fully in its governance. The resulting proposals for yard, block and street committees – discussed in more detail below – were aimed at creating an answerable, effective system of local management, which ensured that the poor would have recourse, would be treated with respect, would not experience discrimination and would be persuaded to act in more disciplined ways.

Like the trade unions in which Mayekiso had been politically educated,[8] the committees were to be based on the material conditions and experiences of ordinary people, but contained within them a clear vision of practical alternatives. The mechanisms of electing representatives, of holding meetings for ordinary residents, of hearing their grievances at the grassroots and of passing them through hierarchically organised structures in order to find solutions were new and came from Mayekiso's trade union experience. In the envisaged popular democracy it would be 'the people who will decide how much to pay and what housing structures suit their pockets' (*New Nation*, 9–21 May 1986).

One observer's impression of the AAC was this:

> The idea was very much the local services, the local situation, and if one looked at the yard committees and things like that, it was grass roots representation dealing with local matters ... it wasn't usurping or taking over the power or the state or setting up some sort of private organisation that would run ... it wasn't that at all. *Did you get the idea that the purpose was to work within the existing system or to put up structures alternative to the existing system or in opposition to it?* Can I say work within the existing system, very much the acknowledgement of the system, the acknowledgement that the state has power and is in control. (R. Valente, M4225–6)

Mayekiso made it explicit that the AAC was based upon trade union structures. Most of the people were workers, he said, 'so the structures were based along the lines of trade union structures – accountability, elections every year and so on'. The function of the AAC, he said was to:

> coordinate the affairs of the township and to deal with the political and social problems. For example we have begun to deal with the problem of unemployment. We are planning to have unemployed cooperatives in each and every street, so that everyone who is not working will be doing something for the community. We are also looking at child-care structures, transport problems, cooperative buying and a first aid system – maybe in each street there will be one person who will learn first aid.

Did workers have an important role within the AAC, he was asked?

> Alexandra is very different from other townships as the majority of people living there are workers. Unlike Soweto, we don't have rich businessmen. Workers are directly involved in the various committees and they bring with them experience of unions' democratic structures. We believe that our struggle must be led by the working class and therefore workers should play a greater role in community organisations. In Alexandra shop stewards play a leading role in the community by being elected onto block committees and so on. So there are

direct links with organised workers. (*SA Metal Worker*, 3 June 1986)

The symbolism adopted by the AAC reflected its view that Alexandra was 'basically a working-class place'. The red flag would be used to 'symbolise the workers struggle', so that 'the logo, emblem, flag colour should be used as an organising feeling (Moses Mayekiso, M2962). Their slogan would be 'The Struggle Must Continue'.

In articulating his notion of a 'sensible Utopia' Mayekiso was shrewdly able to tread the fine line between collaboration and resistance. To some it might seem that what the AAC proposed was no different from the many more conservative proposals about township development that had preceded it. But in fact this was pragmatism rather than simple collaborationism. While adults regarded it as impossible and immoral to work within the system of black councils, Mayekiso also realised that they, like many of the workers he had helped organise, did not want to become sacrificial lambs, to go underground, to participate fully in what they saw as the populist politics of Nationalism, or to give in to youth millenarianism. The AAC philosophy depended more on the realpolitik emerging from this set of motives than from any desire to collaborate.

THE DISPUTED MEANING OF TERRITORY: YARD, BLOCK AND STREET COMMITTEES

As opposed to other townships, then, in Alexandra, a clearly organised adult voice came to rival that of the youths. One of the things it expressed – like the voice of the youth – was a powerful consciousness of the importance of space and territory.

Mayekiso envisaged that in the long run grassroots mobilisation would lead to the building of a township-wide organisation: 'In [the] inaugural congress the decision would then be taken that there should be an organisation for the whole of Alexandra' (Moses Mayekiso, M2929). This was, he knew, a slow method of organisation but one that could prove more resistant than the utopian way to oppressive police and state action. Mayekiso made the conceptual leap from factory floor to enclosed township, and saw how spaces in the township, already so vivid a part of youth strategy, could play the part that shopfloors played in the unions in which he had been politically educated. Thus they could provide a means for adult taming of youth excesses and the mobilising of the general population.

To Mayekiso it was the yard rather than the shop floor which was the locus of a particularly harsh kind of suffering that could be alleviated by local organisation. Organisation must stem from experience, based upon the sentiments and meaning that underlay the grievances of the people. However these ideas had to be 'sold' to the residents – they did not emerge from them. This accorded with union notions of working from experience but leading it into organised directions.

> It is just like the unions started. They did not just become democratic from the onset. There would come perhaps two or three people together who will realise that there is a need for an organisation which would cater for the grievances of the people. Basing all that on the grievances that they already have and have seen already from the other people, you cannot build an organisation in a vacuum without any need for grievances. (Moses Mayekiso, M2333)

The top body, the AAC, would be 'run by the people themselves' in a popular democratic manner. To solve the people's multiple problems Alexandra was to be redesigned spatially, to be divided up and organised by elected committees, each with its own set of duties, based upon the yards, blocks and streets in which people lived. These newly defined spaces would become the units of a new political order. Marshals would be appointed. People's problems would be listened to and acted upon. Alexandra would be united, regardless of belief, colour, age and religion; it would be 'conscientised' and disciplined as a result of the new structure, which would ensure mass control of the struggle and proper democracy based on experience and everyday life. The AAC planned to have unemployment co-operatives in every street, child care structures, transport problems, co-operative buying and a first aid system. It developed sub-committees, too, on such matters as sport, media, housing, pensions, education and catering. Committees on 'women', 'youth' and 'surveillance' were also proposed but seem not to have materialised.

The system of yard, block and street committees, rooted in popular needs, would provide the foundation for a grassroots democracy based upon spatial representation; using a pyramidal structure, it would build up to an annually elected leadership.[9] Adults invoked such ideas as 'building a spirit of togetherness', 'Build unity, love and respect within people'; helping the needy and bereaved; settling differences and disputes that existed in the yard like tribal fighting and witchcraft. 'We want a happy community in Alex that loves one another.' They mentioned 'discipline in the yard' as a specific problem – key points of such discipline were 'Loyalty, Respect, Dedication, Devotion, Self Control, Time factor, and Responsibility'.[10]

Street committees had in fact been formed in many other areas, particularly but not only in the Eastern Cape,[11] but these were often under the control of youths rather than adults. And only in Alex did the phenomenon known as the yard committee emerge. These structures permitted an unusual degree of adult representation and participation, as well as a brake on youth utopianism and spatial power.

Yard committees rapidly spread. By April/May most yards had representatives and the yard committees 'were, in many cases, active and working well' (A. Sebola, M2773) – perhaps not surprisingly considering that the yard was the space most organically linked to the everyday lives and needs of

Table 8: Functions of yard, block and street committees

Yard Committees	Block Committees	Street and Avenue Committees	The Alexandra Action Committee (AAC)
To promote peace and discipline in the Yard	To do all that is mentioned as the duties of the Yard Committee in a broader scale for the block	To deal with matters not dealt with at block and yard committees	To deal with matters not dealt with at Yard Committees.
To <u>unite</u> the people in the yard.	To tackle unsolved problems from the yard Committees of that block.	To deal with all matters that affect the Street people	To solve matters/ problems not solved at Street Committees
To encourage <u>comradeship</u>/brother-hood and working together as family of the people in the yard	To discuss residents' problems needs and requirements – – family, interfamily, house to house, hooliganism, crime, hazards, crisis unemployment, rent etc.	To deal with matters referred to it by Block Committees	To deal with matters dealt with at Yard, Block and Street Committees on a broader scale
To defend each other when there is a need – against any enemy attacks	To introduce harmonious relation-ships amongst residents through discipline and work-ing together	Street marshalls are responsible to this committee	To coordinate all committees
To look to the cleanliness – clean the yard of dirt and crime	To promote family life, accommodation and food for all	To deal with matters dealt with at yard and street committees on a broader scale	To coordinate all activities, in relation to problems in the township – e.g. Education, unem-ployment, welfare, cultural, unity, com-radeship, solidarity, political and social
For people to help each financial, physically, morally and otherwise	To deal with matters mentioned at Yard, Block and Street committees in a broadened way for the whole township		To deal with outside bodies
To look to the welfare of the people in the yard			

Source: Minutes of an AAC meeting held on 2 February 1986; Mayekiso trial, CTH archives.

ordinary residents (A. Sebola, M2773). One observer felt: 'There is a communal spirit and neighbourliness spirit' which 'starts right from the yard where you live as neighbours' (R. Mashego, M4240).

> Because we live so close next to each other we become very close to each other, know each other's problems, form ourselves into societies, burial societies, involve ourselves in financial assistant groups which are called stokvels and help each other during the time of bereavement by contributing money, being supportive to the bereaved. (R. Mashego, M4240)

These things are characteristic of all townships, but:

> in Alexandra from the viewpoint that it starts right from the yard where you live as neighbours. *So the start of the structure is different in Alexandra, it starts in the yard?* Yes. *Where in other areas it may just be a group of people getting together?* Yes. (R. Mashego, M4241).

So yards had not been simply the basis for suffering – they already had organisational meaning to the people.

This did not mean, however, that yards were in any sense sites of previous political organisation. The apartheid years had reduced them to apathy.

> The services were poor, there were promises of better houses and which wasn't coming on. We could go along with rubbish bins in the streets not collected and our yards are dirty, I can start from our very own yard, we didn't care whether our yards were clean or not, it was an apathetic state. (R. Mashego, M4243)

Overcoming this apathy was one of the great achievements of the AAC. How was 'consciousness raised'?

> I think [through] our discussion in the yard because it detailed directly what affected us, the things we were aware of but which we just didn't have, we just couldn't say, we thought it was somebody's responsibility. *Now who was the person who verbalised, who put into words your needs and who triggered this activity in the yard? Was it Mr Mayekiso?* No he just highlighted that we can go back into our yard and highlighted the type of problems, an example which can be given like you can clean your yard, be supportive to each other. (R. Mashego, M4246–7)

Perhaps because of this rootedness in daily life, AAC success in the yards was considerable given the short time they were able to act relatively freely and given the fact that they believed things should be done slowly rather than hastily. Elections of representatives took place, and meetings to discuss and handle grievances were held (*in camera* Witness 23, Z1676–96). Because it was important that this be a gradual process, Mayekiso himself saw it as separate from the rebellion and said it had been 'disturbed' by the Six-Day War (Moses Mayekiso, M2956).

Mashego's yard formed its own committee when the very first AAC public meeting took place in February. At this meeting the AAC set out to get adults to buy into the AAC way of doing things, forming yard, block or street committees. The adults were keen:

> They were very much eager to participate ... Some said that the yards in the township are filthy so if they can work collectively their yards will then be clean. Others said they do not trust one another because they accused one another by witchcraft ... And some said some of their toilets had broken doors so it is their responsibility if they can come together to repair those doors. And others were very much concerned if fights arising due to different tribes living in one yard. So they felt that this committees will bring them together and they will promote peace. (A. Sebola, Z2713)

Throughout the township adults were encouraged to go out into their yards and organise, and within a week return with their nominations.

> It was a grass root upwards where every member had to go back into his yard, look at what their real problems were in the yard and prioritise them. Like we thought our yard was very dirty. We thought we could community more in the yard, that would break that apathy because we knew each other but we just saw each other and we realised that we should keep our yard clean. We should attend to our immediate problems like adding extra lines because we used one line, no one ever thought of expanding more and giving another chance to use his line. We were more concerned about our children, we could leave our children with our neighbours and would know that our children are very safe with our neighbours. We knew that we will be concerned if one is safe. And there was another element of being of alerting each other of thugs or enemies in the yard, so that we must just alert each other and be aware that there is someone in the yard, perhaps unknown people ... someone coming to knock and break in or an unknown person who we will suspect is just coming into harass you and after a house was bombed in the township we didn't know who could be the next victim of such bombing ... There was cooperation, unity and trust in each other. We were just like one big family in the yard ... we started cleaning in our yard ... We made a little park and there is the time when the night soil wasn't taken in our yard, we decided to dig a hole in the yard so that we should use that hole. (R. Mashego, M4245–6)

Officially the functions of yard committees were:

All the people in the yard constitute a committee. The people in that yard should make decisions that affect their lives like housing, problems, health, cleanliness and to settle any differences and disputes that exists in that yard. Differences like tribalism, fighting and witchcraft. We want a happy community in Alex that loves one another, always help the needy and bereaved. (Exhibit G, quoted in P. Tshabalala, M3822)

They had weekly yard committee meetings, where:

we discussed how to organise ourselves in cleaning our yard. We discussed some of the little quarrels which erupted in the yard and we also planned to create a park in front in our yard ... the youth was involved ... When there was conflict in the yard the person who had the complaint will tell the yard rep and the rep will call all the yard committee members and be seated there with both people and the complainant will say what he feels and the other one will also answer and will do it in a sort of a discussion coming up with ideas and suggestions of how it could be handled. *And would you say this is a sort of a mediation process?* Ja, a mediation process. *And was it successful?* It was successful. (R. Mashego, M4253–4)

Albert Sebola said that in his area yard committees were explained to a meeting of adults and youth together. It was explained that in any one yard there may be thirteen to fifteen families;

and people living there of different tribes and sharing two or three toilets so as the yards used to be filthy ... So if the people can come together and to see to it that the toilets are clean and the yard and that they must trust one another and be responsible and unity ... The yard rep was a person whom the people living in the same yard should come together and then elect their yard representative... And the yard committee would come out from the very same meeting ... A chairman would be elected ... the secretary too, and the treasurer ...The yard representative would be elected again from the very same people in that yard. And then he will see to it that the yard is kept clean the toilets are clean also. (A. Sebola, Z2635–6)

Yards still had 'standlords' charging high rents, a problem which yard committees also tried to address:[12] 'Whistles were blown whenever someone came into the yard to harass a member of the yard. This whole new system changed people's respect in one another. And it brought us closer together.'

Paul Tshabalala, one of the AAC accused, said that it was after the funerals following the Six-Day War that people really started talking about yard committees. People, he said, were 'taken up by that'.

People in the township are rather too tribalistic, choosing between

Sothos and Zulus and so on and they believe very strongly in witchcraft. When I looked at it I realised that that is something that would bring the people together ... when people talk of democracy this is what they are talking about, because one would find that people have lived in the same yard for ten years, but as neighbours they are at loggerheads ... Sometimes they quarrel over something useless such as the toilet and this would continue up to where there is witchcraft in it. (P. Tshabalala, M3820)

He initiated the move to form a committee in his yard, where ten families lived. Each family sent two to four people to the meeting, at which it was his mother who was elected chairperson, and one Grace Kambula as vice-chair.

As we discussed it we discussed as something that we were doing for ourselves in our yard. We discussed as to how the yard is to be maintained, especially on cleanliness. We discussed in a general way about the behaviour in the yard. We also discussed that should any death occurrence in the yard, we have to collect for that person. We discussed further that in our block we must help one another with people in the block.

The yard meeting generated a great deal of interest and the idea impressed all those present, who preferred their locally forged idea of yard committees to that of block to street committees. The yards worked, he claimed:

There used to be quarrels before 1986, but after those meetings I did not hear of any quarrel ... [once] we sat and discussed ... about the toilet, which was broken and we decided that it must be fixed and we even built another toilet for ourselves in our yard. (P. Tshabalala, M3731–2).

They liked the fact that they solved their own problems and that no one came 'from outside' to solve them.

How revolutionary were yards? In some respects, they were formed upon the lines of earlier patterns of authority and control. One yard-dweller said that only standholders and their families had been eligible for election to the committee (R. Mashego, M4266–7), while yard representation allowed the adults – even the elderly – to reclaim some authority from youths. In many cases, as we saw in the case of Paul Tshabalala's yard, these were senior women. In others they were older men, 'elders'.[13]

Who gave that instruction? It was an elderly man who stays at that yard [his own yard] ... He instructed us as an elderly man and whenever he gives instructions we have to carry them out ... He is a rep ... He is the oldest on the yard, the one who is looking after us. (*in camera* Witness 19, Z1431–7)[14]

Albert Sebola's yard had an elder as the representative, Mr Nkulu, appointed by:

the people in our yard who gathered in our yard so we elected him ...
As a representative of our yard he was supposed to inform us if there
are any developments maybe concerning the organising of people ...
concerning the burial ... I think as an elderly person he attended the
meetings of the burial committee ... He approached me as a young
man staying in the yard ... He said 'here is a pamphlet, will you please
collect money in the yard'. (A. Sebola, M2569)

A 65-year-old man gave evidence that in May parents in his yard were
called to a meeting at Fourteenth Avenue, in a church. He went there and
found other parents there. The purpose was to elect members of the block,
for Fourteenth Avenue between Ruth Road and Rooseveldt Road. He and
three others were elected. They were told that they were responsible for the
problems of that section.

Yards also sometimes bridged the generation gap between youths and
adults, because the younger people took part in the yard committee projects.
One woman's ideal was that the yard committee would help in forming 'this
big family within us who live in the yard' (in camera Witness 23, Z1676–96).
Strangers would immediately be recognised and in times of crisis yard
members would blow whistles to alert members of the yard.

But this building upon existing social ties and networks, it could be argued,
rendered the yard committees more powerful, and thus more capable of
providing a sustained resource to challenge the state. Certainly that is how
they were perceived by the state (although this was denied vigorously by the
defence) (A. Sebola, Z2848).

Block and street committees were intended to be the next stages up from
yard committees, and to be constituted by representatives, and some indeed
did exist.[15] However they both appear to have had less resonance with
ordinary people's experiences. The block committee's purpose was, said
one resident, to 'see to it that the block is kept clean and that no fights are
there, people must not fight and that at that block there must be peace' (A.
Sebola, Z2677). But block meetings also appear to have been venues at
which larger township issues were raised and funnelled down to the yard
level. At one block meeting, attended, according to Obed Bapela, by 200
people on 25 May 1986, he gave out a pamphlet indicating the issues which
were to be brought back to yard level. They included the rent boycott, the
consumer boycott, isolating the police, and bringing back or isolating
children that were attending boarding school. This appears to have been an
example where yard representatives expressed their own views quite strongly,
supporting only the rent boycott amongst all the various items, and deciding
that people's courts 'should be abolished and there should come out people
to volunteer to go and tell those people to stop the people's court' (O. Bapela,
M3965). Bapela says he went, soon after this, to the Nineteenth Avenue
court to convey the message. Street committees, too, had a similar function.

The whole system was intended to culminate in the AAC itself: *'And what, is there anything above the street committees?'* 'Yes.' *'What is that?'* That is the adult organisation ... Alexandra Action Committee' (A. Sebola, Z2712).

Mayekiso saw it as a smoothly operating matrix:

> Streets, flats, hostels, shacks and buses are organised from floor up to area committee. Representatives receive their mandate from the people via these committees. They report back after discussing the issues at hand with other committee representatives ... Major decisions are already taken concerning rent, refuse removal, peoples court, the attitude to and reintegration of the resigning councillors into the community and the redeveloping of the township. (Report on SASPU article, April–May 1986)

A DIFFERENT KIND OF DISCIPLINE?

Thus to the adults, liberation and emancipation would be achieved through discipline, order and systematic organisation. Rooted in older traditions of African nationalism, they supported and endorsed the charismatic leadership of Moses Mayekiso, and even accepted his casting of their needs into a mould taken from his experiences in the highly rationalistic black trade unions of the time – a more directly democratic style of politics compared to that of traditional African nationalism. Flowing from this, the AAC had developed very different ideas about people's courts. One observer of the rebellion believed that the AAC was entirely separate from the people's courts:

> *From your conversation did you get that impression that they were behind the people's courts?* No definitely not. Definitely not. I never got the impression that they were involved, instrumental or in any way as an Action Committee, involved in peoples courts. (R. Valente, M4227)

The AAC had in fact officially condemned corporal punishment:

> as unacceptable to the community and resolved to stop people practising this, especially at number 31, the youth grouping headquarters. There were also reports of people being lashed at the so-called peoples courts at youth quarters. The meeting raised the problem of the PC not clearly under any organisation's control, which caused some individuals to lash offenders. (Moses Mayekiso, M2973)

And Mayekiso himself was adamant that he did not believe in corporal punishment (R. Valente, M4180–1). 'I do not believe that corporal punishment can put a person right. I saw it as something that has not effect because it goes together with violence,' he said. Instead, he argued that investigations such as those in people's courts required 'trained people' (Moses Mayekiso, M2974), and he deplored the fact that courts were, he said, sometimes giving as many as ten lashes, that there were bribes involved in many cases, and how 'tsotsis became involved' (Moses Mayekiso, M2976). His ideas about discipline were derived from the notion that an alternative to the harsh 'capitalist discipline' many people experienced would be one which was more 'progressive' and 'democratic'. It would be gentle and yet firm, based upon mutual respect:

> Discipline is the way you relate to other people with a conscious under-
> standing behaviour, manners and respect ... discipline is being used to
> make some of us to accept the values and ideas of this present capitalist
> society. Therefore when one's talks of discipline people thinks of being
> shouted at, punished, etc. THE DISCIPLINE OF PROGRESSIVE
> PEOPLE DIFFERS COMPLETELY FROM THE ONES WE ARE
> EXPOSED TO TODAY. When we say we are activists or when we
> say we want to change our society and transform it to a new social
> order, we need disciplined activists who are or who will be performing
> that particular assignment. As activists we are accountable to the
> people we represents, lead and to the organisations we are building for
> them. How can then we be disciplined: 1) our behaviour in those organi-
> sations and outside them 2) how we understand our people and our
> relations to them as activists 3) how we respect their views and aspira-
> tions and encouraging them but not by condemning or discouraging
> and calling them by names that can damage their credibility.[16]

Insofar as adults supported these ideas about discipline it was probably more because of their worries (particularly amongst older men) about the overturning of age and gender hierarchies and their desire to reinstate the status quo – to restrain young people, to support men, and to keep women under control – rather than because of the existence of nuanced views on the evolution of democracy and humanism (P. Tshabalala, M3765). Even one of the AAC's officials and an accused in the Mayekiso trial, Paul Tshabalala, had felt that the Six-Day War had led to a 'loss of control':

> After the youth had taken powers into their hands, when a person goes
> to the youth to lodge a complaint they did not want to hear anything.
> They would take a person and lash him in the street. That thing seemed
> to introduce a changing life in Alexandra. (P. Tshabalala, M3759)

He did not like what the people's courts were doing. Neither did the people in the Seventh Avenue yard, who would often hear people crying as they were lashed. 'At times they would go to these boys and try to talk to them' (P. Tshabalala, M3839).

> I heard, people came there with complaints and they were taking the
> side of the person who was lodging a complaint. One would find that they,
> without asking any questions, they would just take him into the passage
> and administer corporal punishment there. (P. Tshabalala, M3767)

Youths were not the appropriate people to restore the kind of order that was required.

> The youth are not properly trained people to handle people's problems. Even if it is an adult that they must deal with problems and there should also be lashing, that was not right and that a person untrained to handle such matters would not be right. And they also had no proper administration, which would help in investigating the problems they were dealing with, and they also have no administration just like we have the courts and the police. That would not be a right thing. (Moses Mayekiso, M3677)

Claims made by AAC members at their trial that they were always and consistently vehemently opposed to and entirely separate from the youth-run courts were a little shaky – for nobody could escape the engulfing nature of youth authority. We know that individual AAC members were in fact involved in what appeared to be people's courts, and at least one court was run in their name, at Seventh Avenue. But AAC leaders insisted that they had attempted to introduce less punitive notions of control than those emerging in the people's courts that 'flogged' (R. Valente, M4180–1), claiming that they based their strategy upon their rationalistic conception of discipline. We know that they did try to stop youth courts after what Richard Mdakane called 'the decision of the entire community that the people's court must be closed' in June 1986.[17] This they found difficult (R. Mdakane, M2629).

> It is difficult to stop what you did not start, because these people's courts were started spontaneously by the youth, which caused that even after sending the people to go and talk to them, they came back telling us that the people are not prepared to stop it.

Several members of the AAC were heavily involved in what appeared to be people's courts – some of them women. Besides the well-known figure of Sarah Mthembu, discussed earlier, Mapule Morare, for example, 'used to help' in the courts (R. Mdakane, M2519). But the AAC was at pains to make a distinction between their own courts, which they called 'mediation courts' and the more violent ones run by the comrades. Thus quite early on Mthembu began to hold counselling/mediation sessions in her own house, away from the goings-on in the shack – her home was to become the more stable 'helpful' Alexandra Action Committee-run 'mediation' court (R. Mdakane, M2194). At Seventh Avenue, there were actually two courts – one 'mediation' court in the main house, and a second 'people's court' – also called the 'sjambok court' – in the shack outside. In the mediation court people were encouraged, said Mayekiso, 'to come together and discuss their problems', and corporal punishment was not used. (But later we shall see how Paul Tshabalala, an adult and senior member of the AAC, did indeed recommend lashes.)

The Seventh Avenue mediation court was far more respectable than the sjambok court in the *makhukhu*. If not formally run by the Alexandra Action Committee (an allegation which was strongly denied in the Mayekiso trial), it was at least run by people close to it or members of it, and strongly influenced by the Mayekiso organisation whose roots lay in trade union rationality. It tried to emphasise good governance for the township, self-discipline and rehabilitation of the fallen. The mediation court only met in the evenings as the adults who ran it worked. (The 'shack' court met all day, as it was run by unemployed youths.) Mayekiso's vision was that the mediation courts would mesh with the yard system. Yard reps saw their duties as 'to solve other peoples troubles like when people were fighting we had to settle that dispute' (*in camera* Witness 23, Z1678–9). One yard rep said that if this failed 'the matter would be referred to the higher committee, the street committee'. Those premises which did not have reps had to be visited. 'We were given addresses of those places and we went there … in order to find out why those people did not attend the meeting … We were told that if we get those reasons we should take them to the Headquarters' at 15th Avenue.' They went there and found 'schoolboys'. They wrote the reasons down: 'One of them was that the people in a particular yard were scared to elect a rep as one of the women there had a relationship with a policeman and they were scared she would tell him. He reported some others too – complaints from the yard. Theft, collaborators, and so on' (R. Mdakane, 2521).

A hierarchy of courts was envisaged:

> There are little courts and central courts. Each yard has a committee which deals with its own problems. If that Committee cannot solve the problem it is taken to the block committees. If it cannot be solved there it is taken to the street committee and then to the Action committee. All these committees are acting as courts. People at the central court are delegated to receive complaints and to mediate. We are not really acting in the same manner as the present courts. We would like people to come together and discuss their problems. (*South African Metal Worker*, 3 June 1986: 139)[18]

Here, as in the youth courts, the participation of women was not surprising. Women liked the courts because they helped defend them against absconding or drunken husbands.

> It is that the women were getting help when their men were no longer giving them money or supporting their children, and that when they sleep out at places where they liked, the women used to go to the people's court and the people they find at the people's court were able to help them. (R. Mdakane, M2521)

What were the sentences? The ideal was non-violent:

> In Alexandra this is problematic, because how do you sentence a person? We do not believe in corporal punishment, but we have been lucky because people listen to whatever decision is made there. If the person listens then we don't need to implement any punishment. (Moses Mayekiso, M3068–9)

But courts soon came up against the problem of non-compliance with the gentler persuasive methods used:

> We have been discussing punishment for the person that does not listen, but we haven't reached a solution. However, the 'necklace' will never be used because we believe that the courts have an educational function. They are there to politicise the offender. Most crime in the area is caused by the capitalist and apartheid systems, so we tell the offender that he mustn't allow himself to be used by them. (ibid.)

Sometimes attempts were made to punish through shaming the guilty:

> Our method of punishment in our committee system is bringing to the notice of the person that the people are looking at him in the yard or by the committee, as well as the block. The mere fact that he is taken to the block or yard committee and face people with the filth he had committed, that thing would embarrass him. That would serve as a sort of a punishment, as well as that isolation. If he no longer wants to listen he must be isolated in the yard or in the block. (ibid.)

But the mediation courts were not entirely non-violent, and many AAC members did in fact participate in violence, although perhaps with less sanctioning from their leaders. 'When they [the men] are fetched,' said one participant, 'at times they are to get a little lashing' (R. Mdakane, M2521). And Mapule Morare, an AAC executive member, actually lived in the same yard as Sarah Mthembu, and would go and try to prevent 'too many' lashes being given (Moses Mayekiso, M2978).

The mediation court had nine or ten 'high school note books' in which records were taken, and these, too, seem to belie claims of consistent non-violence. In one case, presided over by two leading AAC members, five 'heavy' lashings were prescribed as punishment (R. Mdakane, M2633). Thus when Paul Leropile was brought before magistrate Paul Tshabalala by his neighbour Frieda Majadibodo, the notebook recorded that he had been 'lashed', for 'ungentlemanly conduct'. Leropile had, said Frieda, called her a witch and struck her with 'a rim and a brake', injuring her hand and foot. Leropile denied having hit her, but Majadibodo was both adamant that she had been injured, and insistent that the court do something about it, preferably something in the way of corporal punishment. She:

> stood up. She was shouting and insisting that he had assaulted her. She further said … we are doing nothing. 'I will look for better people

who will kill him'. We tried to convince her not to think of such things. We realised that she is not going to be dissuaded from her stand. (P. Tshabalala, M3772)

But according to the AAC, the recorded lashings were a ploy, to satisfy Frieda's lust for physical punishment and to prevent her from trying to get the accused killed at the more dangerous shack, and in fact the accused was never actually lashed:

> We decided to get into the house and have it written that this man must be lashed ... We wrote it down in the presence of Frieda and we signed and we said we will deal with him. She was hesitant and did not want to go. She wanted to see to herself when this person was lashed. We told her that she will not be able to see that, because it is a man and she is not supposed to see his buttocks. (ibid.)

The vengeful motivations of women such as Frieda may in other words, have been sidestepped, if this is true.

Paul Tshabalala described some of the cases in which he attempted to mediate, and it appears that the temptation to resort to corporal punishment may have grown when it became clear over numerous mediation sessions that courts without sanctions were powerless. When one complainant said her husband had tried to 'chop her with an axe', that he was perpetually drunk, unemployed, and did nothing in the house while she was at work all day, Paul simply 'recommended' that the man should stop drinking and that the woman should try to be more tolerant. We have no further records of this case, but common sense would suggest that compliance with these instructions was probably minimal. When a complaint was made that two 'groups of youths were fighting' with 'golf sticks and pangas' Paul 'found out the root of the story' and 'dealt with it in a way that prevented the two groups from killing each other' (P. Tshabalala, M3740–4). But how sustainable was such an approach over time? In one case of which we have a reasonable record, described in Moses Mayekiso's trial by *in camera* Witness 10, the parties returned numerous times to the court and appear never to have resolved the matter. This witness sheds some light on how the mediation court actually worked. It appears to have been similar in form and structure to the sjambok court, but with a gentler tone and a more peripheral presence of threatening young men.

He said he and his wife had marital problems because 'she used Bantu medicine and he did not'. He said that she had brought their problems to the attention of the court and one day he received a note which read: 'Please report at 31 Seventh Avenue on Thursday 10-4-86 at 6 pm in connection with your wife's belongings.'[19] He got a 'fright' and went to the police, who said they had not called me and I had to go to the address shown. He went, and:

> found many people in the yard ... I approached a person and told him

that I had been called there ... He showed me a hut built of corrugated iron and told me that I should go in there ... When I entered I found people seated on benches. There was candle light burning inside and I found my wife present. I found a girl whose age I estimated to be 18 or 19. She was the one who was asking us questions like a magistrate. (*in camera* Witness 10, M431–2)

He and his wife 'were asked as to the cause of our quarrel' and we were later told that 'we must go and live together as man and wife again' (ibid.). They did not agree and did not move back together. Then 'they' again came to his house and called him to the court again. His wife was there again. 'This time I found an older woman who also questioned me like a magistrate ... We were asked why do I not make it up with my wife ... My wife then came back for three days and left again.' They called him a third time, and this time his trial was presided over by an older male 'magistrate'. Again they told the wife to go back to the house. She refused (*in camera* Witness 10, M433–4). The younger boys present said 'they had sjamboks and said if I do not reconcile with my wife should it be found that I was at fault I would have received a hiding.' But he said he:

no longer had the wish [to reconcile] because she had been using what I do not use, but I was scared of these boys ... She had previously told me she would go to them and they would come and lash me. She was using medicines, witchcraft. I did not like it in my house. I do not use this stuff. (*in camera* Witness 10, M437)

No resolution to this case was recorded, and certainly no mention of physical punishment was made.

Paul Tshabalala's description made the mediation court appear more like a marital and personal counselling session. One day he went to Sarah Mthembu's home (not the shack on the same property). Most of the people present seem to have been women:

I went to house in her lounge. I found people there, about four. They were seated in a divided room. In the lounge there were three women. I went there and Sarah introduced me to them. There was another woman there, there was a coloured woman who was talking a lot there. Sarah introduced her to me. They then ordered us to sit down, myself and Fana Twala. She then said to this woman she must relate the problem with which she had come. This woman then said she had a complaint. Her husband refuses her sex, but he gives her money and maintains the children ... the counselling she received was from the coloured woman. She said, seeing that things are like this, we can see that there is a problem and suggested that she goes back and discuss the matter thoroughly with her husband. If there is still a problem she would volunteer and go to their house. (P. Tshabalala, M3751–2)

He would visit the house frequently, hearing mainly marriage and house-hold cases, mediating quarrels and giving advice. Most complainants were women, and many complaints were about men's failure to pay mainten-ance: 'a woman would come and say the man does not bring money at home'; and Sarah would deal with the 'bedroom problems'. There were quarrels between girlfriend and boyfriend; or between neighbours in a yard. One complainant, a man, wanted to divorce his wife and force a young lodger to leave his home, because the lodger was 'unemployed, does not work and he smokes dagga and he has seduced the daughter of a neighbour'. But his wife said it was the husband who was at fault, and that he just 'wants to have sex with my child'. The mediation, run by Tshabalala, consisted of:

> telling them about how important responsibilities are. We told him that if he chased the child out of the house and finds him dead in the street, although it is not his own child, but it comes to the same that he is his child, and we asked him to give him a chance ... [he] ... did try and he freed his heart ... I told him that divorce is not anything that can build our community. (P. Tshabalala, M3776)

In another case, one Johanna had had a love affair with Mr T., the husband of one Margaret. Tshabalala was clear that this kind of behaviour was unacceptable and spoke harshly to Mr T.:

> These were the things that I wanted to put right. Many of the corpses in Alexandra are caused by the extra-marital behaviour of men and wives. I regarded that as serious, because it might bring in many things ... After our discussions with him T. realised that what we were saying was true. T. then said we must have it written down in order to make sure that he will no longer go to Johanna and Johanna must also have it written that she will no longer come to him. (P. Tshabalala, M3779)

Unlike the trials in the sjambok courts, these sessions appear to have been far less theatrical, ritualised and procedural, although Sarah appeared to be playing a leading role, and would sometimes take notes. In spite of the fact that he considered it his responsibility to hear so many cases from women, Tshabalala's notions were, as we have seen, fairly patriarchal. The media-tion court appears to have concentrated on getting 'both sides of the story' and requiring the complainants to be 'more reasonable' – a quite different approach from that of the youths, who would often take the side of the women against the men, and subject the men to brutal beatings.

CONCLUSION

The adults had a certain romanticism in their view. But their Utopia would be a modest, local one – life in their township would be made better; disrupted social relations would be restored. On a broader scale, the evils of apartheid would be ended but more as a result of the moral force of the justness of their cause than of any clear strategy (leaders, of course, had a greater vision of this, and believed that the sum of numerous local insurrections would overturn the state). Within Alexandra, these ends were to be achieved through reorganising the space of Alexandra in a way designed to promote a local democracy, in which all of the poor residents would have a say in their own daily lives and a means of rectifying their problems.

The function of the AAC would be to co-ordinate the affairs of the township and to deal with its political and social problems. Like the comrades, these activists drew upon the ideas of the burgeoning left-wing culture of the time – with its varying and various discourses of non-racialism, trade unionism, feminism, Marxism, democracy, and answerability – but their style was practical rather than utopian or theatrical, peaceful rather than violent, patient rather than impulsive, seeking to mobilise around people's experiences rather than their own moral outrage, and participatory rather than tyrannical. The ideas of respectability, which had long prevailed amongst the older generation, permeated their culture even as they rebelled.

Significant as these developments were for the possible evolution of a democratic culture, authoritarianism was far from absent. Democratic participation at grassroots level did not preclude a powerful impulse towards organisational centralism at the top. Instead of gang-like violence and the rule of fear, these leaders promulgated an ideology of consensus, but ensured their own hegemony within it.

The adults worried about and tried to control the 'indiscipline' of the youth. Like the youth, they sought to impose a spatial template upon the township, but theirs was based upon the yards, blocks and streets within which ordinary residents' experiences of life were located. Like the youth, they created courts as an aid to reforming the perceived decadence of the culture of the township – but adults remained in charge within them, and their methods were conciliatory rather than punitive.

The two forms of mobilisation – millenarian and rationalist – overlapped in the messy reality of day-to-day politics, of course. Some participants in the world of 'adults' were in fact extremely young. Youth experiences of organising and mobilising were brought to bear in adult groupings. At times the two kinds of people's courts were hardly distinguishable. Adult ideas of yard, block and street organising were rapidly appropriated by youths. Furthermore adult leaders, in their search for a centralised consensus, incorporated and tried to tame youth initiatives through repeated attempts at forging structural unity between the disparate interest groups of youths, adults, men, women, school pupils and others that had emerged in Alexandra during the previous few years. They were, for a short while, successful.

9

NATIONALISM AND THEATRICALITY

A funeral seemed to be a bioscope in Alexandra. People used just to attend when any person has died ... when people see a funeral they just come in big numbers. When they see people go in a certain direction for a funeral they just go there. (P. Tshabalala, M3877)

I think, according to what I saw, people were mobilised by the Six-Day War. Like myself, I used not to attend funerals. Thereafter I started attending funerals, even uninvited. (P. Tshabalala, M3878)

An overarching, more universal narrative overlay the more parochial activities of youths and adults who were attempting to construct their own Utopias. In fact to the South African and even international public, much of what youths and adults were doing remained hidden – confined to the private world of the township – except for the occasional report of a spectacular act. What outsiders saw instead was the enacting of a more public struggle the power of which resided in the fact that it spoke directly to the state and to 'history', and appealed to the narratives of suffering and emancipation in universalistic terms, using street theatre in an overt manner and encouraging the development of an ever larger audience. Nationalism provided the central organising storyline for this display. Building upon the national and international ideas of modernist emancipation from racism and colonial oppression, it sought to present townships as symbolic spaces from which an undifferentiated mass of the suffering and the helpless deserved to be liberated.

African nationalism appears at first glance to have little in common with the first nationalisms – those in Europe – in which language, religion, literacy, territory and/or ethnicity played a constitutive role. It is usually viewed as a reactive form of political movement, developed in response to the 'outside' forces of colonialism rather than processes internal to the societies in which it emerged, and thus unable to sustain itself beyond the immediate post-colonial period. However African nationalism in South Africa may represent an exception to this. Its deep historical and popular roots and its multiple ideological and cultural resources have rendered it a powerful and unifying force with the potential to survive beyond the moment of liberation.

In order to engage with popular consciousness and to make a legitimate public case, nationalism needs to provide a convincing narrative formulation of what the 'nation' is, where it came from and where it is going. Unable to resort to the ethnic romances or religious legends which underlie many other nationalisms, African nationalists have variously identified the nation as synonymous with other things. One is 'blackness', a quality said to be innate but requiring purification and emancipation from white contamination and control (as in Black Consciousness and Black Power movements). Another is a primordial 'innocence', which requires liberation from modernity's corrupting influence (as in Africanist movements). A third is 'martyrdom', which is said to lead to a suppressed and barely contained anger, and which requires violent retribution (as in militaristic revolutionary movements, often with a Fanonist influence). Another is 'rightlessness' (as in most anti-colonial franchise-based movements), and another 'populism', in which large and intractable forces (the state, money, Jews, whites) control and manipulate the small man and must be brought down (also present in anti-colonial movements). All of these major themes, and more, were present in the South African struggles in the 1980s, sometimes overlapping, sometimes in conflict, and to varying degrees. Most of them survive today.

Thus the broad patterns of African nationalism did not portray the world of experience in monolithic terms, but contained within them multiple sets of ideas and visions. Furthermore, each of these discourses manifested itself in different political and social institutions and patterns of behaviour. The still-banned ANC presented the emerging struggle of the 1980s to the people it was attempting to mobilise (as distinct from those it was trying, say, to lobby in the United Nations). We have already shown in Chapter Five how, out of the public gaze and in its illegal publications, the ANC itself used the rhetoric of revolution, with its chief motif being that of the 'people', whom it claimed to embody, in struggle against the immoral 'regime'. In its clandestine publications it called for 'People's power: struggles against dummy institutions' (*Mayibuye*, 9 September 1984), casting the struggle as a 'people's war' in which the 'regime' was 'pinned against the wall'. Within this binary relationship of people versus regime, townships were the cauldron of revolutionary creativity. Alexandra's struggle was portrayed as part of this: 'The people of Alexandra have demonstrated for an end to police repression, and the whole town became a no-go Zone in march for the funeral of those shot by police,' said *Sechaba*, while the townships as a whole were said to be establishing 'emerging embryonic forms of self government and popular power, and the creation of people's committees'. There was an apocalyptic aspect to the ANC's way of portraying events. The townships now had no-go areas, and apartheid was becoming 'unworkable', as 'the country is rapidly degenerating into a state of complete ungovernability'.

people's courts and street committee systems constituted 'a peculiar form of dual power', in which 'organs of self-government and popular power' were 'challenging the apartheid authorities for control of these areas. These should be transformed into mass revolutionary bases, through which we can realise our strategy of people's war' (*Sechaba*, April 1986).

ANC ideologues did not claim credit for the tactics used by the youth, but reinterpreted youth resistance in revolutionary terms (R. Kasrils, *Sechaba*, May 1986). The people's 'improvised tactics', they said, included barricades; trenches; barbed wire; tactical street fighting; people using the labyrinth of township lanes and streets to lure the enemy into ambush; petrol bombs; knives; using the enemy's own weapons against them; and what they called 'rough justice' against community councillors and informers.[1]

Powerful and reassuring as these ideas might have been to the youths reading them or listening to Radio Freedom in secret, they did not provide an obvious means of facilitating mass mobilisation. This was instead provided by another manifestation of nationalism – the ideas about protest, many cast in nationalistic terms, and long suppressed by apartheid laws, which had revived in the climate of National Party 'reform'. This version emerged particularly after the establishment in 1983 of the lawful United Democratic Front (which was effectively a front, but one with its own social roots and momentum, for the still-banned ANC). Instead of using apocalyptic rhetoric, the UDF portrayed its struggle as a far more 'morally serious' one, incorporating religious liturgy and symbolism and older more sober ANC ideas, such non-racialism as well as those embodied in the 'Freedom Charter'. This lent the name 'charterism' to the UDF ideology, which launched a bid for 'human rights' within an emancipatory framework. The distinction between the two forms of framing of nationalism – the apocalyptic and the emancipatory – was a significant aspect of the mobilising capacity of this era. In UDF vocabulary, articulated by Aubrey Mokoena, prominent UDF activist and former Black Consciousness leader, the struggle required that people:

> remember our leaders on Robben Island and we must pray, but when we pray we must not do so like the missionaries who said we must close our eyes while they pull the land from under our feet. I would like to call upon you to pray like revolutionaries with your eyes wide open because I believe we can never win the struggle unless God is amongst us. (Lodge and Nasson 1991: 50)

At one UDF meeting at Soweto's largest church, 5,000 people stood and repeated the Freedom Charter after Tiego Moseneke, black student leader, as though it were the liturgy. The Reverend Allan Boesak's rhetoric was, unsurprisingly, rooted in Christianity, but called for 'rights': 'We want all our rights, we want them here and we want them now,' he said (Lodge and

Nasson 1991: 48). Frances Baard, an older activist, said that one of the early
UDF rallies reminded her 'of a song we used to sing at school – it was "land
of hope and glory, mother of the peace"'. Archie Gumede said he was
inspired by Moses who 'led the children out of Egypt ... there is simply no
reason why the people of South Africa cannot move out of the apartheid
state into a state in which all shall be free and the people shall govern'
(Lodge and Nasson 1991: 48–9).

UDF, religious and other leaders from within and outside the township
saw their constituency in this case as the 'mass' of the people, whose human
and civil rights had never existed, or had been removed, or 'trampled upon'.
Their ideology proved eminently suited to mobilising this mass – much
more so than the clandestine ideas of the ANC itself. Using the technique of
constructing a front out of multiple existing organisations, the UDF grew
rapidly and successfully plied the path between legality and the taste of
illicitness which was required to attract militants amongst the youth. Five
hundred and sixty-five youth, student, worker, civic, women's, religious and
political organisations attended its first launching rally, and over the next
four years it grew rapidly. Whereas in late 1983, writes Seekings, there were
fewer than fifty youth organisations affiliated to the UDF, few of them with
a membership higher than 100, by mid-1987 the UDF youth 'umbrella'
SAYCO was:

> claiming 1,200 local affiliates, with a signed-up membership of over
> half-a-million, and a support base of two million ... Even taking account
> of considerable exaggeration, there was clearly a massive growth in
> terms of both organisations and membership. (Seekings 1991a: 41–2)

Although Seekings argues elsewhere that the 'triumph of charterism'
occurred as early as 1983–4, when he suggests it achieved dominance in
oppositional politics, this is perhaps a little early. Certainly in Alex other
forces prevailed for a while longer, at least parallel to and at times overlapping with 'charterism' (Seekings 1991a: 185ff). Perhaps what is important to focus on here is not the organisational prominence of the UDF but
whether its nationalist and emancipatory rhetoric captured the mass ethos
within individual townships. This took a little longer, and entailed a
complex process.

THE NATION ON STAGE

The broad themes adopted by social movement organisations require much
more nuanced interpretations by nationalist ideologues and mobilisers if
they are to speak to the mass of the people. In Alexandra the skill required
was to translate the master narratives of nationalism as a whole into more
detailed tales of life as it had been experienced by the residents themselves;
while at the same time to give them a universally recognisable character.

One symbolic means through which this was done entailed the metaphorical portrayal of the township – and by extension the nation itself – as a 'family' living out a tragic drama.

The family's parents were virtuous, hard-working and hard done by. The children were wayward and undisciplined. The tragedy consisted in the family's persecution from without. Its children were killed; its elders mourned them. Its defenders were the forces of moral good – the church, older patriarchs and matriarchs. Its worth was sustained through its nobility in suffering.

This tragedy was enacted on the public 'stage', through the use of street theatre. Earlier it was suggested that very few urban settings lent themselves to political theatre in South Africa, but the mid-1980s proved to be an exception. Like the comrades in the people's courts, the mass of Alexandrans usurped an unquestionably acceptable ceremonial ritual – in this case the funeral – and turned it into political theatre. This involved huge numbers of Alex residents, and the concomitant use of space in a much more flowing and public way than had, for example, been the case in student protests, bus boycotts or other mobilising tactics. The ritualised and newly transformed spaces evolved during the Six-Day War were consolidated as such. New ideas as to how to handle and control space were developed, and the AAC spatial strategy outlined above was mobilised to an extraordinary extent, not only consciously 'from above', but also as a result of more spontaneous expressions of anger by the general population. A new type of crowd emerged – a larger one, more subject to ritualised control, and more predictable in its behaviour. The interplay between this crowd and the media stimulated it to develop and behave in ways designed to communicate to an increasingly national and international public as well as to its own constituency.

We know that during the evolution of this vision, youths were highly visible: 'They were everywhere.' The atmosphere was extremely tense, with police and youths treating each other as enemies; the central protagonists in the emerging drama (P. B. Botha, Z294–301). As more youngsters and activists were killed, the emerging sense of a commonality of suffering, located within the compact 'space' of Alex, and mobilised through the use of that space, contributed greatly to the period of consolidation of the upheavals originally caused by the Six-Day War.

The street theatre reached its epitome in the ritual of the funeral, which grew in scale and meaning as more deaths occurred. Massive spaces came to be used to hold enormous funeral ceremonies. On 4 and 5 March 25,000 attended the night vigil and 40,000 the 'Mass Funeral' respectively of residents killed in the Six-Day War, held in the stadium, now the actual and symbolic centre of the township, and at individual churches. This represented a substantial portion of the whole township, and the occasions

marked the beginnings of community mobilisation on a scale never seen
before. At least thirteen funerals or other ceremonies perceived by residents
as having a community significance, were held between January and June.
In the period February to April were included five major meetings attended
by substantial numbers of the entire population of Alexandra. Funerals
became a regularised part of township life, expressing a particular kind of
'community grief':

> *Now was it also traditional to hold funeral services in the stadium?* Yes it
> was traditional because I remember I think it was in 1979 or 1980
> where the late Jakes Nkosi, his service was held at the stadium. *Well,*
> *was everybody's service who had died held at the stadium or only certain*
> *people?* I can say certain people. *What type of people would have a service*
> *at the stadium?* As I have given an example of Jakes Nkosi, as he was
> well known in the township. *Yes, was it then the funerals of people who*
> *were well known?* Yes. *And when a funeral service was held at the stadium,*
> *in the township would it be regarded as something of importance to the*
> *community?* Yes, that is so. (A. Sebola, Z2544)

Political funerals were, it has been argued elsewhere, vital for mobilisation in townships, for they: 'provided the opportunity for ideological mobilisation and the redefinition of township politics through the integration of
local struggles into national politics' (Seekings 1990: 277). Their religious
core and justification provided a legitimate link between the parochial and
the national. They were presided over by national political and church
leaders. They gave the events a 'wider political and moral significance' as
well as a Christian meaning in many cases. Activists from other townships
attended; and they were rallies, with 'freedom songs, slogans, colours and
other symbols of the liberation struggle and more particularly the banned
ANC'. Funerals brought 'national political struggles and the ANC into
township politics more effectively than national political organisations ever
had in the past' (Seekings 1991a: 277). The streets of townships were
redefined, with use of oppositional flags and symbols, freedom songs, poetry,
speeches, music and symbolically important figures within them – and this
time with the passion that came of public and widespread grief at death, or
in many cases the murders of activists.

Each funeral, march or mass meeting expressed the narrative of the
township as innocent and persecuted family within a nation seeking
emancipation and rights, and there follows an analysis of the dramaturgical
processes through which this was achieved. Achieving dramaturgical power
does not happen by accident and in the case of Alexandran funerals many
different means were used to create political theatre out of political tragedy
and to translate the varied emotions of grief, anger, revolutionary passion,
or even apathy into public and theatrical means of communicating power.

Table 9: Funerals, ceremonies and mass meetings in Alexandra during the rebellion

Date	Reason	Night vigil	Venue and subsequent action	Estimated numbers	Main speakers	Police action
Not certain	Funeral of MK Cadre Vincent Tshabalala					
11 January	Funeral of Richard Padi		Followed by riots			
15 February	Funeral of Michael Diradeng	Diradeng yard	Stadium plus march	10,000	Mayekiso, Theresa, 'Moeder', Michael's brother	Teargas, bullets
15 February	Funeral of Jerry Kanaka, Apla Guerilla					
18 February	Community protest at killings in Six-Day War		Stadium plus march	30,000	Tutu, Mogoba, M. Buthelezi	Calm
21 February	Report-back on meeting with Government from Tutu		Stadium	40,000–45,000	Tutu	Calm
5 March	Mass funeral for 17 killed in Six-Day War	Home, churches and stadium	Stadium plus march	30,000	Mkhatshwa, Boesak, Naude, A. Sisulu, Chikane Speech of W. Mandela read	Rioting
15 March	Second funeral for additional 3 or 4 killed in Six-Day War					
4 April	Funeral for anonymous boy	Yard	Yard and streets	1,000–9,000(?)		Calm
23 April	Mass meeting after vigilante attack		Stadium plus march			
17 May	Mass funeral for victims of vigilante attack	Churches	Stadium	Stadium full		
18 May	Ceremony by whites		Streets and cemetery	250–1,000		
21 June	Funeral of Jacob Mabisela					
28 June	Funeral of 'Jingles'					

Other analysts in other contexts have pointed to the processes of: 'Formulating roles and characterizations, managing performance regions, controlling information, sustaining dramatic tensions and orchestrating emotions' (Benford and Hunt 1992: 37).

Protagonists and antagonists compete 'to affect audiences' interpretations of power relations'. Scripts need to be written, *dramatis personae* developed, dialogue constructed and direction given. Props are used, acting techniques employed, elaborate staging planned, including complex backstage directions; and actual performances given. Furthermore, in order for political theatre to be sustainable and effective, those taking part must be convinced of the necessity for 'dramaturgical loyalty' – an allegiance to the defined goals of the performance and the movement of which it is a part. People who 'over-act'; who 'break ranks' by performing outside of the agreed script; who parody the performance; or who misperceive or misuse the nature of the occasion, must be 'disciplined' in order to sustain a unified image. Because scripts are sketchy and political theatre depends on the participation of large numbers of ordinary people without formal scripts themselves, a great deal of weight must be placed on the interpretive capacities of those at centre stage. Skilled political performers need to be placed at the forefront of the show; people who are capable of a sophisticated interpretation of symbols and events, and who can adapt their performance according to the requirements of the occasion in order to keep dramaturgical loyalty intact. And of course interpretive work is important:

> [it] identifies who had and who lacks power, portrays how it is wielded, presents an alternative vision of power arrangements and articulates how such transformations might be realised. Movement interpretive work thus stimulates audiences to redefine their situations as unjust and mutable so that existing power structures can be altered. (Benford and Hunt 1992: 48)

Good interpreters resemble Gramsci's 'organic intellectuals', because they can ensure that the performance is congruent with the experiences of the audience and its cultural heritage.

THE PLANNING OF PERFORMANCE

Youths, adults, nationalists and other leaders spent a great deal of effort in ensuring that the funerals and mass meetings of this period in Alexandra were effective dramatic performances, each organising group contributing its own vision of what would constitute effectiveness. To youths, the martyrdom of the young must be the predominant theme, and these martyrs must be defined as the children of the township as a whole, rather than those of individual families. Most of the families concerned did not hesitate to adopt this redefinition of their dead as 'children of the township'. But in some cases youths compelled families to bury their dead at the communal funerals – even where those concerned had not actually died in the struggle. For example, Joseph Meyers had died during the Six-Day War but had not in fact been killed by police.[2] His family wanted to bury him privately, but the comrades told his brother that they should not do so or they would 'burn their house'. 'We must make it one mass funeral, one burial, with everybody buried that day. They said he was a soldier; he must be buried together with the soldiers' (*in camera* Witness 21, Z1557ff). The comrades even put the name of Johanna Hlubi – who had been necklaced by a mob of Alexandrans – down for burial at the first mass funeral, but she was in fact buried later, by her family.

The comrades also wanted funerals and meetings to display the community of Alexandra as united in grief – another variation on the theme of township as a family whose children had been martyred. To this end they marshalled the people to the stadium using a combination of encouragement and coercion.

To most, the public and theatrical nature of the funerals and mass meetings provided a most acceptable and desirable means of expressing their shock and grief. To others, persuasion was necessary. Cars with megaphones would travel the streets before each event, calling upon people to attend: 'We were told we have to attend because people had died and we cannot throw our hands, wave them away with our hands ... we blacks must not disregard one another. That is why I went' (R. Mathibela, M966).

Some felt that they had been forced by sjambok-wielding comrades to attend – yet another inversion of generational authority. One policeman claimed that he saw a great deal of coercion being used: people were 'forced to go to the stadium. They did not come voluntarily ... I saw people walking in a crowd, being followed by others, driving them' (M. Nxumalo, M248). And one resident said of the May funeral: 'They [the comrades] woke us up and took us out of the house and said we must go to the funeral ... They were going about saying: come out, come out of the houses, come out of the houses, and they had sjamboks ... they also had pangas' (J. Nkuna, M452).

Adults had a different vision of how the drama of each event should be constructed. In keeping with their 'bureaucratic rationality' and emphasis upon organisational answerability, and their concerns about youth 'excess' and violence, they set up 'organising committees', sub-committees and coalitions in advance of each large meeting. In the case of the 5 March funeral, the organising committee – the 'Mass Funeral Committee' – included 'well-known community leaders and priests'(Black Lawyers' Association 1986) and a range of very local organisations.[3] One of the purposes of this kind of committee structure was to ensure the legality of the funeral. A delegation of respected clerics and community leaders approached government authorities and obtained permission. The conditions set by the authorities showed that they knew perfectly well what the theatrical power of such an occasion would be, and they stipulated that only ordained ministers would be allowed to speak, that there must be no banners or singing of freedom songs, and that coffins should not be carried on people's shoulders, but conveyed in vehicles (*The Sowetan*, 5 March 1986).

The organising committee worked within these restrictions to develop a planned, set ritual, to place what they thought of as appropriate figurehead speakers at the centre of attention, and to cast township grief in the mould of dignified passive resistance already implicit in UDF discourse. Pamphlets were printed, T-shirts made, marshalls appointed, funds collected and the ceremonial order planned.[4] The committee was particularly astute in making sure that the 'audience' for the theatrical occasion would be international as well as local and national. Speakers were to include the Reverend Allen Boesak, presidents of the World Alliance of Reformed Churches; the Reverend Beyers Naude, the general secretary of the South African Council of Churches; UDF president Albertina Sisulu; COSATU president Elijah Barayi; and UDF executive chairman, Curnick Ndlovu. Foreign embassies would also be sending delegations (*The Citizen*, 3 March 1986). There was a ban on the media, which was a difficult one to cope with – theatrical occasions such as these require public acknowledgement and often only attain a 'reality' when they are reported on in ways that reflect their intentions. Nevertheless, verbal reporting was not banned, and the organisers would have to be content with that.

A second funeral organising committee or 'crisis committee' was formed for the May mass funeral. A similar range of organisations came together, and an elaborate series of sub-committees (a media committee, catering committee, finance committee, burial committee and marshals' committee), was created, indicating a growing sophistication in the management of public drama (O. Bapela, M3953). The committee opened its own office and bank account, planned distinctive T-shirts for marshals, purchased groceries for each bereaved family, elicited the help of white sympathisers, and negotiated with the authorities, with undertakers and a variety of other groupings (O. Bapela, M3954–6). Funerals and mass meetings were planned in detail. Night vigils were organised for each funeral, and provision made for processions through the street, and ultimately to the cemetery. Buckets of water were strategically placed in the streets (instead of at the deceased's home) so that the large numbers of people could wash their hands after the burial, as was traditional; and plans for the dispersal of crowds thought through.

The police and the army were as much part of the theatrical performance as were the mass of people (indeed funerals consisted of what Canetti might call a 'double crowd' where both sides are important) and their leaders made their own spatial and theatrical decisions accordingly. After the first mass funeral, for example, army authorities immediately moved to close down the use of the stadium as a venue for mass meetings:

> Yes, we saw within days of the first funeral, early in this whole problem period, that this was the place where mass meetings were and from where they emerged to commit all sorts of deeds afterwards, like throwing petrol bombs, attacking people, hijacking and so on. So we occupied the place 24 hours a day with a force. (Colonel Holland Muter, M712)

In fact army strategy was not directly repressive, and they often withdrew to the periphery of the township for funerals and mass meetings, concentrating on containing these occasions rather than stopping them.[5] In preparation for the 5 March mass funeral, army personnel had reconnoitred the situation the previous day from high ground surrounding the township, using binoculars, telescopes and a television camera, and decided to form a cordon around the township, with certain single vehicles being located inside, but not to place any soldiers in the stadium itself or around it (Colonel Holland Muter, M701). This mass funeral went off peacefully (*The Citizen*, 6 March 1986).

Journalist Jon Qwelane described the 17 May funeral, for which the army appears to have planned a more interventionist role:

> The security forces were in Casspirs, armoured personnel carriers and trucks, and also on horseback. They kept a close watch on the funeral of eight youths who had died in the night raids by masked men. Each coffin was draped in the flag of the outlawed ANC and the procession followed two youths who carried a large flag of the organisation. Thousands of people jogged to the cemetery where they found a long line of policemen and soldiers standing on mounds of earth overlooking the graveside. Mounted soldiers were nearby, and many police and SADF vehicles were in positions around the troubled township. (Jon Qwelane, *Sunday Star*, 18 May 1986)

The police, as we have seen, had always been more interventionist than the army, and this was to continue here too. On one occasion they clearly indicated that they, too, were aware of the power contained in theatre – they approached some of the bereaved families to dissuade them from having their children buried 'in a group', in a 'mass funeral'. On another they tried to scupper plans for a mass funeral by removing the bodies concerned:

> Eleven corpses, victims of the unrest, had disappeared from the Government mortuary, leaving only two to be buried at the planned second mass funeral. The Alex Funeral Coordinating Committee believes that the bodies may have been taken to prevent a repeat of the first funeral held ten days ago at which 17 victims were buried and which was attended by some 60,000 people. (*City Press*, 16 March 1986)

It is possible that the police encouraged mortuary attendants to give the bodies to the families for individual funerals. Certainly that was widely believed at the time and rumours of this type of behaviour were repeated at more than one funeral.

NIGHT VIGILS

Each funeral was preceded by the traditional night vigil, which became part of the build-up to the climactic event of the funeral itself. They were not publicly theatrical but their religious significance for those taking part lent them a considerable aura, while they provided an opportunity for the symbols and rituals which were to be used in the next day's events to be rehearsed, and for popular emotions to be captured and channelled. There were reports of youths compelling residents to attend and remain at the vigils all night, and some substantial mobilising techniques were used in one case, in which the vigil was attended by young people from all over the Transvaal (O. Bapela, M4033). Some night vigils were, as was customary, held in the deceased's home where tents were sometimes erected – as in the case of Michael Diradeng's. The larger ones gained more theatricality by being held in the stadium itself, or in churches. Poetry was recited, speakers condemned the deaths and consoled the families, and a great deal of singing took place, from dusk until dawn (S. Mabaza, M1038).

> Mourners packed tightly into St Michael's Anglican Church ... About 1000 people crammed into the church ... and between 3000 and 4000 packed the church courtyard and narrow streets nearby. Police and SADF members armed with shotguns and rifles patrolled the area in armoured personnel carriers, and parked in front of the church. Police ordered the outside crowd to disperse but the reverend pleaded with them and promised calm. Mourners chanted slogans in support of Umkhonto we Sizwe. (J. Nkuna, M450)

At one vigil Moses Mayekiso spoke: 'He said we must not allow the Boers to get on our shoulders. This land belongs to us ... he further said that we must not go to work and wait until the corpses have been buried ... He said Mandela is our father. He is coming to rule this country.' Other speakers seemed to be 'ordinary people who were giving one another a chance to make speeches' (J. Nkuna, M450). This (hostile) witness said that not everybody joined in the singing willingly. The comrades 'taught us' the songs. 'I was afraid that they would thrash me if I do not sing, because every time they came near you they insisted that people must sing, sing, sing' (J. Nkuna, M465). They also, she said, 'burnt police clothes' during the night.

The police duly played the role of antagonists at the Diradeng vigil by throwing teargas into the singing crowd twice during the night, and pro-voking the Six-Day War itself, while the army's stand-off strategy was made clearest in respect of the vigil for the 5 March mass funeral:

> The whole plan was that we would leave the people to have their night vigil within the limits of the law, and my troops were specifically instructed to stay away completely until they received instructions to act, should it be necessary. (Colonel Holland Muter, M698)

They stood by in case the police could not cope, believing that 'the night vigil is a very sacred ritual in black tradition, and it would create unnecessary trouble to go there' (Colonel Holland Muter, M700).

However crowds are notoriously unstable and treacherous, as Alexand-rans knew only too well from their experiences of the Six-Day War. They erupt, they favour violence, and they grow in unpredictable ways. Obed Bapela remembered his own personal experience of this when, at the 4 March night vigil before the first mass funeral:

> At the stadium, whilst people were singing and they were full, there were people running towards the north, in the northern direction of the stadium. One person shouted and said, 'There is a person that is going to be lashed. It is alleged that he is an "*impimpi*" [informer].' I ran and climbed onto the truck on which the sound system was put and took the microphone, and shouted that the marshalls should go and rescue that person. They ran and came back with that person. We noticed that he was still very young. He was about 15–16 years of age. He came with a crowd that was surrounding him. They said they knew him. He stays out in Tembisa and they came with him from Tembisa and that person is an '*impimpi*'. He also has a tape in his hand. I said, 'Let us see the tape'. We took the tape, played it to him what was recorded on it. It was just songs and speeches that were made by the people. Then the people said 'Can you see now that he is an "*impimpi*". We have to burn him.' I pleaded with them and told them that it is not so. He may be liking those songs, that is why he has taped them for himself and that we should have respect for the service. That because we have lost children and people of Alexandra this thing must be conducted peacefully without bloodshed. We will then take the tape, give it to the marshalls for storage and they should leave that boy and for his safety I suggested that he should stay near the marshalls and the crowd should move away and go and stand where they had been standing. Then order was restored and the service continued. (O. Bapela, M3924)

On every one of these large occasions, there were moments where mobs appeared to be about to erupt. At the 17 May funeral, youths 'hijacked' coffins from one vigil and brought them to another, in defiance of government permission having been granted only on condition that vigils were held separately (Moses Mayekiso, M3030–1).

After each night vigil, the private would spill over into the public. Canetti believes this is typical of the behaviour of 'closed' crowds, which will suddenly erupt, seeming 'to overflow from some well-guarded space into the squares and streets of a town where it can move about freely, exposed to everything and attracting everyone'. Members of the crowd are, he says, driven by 'dissatisfaction with the limitation of the number of participants, the sudden will to attract, the passionate determination to reach all men' (Canetti 1962: 23). Indeed mourners would march through the streets early in the morning, from night vigil to funeral, church to stadium, carrying coffins and singing and chanting. Zealous comrades and marshals in their special T-shirts, would use this occasion as an opportunity to mobilise those residents who were not already part of the crowd, using loudhailers, going into houses, sometimes using force (A. Sebola, Z2570).

THE MAIN PERFORMANCE

The funeral itself became sublimated into notions of peace and justice, and the row of coffins became a symbol of the fight for liberty, like the crosses in a military cemetery. (*Sunday Times*, 9 March 1986)

Political theatre may have planned scripts, designated performers and appointed directors, but when successful it generates its own inner creativity, and its participants begin to write their own scripts. It evolves its own poetic forms and visual language, surprising and moving those who observe it and who are able to read its myriad overt and subliminal messages. The funerals and mass meetings in Alexandra in this period achieved this type of success, the tension between volatility and conformity casting a compelling spell over all who attended.

On these occasions huge crowds of people thronged to the churches or the stadium – relatively protected places where they could express their otherwise internalised anger, grief and hatred of the unjust world in which they lived. Crowds provide the one environment in which the natural fear of touch, invasion and pain can be overcome (Canetti 1962: 16). Crowds had to be assembled into these large gatherings as on other occasions. Youths were once more the marshals, the assemblers, and the retainers of the crowd, using their usual range of loudhailers, door-to-door visits, pamphlets and force.

Unlike the forms of mobilisation used in the actual uprising, the funerals and mass meetings set out to achieve not simply the creation of crowds, but their domestication. They enabled the creation of:

an obsequious flock ... The faithful are gathered together at appointed places and times and, through performances which are always the same, they are transported into a mild state of crowd feeling sufficient to impress itself on them without becoming dangerous, and to which they grow accustomed. (Canetti 1962: 31)

Thus in spite of the volatility of the street crowds, most night vigils, funerals and mass meetings were relatively peaceful. Their symbolism rested in their size and demonstration of mass mobilisation, rather than their capacity to mobilise violence. The planning and orchestration of the events made it possible to control the mob and provide more regularised means for the expression of anger. Senior African politicians and church-men and women would address the community, with the intention of expressing emotion in acceptable ways, or even 'calming things down'. They did the latter by offering to mediate between the community and the authorities, or by attempting to alleviate the behaviour of the police or army. They were, it seems, attempting to capture the local rebellion for the broader nationalism for which many of them stood.

> The marshalls controlled the people. They forced them to go to the stadium. We saw them take cars from people – I remember a bakkie taken from a person. And they sort of chased people from house to house to the square. They drove people themselves in the vehicle to the stadium. Some of them had sjamboks and knobkieries. (Colonel Holland Muter, M702)

Adults, priests and recognised leaders 'worked hard to preserve calm'. When youngsters seemed to be getting out of hand at one funeral, Father Mkhatshwa, the MC,

> quickly ceded the microphones to one of the younger leaders to calm the comrades with chants and songs and gentle exhortations. The technique works; there is still a layer of young leadership that com-mands the respect of the blood-soaked teenage comrades who have become addicted to the horrors of the necklace and the panga, but it does take work. (Colonel Holland Muter, M702)

A latecomer to a funeral would find the stadium transformed into a theatre for the domesticated crowd. It would be packed with people and filled with a variety of cultural symbols and political styles (Colonel Holland Muter, M841).

> Alexandra is ringed with steel, inside, it is as peaceful as a cathedral in the middle of the war ... Everything else in Alexandra stood still. Not a car moved in the streets. Helicopters kept flying over the stadium but the unity of the people was so fiercely comforting there was no fear in the stadium ... It seemed so peaceful and untypical that I could hardly believe this was Alexandra (or South Africa). Many had come in trepi-dation of being shot. (*Sunday Times*, 9 March 1986)

In each ceremony set rituals would be overseen by a formal master of ceremonies. The opening ritual was often a procession, led by youths, sometimes in military uniforms, carrying (usually illegal) flags and banners:

The comrades turned up in force, loping in cohort around the stadium, arms raised in the ANC salute. A third of them, I estimated, were under 10. Their mood seemed to me febrile and untrustworthy. There were quick flashes of anger, a suppressed hysteria close to the surface. (*Sunday Times*, 9 March 1986)

Wreaths would be laid, prayers said and, most importantly, speakers would address the crowd. Speeches at funerals and mass meetings were important mobilising devices, and were both passionate and highly politically charged (P. Tshabalala, M3879). Different discourses were used by different kinds of speakers. Some would be humble residents who would act as community storytellers or poets, presenting the narrative of the events that had led them there and consoling the crowds (I. Hattingh, M660). Others would be eminent political figures whose rhetoric was that of civil rights, and whose metaphors were those of the 'nation as family'. A third type, ministers of religion, would give moral directives and evoke symbols and thoughts on a larger scale or canvas.

At one funeral the speakers included all three types, eminent whites as well as blacks. They included the secretary general of the South African Council of Churches, Beyers Naude; Johannesburg's Catholic bishop, Reginald Orsmond; Curnick Ndlovu and Frank Chikane of the UDF; Albertina Sisulu, UDF leader, and wife of the jailed African National Congress leader Walter Sisulu, and Mike Beea of the Alexandra Civic Association. Present and prominent were Winnie Mandela – who could not speak publicly because of a banning order, but whose words were at some of these meetings read out by others, and members of the Release Mandela Campaign (Black Lawyers' Association 1986). The South African Council of Churches' secretary general, Smangaliso Mkhatshwa, led the funeral service (*Business Day*, 6 March 1986). Letters of support and condolence from eminent figures such as ambassadors, leaders from other townships and cities, and a range of political, religious and cultural organisations, were read out.

Thus in many cases, the mass occasion included people from outside Alexandra, whose symbolic presence was recognised as being important. The report on one such funeral emphasises its capacity to embody symbols and ideas which extended far beyond the borders of the township and which included the legal, the illegal, the national and the international, the religious and the political:

Dignity, anger and protest reigned at the funeral and mourners included representatives from embassies such as those of the United States and Britain. Amongst the mourners were representatives from civic, youth, women and students organisations from Atteridgeville, Soshanguve, Mamelodi, Kwa Thema, Duduza, Ermelo, Witbank, Soweto, Tembisa and other parts of the country. The stadium saw intense emotions as seventeen victims were laid to rest. (Black Lawyers' Association 1986)

On such occasions, the centre of the stage would be occupied by the coffins themselves, usually 'draped in the African National Congress black, green and gold colours and guarded by khaki clad youths' (Black Lawyers' Association 1986).

The stadium crowd constituted a volatile audience 'within' the theatre. The funeral was not simply a theatrical performance in its own right, but also a play within the broader play of the fight for recognition of the Alexandran, and indeed the South African struggle, by the national and international public. 'Huge banners and flags were hoisted, among them the Soviet Union flag with the hammer and sickle emblem, the Azanian Peoples' Organisation flag and the African National Congress flag' (Black Lawyers' Association 1986). 'I was in the presence of death ... and in another world where the Government writ no longer rules,' wrote a journalist (*Sunday Times*, 9 March 1986). Cameras, the ANC and the Communist Party were all banned – but all turned up, he said.

> The immense red banner of the CPSU (not the Communist party of SA but the real thing) rose dramatically above the crowd midway through the ceremony. By that time there was no hope of escaping from the throng, so the Christian ceremonies were conducted under the hammer and sickle. The coffins, a mind-numbing row of South African corpses, were draped in the green, yellow and black colours of the ANC. (*Sunday Times*, 9 March 1986)

A placard read: 'Allan Boesak please assist us to get away to undertake military training in Zambia, Angola, Swaziland, Lesotho, Botswana soon' (Zwane trial report, Z1503-4). One T-shirt said not only 'Alexandra Massacre' but also 'all power to the people', 'no easy walk to freedom' and 'forward ever, backward never' (Zwane trial report, Z4133). 'Everybody' wore them (*in camera* Witness 20, Z1501ff). Flags displayed slogans such as 'Forward to People's Power' and 'The People Shall Govern'.

The police and suspected spies were unwelcome: 'What is the police doing in our funeral because it is our comrades we are burying. Go away now,' said one placard. Another said: 'Away with Mothibe and your wife Theresa' – referring to the hated policeman and his suspected *impimpi* wife, Theresa Maseko, soon to be necklaced (*in camera* Witness 20, Z1503–4).

The set was enriched by the crowd, which played a role similar to that of a Greek chorus: 'and the crowd from time to time chanted "Viva Oliver Tambo", "Viva Nelson Mandela" or even, once, "Viva Joe Slovo"'. (*Sunday Times*, 9 March 1986)

The volatility of the crowd sometimes spilled over into disruption. At one funeral, the service, which was conducted by Father Smangaliso Mkhatshwa, the secretary general of the South African Catholic Bishops Conference, was temporarily disrupted as the crowd started ululating and singing and chanting various slogans (Black Lawyers' Association 1986). At another, the occasion moved briefly from symbolic to physical resistance when one youth fired from the crowd. Journalist Sipho Ngcobo remembered how:

> A salvo of gunfire from its ranks sent the advancing police scattering for cover. Police frantically took refuge in little ditches and under the trees, amid shouts of: 'Dit is die AK' ... I dived, hands first, behind the car of a foreign television crew. Next to me, also taking cover, was a young policeman, about 22 years old. His hands gripped his gun. He was shaking. Looking at my hands, I realised I was shaking too. At least I shared one thing with the policeman – fear. (*Business Day*, 24 April 1986)

He could see a youngster of about 18 armed with an AK47, who darted from one side of the road to the other, firing intermittent volleys. One policeman was shot in the stomach.

Each of the different types of public discourse engaged in at funerals may be viewed as an 'intentional construction' – something which follows rules, employs devices and utilises strategies to accomplish its purpose. An intentional construction of this sort, argues Wuthnow, does not simply articulate a theme, but couches that theme 'in a framework of parallels and contrasts, frames it within certain categories that deny others, and implies various relations between the speaker and the audience' (Wuthnow 1992: 10). But whereas speakers in a more ritualised and fixed setting, such as a church service, are able to pursue their 'intentional constructions' more or less unhindered, on occasions such as these, where the theatrical performance is to some extent being constructed as it occurs, and the crowd would act as the chorus, events would take a more spontaneous course. Thus the crowd played a vital role in the creation of an appropriate script for the variety of speakers who addressed them. They would cheer, jeer, ululate, chant or sing, depending on the speaker, his or her symbolic or political significance, and whether what they had to say accorded with what many seemed to be aiming for – a moral consensus within the meeting. At the April 23 meeting:

> Still seething with bitterness at the events of Tuesday night, thousands of residents staged a massive work stay away the following morning while the township's school children boycotted classes. Later in the day they all trooped in their thousands down to the local football stadium where the night's activities were roundly condemned and the concept of 'self-defence committees' was mooted. The people packed in the terraces of the stadium shouted deafening approval for the proposal, at the same time rejecting claims that the violence was the work of inter-community rivals. (Jon Qwelane, *Sunday Star*, 27 April 1986)

Political poetry – sometimes by Alexandra's 'people's poet' known as 'Jingles' – was read, discussing the living conditions of black people, venerating the leaders of the struggle and condemning police actions saying the police 'must stop shooting small children' (description in Zwane trial, Z1503-4). One schoolmistress called 'Jeanette' was said to have recited poems 'saying whites are dogs'. The poetry too would often refer to the father figures of African nationalism – Nelson Mandela, Oliver Tambo, Walter Sisulu (*The Star*, 24 April 1986).

The songs sung by youths at funerals were typical of the nationalist repertoire (Exhibit QQQQ, Zwane trial, PJ archives). The song-style lent itself to mass participation, for the main singer would sing a line and then the audience would follow his lead. '*Where did you learn the freedom songs? ... The very same day ... These songs were not written on anything, but they were easy to be followed*' (P. Mogano, Z4458-9).

The motifs of oppression, freedom, the benign father and sometimes mother figures of nationalism, innocent suffering and martyrdom by the 'children' of the nation and the biblical idea of a 'way' to freedom, were all themes within them:

> Oliver Tambo talks to Botha
> So that he can release Mandela
> Winnie Mandela talks to Botha
> So that he can release Mandela
> Mandela to lead the oppressed people
> Mandela to lead the oppressed people

Africa's children were innocent and in need:

> We the children of Africa need Freedom
> We the children of Africa need Freedom
> Freedom, Freedom, we don't have
> Freedom, Freedom, we don't have
> It doesn't matter whether we are arrested
> But we need freedom
> It doesn't matter whether we are shot
> But we need freedom

Their leaders were benign fathers:

> Our Father Mandela, Our Father Mandela
> We are being shot by the police
> We are being shot by the police
> We don't know what we have done
> We don't know what we have done
> Our Father Sisulu, Our Father Sisulu,
> We are being shot by the police

We are being shot by the police
We don't know what we have done
We don't know what we have done.

'Freedom' was the undefined goal:

Rolihlahla Mandela, Freedom is in your hands
Show us the way to freedom
In this land of Apartheid
Mandela, Mandela, Freedom is in your hands
Show us the way to freedom
In this land of poverty. (Exhibit QQQQ, Zwane trial, PJ archives)

Those less eminent members of the Alex community who spoke – relatives, friends or comrades of the deceased, or members of local committees and churches for example – would adopt a local tone, telling the stories of the hardships people in Alexandra itself had experienced rather than constructing interpretive metaphors. Sebola described how at Michael Diradeng's funeral:

there was an old granny who related how Michael was killed ... she was at the centre of the stadium ... She spoke through a loud-hailer ... She said Michael went to Jazz Stores and he was to change a bottle of cold drink, therefore a fight broke out between him and the security guards ... There were other speakers. Michael's brother related how Michael grew in Alex. (A. Sebola, Z2543ff)

'Theresa' – at that stage still boldly under cover – also spoke at the Diradeng funeral, 'condemning and chanting slogans, and reading the wreaths' (A. Sebola, Z2543ff). She said 'Boere, Boere, Comrades, when I see Botha I get upset, I feel like vomiting' (J. Nkuna, M451 and 470–1).

When politicians spoke they adopted the much more basic Nationalist discourse of peace and human rights in a context where violence was a tempting option for all. On the one hand they, like all the adults present, attempted to calm the crowds. Albertina Sisulu, at one rally, for example, emphasised that the people's own brutality should be curbed: 'We should not kill one another with tyres,' she said. 'If any person has done wrong we should sit down and discuss. The problem must first be solved before a person can be said he is wrong.' Elsewhere she said, 'There is no need to be carried away by hooligans,' while an ex-political prisoner at the same meeting pleaded with the people, particularly the youth: 'Don't go on the rampage all over. Those people up there have heavy weapons. It gives me pain; it makes me not to sleep when I hear they are shooting our people. So don't go on the rampage.' Politicians also condemned the unacceptably high levels of government brutality. But implicit in their discourse was the apocalyptic vision of the ANC. They would suggest that 'black patience was running out', that violence 'would eventually erupt'. At one of the most important rallies of the period, for example, 'Speakers called on the Government to unban the African National Congress, release all political prisoners and negotiate with credible black leaders.' Others said that time was 'running out for the government to solve the country's problems peacefully'. Sisulu said here that South Africa's problems could not be solved 'by bullets and troops patrolling the townships in a show of force', and Elijah Barayi said that the killing of people in the townships would not stop the people's realisation that they were oppressed but would 'nourish their hopes'. The government should renounce violence because it was the violence practised by 'the system' that ended in funerals such as the present one'.

They, too, would refer to the central symbol of the nation – or the township – as a 'family'. In many of these ceremonies the notions of childhood, motherhood and family belonging were emphasised. The idea of the 'mother of the nation' was prominent. 'Massive cheer for mothers of the nation' (*The Star*, 6 March 1986). Indeed, at this stage Winnie Mandela *was* the nation – her very demeanour and clothing indicated that she sought to embody it:

> The crowd roared approval when banned activist Winnie Mandela walked through the crowd, her head shaded by a large floral wreath in the shape of Africa and bedecked with the ANC's green, black and gold. (*Business Day*, 6 March 1986)

Winnie Mandela appeared, wrote one journalist, to be 'a South African Evita, bringing glamour and beauty into the drab lives of her people'. In her speech, read by Frank Chikane, she focused on the family, saying, 'The grief of the families is subsumed in the longing for freedom, the demand for justice and the hope of peace. The grief of the families is taken up in the wider agony of a people who have been unfree too long.' Albertina Sisulu developed this theme. She said, 'All the mothers of South Africa, black and white, they should join hands and then mothers of the white children you must not allow their children to kill their own black brothers in the township,' while Chikane himself 'reminded the mourners that the seventeen coffins before them did not represent statistics but housed bodies of people who had been children, mothers and fathers'. An AAC woman echoed this theme, saying, 'Women must take their shawls and tie them around their waists to go and look for their children because children have disappeared, some have died and the children cannot be found' (J. Nkuna, M496).

Churchmen and women were less ambiguous about violence than were politicians and residents. None of them implied that the time for popular violence would eventually come or that it was a looming threat that could be used. Instead they conveyed a clear preference for passive resistance, emphasising discipline and control amongst the masses and placing their faith

in God to liberate them. 'You are true fighters for freedom,' said Mkhatshwa to the crowds at one rally, 'You are disciplined, I am proud of you.'
Bishop Tutu, supported by eminent churchmen such as Mkhatshwa,
Mogoba and Buthelezi, could have been awarded his Nobel Peace prize for
his role in Alexandra alone, so firm was he on this matter, comforting,
cajoling and calming the crowd, portraying himself as staunch 'father' to the
masses, and risking his life and reputation amongst youths deeply hostile to
the passive resistance message. At the 18 February mass meeting he 'pleaded
with the people to control their anger', promising to take their demands to
the 'higher authorities'. 'Tutu saves the day,' wrote one Alexandran journalist. He said: 'As your leaders and parents we cannot stand by and watch
people pointing guns at you and shooting you. It is important to remember
that we are dealing with people who have guns. So we need to have other
strategies which will not make us cannon fodder.'

> We as your parents know that we have failed to lead you. We know that
> you are brave. But I want to ask you one favour, go home peacefully
> and the SACC will take your grievances to the authorities. When you
> go home please do not go in groups of ten or eight because there are
> people waiting to do terrible things. We do not want to give them that
> chance. We believe in God who is powerful. We know that He is going
> to free us. There is nothing wrong in struggling for your liberation.
> What is important is to use strategies which one is not going to regret
> when read in the history books in days of freedom. (*The Sowetan*, 19
> February 1986)

The crowds applauded when he said, 'We are on the winning side, our
cause is just, and we will succeed against the evil system of apartheid.'
Impatient bands of youths behind the truck on which Tutu stood were
incredulous when Bishop Tutu said black people would be free. 'When will
we be free,' they chorused. When he said he and his delegation had secured
assurances that residents would not be harassed, some elderly people joined
the youths and said Bishop Tutu had allowed himself to be lied to by the
police. 'They are harassing us right now. We don't sleep at home,' said the
youths. 'The police are lying. They conduct night raids and take our children
away. Many of them no longer sleep at home,' protested the parents.

Tutu was booed. At the subsequent meeting where he reported back to
the crowd, and had to explain to them that his negotiations with the government had not been entirely successful, their reaction was even more hostile:

> On Friday afternoon an even bigger crowd of 40,000 turned up to hear
> him report on the talks – and his magic failed to move the masses. By
> the time the delegation of churchmen left the stadium, tempers were
> such that a gang of youths blocked Bishop Tutu's path before he
> reached his car and demanded to know from him where they were

supposed to sleep because 'the police harass us and raid our homes every night'. The bishop stopped to talk to the youths, who were clearly unhappy with the state of things. He appealed to them to be calm and take what he and other churchmen said, 'because we are your leaders and your parents'. The youths were sceptical. Crowds had earlier refused to allow Tutu out of the stadium. Tutu told youths they must not spark a fresh wave of violence. But youths said 'as soon as you leave here we will deal with the police in our own way because they are merciless. (Rich Mkhondo, *The Star*, 22 February 1986)

The Reverend Peter Storey observed the crowd's pain:

I wish every white South African could have been at the Alexandra stadium to see what apartheid had done to the future generations of this country ... I was saddened by their sullen faces. There was agony in more than 45,000 faces, I saw how they hated the system. One could see that they wanted something positive done to remedy the situation. (*The Star*, 22 February 1986)

This particular ceremony proved not to be as cathartic as others.

THE USE OF THE STREETS – AFTER

As had been the case with night vigils, once the core ceremony of each occasion was over, the crowds of Alexandrans found themselves in a condition of liminality. The enclosed and relatively controlled ritual had ended, and the streets beckoned. It had been at this stage of the Diradeng funeral that the Six-Day War itself had erupted. After the visit to the cemetery the crowd had divided into at least four singing and chanting groups, and violence began (Wilson Moses, M369ff). Mechanisms of controlling this dangerous time in the crowd's life cycle had been devised – but the adults, the organisers, the police and the army were all aware of the risks. Paul Tshabalala could sense the tension as the 5 April funeral crowd formed a procession to walk to the cemetery:

As we went down to the cemetery I realised that according to the situation that there could be danger and we realised that the only thing to do was to walk in front and to try to control, because the allegations were that the youth at funerals usually throw stones at the police and the police would start shooting ... I ... became the person to protect these people and otherwise stones would have been thrown and I would have fled. (P. Tshabalala, M3884–5)

On another occasion, the ceremony ended in a ritualised use of the streets, followed by the inevitable breakdown (*The Star*, 6 March 1986). After the burial, people started going home in groups, and the order disintegrated. One group stole a bulldozer, and burnt it. Others turned over cars and burnt them once inside the township (J. Nkuna, M702ff; *Business Day*, 24 April 1986).

On two occasions – the funerals of AYCO member Jacob Mabisela and of the already mentioned people's poet, 'Jingles' – the police appear to have seized the opportunity provided by this liminal period to 'hijack' the funerals.[6] In the case of Jingles:

> It was said that the boers took the coffin of the deceased by force ... They went to bury it ... What I heard is that people did not reach the graveyard, the police came and fired teargas and people dispersed actually and ran in different directions and the coffin was then taken by the police from Jingles' place to the graveyard, they took the coffin to the graveyard and buried it. (A. Zwane, Z3798; see also Z4109– 10)

CONCLUSION

The power of nationalism lies in the nature of its symbolic repertoire. Nationalism is unlike the more sterile symbolic offerings of such mobilising ideologies as Marxism or trade unionism because of its profound relationship with the inner self of ordinary people – its capacity to stir 'the deepest roots of their emotional being' (Wilhelm Reich, quoted in Boggs 1976: 35). It is immeasurably strengthened by the presence of a substantial 'protonationalism' in popular culture – a range of religious or other cultural expectations which render nationalistic messages plausible and attractive (Hobsbawm 1990). We have seen that memories and habits of resistance in Alexandra had deep roots in the past. These were always woven together with a broad set of claims to rights and freedoms which were compatible with a nationalist vision.

In this case, the nationalist repertoire was more extensive, theatrical and symbolic than any others in the township and constituted a significant part of the township's capacity and willingness to mobilise. It was a-temporal. It did not pose an idealised future, but embraced the older central motifs of 'the people', church, nation, family, suffering, martyred womanhood and a generalised sense of martyrdom. While the youth and adult groupings were combative and divisive, African nationalism was defensive and unifying.

The power of nationalism in Alexandra, and its capacity to 'trump' the ideologies of the local movements, was immensely strengthened through the theatrical forms through which it was expressed. Vital to the magnification of nationalistic – as opposed to local youth and adult – claims was the part played by the local and international media. Clearly good political street theatre needs the media. It works best if it is able to ensure that the media provide publically accessible interpretations of its claims. But this is a factor outside the control of performance planners. While they seek to ensure that the media interpret their performances in ways that are congruent with the intentions of the activists concerned, the media have their own agendas.

In Alexandra, not all of the performers' intentions were reflected in media reports of the situation. In particular, nationalism tended to trump local visions. While adults and youths sought to use the mobilising power and legitimacy of public funerals and ceremonies to gain wider public acceptance for their 'local' utopian visions (adult organisations would bid for supporters; militant youths would toyi-toyi, display posters with specific local meanings rather than broadly symbolic ones, and loudly express their resentments at what they saw as the conservatism of national leaders), the press did not quite see things the same way.

Of all the South African township revolts, this was the one made most visible to local and world audiences through widespread media reports. Alexandra became one of the symbols of the struggle against apartheid. Mayekiso's international connections and trade union networks, the location of Alexandra in Johannesburg (making travel there relatively painless for journalists), the long-standing connections between Alexandrans and influential white liberals and the adoption of the rebellion by prominent churchmen and politicians, all helped make this possible.

Residents were sharply aware of the role played by journalists in bridging the gap between the local events and the international audience; one journalist described how the nun sitting next to him at one funeral reacted:

> 'Kuluma, speak', she cries. She glances self-consciously sideways under her lashes to see if the message from the township, the cry for peace, has been heard and understood, and if it is being faithfully recorded in a battered notebook, so that everybody out there, in the peaceful suburbs beyond the ring of steel may hear it. (*The Sowetan*, 7 March 1986)

In spite of efforts by local activists at bringing their own agendas into the 'theatre', the overlay of public nationalism was too powerful for this to occur to any significant extent. Nationalism, as always, was opportunistic, it was of long standing and it could provide an overlay and a disguise for the syncretism that underpinned the private world of township residents. At the same time it was widely appealing – not only to township residents but also to those millions all over the world who supported the ending of apartheid. Thus when journalists ensured that the 1986 events gained considerable publicity, both nationally and internationally – and the Six-Day War hit the international press in a big way, making major news on British TV, making the front page in all of Fleet Street – it was to the readily available and more familiar nationalist symbolism that they turned, finding it difficult and sometimes a little politically awkward to cope, perhaps, with the complexities of Alexandra's multi-layered struggle. Nationalism appropriated the public version of what had been happening in the township.

Thus Mojalefa Moseki, a resident and journalist, described one of the funerals in clearly nationalistic terms. He had, he said:

> never seen so many well behaved people in my entire life ... It was a *big family, sad, but close and most touching.* ... *Whites and blacks* from all parts of the country were there. The day before the funeral youths in all types of vehicles drove into Alexandra ... Thousands gathered at the stadium for this night vigil that went on until early Wednesday morning. ... *the whole of Alexandra was involved.* Some people were given places to rest and sleep. *The township was united* as friends and strangers helped and comforted the other ... March will be recorded as *historic* in the life of this township that has a *proud heritage of resistance.* (*The Sowetan,* 7 March 1986) (my italics)

This was the type of language most commonly used to describe the events – an interpretive legacy which remains until this day and which contrasts strongly with the utopianism of the local movements themselves.

Nationalism was more than an ideology embodied in the UDF and expressed in 'theatrical' venues within townships. Its ideological and cultural magnification had real institutional implications. For one thing, it was a self-generating discourse, a compelling frame. Some elements of its language were accepted across societal divisions without much variation – for example, calling everyone 'comrade' was an essential ingredient of the repertoire of the time. And keeping within certain tactical boundaries – for example by refusing to take part in any structures promoted by the government – was required: the culture of the boycott was so deeply entrenched that it could not be transgressed.[7] The flexibility of the ideas contained within the nationalist vision gave it its greatest power. Millenarian youths and 'rationalist' adults could use the same terms and mean different things by them: adults could interpret 'organs of self-government' to mean an absence of crime and a smoothly operating township (O. Bapela, M3971). Youths would interpret the phrase to refer to the establishment of a fully 'liberated zone'. Some of these differences could be a reflection of the defence strategy in the trial, but there were genuine differences as well. This commonality of repertoire, together with the magnetic power of the nationalist theatre, predisposed Alexandrans of both generations towards unifying tactics.

Organisational connections between the two strands of the rebellion – adult and youth – had first been mooted in 1984 (Moses Mayekiso, M2701). These early impulses towards unity had been sidelined during the high points of the revolt, when youth and adult forms of mobilisation took divergent paths. It was only later that a more serious merging of strategy and tactics began to develop. The crisis committees which had arranged funerals were the least institutionalised example of this. Later, two remarkable 'workshops' were held in the township during the months of the struggle, which took unification further. Held under the organisational impetus of the AAC, they set out to try to forge unity by drawing together 'all progressive organisations' within the township. These workshops illustrated one of the most striking features of the South African struggle for liberation (and post-liberation consensus) – the centripetal forces which brought together otherwise mutually extremely contentious factions. Through them the AAC tried to promote the idea that the revolt should be about the township 'governing itself', rather than the youth idea of township 'ungovernability'(P. Tshabalala, M3798). The workshop in April, for example, was attended by all the key players, including the wilful youth groups.[8] The AAC presided over a process through which the fragmented youth groupings were to be drawn together, and whereby they, in turn, would link up with adult organisations. Thus those invited ranged from the most militant youth groupings to the moderate Alexandra Residents' Association. In his trial, Obed Bapela suggested that the motivations for this were 'adult' in orientation (O. Bapela, M3947–8) and that the workshop's outcome was to promote adult rationality under the auspices of the AAC.[9] The workshop endorsed the idea that strategies initially forged within the Alexandra Action Committee should become dominant, and that the AAC itself should oversee this process. The AAC was 'unanimously elected the sole representative of the Alexandra community', thus giving institutional form to the nationalistic ideology of solidarity (*The Sowetan*, 10 June 1986).

10

FROM VICTORY TO DEFEAT

In those days we thought that liberation was just at the brink. We were moving in Alex. We used to call the whole of Alex 'Beirut' and we used to call Sandton 'Lebanon' ... we felt that now we shall exercise the first part of the Freedom Charter: 'The People shall govern'. We were having our People's Courts. Even police were complaining that they would lose their jobs because there were no reports of rape etc. (DP, quoted in Carter 1991a: 182)

Three months after the rebellion had started, Alexandra was a changed place. In the *Sunday Times*' view, the 'comrades' were a 'faceless group of hard-line militants who aspire to rule the township', who had 'called on blacks to "isolate collaborators socially", to "refuse to serve councillors and their families in their shops" and "to end all personal relationships with police and other collaborators"' (*Sunday Times*, 27 April 1986): 'Wide-eyed township dwellers talk of "people's courts", where the comrades dispense their medieval justice – often condemning victims in absentia, with the dreaded 'necklace' as the symbol of their revolution.' Angry white business-men talked of forming vigilante groups to curb the wave of crime and vandalism which had seen the open looting of some white owned shops and the hijacking of cars. The leviathan which was the apartheid state found itself unable to govern the township and a crucial plank of its 'reform' strategy had collapsed. Councillors had resigned en masse and no form of even vaguely legitimate governance was actually in place.

Significantly, the state had not successfully replaced by force the legiti-macy that had been lost. The police station itself was rendered ineffective and police would tell complainants who approached them to 'go to the comrades'. The police experienced this as a period during which they were harassed, marginalised and weakened. They could not, said one policeman, even stop in the township to talk to a friend. They were termed sell-outs, could not buy goods at shops or use roads in the township, and their children could not attend schools. Residents 'subjected themselves to the authority of the comrades' (P. B. Botha, Z301). The final blow came when the mayor himself, Sam Buti, and the three remaining councillors resigned on 22 April, making Alexandra the fourth Council in the country to collapse completely and the first in the core urban centres of the Witwatersrand (*Business Day*, 23 April 1986).

Adherents to each discourse of rebellion interpreted this in their own terms. Thus many youths overestimated their success, believing that a Utopia had indeed been set in place and Alexandra was now, in accordance with the calls made by the exiled movements, liberated and 'ungovernable'. People's power had prevailed. It was a period of the 'rule of the comrades' (A. Sebola, Z2305). Many residents and observers believed that the state itself had been weakened:

> In 1986 Alexandra was a liberated zone. People no longer took their complaints to the local police station. The people's courts were established. The people's power was imminent. The people had taken the initiative from the state and they were battling the state. The state only responded to the moves of the people. (LK, quoted in Carter 1991a: 181)

But the adults did not go along with this apocalyptic view of what had happened. Fully aware of the real power of the state, the accused in the Mayekiso trial seemed to agree that Alexandra was not a 'liberated zone' (Mzwanele Mayekiso, M4087). The adults instead claimed more modestly that they had brought order to the township in accordance with rationalistic principles. Yard, block and street committees had been established. There were mediation courts in each yard, trials were being held, and a committee system was fully in place. Ninety per cent of Alexandrans, they said, supported them.[1] Mzwanele Mayekiso believed that what he called 'AAC hegemony' existed in the township by late April.

> The AAC had political hegemony in Alexandra, and was a household word. This status was a result of the sophisticated system of organising we used. Issues that we were dealing with were not only political repression, but also socio-economic. There was no other system like it in the history of Alexandra. (Mayekiso 1996: 22)

Mayekiso's own vision was often broader than that of those whom he organised. Once the Town Council was out, he started to think of how actually to govern the township. He began to ask questions like:

> With the collapsing of town council what should the action committee do to run and govern the township democratically. a) running of churches etc, b) collecting of garbage c) repairing of roads d) allocation of houses to the people (development of area) e) removal of coloureds in the township and f) the organising organs of people power. (Exhibits F20–2, Mayekiso trial, CTH archives)

On 29 April the AAC claimed in a press conference that it had achieved 'grass roots control' of the township. AYCO supported this claim – its president said, 'Alex has its own political system'; 'although we have taken over some law and order functions, our aim is not to mete out punishment, but to educate and restore the right values within the community.'[2] Mzwanele Mayekiso linked the success of the AAC to its analytical sophistication, which in turn had led it in strategic directions which united the generations and the classes of the township:

> How do we explain the AAC's success during those momentous weeks and months ... First ... it was crucial for the AAC to establish the proper relationship between the youth and the adults ... [secondly] it was also logical to carefully plan the role that disciplined youth would have in organising their community. Once the link was made, parents began to have the confidence to come to meetings. That was the single key breakthrough. And that breakthrough was based on the way we understood the dynamics of Alexandra, which was based on class analysis, but which had a mass line ... Class politics were crucial to our project. (Mayekiso 1996: 22)

To him it was not the Utopia of the revolutionary youth that had prevailed but the ordered 'commune' of the parents, the 'disciplined youth', and the AAC. Indeed, quoting Marx, he later separated his ideas from utopian ones quite explicitly.

> The working class did not expect miracles from the Commune. They had no ready-made utopias to introduce *par decret du peuple*. They know that in order to work out their own emancipation, and along with it that higher form to which present society is irresistibly tending by its own economical agencies, they will have to pass through long struggles, through a series of historic processes, transforming circum-stances and men. They have no ideals to realise, but to set free the elements of the new society with which old collapsing bourgeois society itself is pregnant. (ibid.)

However the hold that the rebels, whether youth or adult, had over the space of the township was in fact extremely tenuous. In reality, the momen-tous press conference, at which Moses Mayekiso claimed 'grass-roots control' of the township, was not what it seemed – it was as much a defensive response to the invasion of Alexandra by murderous vigilantes as a reflection of genuine power. The rebellion began to collapse just as its proponents claimed it had reached its pinnacle.

Some of the weakening of the rebellion took place as a result of inner decay. The rebels found that from very early on it was difficult to sustain the uniformity, even purity, of purpose that they sought beyond the period of actual mass meetings, marches or funerals. At AYCO and AAC meetings activists complained of passivity, 'neutrality' amongst the general township population, and constantly attempted to find ways of persuading people to join their cause. While leaders were restrained in this, their followers were sometimes less so, hence the numerous reports of youths 'disciplining' adults, forcing them to attend meetings, to boycott stores, or to participate in other events – too many for such reports to be dismissed or ignored. Ordinary adult residents found themselves torn between their basic sympathy for the cause, and their anger at what seemed to be a total loss of adult control over youth behaviour.

The public and symbolic nature of spatial power lent itself to similarly public and symbolic parody, a profoundly undermining occurrence. We have already seen how before long, the anti-crime campaign had deteriorated. Criminals themselves started patrolling the streets, dressed as comrades, mimicking the comrades' songs, slogans and clothing; but instead of disarming the population, they robbed and attacked them. 'True comrades' as well as AAC adults were deeply disturbed by this.[3] 'Comrades' and '*tsotsis*' began to become indistinguishable and the sinister '*comtsotsi*' ('comrade-gangster') became a bizarre feature of life in the township (P. Tshabalala, M3849). As people's courts slid into becoming kangaroo courts, over-zealous comrades sjambokked the 'guilty', and crime began to burgeon,[4] the youth began to appear to be beyond reform. To this inner fragility of the rebellion was added a far greater threat to its survival.

THE OCCUPATION OF THE TOWNSHIP

This side it is very bad there's dying everyday as you have heard over the Radios. There is real fighting here, there's not even a chance to flee because the location is surrounded by the Army. Soldiers are well armed. It is becoming bad every day there's no longer going to work. I am not frightening you I'm just relating a story. We still live despite that.[5]

The response of the government to the rebellion's successes was multi-layered. Because the state was internally divided, the township was subjected to the ambiguous forces both of the reformism advocated by some, and of the repression which others attempted to sustain. Having lost what little legitimacy it had had, it was forced to resort to rule by fiat on the one hand (by having to appoint a colonial-type 'administrator') (South African Institute of Race Relations 1987: 119), and to various types of repression on the other. These responses represented a considerable retreat from the reformist agenda, and taking into account the fact that similar rebellions were occurring all over the country, a blow to the government's attempt to pre-empt majority rule through a legitimating strategy of urban co-optation. But this was not quite how it felt to the participants in the rebellion, who experienced government responses at first hand.

The state could mobilise several different types of power: the much derided and controversial new Municipal Police formed by the Council under Sam Buti; the South African Police; the Defence Force; and finally, the unleashing of vigilantes, all represented brute force. In addition, it used an extensive network of spies and informers, the weapon of propaganda,[6] through the government controlled SABC, and the wide range of punitive laws available to it to detain, and eventually actually arrest and try rebels.

One of the original reasons for spatial segregation had been to facilitate control – and although the rebels had used the township's design to their own advantage, its original function was never lost and easily resurrected when it came to repression. The township was, from the time of Mayekiso's claim to control Alexandra, effectively occupied by the army and ongoing police patrols (in spite of the eviction of the police, they continued to patrol, although they refused to undertake regular duties of taking up cases and so on) (R. Mashego, M4257–8, amongst others). An air of surrealism pervaded this small and congested place, where disproportionately huge Casspirs trundled along the narrow rutted streets and youths attacked them. Police and troops used to patrol, and during the night they used searchlights, placed on either side of the township, glaring all night, lighting up the otherwise dim streets. The troops would 'drill' in the streets, often at night. House to house searches took place from soon after the Six-Day War (*Sunday Star*, 23 April 1986). The army also occupied the symbolically vital stadium:

> They stayed, actually they camped there in the stadium and the stadium is meant for playing football as a result we could no more play football because they occupied it ... the army troubled us there in the location and made life difficult for us there in the location. (A. Zwane, Z4248)

They used the stadium as a base from which to make forays into the township: 'By day 500 army and police move through the township. By night they switch on their spotlights and patrol and then move back in to the stadium.' They also set up a tented camp outside the township, where ammunition, hippos, army trucks, Casspirs and other vehicles were housed (anonymous statement, Zwane trial, PJ archives). The army was hated and often attacked. One police witness said in the Zwane trial:

> No 'soft' [regular] police vehicles could go into Alexandra; only armoured vehicles, namely Casspirs, were used ... The so-called 'comrades', the young blacks in Alexandra, would attack any vehicle which belonged to any state department, the police and the army, with petrol bombs or stones ... what normally happened was that the youths formed groups of about 100 and ran on to the streets. When a police vehicle, and now I am talking about Casspirs, came along to chase them away then others from the sides of the streets between the houses would stand with petrol bombs and stones and throw them at the vehicle. (Lieutenant Zeelie, Z388–400)

Patrols were particularly feared and hated:

> We fear them ... the attitude of the youth to the patrols was one of fear, antagonism and anger ... Certain groups of youths ... the extreme groups of youths whose anger would consume them and they would respond by stone-throwing, violence, digging holes and ditches in the township, in the roads, to prevent the patrols from making their patrol. Other youth would be afraid and hide, but in general everyone had a united feeling against the patrol ... The patrols were seen to be unnecessary and would actually be accused of initiating the anger and the violence ... perception would have been that in a turbulent situation like this I would see the patrols as inciting rebellion amongst people but I would also see that it wasn't just the patrols, it was also the deep anger and hurt and frustration of people over many years breaking out. (Father Cairns, M4360–1)

The climate of fear spread:

> Today parents are afraid to send their children to the shops. Youths are no longer seen playing football in the dusty streets. Police and army vehicles patrol the streets day and night. It is a real war against the unarmed residents of Alexandra. 'Death – our game, Jail – our home' is what the angry youths in South African townships are saying today. (*Alexandra Speak*, 15 May 1986)

In spite of these harsh experiences, the army, in fact, represented the face of 'reform', and had come to the township with a different basic ideology from that of the police. In many townships it was felt that their presence was marginally more tolerable than that of the often far more brutal police.

> I was at my mother's place in 7th Avenue, when there was no water and people wanted to go to the neighbouring factories to get water and the police refused. But the army came to their rescue and indicated that the people should be allowed to get water. *So the army, what did the army do?* They intervened; they asked people to be allowed to get water from the factories. *Was there a difference in the attitude of people towards the army and the police?* Yes, the people came to see the army as more helpful than the police, they knew they could get help from the army than from the police. *And what was the attitude towards the police after the six-day war?* The attitude towards the police was that of anger. (R. Mashego, M4258–9; M4275)

COUNTERATTACK

The evil system of
Apartheid is oppressing
the blacks of Africa.
When residents puts
Some demands the
Answer is the bullets
Teargasses, birdshot
And deaths to the people that's what
The government is.[7]

Balaclava man
I know you like to take my life Balaclava man
Do it balaclava man.
Petrol bomb my Mother' house, balaclava man,
But the spirit of freedom will never fall into the sea.
Balaclava man I know you are looking my step
I know you like to kill me because I am against Apartheid
Do it Balaclava,
(this) is your chance
But the spirit of Liberty will never fall into the sea.[8]

Important as these various controls were, particularly for the long-term, they were not sufficient on their own, and the rebellion was effectively ended, not by the authoritarian actions of police or army, but through a bitter, vicious counter-attack mounted by a mysterious group of 'vigilantes', almost certainly organised, manned and powerfully backed by police (Haysom 1987).[9] This, too, parodied the 'spatial' motif, but much more cruelly. The action of the vigilantes took an ugly, personalised form. The police, both municipal and national, many of them long-standing residents of the township, were filled with resentment at their treatment – the murders and necklacings, the gutting of their houses, their ostracism and finally the driving of themselves and their families from their homes. Encouraged by the growing right-wing vigilantism throughout the country (reinforced by pro-repression forces within the state itself), they themselves launched an anonymous attack upon the township one fateful night.[10]

It was a Monday, 21 April, the day that Sam Buti and his town councillors had resigned. That day, the consumer boycott had become more violent, with crowds of youths gathering in front of shops preventing people from buying. Generalised violence within the township had accelerated – trucks had been attacked, stones thrown, and vehicles burnt. That night an eerie darkness spread through the township. The army lights were mysteriously absent: 'There used to be search lights in the township. As soon as it is dark there are these search lights which are lit … but on this particular day those search lights were switched off. They were not there.' Roadblocks were operating but many were surprised at how violent they had become – some cars were overturned and the police manning them swore and abused passengers. They did not seem to be the usual police (Wilson Moses, M351; Moses Mayekiso, M2990–3005; Father Cairns, M4362). Then sinister groups of heavily armed white and black men – carrying teargas canisters, pangas, stones, iron bars, knobkerries, petrol cans, pickaxes, sjamboks and/ or guns – dressed in the distinctive blue of the police, but also wearing masks, or *doeks* (headscarves) or trying to imitate or parody 'comrades', launched a major offensive upon the places, people and spaces which had been central to the revolt. They were assisted by men in Casspirs and vans. Observers estimated there were 200–400 of them. Some shouted '*Bopha* comrade' –'comrade, come out' – as they attacked. Others said, 'We are the Kabasas, and we have come to fight' or 'You are the dogs who do not want the police.' Some whites had their faces painted black and wore balaclavas. At times during the attack they would gather and mockingly sing freedom songs (*in camera* Witness 10, Z1298ff; vigilante attack file, Mayekiso trial, CTH archives).

This was also a theatrical affair. It was a night of widespread murder, destruction and terror. Activists were killed, their homes destroyed. people's courts were burnt. Seven activists were shot dead, and forty-seven were injured through assault, gunshots or beating. Specific addresses of activists were targeted. Most of these were totally destroyed by fire. Others were damaged by stones, bricks and sticks. Dozens of cars were attacked, burnt or smashed. Taxis and fruit-sellers' stalls were destroyed.

> Gangs of armed black marauders … came shortly after dusk and wreaked havoc. They shot, burned, killed, assaulted and taunted their victims as homes burned and women and children screamed. Some of the families were trapped inside the burning structures, their tormentors at the ready outside for anyone who dared to break out. Some families broke the burglar proofing on their windows to enable their children to escape the raging fires and the threatening men outside. (*Sunday Star*, 27 April 1986)

Wilson Moses remembered:

> I went into a shebeen, sat there and enjoyed a beer, one beer. I all of a sudden heard shots being fired outside. We saw many people coming and they were being followed by police vehicles. It seems as if there was fighting … It was the people and the police, and it was at night.

Later he says he also saw about 100 or 150 youths coming up Selborne Avenue, being followed by the police in ordinary cars. Police were firing shots. Youths were throwing stones. There was 'running and stopping, running and stopping'. He says he heard that about 200 people in blue shirts hanging out of their trousers were going up Forth Avenue singing comrade songs/freedom songs. 'We drew the curtains and closed the doors for fear that these people might run into the house … Thereafter I went home' (Wilson Moses, M351). The youths ran from house to house, waking up the residents, shouting 'wake up, wake up the makabasas are attacking us'. People rushed out of their homes:

> People were near me, I was aware that people who were near me had their lights on … *Now did you go back to bed? …* No I did not … because there were various groups coming. When one group leaves another group would come and when it leaves another group would come and when it leaves another comes. (L. Nkuna, M454ff)

First attacked were taxi drivers and passengers, who were beaten with axes, pangas and guns. As they were beaten, attackers said, 'You are the people who drove us out of the townships' (*Speak*, 15 May 1986).

> Residents left their flats to witness the commotion. The group started singing some freedom songs and even chanted political slogans. Some even shouted 'Ke rona ma comrade a macha' (We are the new comrades). As they did so they displayed an assortment of weapons and shouted at the residents to 'get into their homes and stop watching them since they were not a bioscope'. (Black Lawyers' Association 1986)

They started firing shots at random and residents disappeared into their homes. Johanna Maphosa, an itinerant fruit and vegetable seller with her two young children by her side, was one of those at the taxi rank:

> This large group of people came by. They began assaulting us, and in the commotion my children fled. I don't know where they are now. I was hit with a very heavy object smack between my upper lip and nose. It tore off all the flesh. I was knocked unconscious. (Witness statement, CTH archives)

Then the group split into numerous smaller groups of about fifty to 100 men, and went for various strategic points. They attacked homes, properties and even families of activists and leaders of the community. At 7.30 p.m., the invaders attacked the first people's court – at the 31 Seventh Avenue yard. First, they set alight seven or eight cars parked outside. Sarah Mthembu, Mzwanele Mayekiso and several others were inside Sarah's house, holding a meeting at the time and Sarah remembered hearing the attackers. She looked out and saw men in police uniforms, mostly black, armed with guns, knives and pangas, and followed by a hippo. She was terrified when bricks and stones rained all over her house and smashed all the windows.

She and her family broke down their door to escape the attack, and ran to an adjacent lodging. But the marauders followed and set fire to the house and everybody inside was trapped. She said:

> We jumped through the windows and outside I became more certain our attackers were not civilians. I also recognised a man who was guiding the attackers on their path of destruction. He is a local shopkeeper whose business has been singled out for boycott. (Mayekiso 1996: 47)

When the attack began Mzwanele Mayekiso jumped out of a small back window, crawled into an alleyway and found himself on top of a dead body.

> This was the closest I have come to losing my life in the struggle. We ran across several streets, and regrouped elsewhere, raised the alarm, and began to defend the area. But the attack was simultaneous, happening all over, especially at the homes of activists. (Mayekiso 1996: 48)

One of Sarah's neighbours also tried to escape, but police chased her, caught her, stabbed her and fled. Petrol was thrown over the houses which were set alight and destroyed. Another neighbour, John Grant, helped his wife and seven children escape while his house burnt down:

> Mrs Jizabelle Grant pushed her seven children through a window, she and her husband scrambled after them, and their home burst into flames. With a year-old baby on her back, a 14-year-old handicapped son and five other children in tow, the 36-year-old mother ran through the dark and dingy streets of Alexandra Township. She jumped high fences and ditches to seek refuge with her neighbours. Her husband John stayed behind watching their home and car being razed. (*The Star*, 25 April, 1986)

The attacks were well-planned and speedily executed. By 8.15 p.m. the vigilantes had reached the next target – the Eighth Avenue yard presided over by Mike Beea. Mrs Beea remembered that her door was kicked open and two men wearing powder blue shirts and dark trousers, one carrying a panga, asked where the father of the house was and started searching for him. She was threatened; they hit her in the face, shouting that they would burn the house down – which they proceeded to do. Other homes in the yard were also broken into, set alight and attacked. Children were sjambokked, shots were fired, and adults were assaulted. Twenty-year-old Virginia Pitso was outside the house, when a bullet hit her in the stomach. She survived.

While the Eighth Avenue court was being destroyed, a further forty or so men went to Linda Twala's yard in Seventeenth Avenue. His neighbours were attacked and their homes destroyed; Twala's own home was set alight while his children fled. Many assaults and attacks took place after the attack on 31 Seventh Avenue, as the group walked down the street. Moses

Motshwandi was driving along and was confronted by a large group of men who were followed by a hippo. The men were carrying long poles and as they came upon his car they shouted, 'Yes comrade'. Someone in the crowd shouted, 'That is Moses, leave him alone.' But the men were already in a frenzy and attacked him. He was shot in the neck and shoulder.

The men continued to march around the township attacking, stabbing, beating and shooting people, burning cars, throwing teargas canisters through windows, and destroying homes while singing freedom songs and shouting slogans.

Maria Malakoane and her boyfriend, Ace (Uys) Hlongwane of the ACA, were at their home in Second Avenue. There they could still hear the commotion in the streets. Uys went out to see what it was.

> He came back almost as soon as he went out. He was clutching his chest, saying he had been shot. I asked who had shot him, but he collapsed. More shots were being fired at our house, and they were smashing windows. I crouched behind a wardrobe and then lay flat. The attackers burst in and asked me where Uys kept his gun and the minutes of the Civic Association meeting. I said I did not know he had a gun, nor where he kept minutes of any meeting. (Witness statement, CTH archives)

The men were by then pouring petrol inside the house and at her denial of any knowledge of a gun and minute book they said she must also be soaked with petrol and set alight. She was hit on the head with a heavy object and heard the rest of the men screaming outside that Uys should be killed. Their home was gutted and Uys burnt to death inside the blazing house. Miss Malakoane said: 'When everything subsided I noticed a Hippo just outside our yard. The occupants of the vehicle did nothing, and just watched as the fire destroyed our home.' One Beatrice Mampane was summoned to Hlongwane's house, and arrived to find his body burnt beyond recognition. The police and army then came in large numbers, wrapped the body in a blanket and refused to allow her to take it. The body lay in the house for five hours.

By the time Moses Mayekiso got home from a meeting in Johannesburg, the main attack was over. Mayekiso was travelling with his wife and comrades when they

> came across a group of people in police uniform ... whom we believed were police. They had knopkieries and iron rods. Some had firearms ... They had powder blue shirts and blue trousers. Some were in civilian clothes ... When we were near them they stood in the road and blocked it and they started striking the car with the sticks they had and demanded the driver to open the window. He opened it. They asked us where we came from and they were rough in their speech. We told them we were coming from town. Some at the time were forcing to

open the door of the vehicle and it did open, and they shone a torch inside. They started swearing and asked us why we travel at that time. They started hitting people inside the car and the driver drove from there, took off very fast to get away … It was at night and my estimation of them was … between fifty and a hundred. (Moses Mayekiso, M3990ff)

As they drove off, they saw another similar group, and then they came across a large group of local youths, who said that the mysterious strangers had attacked many places and killed people, and that they wanted to find them:

The youth were very upset. They were in a fighting mood. We told them not to follow those people, because they were armed, but they did not listen. They proceeded … We decided to go to Seventh Avenue where we had heard that many places had been attacked there. There was a fire brigade there, extinguishing fire from burning houses. People were just full up there. Some were crying, saying people are finished. They were attacked by the police. (ibid.)

He went to his own house, and found that it had been petrol bombed. He drove around and saw many other burnt-out homes, mainly belonging to activists, and a dead body in an alley. He went to the clinic, where he found dozens of injured people and blood everywhere. As he continued to drive around the township, unknown gunmen started firing and he fled, and spent that night and many other subsequent nights on the run. After his attack he did not sleep at home until his arrest, and nor did his wife. The vigilantes had said they would come back. 'I realised that I was myself in danger … Concerning my life I realised that I was not very safe' (ibid.).

RETALIATION

The next day Alexandra was sealed off, as it had been in February, by the army (*in camera* Witness 10, Z524). The whole community was abuzz with the events. 'One would come across a group of people, discuss it a little, and then pass on' (*in camera* Witness 10, Z524). Emotions were very high. A meeting in the stadium was called and various plans for self defence – the use of Youth Groups, area committees and street committees as the nucleus of resistance, the building of barricades and the digging of trenches – put forward in response. With AYCO taking a decisive lead, it was not long before new people's courts – including the notorious Fifteenth Avenue court discussed earlier – were established to replace those burnt out. Street committees re-emerged more powerfully than ever before. Youth Groups were strengthened. That night, said Mzwanele Mayekiso, 'we organised our street committee system into action' (Mayekiso 1996: 21).

The streets were barricaded using barrels and burnt out cars, and trenches were dug, by young and old alike.

Eyewitnesses in Alexandra township, scene of bloody clashes in the last few days, said people were building what they called 'tank traps' on several of the main dirt roads. 'They are digging holes in the roads and camouflaging them with tarpaulins in the hope some of the armoured police vehicles will drive into them,' one witness said. 'It's not just teenagers doing it. Everyone seems to be involved as if it were some kind of community project.' He said several blacks were seen carrying petrol bombs although none had yet been used. (*Sunday Times*, 27 April 1986)

One of Carter's informants said that the idea of digging trenches had been imported from similar experiences elsewhere:

We used to dig a trench across the street. After digging it we'd put a string across, with petrol bombs in the hole. Then when a Casspir came the bombs would explode. We knew of these trenches from Cradock, because that was used in Cradock ... We would stand on the one side and sing. Then when they turned into the road they would see us, and when they went into that trench we would attack them ... You would have people who were brave enough to throw a petrol bomb into a Casspir. I wasn't brave enough. (DP, quoted in Carter 1991a: 180)

Journalist Jon Qwelane visited the township on the Sunday, a few days after the attacks and found:

Bands of men and youths dug deep trenches across many streets of Alexandra yesterday and by nightfall most sections of the township were inaccessible to vehicles ... The trench diggers did not hesitate to say for whom the dongas were intended – 'those troublesome hippos which raid us every night and we hope they all fall in'. An awful smell hung over some areas of Alex yesterday as uncollected night soil buckets and dustbins overflowed. In Eighth Avenue the buckets had been tipped over and waste littered the road. Youths blamed 'the enemy' for this. (*Sunday Star*, 27 April 1986)

Resistance seemed to have grown rather than diminished as a result of the attack. According to Mzwanele Mayekiso, 'This was the height of people's power.' But this was a naive view in the face of the power the state was now prepared to exert. The barricades and trenches were but feeble obstacles to army Casspirs. A journalist described the situation on Wednesday 23 April:

The town has the tragic appearance of being at war. Burnt out shells of vehicles are pulled across the rutted and untarred streets by rioters in an effort to hamper patrolling police Casspirs. They are as effective as a man trying to hold back the sea with his hands. The giant police armoured vehicles – some gaily painted in canary yellow – push through as though they weren't there. Despite the menace, however, it seems in many cases almost a game. A few stones are lobbed casually from the shadows. Police fire teargas canisters at groups of youth who quickly scatter, dampen the canisters and then return to taunt the police. 'Come out you cowards' shouts a young policeman. The answer is more stones. Minutes later what sounds like a shot rings out. A police patrol van seems to be the target. 'Get out of here' screams a constable to Pressmen. No reaction. 'They are shooting. Get out of here'. Still no response. Within minutes three Casspirs arrive on the scene. Teargas canisters are into the air [sic] falling among the houses and barricades. In the confusion, the Casspirs bulldoze through the barricades and smoke. The youngsters scatter as the police dismount to clear the obstructions. Round Fifteen. (*Sunday Times*, 27 April 1986)

Journalist and resident Mojalefa Moseki remembers a vicious gun battle that took place:

It is 3.30 on Monday morning, April 28, in Alexandra Township. A disturbing and eerie silence over the township haunts me in my vain attempts to fall asleep. A fearful scream cuts through the silent, dark streets, and puts paid to my attempts at falling asleep. I am wide awake and jump from bed. It seems the entire area in which I live was lying in this fearful silence waiting for something to happen. It did. The juddering sound of gun-fire a few streets away ruptures the silence. I pull on a shirt and a pair of jeans. The gunfire continues as I walk and then duck into the dark street. I would rather die out there than in my bed. I decide to creep as if this was the frontline of a war zone. A thunderous explosion rocks the township; it is heavy gunfire with the crash of thunder and a haunting echo. I feel dazed and my sight fails me. I cannot see through the dark that envelops me, despite the bright moon. Alexandra remains as dark as its nickname, 'Dark City'. I play it by ear as I sneak through the streets until I come close enough to judge the goings on. A hippo like vehicle and other vehicles travelling on Hofmeyr Road come closer. There is gunfire around the area, but no visible target. Answering guns shatter the night. Gun smoke smells all over the place: People are standing at the gates of their yards as I walk home. Next morning everyone goes to work, and talks about the gun battle. It is as if they are discussing something they saw on television. Some say two youths have died. Others claim two policemen were also shot. As I make my way to work, the place is crawling with military and police vehicles. At the soccer stadium in 12th avenue some soldiers are casually playing a game of soccer. More than six army vehicles, some of them looking like small tanks, are parked near the stadium. Some officers on top of the vehicles are scouring the township with binoculars. Another is taking pictures through a long lens camera. But ordinary life is also 'pulsating'. One woman in a taxi: 'It is like living in Beirut.' She was talking about the police and the army units, almost everywhere in the township. It is indeed impossible to walk through the narrow streets without having to stop for a Hippo, a Casspir, a vehicle called a 'Yellow Mellow', or a Land rover carrying heavily armed policemen and soldiers. I have survived many disasters that befell the place. But today I believe I am living through a nightmare. (*The Sowetan*, 29 April 1986)

It was in this battle that Zephaniah Mdakane, brother of treason accused Richard Mdakane, an AYCO member whose home had been destroyed in the vigilante attack, died (*The Star*, 29 April 1986; *The Citizen*, 29 April 1986). Emanuel Nkubeni died in the same battle, while a third man was seriously injured and arrested. Several policemen were wounded. Their version of events implied that Mdakane and his friends were probably fully armed ANC cadres:

Police are investigating the possibility that the three men involved in the gun battle are responsible for previous attacks on police in the troubled township. Police action follows information which they investigated, arriving at the three roomed house at about 4.20 a.m. As the police team, a lieutenant and a Warrant Officer, were knocking at the door someone opened fire at them from another room through the door. Another member who accompanied the two policemen immediately retaliated and the gun battle was over shortly afterwards. After the shootout the two wounded policemen and the wounded black occupant were rushed to hospital ... Bystanders, woken by the fierce gun battle, said several other occupants of the house were taken away by police who are believed to have found firearms in the house. (*The Citizen*, 29 April 1986)[11]

These militaristic operations, combined with the shock effects of the vigilante attack and carefully targeted arrests, appear to have succeeded. After a few days during which violent eruptions were followed by police retaliation – there was strong evidence, said *The Citizen* (26 April 1986) that black policemen were taking revenge against 'radical elements' – and army invasions, and by at least three further deaths of activists and widespread detentions and arrests, Alexandra had quietened.[12] Residents went back to work, and pupils returned to school. The barricades were removed by police, guards were set up around all factories; and some key AAC members – John Grant, Maria Mthembu and Obed Bapela – had been detained. A 'virtual state of siege' had been consolidated.

> Last night Alexandra was quiet but very tense and streets were empty. Selbourne Avenue, the township's main street, which youths had barricaded during the day, was deserted. Wrecked cars were still there and smoke, apparently from smouldering tyres, was still in the air. Families had apparently locked themselves in their homes and many homes were in darkness. (*City Press*, 27 April 1986)[13]

The siege was punctuated by random attacks and battles, some of them highly theatrical.

> An unknown guerilla held about 200 unarmed cops at bay for almost 30 minutes during a shootout in the heart of Alexandra township this week, wounding at least one cop. Hidden among a crowd of about 10,000 residents, the guerilla rattled off shots at a police patrol. (ibid.)

Surrounded by defiant residents, the guerilla held a mini-army of cops in Casspirs, Mellow Yellow buses, trucks and Land Rovers, at bay, firing from behind a barricade of burning tyres. The police eventually retreated. One policeman was left badly wounded in the stomach; the guerrilla withdrew unharmed. This shootout was filmed by camera crews from foreign media, and was billed as 'the climax of two days of death and destruction in Alex'.

The UDF called for the formation of 'street defence committees ... on every street, on every block, in every township to defend themselves against those who lurk in the dark with petrol bombs and hand grenades'. Because it was illegal for blacks to own firearms, a communications system at grass roots level should be set up, where immediate help could be called for from neighbours if attacks were made (*The Citizen*, 25 April 1986). By 27 April the AAC had issued a statement strongly condemning the ongoing police action in Alexandra, and appealed to the authorities to stop 'harassing their people'. Since the vigilante attack, they said, the police had maintained a high profile and continued to harass, intimidate and detain residents (*The Citizen*, 27 April 1986). Police began to raid activists' homes for documents such as bank books, minutes and other records, presumably beginning to prepare for their treason cases.

In his press conference on 29 April – the conference with which this chapter opened – Moses Mayekiso claimed that at least eighteen people had been killed by police during and after the vigilante attack. These figures were later vigorously disputed by police, who claimed that no more than five had died as a result of police action. It is against this background that his claim to 'grassroots control' of the township needs to be understood. Mayekiso took a defiant stance, claiming that the attacks had been directed at the constructive and productive efforts of the community to bring order to the troubled township: 'Crime has died since the Alexandra Action Committee took over the administration of law and order.' He said that:

before the committee organised the people of the township, crimes like rape, murder, robbery and assaults were common. Police could not deal with them effectively ... What we did was organise the youth and form the AAC ... We also remind them that they should not cause hardships for other residents, as we are already made to suffer by the government. We also tell them that we would not like to see ourselves handing them over to the police as we believe we can solve our problems by ourselves. Indeed, Alexandra is more stable than many townships which have horrifying crimes reported in the media. Today it is possible to move around Alexandra at any time of the day and night without fear of being molested. There are no longer cases of unknown bodies in the streets. We have succeeded where police have been unable to for the past years. (*Sunday Times*, 4 May 1986)

He said that the responsibility for the state of siege lay squarely with the police and that the innocent community was simply defending itself against armed attackers:

There is no unrest in Alexandra. People react to an ugly situation. That is why we have started defence units in each street and blocks of houses. We patrol our township by day and night ... Trenches have been dug in strategic places to stop or minimise the speed of the vigilantes. Everywhere they go, they will meet with obstacles. (ibid.)

The destructive and murderous nature of the vigilante attack, as well as the mystery as to the precise identity of the attackers, became a matter for national debate. Opposition MP David Dalling raised it in Parliament on 30 April (*The Citizen*, 1 May 1986), claiming that 'there was overwhelming evidence that the latest round of violence in Alexandra Township was planned and executed by policemen and their friends'.

Alexandra looked yesterday like a scene from the movie 'The Killing Fields'. A leadership vacuum exists as every known leader has fled, fearing death at the hands of the police ... Houses belonging to leaders have been gutted, burnt out cars litter the streets. Local business has virtually ground to a halt. The pall of death hangs over that community. What has happened there is nothing short of madness ... Unless this insanity is stopped, and quickly, Alexandra will experience a new dark era which for years to come will bear the fruit of bitterness and hatred.

Ironically, the attack had the effect of permitting outsiders to cast the complex and multi-layered rebellion in simple terms – this was a clear case of good versus evil with no room for ambiguities. Perhaps it is not surprising that when the Truth Commission – an institution which was based upon binary conceptualisations of this sort – was later to turn its mind to the rebellion, it was the vigilante attack that took up the most space in its report.

THE FINAL CLAMPDOWN

For weeks afterwards skirmishes continued between police, the army, activists and ordinary people in the township, and the rebels continued to attempt to assert their authority. Police launched a massive crime prevention drive during May, which resembled another military operation:

> Getting into Alexandra yesterday was like getting into Beirut. Getting out was like leaving prison. More than 1,670 troops, backed by troop carriers, Casspirs and trucks, turned this trouble-torn township into a war zone for the umpteenth time this year, conducting house-to-house raids and searching every living soul moving in and out. Security force roadblocks stopped all vehicles and people entering the township, but took an even closer look at those leaving the township. A *City Press* vehicle was stopped five times yesterday. The searches resulted in yet another stay-away by Alex residents – but this time it was because of the security forces. Their continual searches – up to six checkpoints in some township exits – meant some workers only got out of their home township by noon.' (*City Press*, 11 May 1986; see also *The Citizen*, 12 May 1986)

The security forces tried to capture the support of adults disillusioned with youth excesses by publicising a hot-line for people to call to report anybody 'disrupting their children's education'. But as Moses Mayekiso said: 'The security forces are the ones who have made life difficult. Residents can't go outside after sunset and for the past few weeks we have been hearing gunshots in the dark. Searchlights manned by the police make it difficult for people to sleep.' One newspaper reported that twenty-eight people were arrested over the weekend of the raid and that the township was still being patrolled by a large contingent of police and army, and roadblocks and searches continued. White businesses were being guarded; and soldiers in trucks had made a base for themselves at the local stadium (*Business Day*, 13 May 1986). Far stricter controls on funerals were introduced.

This local repression was ultimately overshadowed by the declaration of a national state of emergency on 12 June, which was followed by the detention of at least 3,000 activists throughout the township – many of them leading members of the AAC, AYCO and ASCO (Carter 1991a: 185). The emergency was 'unprecedented in its comprehensiveness' and outlawed practically all forms of mass mobilisation, even imposing curfews in some areas. It marked, said one commentator, 'the end of one phase of the popular struggle and the beginning of another' (Murray 1987: 430). In the country as a whole, 22,000 were detained in the first five months of the emergency,

40 per cent of whom were under the age of 18. The police were indemnified from any prosecution for actions taken under emergency regulations. Youths went into the underground movement, 'which swelled to bursting point' (Johnson 1988: 63).

For the Alexandrans who were arrested the emergency had one unintentionally productive consequence. For the first time, many activists in jail were thrust together, leading to a new harmony of purpose and understanding. One, Saths Cooper, said that:

> the Emergency has been a blessing. It has forced common ground between different factions. They have had to acknowledge that they've got something in common and that the luxury of attacking each other – even verbally – cannot continue. (Johnson 1988: 67)

Activists had also been forced into the realm of secrecy:

> We must admit it is very hard. We are operating under very trying conditions ... The security police ... even roam the streets at night now and go to the shebeens ... Our organization is underground .. we are holding meetings underground ... we can't move around freely, but we are still organizing the youth. We just arrange a meeting point and move from there to a venue ... Our support is still strong. People [had been] mobilised and conscientised and the next step was to organise them, to get them into structures. Now we are having to talk to people about the clampdown and how it affects the struggle. (*Weekly Mail*, 29 August 1986)

Few activists could live in the township any more. Overtly rebellious behaviour was no longer possible and a major reassessment of resistance strategies was undertaken. Youth politics suffered most in this realignment, as most groups were forced into alliance politics of one sort or another. Alliance politics became the order of the day in the case of youth, workers and even non-UDF groupings (with the tragic exception of the IFP) (Johnson 1988: 79ff). But at the same time large sections of the youth retained their commitment to violence and formed gangs or underground organisations; and began to commit themselves to militarism in a manner not seen before (Marks 2001).

By August, while Alexandra was not completely 'normal', the township was relatively stable. The rebellion had lasted six months in all. In that month the police returned to their homes. Five months after the Six-Day War – in September 1986 – two separate groups of key activists (one group of nine youths and one of five adults) were arrested. Charges of treason and/ or sedition and a series of others were brought against them. While previous detentions of activists had been short-term and had tended to enhance their radical reputations in Alexandra, these serious charges, when combined with the assault upon the township by police, proved crippling.

By September, too, a Joint Management Centre (JMC), part of the state's National Security Management system, had been established to administer the township. The rebels' belief in their own infallibility rapidly faded, and one comrade remembered the whole rebellion as a delusion: 'In 1986 [people] were fooled into believing that they were governing themselves. They believed they had power in their own hands' (BM, quoted in Carter 1991a: 78). The dramatic performance of the revolt had come to an end and the briefly imagined theatre of revolutionary scenes and Nationalist spectacle within which it had been staged, the township itself, reverted to the mundane.

11

MEMORY AND FORGETTING

The rebellion was one amongst the many that contributed to the eventual demise of apartheid. The attacks upon township space and authority made it obvious that the establishment of an even marginally legitimate form of rule in townships was not feasible within the framework of apartheid once the older authority of paternalism had been removed. Power had to rest with the army and the police, a situation which was impossible to sustain as a long-term form of governance. Barely four years later, Nelson Mandela was released from prison, and the new ANC-dominated order began to emerge.

This study does not pursue the story of resistance and struggle in Alexandra in particular or South Africa in general after the rebellion had ended. The story of this particular uprising stands on its own – emblematic of the challenges to authority which the apartheid state experienced in the 1980s. Instead, it now turns to the question of how this event was constructed by the ideologues of the transition, how its participants presented it at their trials for treason, and how it was more 'officially' remembered in the subsequent ten years.

NARRATIVE AND MEMORY:
FROM TRIALS TO TRUTH COMMISSION

In what ways did officially sanctioned narratives construct the revolt, both as a private experience and as a public occurrence? Did the three 'frames' of collective action survive to constitute three 'frames' of memory?

The recording and remembering of the rebellion had begun before the flames died down. Academic theses, memoirs and newspaper reports flourished. It was not long before it became clear that everyone wanted this to have been a Nationalistic uprising, and most press reports tended to reproduce the public Nationalist narrative, treating other events in the township as exceptional. The ANC propaganda machine was part of the Nationalist appropriation of events. To the ANC it had been 'the consequence of a grand revolutionary conspiracy' to replace the apartheid government – created and guided by themselves (Carter 1991a: 6).

> Even the least attentive study of the situation in South Africa will show that taking place almost simultaneously with ungovernability is the

creation of a new type of governability, that which is exercised by the people. Places like Port Alfred, Lingelihle, KwaNobuhle, Mamelodi, Alexandra and others ... provide the ground for the growth and development of our people's army and for the escalation of our people's war. (Mzala in *Sechaba*, September 1986: 12)

The 'organs of people's power' had emerged as a result not only of subjective momentary conditions 'but also by the objective level of our revolution towards seizure of power by the people'.

Let the racist magistrates and lawyers shout their lungs out in scorn of the 'necklace' method of punishing collaborators, let them call the People's Courts 'kangaroo courts' if they want to, but we shall always reply to them by saying: when we say power to the people, we also mean the right to suppress the enemies of the people, we also mean the country's administration and control by the ordinary people. (Mzala, in *Sechaba*, September 1986: 13)

Additional narratives of the revolt came to be constructed within two other worlds, both of which took a theatrical form: the courtroom, where in 1986–7 the key treason trials involving activists were held; and the Truth Commission, where ten years later a different memory of the township more broadly and of the revolt in particular was evoked.

CONSTRUCTING THE TRIALS

In May, June and July multiple arrests had taken place in Alexandra.[1] Two major trials followed. Moses Mayekiso and four other members of the AAC leadership, and eight comrades from the Fifteenth Avenue court, were brought to court in two separate trials. All were charged with high treason, alternatively with sedition and subversion in terms of section 54 (2) of the Internal Security Act of 1982. They were said to have conspired with the ANC, COSATU, and the UDF to seize control of Alex and render the area ungovernable.

The two trials took place while the old state was still in existence and while it continued to display an ambivalent approach towards reform, as well as a frightening capacity for repression. The trials stand as imperfect monuments to the rebellion and also reflect these conflicts within the state. During the actual trials and the mounting of the cases, significant shaping of memory took place. The thirteen accused from the two trials were in the same communal cell, for one thing. And then the lawyers, particularly for the adult case (called, after its chief accused, the Mayekiso trial), some of whom were trained at the University of the Witwatersrand, where Marxist and Gramscian academic discourses were prevalent, sought to cast the whole event in a sociological light, and used sociologists, including myself, as expert witnesses. We portrayed the rebellion as a form of collective action, resulting from the structural situation in which the inhabitants of the township found themselves, and argued strongly against the state's assertions that it had been the result of a conspiracy, an ANC plot, or evidence of treasonous and illegal activity. The lawyers spent hours going over the case and attempting to give meaning to it. So trial evidence was not only shaped by factors such as fear and state manipulation, but also by the construction of a narrative of the revolt which reflected contemporary academic concerns about resistance, collective action and popular consciousness. This narrative came to infuse the evidence given by the accused.

The portrayal of the revolt was rehearsed and meticulously constructed. As Mzwanele Mayekiso said: 'The preparations with the lawyers were rigorous. Like an actor who learned the role, I knew what to expect' (Mayekiso 1996: 34). In it, most of the violence which had taken place was blamed on 'wayward youth'. The adults were, by contrast, portrayed as sensible seekers after justice for their people – idealists with a broader vision than that of the 'disreputable' and 'uncontrollable' young. The causes of the rebellion were attributed to broader social as well as economic factors and a sense of the nature and existence of the private social world of the township was conveyed in the defence argument. The judge was not unsympathetic to this approach, and at times a relatively cosy atmosphere of clever jokiness pervaded the courtroom. It was difficult for the state to sustain a case of treasonous or seditious activity in the face of evidence of the adults' patently constructive activities and the unclear relationship between the ANC and adult ideology. The state itself had not penetrated the private world of the township sufficiently to distinguish between adult 'democracy', youth 'utopianism' and the more generally pervasive nationalism.

By contrast, in the youth trial the prosecution emphasised the brutality, randomness and wilfulness of the youths' anti-crime, people's court and consumer boycott activities. Their own community, it was argued, had suffered most, although their aims also coincided with those of the ANC's strategies of ungovernability and people's war. The defence relied on exposing contradictions and weaknesses in, or simply disputing, prosecution evidence, as well as portrayals of the youths' lives of hardship and suffering in the poverty stricken township. Moments of aggression and disbelief on the part of the prosecutor were met with hostility or angry withdrawal on the part of the accused. Although the defence did try to deflect responsibility for the better documented of the more vicious youth activities onto others, this was difficult to sustain, and anybody who followed the trial knew that its evidence could not be embraced within a sanitised version of what had happened. Not surprisingly, this trial was barely reported publicly and remains little known.

It was the adult trial that occupied the public stage. It became something of a cause célèbre, both nationally and internationally. For a time the activities of adults appropriated the 'public' ground. International support, said one of the accused, was 'crucial'. The United Auto Workers Union in the US took a particularly active role in mounting an international campaign, as did many other trade unions, while the then US ambassador attended the trial frequently. The trial was widely reported in the South African, and occasionally the international, press. In Britain support for the Mayekiso trial was in fact divided, with the official anti-apartheid movement, influenced by its SACTU wing (the ANC union movement which the chief defendant Moses 'Moss' Mayekiso had not supported) deciding:

> not to take our case seriously, using the argument that the Mayekiso treason trial promoted personality cults. There were also allegations that Moss was a workerist, and yet the rest of us came from the Congress of South African Students and other groups from the Congress tradition, which always held the Freedom Charter banner very high. (*Non-Stop Against Apartheid*, monthly bulletin of the City of London Anti-Apartheid Group, October 1986. Thanks to Gavin Brown for assisting with this information.)

This was a hint as to the difficulties, which later emerged in constructing a valid 'ANC sanctioned' memory of the rebellion through the Truth Commission. The then controversial 'City of London' anti-apartheid breakaway group, as well as the then British ambassador, provided the main non-union support in England for the trial instead.

The two trials ended differently. While the youths were acquitted of treason, they were found guilty of sedition and most of them were imprisoned.[2] Few knew of their plight.

All of the adults, on the other hand, were found not guilty. The prosecution, it was found, had failed to prove that the accused had been responsible for the establishment of street committees and other 'alternative structures', or that there had been a conspiracy with the ANC to render the township 'ungovernable', and the five adult activists were released to great public acclaim in April 1989. The 'sociological defence' had worked.

The overall effect of the two trials was that the contributions to the revolt of the main rebellious groupings were startlingly misremembered. The adults came to be thought of as victors on behalf of public nationalism, whereas in fact they had pursued their struggle to a certain degree independently of the nationalist 'frame'. Even greater distortion accompanied the construction of the story of the 'less palatable' actions of the youths, who became profoundly marginalised in the public and private memory. Youths who had taken part in brutality and violence were portrayed as the 'other'. Their actions were not perhaps forgotten entirely, but increasingly came to be thought of as outside of the virtuous realm which adults claimed for themselves. The fact that the 'sensible' revolution had depended upon the youth movement was downplayed. Instead a working misunderstanding was cultivated concerning the respective roles of these two strata.

Together, the press and the trials had by now engendered powerful public myths about the township and its people, to add to those that already existed. Even today, the story of oppression and resistance in the township is already frequently told as part of the litany of African nationalism – its civil religion. It is also embodied in numerous published writings, and in a variety of unpublished theses and dissertations already widely used in this study. By the time the Truth and Reconciliation Commission (TRC) had been established, the public myth was something like this:

The nationalist myth of Alexandra (before the TRC)

Alexandra has always been a sadly neglected township, and for this reason, and because it was unlit, was called 'Dark City'. However it had always had a strong sense of its own 'community' and of belonging, in spite of the fact that violent and criminal youth gangs had often plagued the township. This 'community' was at times indistinguishable from the 'nation' – belonging to the community meant belonging to the nation. And the nation, in turn, was often indistinguishable from the ANC. Indeed prominent and famous ANC figures, including Nelson Mandela, had actually lived in Alexandra. Alexandra's residents had suffered but were very brave. They had constantly experienced poverty, crime and hardship, and yet took part in courageous bus boycotts and squatter movements in the forties and fifties. They resisted government attempts to remove them more than once. They, guided by the ANC and their own local leaders, and in the face of terrible repression and provocation, about which numerous tales abounded, mounted a local revolution in the mid-eighties, followed by a famous treason trial in which the accused were victorious. This was followed by the tragic conflict between the ANC and the IFP in the late eighties and early nineties, and the appalling overcrowding and rising social tensions as thousands more squatters, including 'foreigners' moved in after the ANC was unbanned. The ANC's ascent to power in 1994 was in part due to the heroic struggle of Alexandrans, and although today they continue to live in great poverty, plans will soon be under way to rebuild and upgrade the township. The people are cynical of such plans, but hopeful that they will come to fruition.

THE TRUTH COMMISSION: A NEW PUBLIC MYTH?

When, in 1996, the Truth and Reconciliation Commission held a special hearing on Alexandra Township, a different configuration of narrative and memory emerged, through a different series of processes. A great deal had happened in the interim. The main activists had moved on, some into key

258   THEATRES OF STRUGGLE AND THE END OF APARTHEID

government positions and others into professional jobs. Some remained active in grassroots politics, while still others remained marginalised and unemployed, as did most of the population of the township.

But most importantly, the country had been liberated and a new government had come to power. Alexandra itself had voted overwhelmingly for the ANC in the 1994 election. Nationally and in local contexts the ANC rapidly sought to establish itself as the legitimate, hegemonic, party, using history as part of its comprehensive bid for power. Public Nationalism was rapidly appropriated to this end. The rebellion was still not forgotten, but gradually came to be thought of as part of the public history that the now ascendant Nationalists sought to construct.

The Truth Commission's Committee on Human Rights Violations took thousands of statements from victims of apartheid, hundreds of them residents of Johannesburg's townships. People were asked to come forward if they or their kin had been killed, abducted, tortured or severely ill-treated for political reasons. The commission defined such experiences as gross human rights violations and undertook to investigate them through its Investigative Unit, aiming to find out who was responsible for these, how and why they happened; and to hold public hearings. The Committee on Reparation and Rehabilitation would receive the information thus derived, consult with 'communities' and make policy recommendations to the president for appropriate reparation to victims. So far, a minute proportion of these reparations have been paid, discrediting the entire process quite fundamentally. However the importance of the rituals held to hear evidence should not be discounted because of this, as they played a significant part in shaping subsequent perceptions of the events of the rebellion.

Twenty-two Alexandran residents were invited to present their testimonies concerning resistance in the township between the 1960s and late 1980s. The commission chose to use the method of cultural ritual rather than that of legal procedure to carry out its purpose. How were the already established myths and narratives embedded in the ritual? What definition of 'community' did the ritual embrace? What did it allow to be said, and what silences did it permit? And what patterns and types of storytelling accompanied it? The patterns of ritual clearly would have had profound psychological effects upon the participant who sought catharsis. But they would also have had significant social effects upon the longer-term meanings given to the crucial period of the mid-1980s.

The Truth Commission hearings tended to resemble what Durkheim calls 'the piacular rite', which has an ambiguous nature. Normally embodied in such occasions as funerals, the marking of drought or plague, or the occasion of a poor harvest, the piacular rite is both positive and negative. It is 'negative' in that it permits the separation of the sacred from the profane and of the individual from the collective. Most importantly for our purposes, it allows for the replacement of individual representations by collective beliefs. But it is also 'positive' in that it allows the worshipper to bridge the gap between himself and the object of his cult, by encouraging recall and the construction of myths. It allows expiation, but also brings to the fore 'sentiments of sorrow or fear' about 'every misfortune, everything of ill omen' (Pickering 1984: 339ff).

In order for rituals to bridge the gap between the personal and the social, they require the use of sacred ground, the gathering together of an 'assembly', and the definition of a purpose: 'the gathering of people seeking the same goal and vibrating with the same emotions' (Pickering 1984: 324). Rites remake individuals and groups morally – and therefore have power over things. 'They have a profound effect on the participants as individuals and as a group, intellectually and emotionally.' Participants take away a feeling of well-being. 'Men are confident because they feel themselves stronger, and they really are stronger' (Pickering 1984: 338).

The physical elements of the TRC ritual embodied the commission's function as a bridge between the public and the private. The ceremonial form of the hearing was proto-religious, adding to the emotion it evoked, and was constructed around a variety of carefully chosen collective representations. Each session opened with a prayer, conducted by a religious figure from the community who would then light a candle to symbolise the bringing of the truth. The national anthem followed. Tears would flow; hidden pain would be revealed; terrible stories would be told. Ritual could bridge the realm of the personal and that of the social. On the individual level, the TRC set out to allow people to participate in rites of confession, mourning and making public their private pain and anger. Rather than opting for a punitive approach, it opted for an expiational and healing one. It sought to transform individuals and assemblies of individuals from stances of resentment, anger, hatred and guilt, to those of acceptance, wholeness, forgiveness and confession. In addition, these changes would then, it was hoped, be 'writ large' upon the society as a whole, freeing it from the burdens of unspoken passions and from a possible future age of retribution. This double-sided purpose was not always articulated as such and the gap between the personal/private and the social/public was, it will be argued, bridged in a very particular set of ways, which had their own effects upon memory.

The ostensible aim of the TRC was to bring to the fore the stories of those who had been silenced in the past. But in the case of the Alexandra rebellion, would it, in doing so, simply reinforce the existing myths? To what extent would it actually be able to permit the real complexities of the situation to come through? And to what extent would it create new myths?

Key speakers were included in the Alexandra hearings, not as witnesses to specific abuses, but as 'community representatives'. Thus a person clearly designated as spokesperson for the township, Patience Phasha, opened the proceedings by welcoming the commission 'on behalf of the community of Alex'. The commission, she said, was there to hear an entity thought of as 'the community', of which the witnesses were representative in some way. The 'community' came to resemble the 'congregation': the truth would be spoken from and about it, as well as from and about individuals who were 'part' of it. By referring implicitly and often quite explicitly to an abstract notion of 'community' the hearings thus precluded any reference to the divided nature of the rebellion.

Phasha sketched the main 'community' experiences that she believed Alexandra residents considered to be the central motifs of their suffering under apartheid. The existing myth surfaced. She included the bus boycotts of the forties and fifties, the gangsterism of the fifties, the removals and upheavals of the sixties, the Six-Day War of the mid-eighties, the orchestrated conflict between ANC and Inkatha, and the plight of the displaced people, of the nineties. Clearly Phasha was invoking a story that encapsulated key moments and perceptions of their suffering, to which the audience clearly related. She concluded by linking community, the TRC, God and the nation – arguing that the TRC was there to act as a national lifeline, in a context in which South Africans could express their need for each other and their capacity to work together.

The stories of two others, Benjamin Lekalakala and Obed Bapela himself – who had become an ANC-aligned local councillor – were both presented to the commission as testimonies 'for the community', rather than for themselves.[3] Both indeed claimed to speak on behalf of the community. Unsurprisingly, Bapela displayed wide knowledge of the recent history of resistance and state repression in the township, and gave the hearings a certain weight. He spoke of the need for forgiveness and reconciliation and often referred to examples of human rights abuses that were not inflicted upon him but upon others – reinforcing the impression that he was spokesman for the community.

The TRC's mythologising elided 'community' and 'nation', while it permitted the ANC to claim to represent both. Witness selection itself was part of this.[4] The choice of which witnesses would represent the 'community' was heavily influenced by the ANC – indeed Bapela had, together with his wife Connie, assisted the commission to find its witnesses. As the commission's hearings proceeded, the impression was given that they were the 'hosts' of the occasion. Thus they were thanked in the opening speeches for their help and co-operation; and Bapela, although he gave evidence (but of a very particular sort, as we shall see), did not sit with the rest of the witnesses. This is not to imply that efforts were not made to include non-ANC witnesses who had experienced human rights abuses; nor that the ANC was not a key and highly significant player in the events experienced by Alex residents. But the identification of the ANC with the public telling of the story of Alexandra's past – with the very definition of 'community' – was surprisingly central and to an extent built into the hearing from the start.

A third feature of TRC myth-making was the way in which the existing public myth was modified through the interpretation given of the Six-Day War and its aftermath. Following quite closely the accepted narrative of the time Bapela said it had all started in June 1985. A lot of townships were aflame. There was a lot of activity. 'People' established street committees. There was also a consumer boycott. In January 1986 things started to take off in Alex. There was shooting at 'Jazz Stores'; a young man was killed. This 'provoked the whole situation'. His funeral was held at Alex stadium; then his parents' home was tear-gassed. That provoked the youth. The police became targets. Alex was aflame for six days. Ninety people died.

In all of this, no suggestion was made that the rebellion was anything other than a united uprising by the community, led by ANC-linked leaders. Bapela's own role and that of other adults was put at the forefront. 'How did the street committees start?' Bapela was asked. They began in the Eastern Cape, he said. He had travelled a lot and been exposed to how they worked. He had shared the idea with other comrades. They had tried to get support. They started yard and block committees. The idea 'spread'. They moved from street to street. He was asked if the consumer and rent boycotts were violent – particularly in the light of the fact that the police said they were responding to the violence of the day. They were not, he answered. The police had legal means to respond to consumer and rent boycotts. They did not involve killing and attacking.

He was asked about people's courts. Here, he took the opportunity – the only one given during the hearings – to describe the youths' activities. They came across as having started off 'well' and then deteriorated into more dubious practices. The idea of 'people's courts' had arisen in 1985, he said. They were started by the youth, who formed into anti-crime patrol groups. They took out youths and told them not to drink, fight, and so on. Crime went down to zero. They took many knives and weapons. People started having confidence in youths and brought cases to them. They would bring the complainant and the perpetrator together and give advice. The courts spread. There was no sjambokking at this time. But after the Six-Day War, youths 'got excited' and started to hold trials and prosecutions. There was now sentencing and sjambokking. Bapela distanced himself from these activities, saying that he had not been personally responsible for the sjambokking.

While Bapela claimed that the 'sensible adults' had been of importance to the rebellion, Moses Mayekiso was portrayed as having been of secondary importance to Bapela himself. This presented quite a different picture from that given in the treason trial, where Mayekiso had been seen as the leader and the solid trade unionist, keeping the unruly youth under control. Was this because by that stage Mayekiso had been publicly revealed as a member of the Communist Party, and therefore was perhaps less 'suitable' as a key figure to give evidence of community worthiness and folk Nationalism? He was asked if the strategy of the time had been to form an alternative government. He answered, in contradistinction to the 'sociological' defence of the trial, that the intention had indeed been to undermine the government and to make Alexandra – and indeed the whole society – ungovernable; an admission which could have seen him found guilty in the trial. This had been a just war and a just struggle. 'Now we are liberated,' he said.

Bapela's evidence combined and interwove both the 'adult' and the 'Nationalist' narratives, co-opted them into an ANC version of history, and negated the part played by the youth. The way he distanced himself from the more dubious and brutal actions of the youth followed the line taken by the treason trial defence absolutely. There was to be no admission of responsibility for violent and overtly revolutionary behaviour – even indirect – here. The youth, in this portrayal, had been the architects of their own descent into a sort of depravity. The commissioners reinforced this by asking only if the rent and consumer boycotts had been violent – thus allowing Bapela neatly to sidestep the question of other forms of violence at the time.[5]

The significance of this double marginalisation of the story of the experience of youths – first in the trials and now in the TRC – cannot be underestimated. They were the key actors in the entire revolt, both in Alexandra and throughout the country. And yet these versions of the past obfuscated their role, and any direct or indirect connections there may have been between the youth and the ANC or its surrogates.

Bapela's capacity to tell the story of the revolt gave a weight and coherence to the occasion. He had created a new central 'myth', to which the more personal and fragmented stories of those who were not leaders of 'the community' could be connected. This study now examines the areas of overlap and dissonance between the new, highly Nationalistic, public myth and the private stories of individual witnesses.

THE TRUTH COMMISSION'S 'PRIVATE' STORIES: GOOD AND EVIL WITHIN THE COMMUNITY

With the remaining witnesses the commission undertook a far more difficult task – taking the much more private versions of events of ordinary people who did not 'represent the community', and making them public. An elaborate process was developed to this end. Each witness was accorded a dignified welcome. They were told that their words and stories were very important, and asked several pointed questions. Most testimonies were brought to a dramatic point where the recall of the witness's greatest suffering was reached – and many would break down here. As they wept, women, clearly there for precisely that purpose, would come up to hold and comfort them – but the witnesses were encouraged to carry on, sometimes quite relentlessly. Thus those called, in a legalistic sense, 'witnesses' behaved unlike witnesses in a court. They were more like witnesses to God. This was an occasion when collective, as well as individual, memories and experiences were drawn upon, and emotional displays were common. A strong relationship between witness and audience, and between witnesses and their questioners, developed.

Each was then ceremoniously thanked by the chairperson, who would sum up important elements of the testimony, and indirectly praise the witness. He or she would talk of, say, 'what kind of son you had'; 'what was in your heart'; 'your sad story', your 'gratitude for survival' or your 'spirit of reconciliation'. What did the various pieces of evidence, which had a direct link to the rebellion, add up to? Did they differ from the existing 'public myths'? If so, in what ways? What conceptions of suffering did they convey, and what did these conceptions of suffering imply about the nature of the rebellion?

While 'human rights abuses' were defined by the commission as mainly concerned with deeply personal tragedies, there was room in this hearing for broader issues to be raised, as the discussions of Bapela and Phasha have already indicated. And although they were not the centrepieces of any story, social and cultural matters were clearly part of the generalised experience of apartheid, and part of the discourses within which such experiences were retold. In fact, so powerful were these aspects that they often 'burst through' an individual's story even when they were not specifically being asked for by the commissioners.

The residents of Alexandra were, like most witnesses in the TRC, cast as mere victims. Their extraordinarily courageous, unique and imaginative struggle was almost entirely ignored. The gross unfairness of apartheid; the ways in which whites and blacks were regarded as enemies at worst, or alienated from one another at best; the presence of, and appalling behaviour of, hated officialdom; ignorance; poverty; the uncared-for children and youth; poor education – these things all appeared in the stories of the witnesses. Witnesses felt excluded from knowledge of the workings of courts, police stations, mortuaries, and the other institutions with which they, in their moments of suffering, had to interact. They felt the police were not only violent and murderous, but also deceitful. Maria Makaloane would not forget how they had posed as private vigilantes, tying cloths around their heads to pretend they were *Makabasas*. Guns and bullets were ubiquitous; violence was common. The eighties were a time when the 'people' – portrayed as poor and humble – were cast against 'the police' in all their power and might. As Jabu Malinga said, 'We fought the police with stones and dustbin lids.'

The emphasis here was on the oppressive actions of the police during the revolt, and the vigilantes who ended it. The community, it was felt, had been invaded by the forces of the state. Irene March said that Alex was 'a battlefield' – a phrase also used by others. Dorah Mkihele described how one day the streets were blockaded and people were stopped from going to work. One bereaved mother told of how after her son's funeral 'my daughter and friends were taken away by white policemen'. They were bailed out. In court the police said, 'Let's work quick today because we have to do things. Today we are going to the township.'

Referring to the *Makabasas*, she said that:

> they were there to burn people; people were burnt by police. They had petrol bombs, axes, they were singing. The police – from Wynberg and Bramley – did the burning of houses. I walked behind them. They went to no 31 and 32. Then they went to Second Avenue. The next day white people were taking pictures.

Obed Bapela told the story of the *Makabasas* too – with the greater perspective that he brought more generally to the occasion:

> During that period the police wanted to identify a group to use against us. In April when they could not find a local group they themselves dressed up and called themselves 'Amakabasa' (called after a local gangster). They dressed up like them with uniforms on, though they pulled their shirts out. They came from Wynberg; they entered Alex and attacked all meeting places and houses. They retreated back to Wynberg.

The Alexandra police, seen as invading, deceitful and violent people, were also heartless, said witnesses. When Jabu Malinga had been beaten up until his teeth were loose, he asked who could help him; he was told 'go to Mandela'. When community leader Linda Twala's house had been burnt down, the fire service would not extinguish the fire. Nkosana Mngadi said that when he had had his leg amputated, a doctor from South America working in the hospital had said he was 'Mandela's terrorist'. He asked to be moved from the hospital because of harassment. When Sekitla Mogano went in 1985 to seek the body of one of her two sons, and it was not there, she was told to 'go to Mandela' to find it.

Good and evil were personified in many testimonies. Famous local names, people who had been directly or indirectly involved in the rebellion, were included in the testimonies as points of reference for 'goodness' and, in most cases, 'victimhood'. 'Jingles', Ace Hlongwane, Michael Diradeng – these were important figures in the community and, indeed, in the public narratives of the past. It was they, and their harsh experiences, rather than the participants in the revolt and their courage and imagination, who took centre stage.

Jessie Moquae told about her fiancé, the well-known Alexandra 'people's poet', Jingles. He was shot dead: 'a white Mazda had passed three times. They shot Jingles,' she said. Subsequently, moreover, 'whites disturbed us from preparing for the funeral ... Teachers and comrades were not allowed in Jingles' funeral' – which was at first arranged by the police. The comrades were so angry with this they collected his body again. Then police arrived at Nineteenth Avenue, looking for his body; they threatened to shoot; there was tear gas. The funeral didn't go well. 'The police took corpse and threw it into a hearse,' said Moquae, weeping. 'They stopped the people from going to graveyard. I am proud of him. They had to bury him. At graveyard the reverend came, but people were absent. They took the body, threw it, like any rubbish, and threw soil on top of it.' His 'body was abused'.

Another witness, Montshentshe Matjila, remembered how when the police, posing as the *Makabasas*, arrived: their faces were painted black; they wore berets. People were scared and were told to go inside the house. But instead people tried to go home. The police threw canisters. 'One landed in front of me. I tried to run away. I fell inside a drum.' Two black policemen, including the notorious Mothibe, and four white policemen 'kicked me. They hit me with batons. I lost consciousness. I found myself in hospital. My arm was broken. My teeth were out.' Maria Malokoane told of how she went out on a Tuesday in April 1986, when she saw people in blue shirts and navy pants, with cloths tied around their heads, singing down the street. Later they surrounded her house looking for her boyfriend Ace Hlongwane. They came in and asked for him; they started shooting; they set the house on fire, with Ace inside. He died. They were the *Makabasas*.

Specific policemen such as the above-mentioned Mothibe personified evil. His sin was that he was both of and yet against the community. He epitomised the 'sell-out'. Maria Malakoane said that she had seen Mothibe – whom she knew – amongst the police. He even tried to warn her, saying 'I know you. Get away. We are going to cause damage.' She was injured. 'I was bleeding everywhere.' She went to work the next day. At 4.30 p.m. the police 'shot again'. They retreated. 'The hostel ladies helped me, washed me, reporters took statements.' She had a bullet 'in her bones'.

BODIES, SOULS AND SPACES

In this stark world of good and evil, how was suffering to be defined? Unlike the ideologues of Nationalism, the ordinary witnesses to the TRC did not cast their memories in terms of larger images of community, nation or social movement, but rather on a more intimate, but no less socially constructed, scale. The body, the soul and the personal space provided the main markers of this universe. Bodies were attacked, brutalised and abandoned. Dorah Mkihele told of how her son Jabulani, a 19-year-old with a Standard Two education, 'who delivered papers for Allied', was shot after he left very early to go to work. 'Before he reached the bus stop he came across white police at Twelfth Avenue and was shot by them.' Three people he was with ran away and climbed a tree and 'were shot at until they fell'. Others ran into a shack but were pulled out. Sizakele called an ambulance. The ambulance arrived but the 'police would not allow it'. The police 'finished the rest'. She found out only the next morning what had happened and found Jabulani's body in the government mortuary.

Margaret Madlana's story of physical abuse was brilliantly told. It combined place, event and time, conjuring up a visual image of the events, apportioning blame, and situating it within the known stories about Alex. Like many of the stories told at the commission it was almost biblical in its force and impact. She appeared in front of the commission with her daughter, to talk about her son, Bongani. 'It was February 1986; Monday the seventeenth. I was at home,' she said. 'There were some youths who came to my house. They were telling us to get out of the house. My twelve-year-old son went with the youth. After a while I got worried. I had had no breakfast. I needed to go to my sister, at Fifth Avenue.'

> When I passed Twenty-fourth Avenue, I found a child shot in the yard.[6] They were pulling him. They were white police. He was not dead. They pulled him up and hit him against a rock. They chased us away. I looked back. More police arrived. Mothibe was there ... I passed the place. I told my sister they had killed a young child. She said don't worry, relax. I said how could that happen. Bongani would not do that. I went home. He was not there. I told them I saw the police. I woke up at 5 am. Still no Bongani. I went to the Alex Clinic, and then home. Then I went to Bramley police station. The police didn't listen. I looked at their records. He was still not there. Some had been hit by bullets. They said go to Khotso House; go to the mortuary. I went to his father's work. I explained about the hippos. I took a taxi, and went to the mortuary, not to Khotso house. The taxi passengers agreed. There was a queue at the mortuary.

She went on: '"Mama," they said, "we have seen one child. He came alone and was carried in a hippo."'

> They took me into the mortuary. There were bodies lying on the ground. Bongani was there. I cried 'Bongani you have left me behind' ... They gave me letters for the police and myself. I went and told his father. Mothibe took the letter. He said the child was killed at number twenty-four – the one I had seen. They had photos of him holding a half jack which was a petrol bomb. Therefore the police knew him and knew me – yet they took him to the mortuary alone because they knew me. Most children disappeared and parents could not find them.

Later the commissioners asked her to give more details of his death:

'They hit him with irons,' she answered. 'He may have survived but his head was hit against a rock. He was swollen.'

Searching for a loved one and finally finding his or her body in the clinic or mortuary was a horror which several experienced. Of course such experiences were interpreted as examples of the callousness of the police. But parents also saw it as a reflection of the waywardness of their children – echoing the way in which youth rebelliousness was marginalised in the public version of events. Lesoro Mohlomi's son Reuben had been shot in the eye in 1985 and his eyesight permanently damaged; a year later he was shot dead. His mother had tried to stop him taking part in rebellious events, but to no avail.

> Reuben was a comrade ... it was the Friday before Michael Diradeng's funeral; Reuben wanted to go – but I advised him not to go because he couldn't see clearly and couldn't run. He went but denied it. I was selling alcohol – I asked him to stay home and sell for me. When we heard there were police and bullets I closed the business. Reuben could go. They came and told me he was shot, suspected dead. At the clinic all the bodies were lying in the hall. I tried to drag him out. I tried to talk to him. I took off his shoes, a key and a letter to the President. A nurse came in and said he was dead. They refused to let us into the mortuary. The priests of Alex helped us get the bodies of our children, but only after five weeks.

The phrase 'our children' is indicative of the fact that what Reuben's mother was experiencing was so common as to have become a part of the collective memory of the township. Thus Dorah Mkihele spoke of how 'a big ambulance' went around the township calling people to come and identify bodies. Reuben was, like many others, buried at a mass funeral and the family's mourning became part of a communal process. Maria Makaloane remembered that: 'they were buried – that is many people, seven at a time, though nine were advertised. They were all shot.' Like Reuben's mother she, too, remembers the time lapse: 'they were buried after four weeks,' she said.

The virtual imposition of the mass funeral format upon families meant that the story of one's child or husband's death inevitably became part of the wider story of the suffering of the community. Martha Smiles too, whose husband was shot in the Six-Day War, was drawn into this: 'After three days I realised he must be dead. I found him in the mortuary. He had to be buried with the children who had died, because "he died for his country".'

Mourners for Jingles were not the only ones for whom the denial, manipulation or control of burial rites was abuse – of the body, the soul and of the bereaved. Matsiliso Monageng also suffered greatly in this respect. She said that 'Boers harassed us every day' before Jacob's funeral which was restricted by law to only twenty-five people, and which was held with 'police all around the graveyard'. No buses were allowed, people were stopped from attending, and some were arrested in the church. Those at the subsequent night vigil were tear-gassed, as was the frequently the case. Irene March, too, reported that night vigils were 'very difficult to attend'; and the burial of her son was 'disturbed by teargas'. Similarly, the Reverend Snoeki Mzamo expressed his outrage at the fact that after 'dozens of young people were killed in the Six-Day War of 1986, the magistrate refused permission to bury them in a mass funeral'. But, he said, 'some of our people did not have their own money ... Why did the magistrate do it?' The people were angry and could not stand these restrictions. Mzamo was appalled: 'The burial of a body is a right,' he said.

Personal spaces were unforgivably attacked. The destruction of homes and possessions was also desperately deeply felt by witnesses. Linda Twala, local businessman and patron, spoke bitterly of his losses:

> my home and cars were destroyed; my furniture, my clothes, every-thing when my house was bombed. My children were inside – but my three daughters went into the dog's kennel and were saved.

The fire brigade came but had been instructed not to put out the fire. His neighbour's house was also burnt down: 'I saw my house was on fire,' said Mabusane Moquae.

> It was the police. Children were inside. A neighbour came and helped us try to put on water. A cop came and asked whose house it was. Linda Twala's and mine was the reply. The cop said he had wanted that. We found the children – but had nothing left.

Moquae wept at the memory. 'I worked very hard for my clothes, my furni-ture,' he said. 'Everything was burnt to ashes. It was very cold. It was winter. If you lose your home you are destitute.'

Ntombizodwa Sidzumo talked of the loss of the home her son had lived in when he was driven out by political forces she would not mention. She now lived with five children and four grandchildren in a flat in town. Moko Lephuthing's house was also burnt down. Her son had been a comrade; her husband had helped Civic Association members. She went out after being told armed people were coming from the barracks. It was 22 April 1986. And then 'they' came and told her that her children, her friends and her husband were burnt in her house. She waited for the fire to die out so she could get their corpses. She prayed to God. Her husband came out. Her children were safe. They had hidden in bushes. There were no bodies in the house. Nobody had been killed.

Daisy Mashego was shot in the back while looking for her children in the mayhem following Michael Diradeng's funeral. She described the violence and conflict in the street. People were crying, looking for their kids. She was in hospital for two to three months afterwards. She was left completely helpless, and depended on the Red Cross and on her disability pension. Maria Malakoane, shot in 1986, lived with a bullet in her body for several months until she finally had it removed. But she suffered from constant headaches and was no longer healthy. Sekitla Mogano attributes her loss of health to the deaths of her two sons.

Two of the witnesses implied that the loss of a child was so great a tragedy for parents that they died subsequently. Clearly, the link is indirect. This is, however, surely an indication that whatever suffering occurred in those times was thought of as part of a generally oppressive experience. Maria Malakoane said that both Ace Hlongwane's parents died after he was burnt to death – strongly implying that this was because of the death.

THE TRC MYTH OF ALEXANDRA AND THE FORGOTTEN REBELLION

The stories convey a sense that the community of Alex had been insulted, invaded, damaged and cheated. The people had been cast in opposition to the evil state, embodied in the police. The idea of the community as a spatial and symbolic entity deeply interwoven with the experience of apartheid was an integral part of the memories of the witnesses. This is not quite the same as the public presentation of Alexandra's story, in which the community was a united social force more than a series of spaces and places. But some overlap clearly did exist.

One unintended consequence of this was to exclude from the individually constructed narratives the story of the actual revolt of the 1985–6 period. The impression given by the witnesses is as follows: a cohesive community consisting mainly of older parents and somewhat wayward youth, and surrounded by a series of set rituals – funerals mainly – over which they had no control, was subjected to unbearable brutality. Many loved ones died, their homes were burnt, and their lives overturned.

This version precluded the telling of another story – that in which intrepid youths manned the barricades, reconstructed social and cultural relations, and tried to create alternatives to the governance of the township; in which adults sought to control this uprising and turn it into an example of civic-mindedness, and in which nationalists came to claim the rebellion as part of their teleological march to glory.

Additional ritualised processes within the hearing attempted, not entirely successfully, to bridge the gap between what have so far been portrayed simply as private experiences, and this public myth. Clearly on the personal level, what it meant to be a victim of a 'human rights abuse' was defined by the occasion. But as their testimonies were presented to the hearing, people's lives and stories came to carry meanings beyond the personal. A public sphere was constructed, within which private experiences could become the property of all. As the witnesses spoke, it often seemed as if many were telling of their lives for the first time – in public at least. Experiences such as theirs had been hidden, or only partially brought to light. Oral historians are conscious of the ways in which they themselves take part in a process of this sort. However for an institution as morally and politically charged as the Truth Commission, the complexities are multiplied.

A subtle and complex social process took place. The stories of the witnesses were recalled in ways that were meant to transform their memories and their persons. Their stories were meant to be transposed from the private to the public sphere, the profane was meant to be transformed into the sacred. The hearing contained within it what could be called 'rites of closure', creating a sense of psychological closure in the witnesses themselves. This in turn affected both the audience present and the 'imagined' audience of the general public who would read press reports and watch television, or perhaps ultimately read the commission's report itself. Such a conclusion was 'meant' to occur through the witnesses reaching a stance of 'closure' such as forgiveness.

How did the witnesses think of themselves in relation to their own possible transformation as they came to the witness stand? Two broad possible opening stances could be made – the 'weak' and the 'strong'. One type of weak stance was often unsuccessful from the transformative point of view. This was manifested by the witnesses who appeared mystified by what had happened to them, indeed who seemed lost in a sea of tragedy. In this case their 'weakness' may have been a function of their inability to find concepts to help them make sense of their memories and experiences. Dorah Mkihele, whose son was shot, gave a deeply incoherent tale of the subsequent proceedings in court – a tale that seemed to get nowhere. Her brother had to intervene to help convey her message. And Sekitla Mogano conveyed an air of being mystified. She seemed lost for an explanation of why 'the police came and looked for him' (her son) and said 'he taught others to write on walls'. He was a leader of the comrades.

Fear was another 'weak' stance. Commissioners found this hard to deal with. Ntombizodwa Sidzumo would not mention the people suspected of driving her son away from his home, in spite of being pushed hard by the commissioners. God would reveal them, she said. She appeared to be deeply traumatised, and to have found giving evidence extremely difficult. She could hardly answer when asked if her son had been killed or had committed suicide, saying she did not feel free to do so.

By contrast the other most common 'weak' stance was perhaps the most transformative – that of weeping. These witnesses were comparatively most malleable at the hands of the commissioners. At first they often demonstrated reluctance about self-exposure; they were in turn gently pressured for the sake of reaching the truth. However the listeners here were not psychologists; and even more was at stake than the freeing of the individual psyche from the torment of unacknowledged suffering. Often the unstated aspect of this was that they were pressured in order to allow the community to feel through their suffering. Perhaps their suffering was thus turned into martyrdom, their weakness into catharsis.

Many wept, or broke down and were temporarily unable to continue. For example Jessie Moquae and Matsiliso Monageng seemed to have experienced a painful 'expansion' of the self by speaking to an audience. Their private experiences were now defined as symbolic of a wider experience.

A stance of strength was transformative in a different way. The coping, strong witness was the witness who could most easily forgive. Common themes were those of dignity, the strong woman, the protection of God, the benign presence of Mandela and the luck of having a strong family. Irene March, who had lost all three of her sons, showed no self-pity at all. She had survived, she said, because of her strong family, the gift of love, her neighbours and the presence of Mandela. Ramatsobana Masenya spoke of herself as 'a strong woman': she gave thanks to God and thanks to Mr Mandela.

Another strong stance was that of indignation and anger. Linda Twala's fury was evident as he read out a statement: 'My rights have been violated by the police in the previous government. My home and cars were destroyed. My furniture, clothes, everything. Who were they and who instructed them?' he asked angrily.

Many witnesses cast the relationship between victim and perpetrator in clearly 'binary' terms. Innocence stood opposed to guilt. This stance was encouraged by the mandate of the commission itself, which did not seek out ambiguity. Witnesses frequently felt it necessary to proclaim their own moral innocence. Linda Twala and his neighbour were both keen to emphasise that they were Christians, Catholics, who were at church when attacked. Obed Bapela's testimony was interlaced with frequent emphases on the innocence of himself, his colleagues and at first, the youth. Dorah Mkihele's son Jabulani was with comrades who were 'just sitting there' when attacked by police.

From the strong and the weak witness various forms of closure emerged. The weeping, weak witness reached, it has been suggested, a sort of catharsis; and his or her weeping assisted the audience, too, to attain this state. Other forms of closure included strong statements about the desire for 'truth', and a belief in its healing power. 'Everyone must come forward,' said Jabu Malinga, 'even the Kabasas.' And 'Have the commission called all the people to ask for forgiveness – or maybe they want us to point them out,' said the Reverend Snoekie Mzamo. After he had recalled his house being surrounded by police he asked:

> Where are those police? Why don't they come out? They must come and confess, confess they were Makabasas. This should be part of the commission. I can understand why they did it. They were driven out,

isolated, they could not drink in our shebeens, they could not fall in love with our women, they could not buy in Alex. If they come forward and confess, the community will be very happy.

Obed Bapela had, in the opening speech, made enthusiastic claims about the healing power of truth. But this elicited less than positive responses from the audience present. He named five policemen who owed the commission both information and an apology – including Sergeant Mothibe, now, he said, a preacher and repentant. But, the commissioners asked: 'What about Erasmus and Ndaba and the informers – what will your attitude be when you know them?' Bapela said: 'Some I meet – I am friends already. But they must come and repent to the whole community.' The commissioners asked: 'Does the community share these feelings of reconciliation?' He answered: 'If they come back the community will welcome them.' But the audience jeered at this point. They knew better, perhaps. Sergeant Mothibe had indeed attempted to visit Alexandra in recent months, but had been 'almost killed' according to one informant. Another said he had been stoned.

Some witnesses said they would forgive. They were often those who took stances of strength. To them, truth telling and repentance would lead to forgiveness. Thus Martha Susan Smiles claimed to speak on behalf of everyone when she said:

> People who hurt the people of Alex should come forth, like de Kock, and tell the truth and maybe we will forgive them. I would like to forgive them, because if I do not forgive them the Lord will not forgive us.

Many witnesses would not, however, contemplate forgiveness, as the example of Mothibe seems to suggest. It could be said that these did not achieve 'closure' at all. Linda Twala would not 'forgive or reconcile'. When asked by a Commissioner whether he held out any hope, he answered: 'We need something to motivate us. We had it in the old days. Now we don't.' Jessie Moquae asked bitterly and rhetorically: 'Will I ever forgive white people?' Margaret Madlana, mother of Bongani, was at first passionately unforgiving: 'I apologise before God, but I will poison the white man's children,' she cried.

> I will never forgive in this case. What will make me to forgive is if Sindane and Mothibe come and confess and say sorry to the parents ... they killed children of the wars. How can Mothibe be a minister now? Which children is he preaching to? I will never forgive, I will never forgive, I will never forgive, I will never forgive, I will never forgive.

And later she said: 'We work for them [whites], raise their children for them, cook for them, but they still kill us like dogs or baboons.'

A more common form of closure than forgiveness was that of an expressed desire for reparations. Most demands were extraordinarily modest. Linda

Twala suggested that the 'children who died in Tanzania' must be brought back and buried at home. He said that the government should give families tombstones for the dead. More ambitiously, he suggested that the government should 'create jobs for the school dropouts now unemployed'. Similarly Jessie Moquae wanted the government to 'help us through education'. Obed Bapela, in his more nationalistic style, said: 'We must honour the victims of the Makabasa attack as heroes and heroines on the 85th anniversary [it was not clear whether he meant of the ANC or of Alexandra itself] next year.' He said the government would or should 'declare Alex a presidential project in honour of its people who have carried the flag of freedom since 1912'. Martha Smiles said that the people of Alex should make tombstones for those killed during the Six-Day War. Daisy Mashego wanted a bullet removed from her body – and a house of her own. Very few of these requests were met in the subsequent six years.

Some chose to enact closure through apology. Tlale said to his family: 'I am sorry I burnt the church down.' Obed Bapela rendered an apology on behalf of the community:

> I must say that in the conduct of the struggle there were things that went wrong. But these were not planned. We sometimes succeeded in stopping it, but not always. People's Courts were not set up by us as leaders, but by members of the community. People demanded and wanted them. But unfortunately people got excited. There was great anger after the Six-Day War. Wrongs were committed

Kenneth Manana was now a Christian: 'You have changed, repented,' said the commissioner, 'but from what?' He answered: 'To show that in all that had happened, I now realise that some of those things were mistakes. I had the heart to forgive.'

Some used the occasion to make a general statement. It is not clear, however, whether these qualify as 'closure'. Many of these statements raised more questions than they resolved. Irene March made a statement about the need for crime to end and 'policemen to do the job' of securing South Africa as a home for black and white. Linda Twala was even clearer about this: 'Most of the youth are loitering around the streets. They are our future leaders and must be assisted. We must groom our leaders of tomorrow.' He earned applause for this from the audience, after which he continued. 'Youth,' he said, were 'nice' in those days when they were fighting for the struggle. But today, in these times of drugs, liquor and unemployment, he said, youth 'are no longer nice'. For this he earned further applause. Others made similar links between the high rate of crime in the Alexandra of 1996, and the past. As Margaret Madlana put it: 'Now they, the youth, are with the criminals.' The audience muttered agreement.

Because such statements were outside the terms of reference, the discourse, of the commission, they were perhaps not 'heard' as readily as the main forms of closure. However it was they that earned the greatest support from those present.

CONCLUSION

The Alexandra hearings of the TRC had created a different kind of theatrical venue – a symbolic rather than spatial one – in which the events of 1986 were staged; this time so that they could become part of a newly imagined past. The commission's chief task had been to uncover 'private' stories rather than repeat public ones. Numerous private stories of suffering in the period of the revolt were brought to light, giving great insight into the meanings attributed to the past by ordinary Alexandran residents, as well as permitting some catharsis to take place. But at the same time, the presence of an already powerful public myth of the period, retold in highly nationalist terms during the commission's hearing by one of the main accused in the adult treason trial; the stark opposition the hearing posed between oppressor and oppressed; the way in which the commission cast ordinary people as victims rather than actors; the numerous silences in the hearing, in particular silences about the role of the youth; and the only partial ability of the hearing to achieve closure in its witnesses, together meant that the private stories were only briefly brought to the public view and then resequestered. The perhaps unintended consequence of the hearings was that a new narrative version of the revolt evolved, this time involving an even lesser role for the youth and also downplaying the adult role to the extreme.

The new 'public' myth of Alexandra, articulated by Bapela and by the very shape and form taken by the Alex hearings, placed the ANC firmly and purposively in the lead of a just war. It cast the organically defined and united 'community', identified clearly with the ANC, in opposition to 'the apartheid state'. It reluctantly acknowledged the role of the youth insofar as they were 'good', but attempted to marginalise their 'bad' behaviour. It sought 'closure' through articulating how peace and liberation had been attained, and forgiveness needed to be granted.

The 'private' narratives of the witnesses were much less seamless, but did, it has been argued, form something of a statement. In these narratives, 'community' was sometimes absent altogether. More commonly the township was thought to consist of a series of geographical and ritual 'markers' around and upon which resistance occurs, or an entity subjected to evil, insult, or deceit, usually by the forces of evil, demonised and personified through the image of the *Makabasas*, or Mothibe. The experiences of the witnesses were not so much those of participants in a just war, but those of a suffering people, subjected to loss, abuse, and social oppression.

Like the public TRC narrative, the private ones also tended to marginalise the role of the youth. How the youth behaved in the 1980s was only indirectly referred to. The fact is that the youth of Alexandra organised and led a revolt, whose main contours hardly appear at all in the hearing. No mention is made, except in the most anodyne of terms, of the marches, street committees, Youth Groups and their 'headquarters', mass meetings, *comtsotsis*, banners, placards, songs, renaming of parks, schools and streets, setting up of barricades, hounding out of local Town Councillors, boycotts of police stations, throwing of petrol bombs, necklacings and people's courts. The most well-known spectacular necklacing – of Theresa – was not mentioned. I asked Obed Bapela why this was so and he answered curtly, 'Theresa had been told to leave the township.'

Thus the youth were the absent witnesses to what actually happened in 1986. This does not prejudge what they might have said. We do not know if they were proud of what they did, or sorry for it. We do not know if they felt they had won major victories, or lost. Almost the only way in which their experiences were recounted in the hearing was at second hand – through the tragic stories of parents who lost their children. Thus the question of what the youth were actually doing at the time they were shot or attacked was sidestepped. This both demeaned the youth, and let them off the hook.

The effect of this was twofold. The parents were portrayed as the victims of the brutality of the system. Indeed the motif of 'the victim', not surprisingly perhaps, in a commission designed mainly to uncover the truth about suffering, prevailed. Africans became passive rather than active, in the memories of this era. Young people were spoken of critically, or in the worried tone of the parent whose child has acted waywardly. Closure in these narratives was only partially successful. It was hindered by problematic links to the difficult present, by an unwillingness to forgive, or an uncertainty about precisely how much 'truth' was going to be told by the perpetrators.

Although the hearing allowed these disparate private narratives to be brought into the public realm, it was the much more coherent public narrative that prevailed. It was increasingly formalised, and had already begun to be sanctioned more broadly in the society, or even promulgated by the state. Press reports of the hearing reflected this. Even so, the public narrative only partially succeeded in appropriating the private stories. These remained focused upon the myriad of tragic experiences of ordinary people, cast in quite different terms. They were not usually heroic. They often reflected a sense of helplessness and marginality. A new sequestration of the experiences of ordinary Alexandrans was the result.

12

EPILOGUE

Black South Africa has experienced a cultural revolution, a metamorphosis in values and conventions of the profoundest type ... Young people have experienced an unprecedented moral ascendancy. They are known universally as 'the youth', the legion of black teenagers who for the last two years have provided the shock troops of a nationwide popular insurrection. This has been a children's war. (*City Press*, 20 April 1986, quoted in Johnson n.d.: 1)

If it is true that a people's wealth is its children then South Africa is bitterly, tragically poor. If it is true that a nation's future is its children, we have no future, and deserve none ... [We] are a nation at war with its future ... For we have turned our children into a generation of fighters, battle-hardened soldiers who will never know the carefree joy of childhood. What we are witnessing is the growth of a generation which has the courage to reject the cowardice of its parents ... to fight for what should be theirs, by right of birth. There is a dark, terrible beauty in that courage. It is also a source of great pride – pride that we, who have lived under apartheid, can produce children who refuse to do so. But it is also a source of great shame ... that [this] is our heritage to our children: The knowledge of how to die, and how to kill. (*City Press*, editorial, 20 April 1986, quoted in Johnson n.d.: 62)

Small rebellions sometimes have large consequences. In Chapter 4 it was suggested that space may be a useful source of power, but is an unstable basis for authority. The modernising apartheid state had, by the 1980s, made a bid for greater power by seeking to enter into and control the private world of the ghetto. However, it aimed to do so through the abolition of the older township paternalistic systems, and the establishment of new relationships of authority rather than brute force. The spatial design of the townships, it was suggested, rendered this extremely difficult. The trade union organisation FOSATU had predicted, in fact, that 'anyone who tries to govern a [black] community, no matter how good their intentions, will have serious problems' (Moses Mayekiso, quoting from a FOSATU document, M3049). And indeed, space had proved to be an 'unstable basis for authority' in the case of this township, and many others.

The rebellion has never been forgotten in Alexandra. Together with hundreds of other uprisings in town and countryside it contributed to the eventual demise of apartheid, because it made clear that the establishment by the state of legitimate authority was not feasible. One survey in 1997, the Community Agency for Social Enquiry (CASE) survey, shows that of the dates that Alexandrans thought should be commemorated, the Six-Day War and the vigilante massacre together were the number one choice of almost 20 per cent of respondents, and the number two choice of a further 17 per cent (see Isserow and Everatt 1998: 95).

However, memories of it are ambivalent. In spite of the Truth Commission's sequestration of memory, the rebellion left a legacy of pride. A sense of assertiveness and power, of ownership of the space had for a brief moment been born, and this was indeed a matter for self-respect for residents. But it also left a vivid memory of tragedy. In its 'turning upside down' of many of the features of normality, it left a heritage of normlessness which adults still to some extent regret. Youth are said to still be 'out of control' – even more so now that the 'new South Africa' has come into being and the more noble cause for which the youth of the 1980s fought has given way to crime and social decay.

After the 1994 elections the fundamental change in the nature of the state meant that the 'public' expression of township interests changed once more, placing it in a new relationship with the private milieu of inhabitants. At the same time, it appears that by the late 1990s some of the apparently resilient 'private' institutions of township life had begun to decay.

As apartheid ended, nearly all of the urban initiatives born of resistance in the townships were severely weakened by mass arrests, the burning down of people's courts and the killing of activists. Furthermore, many townships – Alexandra among them – experienced ethnic and political violence on a scale not seen before, in the turbulent years of 1990–4, as the 'third force' provoked and initiated brutal conflict and a war between the ANC and the IFP erupted. Nevertheless, the movement to form civic institutions such as had emerged in Alexandra ('civics', as they came to be called), across townships, survived – at least at first. Indeed, after 1990, when all political organisation was legalised, and the process of transition to a democratic government was formally begun, 'civics' flourished. But as democracy came to be established, so the civics were, in spite of themselves, demobilised. Jones writes of how this process of demobilisation is a common fate of social movements in transitional states:

> As power changes hands ... the struggle transforms from a popular to a democratic one and civics are no longer opponents of the authoritarian state, but are one of many actors in a plural democracy. When the definition of roles that were once held firmly on one side of a dual

system begin to shift, then who takes on those roles and how they are defined become the problem. (Jones n.d.)

New positions, new networks, new definitions of territory and new opportunities change the relationship between claim-makers and government.

Furthermore, from the point of view of popular mentalities, the period saw the 'trumping' of civic and township-based movements and organisations by another form of public expression of private consciousness – the rising tide of an (ironically) disempowering ANC-based African nationalism. This tended to elevate the attainment of state power above the sustaining of links to new, or indeed old, forms of civil society. It has already been argued strongly that there was a dislocation between civic forms of mobilisation and the much older mobilisation 'frame' of African nationalism, and that as memories of the rebellion were constructed, so it was that nationalism prevailed. As the 1990s proceeded, the nationalist discourse became even bolder. By the early 2000s it commanded the public sphere almost entirely.

The emerging relationship between the state, nationalism and the township poor had some elements that could be seen as promising. In post-apartheid Alexandra, there was some effective delivery: for example, of some housing[1] or the payment of compensation to those dispossessed of property by apartheid laws.[2] 'Some improvement' in the conditions of township life – in such areas as roads, housing, street lights in particular – was felt by the majority of respondents in a 1998 survey and, interestingly, particularly by shack-dwellers (Isserow and Everatt 1998). Respondents in some of the poorest areas – shacks and hostels – felt that their local councillor was paying reasonable attention to their needs.

Furthermore, the private world of the poor showed itself to have a degree of resilience in the face of the growing hegemony of nationalism. In most townships, networks survived and were being constantly recreated. Sowetans reported in 1999 in surprisingly large numbers that they found the township 'a pleasant place to live'; two thirds of them had friends within walking distance, whom they visited regularly. Sixty-two per cent had 'received help' from these friends in the previous week. Forty-eight per cent had family within walking distance. These statistics were not confined to the older residents in townships – quite the reverse in some cases. Incoming migrants living in shacks were within easier reach of friends (older residents had stronger family networks) (Morris et al. 1999). Even in the worse-off areas of Alexandra, 46 per cent of respondents belonged to a church group, 37 per cent to a *stokvel* and a significant minority of respondents found it a convenient and relatively cheap place to live (Isserow and Everatt 1998: 80–3).

However, there is evidence to suggest that strong countervailing tendencies appeared in Alexandra in the late 1990s and early 2000s, including features of predation and failure in the system of delivery and a decline in the resilience of the 'private' worlds of their inhabitants. Schizoid mental maps have been one result. The 'millenarian' expectations of the period of rebellion were followed by a period of disappointment and let-down. A full one-quarter of all respondents in the 1998 Alexandra survey agreed, indeed, 'Things were better in the "old" South Africa'! The needs of the poor did not decline but grew in the face of expanding unemployment, by 1997 at roughly 50 per cent in Alexandra, and far higher in the more peripheral townships (*Business Day*, 18 July 1997). Systems of representation at local level were not always effective, and corruption emerged, as it always has done, in the supply of basic township goods such as housing. This was profoundly reinforced by the state's reduction of expenditure in the late 1990s. Cuts in government expenditure in key areas of welfare, to which should be added government incapacity to spend what money it did have, have resulted in a decline in such services as health. The new institutions of the state delivered only modestly to the poor. As early as May 1998 letters were appearing in the press indicating disillusion:

> I refer to the state of our country almost five years after our so-called independence. Nelson Mandela is presiding over the greatest myth ever in the history of South Africa. Using his Madiba magic, he has lulled us into believing that good times are ahead for everybody … Now, almost five years since the ANC's promise to 'deliver a better life for all', what do we have? The grandest theft of our wealth which is now shared between a handful of the so-called 'black empowerment groups' (or, more appropriately, greedy black capitalists) and their white counterparts. (*City Press*, 24 May 1998)

While a majority of respondents in the 1998 survey felt that some improvement had taken place since 1994, a quarter felt that 'nothing has improved'; the levels were higher amongst the poorly educated (34 per cent) and lower amongst the better-educated (16 per cent) suggesting the beginnings of a new stratification in delivery systems. In spite of the fact that large numbers of homes were indeed built by the ANC, the greatest inadequacy in Alexandra township remained that of housing:

> Yes, we can see that they are fixing roads, but that is not major because we need houses … they are the most important things. Streets are not that important, even if they have tried to make them better … with houses they haven't been able to improve them … the local municipality of Alexandra is trying with water and other things like sewerage, but it is not making enough effort in building houses. (Isserow and Everatt 1998: 61–2)

In 2000, new houses intended for Alexandran residents were occupied by illegal squatters angry and resentful at their own homelessness and at the fact that the houses had stood empty for many months. And there were reports of the very poorest people in townships accepting government subsidised houses and selling them soon afterwards to better-off families or even speculators, and moving back into squatter camps (*Business Day*, 23 July 2000; *The Star*, 24 June 2003).

In addition what was delivered did not, it appears, always last very long. In the cases of sewerage and electrification:

> Many residents told of toilets breaking; of unqualified plumbers trying to repair them; of having to walk long distances to find working toilets; those from shacks complained that those with toilets lock them at night to stop others from using them. (Isserow and Everatt 1998: 66–7)

One woman whose house was supplied with electricity spoke of the Hobbesian world of desperate and violent competition for resources that resulted from scarcity and social decay:

> You buy the electric card ... and suddenly you see cable leading to other shacks and you know that you're the only one that has bought units and nobody is supposed to receive electricity. It is for you alone. But you won't say anything because you're afraid that you'll die. (ibid.)

The decay of the civics cut down the recourse that people had in such situations, and civic leaders reported a 'confusion of allegiances' (Jones n.d.). There was once again an emerging sense of disarticulation between private experience and public expression.

This was reinforced by the fact that the shiny new institutions of the liberal state were in many cases increasingly perceived as having little relevance or effectiveness for those at the bottom. Only 1 per cent of respondents in the Alexandra survey mentioned a human rights issue – 'freedom of speech' – as a benefit of the post-1994 period. One township newspaper reader in 1998 saw the new constitution, for all its progressive aspects, as irrelevant, because 'it gives more rights to abnormal people such as the homosexuals, lesbians, paedophiles, and white collar criminals'. Other institutions with the ostensible aim of protecting democratic rights and answerability – such as the Youth Commission, something that flowed directly from the youth resistance of the 1980s – emerged as 'shabby and parasitical'. Extremely expensive, they were seen to have, in many cases, done more to boost the income of a growing nationalist intelligentsia than to articulate the needs and wishes of the deprived (*City Press*, 23 July 2000).

In some areas, systems of local representation appeared to be disengaged from, rather than integrated with, social institutions on the ground. Squatter areas in some cases continued to be preyed upon by the unscrupulous (*City Press*, 23 July 2000). Systems of leadership that emerged during the struggle of the 1980s decayed in many places as the top layer of people was drawn into government systems without deep township roots:

During the negotiated transition the armed struggle was suspended and the political leaders called on the youth to curtail their resistance activities. It is ironic that the materialisation of their goals ... resulted in the marginalisation of these youth. Many of the leaders of the youth movements were lost to power politics in the negotiations, and later to parliament and government, leaving a hiatus in the direction and leadership in the movements. (Dissel 1999: 3)

Growing 'material selfishness' was noted by some as a feature of the post-election period, concomitant with a 'drop in the sense of "community"' (Isserow and Everatt 1998: 53). A pervasive cynicism began to affect the former carriers of social capital – teachers and nurses being the most important of these. The consequent disillusionment added to the impetus of a general political demobilisation.

The resulting groundswell of disaffection at unrealised expectations had, by the late 1990s, been unable to find a constructive outlet and instead revealed itself in crime, family violence, semi-criminal strikes, bizarre semi-millenarian movements such as pyramid schemes, witchcraft accusations and vigilantism, street gangs and generalised violence. Crime syndicates specialising in drugs, car theft and arms invaded townships, where guns were sometimes available at less than R100 each; furthermore, this renewed wave of criminality involved a higher proportion of serious offences than in previous times. Crime – that perennial problem of life in townships – became worse than ever before. 'What main thing has got worse in Alexandra since 1994?' respondents in the CASE survey were asked; 74 per cent answered 'Crime and violence'. A culture of criminality, rooted in the very shattering of bonds that took place under high apartheid, emerged. It appears to have had deeper cultural, familial and other roots than those which provoked earlier moral panics in Alexandra and elsewhere. Police commissioners interviewed about crime in townships said, 'It's a culture of violence, liquor, drugs. They say if you don't drink, womanise or involve yourself in drugs, then you are a *moffie* [queer] ... It's peer pressure' (Rauch 1998: 10). Even the very young 'want to become *makweres* or township bosses ... who flaunt their wealth in the latest BMWs and with massive gold chains. Their bars, clubs and chop shops provide "employment" of a type to draw young people into the crime circle' (*Financial Mail*, 10 September 1999).

Township residents were afraid to go out at night, or even to send their children to shops during the day. The feature of township life most disliked amongst respondents in Alexandra in 1998 was rape (19 per cent) followed by overcrowding (17 per cent), and crime/violence (12 per cent, but the second choice of 69 per cent). One resident made a sad comment: 'We are no longer free in our country. We are always afraid that something bad will happen, even in our homes. When you come back from the toilet, you have to lock the door' (Isserow and Everatt 1998: 82).

The police were perceived as corrupt and the criminal justice system seen by many as too liberal (*The Star*, 31 July 2000). Crime was not only experienced as a terrible hardship, but was also seen to be producing social injustice and inequality. In Alexandra, wrote one irate resident:

> young school dropouts own BMWs, eight per cent of cars and taxis are stolen, everyone knows who the top drug lord is (including the police); drug lords meet in top taverns to make deals; football administrators are part of the syndicates; some people own a fleet of taxis, 80 per cent of which are stolen. (letter to *City Press*, 26 March 2000)

The possibility of reviving, producing and sustaining social capital in this context was extremely limited. The most vivid form of self-organisation that emerged was that of vigilantism, which developed on a scale not seen in earlier times. Vigilante action in Alexandra included threatened 'strong mass action' following the acquittal or release on bail by the courts of four men who allegedly gang-raped two girls, aged 13 and 14 (*City Press*, 25 January 1998); or the time when an 'angry crowd' demanded 'instant justice' against shack-owners suspected of causing a fire which had resulted in the destruction of 100 shacks (*City Press*, 29 September 1999); and many others. There were far more extreme examples of burnings, beatings and houndings in other townships. At one Alexandra residents' meeting about the issue of rape a speaker expressed the extreme frustrations he experienced:

> We cannot wait for new legislation while our children, mothers and sisters are being raped and the culprits walk around as free men. We have lost trust in the police and the justice system, and we are not going to report to them any more. (*City Press*, 25 January 1998)

Another said that 'the police are corrupt and not taking the issue seriously'. Speaker after speaker 'called for action against the alleged rapists, corrupt policemen, doctors who wrote false reports on rape victims and court officials'. The people's courts were perhaps what was needed: 'I think we should run our courts ourselves by bringing back the kangaroo courts,' said one resident (*City Press*, 18 January 1998).

If the experiences of previous times are anything to go by, vigilantism of this sort is far from being the seedbed of a new form of community institution to cope with crime. In its spontaneous form it is uncontrollable and brutal. In its more institutionalised form it has the capacity for rapid decay.

A further response to disillusion and relative powerlessness appeared in many townships in the form of xenophobic and inward-looking panics. In Alexandra in 1995, 'Simmering tensions over the endless flood of foreigners into SA reached boiling point.' In a concerted campaign to drive foreigners out of the township hundreds of foreigners (many of whom were in fact not newcomers) were rounded up and chased out by gun-toting men who accused them of criminal activities including theft, car-hijackings, house breakings, rapes and the illegal supply of arms (*City Press*, 29 January 1995). Frequent attacks upon and often fairly widespread murders of foreigners followed. The CASE survey revealed a disturbing degree of treating foreigners as the scapegoats for the two chief issues worrying residents – those of crime and the housing shortage. 'South Africa is for South Africans only,' said 62 per cent of respondents; foreigners should be repatriated, said 35 per cent.

Townships as living spaces were subjected to middle-class flight, as the formerly white suburbs became available to the burgeoning black petty bourgeoisie (*Financial Mail*, 20 December 1996). Not only did many move out, but those that remained but who had a moderate income moved their children to non-state or formerly white schools, leaving township schools – already profoundly damaged by the depredations of high apartheid, the destruction of white philanthropy and then the era of resistance – vulnerable to further decay.

In June 2000 township residents in Alexandra experienced déjà vu when youth resistance erupted once more in a distorted echo of the 1980s. Five hundred pupils set out to avenge the death of a fellow pupil (and SRC member) shot dead in a rent dispute. The pupils (from one of the same schools which had bred the rebels of fifteen years earlier) rioted, surrounded a police car and threw stones and rocks. In the ensuing violence, a second youth was shot dead and nine were injured. The old repertoire of resistance – petrol bombing, stoning, the building of barricades, the singing of freedom songs and chanting of old slogans, and the dance of protest, the *toyi-toyi* – was revived, but it is uncertain whether as tragedy or as farce. It emerged that the leader of the revolt in fact went to one of the most expensive private schools in the city; that many of the rioters carried arms (largely absent in the 1980s); and that neither the state nor the Alexandran public was parti-cularly sympathetic. The ANC government stated that 'proper grievance channels should be used'; and that Cosas, the organisation behind the protest, was in fact 'run by adults with hidden agendas'. Kader Asmal, Minister of Education, said to the youths: 'We are no longer slaves who have to revolt. We must use all instruments of democracy to achieve our goals' (*City Press*, 11 June 2000). However, when top government officials spoke to a 2,000 strong crowd in Alexandra to try to bring calm, *toyi-toyi*ing students jeered, and their bodyguards were attacked. Cynicism and disillusionment followed millenarian optimism, in this township and elsewhere.

This and similar incidents had perhaps begun to worry some black intellectuals, who sought to remedy what they saw as the absence of 'responsible citizenship' in township life (*City Press*, 4 June 2000). One such intellectual included in his vision the advocacy of the nurturing of social capital quite explicitly (Xolela Mangcu, in *Sunday Independent*, 23 July

2000). One quoted Mandela's statement that what was needed was the 'RDP of the soul'.[3] Another lamented that the 'youth of today' lacked the inspiration and moral commitment of the 'generation of 1976' (Barney Mthombothi, *City Press*, 18 June 2000). Such calls were frequent. But in many cases (and with some great exceptions) these thinkers had become detached from daily township life. Their earlier commitment to the unglamorous world of community development faded in the face of the attractions of the life of the intellectual (to which end further destruction of the old white liberal philanthropists, and now the white left intelligentsia began to take place). Many of these calls remained at the level of impassioned articles, editorials and speeches. The detachment of the private from the public was of long standing, and began to become increasingly deep-rooted.

To the new generation of unemployed and 'uncaptured' youths it may have seemed that townships no longer resembled the semi-colonial living spaces they once were. In their increasing isolation from the public domain they came to resemble the 'impacted ghettoes' of the post-modern US.

At the same time, all the features of post-colonial 'predation' and decay of social capital seemed also to be present. South African urban dwellers may recognise this slightly reworded portrayal by Woolcock of the South Asian mire in their own circumstances – and in writing of a rural setting, he does not even mention crime:

> Most people simply cannot be trusted. Local elites exploit every opportunity. Wages are so low that any personal advancement is rendered virtually impossible. There are schools and health clinics, but teachers and doctors regularly fail to show up for work. Funds allocated to well-intentioned government programmes are siphoned off by local elites. Police torture those suspected of smuggling. Husbands regularly beat or abandon their wives. Utter destitution is only a minor calamity away. Any efforts at improvement always seem to come to naught – development workers are no different – some vanish, absconding 'with all our hard-earned money. Why should we trust you? Why should we trust anyone?' they say. (Woolcock 1998: 153)

Many post-apartheid townships became intractable and violence-ridden places, in which ordinary people made their lives, but in which powerful forces continued to create ungovernability where the political call for ungovernability no longer existed. Here the lethal cultural cocktail of youth militancy, a culture of boycotting, high levels of tolerance of violent behaviour, endemic crime and easily available hard and soft drugs have threatened to shape the new order in destructive ways. The cultural, ideological, moral and structural underpinnings of the drama of the 1980s cannot be wished away; they need to be confronted to help us understand the social decay of today.

NOTES

CHAPTER 1: INTRODUCTION

1. Its history has been reasonably well documented, considering its neglected urban status, although not as thoroughly as the history of Johannesburg's other inner city black suburb, Sophiatown, perhaps because of the lack of official documentation. See Tourikis (1981). Sophiatown's romanticised mythology, perhaps aided by its having been razed to the ground in the 1950s, is also far more powerful.

2. The phrase 'the youth' is common in South African discussions of this period and of South African townships and should be deconstructed. Of course it does reify young people and turn them into an apparently homogeneous category. But as an indication of the power and level of organisation of young people it says a great deal.

3. One perceptive study of the revolt uses the idea of 'counter hegemony' to explain the resulting contestation – but this seems a little bland for a situation in which a semi-permanent legal and moral vacuum came into being..

4. The tone of the times was strongly reminiscent of that described in Hill (1987). This phenomenon was echoed all over the country. To give but one of many examples, in Cape Town during one school boycott, relationships between older staff and younger students were 'consistently and completely overturned', according to Molteno (n.d.).

5. The discussion in this chapter is distinct from that which concerns theorists engaged in examining societies experiencing high capitalism, in which space and time have come to acquire new meanings. South Africa in the mid-1980s, while it had undoubtedly been affected by some of the features of post-modernity, was essentially a modernising society, with strong remaining pre-modern features. See for example Castells (1977, 1983).

6. See, for some suggestive answers to this question in the Irish context, Feldman (1991) and an earlier literature on what was thought of then as 'ghetto revolt' (Rossi 1970, Schlemmer 1968). For a more recent discussion of such 'enclosed' rebellions see Gutman (1982), or Morris (1984). Lash and Urry (1994: 145ff) argue that the American black ghetto has become increasingly spatially 'impacted', an interpretation with which Wacquant (1994) would agree, lending perhaps a special relevance in situations of 'post-Fordism' to discussions of the nature of enclosed rebellions.

7. Steve Davis (1987) suggests that during the struggle, the ANC tried to stage 'performances' of bomb blasts and at the same time not to take lives. But this staging was not entirely successful as a dramaturgical exercise because the government controlled the media, and every time they did this, the media would portray the blasts as ineffectual, or just not report them at all.

8. Supreme Court of South Africa (Witwatersrand Local Division), 1987, The

State vs Moses J. Mayekiso, Paul N. Tshabalala, Richard M. Mdakane, Obed K. Bapela and Mzwanele Mayekiso, before the Honourable Mr Justice van der Walt, (Case No 115/87) (hereafter referred to as the 'Mayekiso trial'). All references to this trial in the remainder of the study will refer to the name of the witness being quoted, where appropriate, followed by 'M' and the page number of the transcribed record; and Supreme Court of South Africa (Witwatersrand Local Division), 1987, The State vs Ashwell M. Zwane, Vusi A. Ngwenya, Andrew Mafutha, David Mafutha, Arthur S. Vilakazi, Albert A. Sebola, Piet Mogano and Phillemon C. Phalongwane, before the Honourable Mr Justice Grosskopf, (Case No 50/87) (hereafter referred to as 'Zwane trial'). All references to this trial in the remainder of this study will refer to the name of the witness being quoted, where appropriate, followed by 'Z' and the page number of the transcribed record.

9. Even as they were happening, Karen Jochelson (1988a, 1988b) documented some of the early activities of the rebels. Later, Charles Carter (1991a, 1991b, 1991c) mined the Mayekiso trial in particular, and supplemented it with excellent interview material to produce an outstanding study of the revolt, used extensively here. Richard Abel (1995) wrote a thoughtful piece on the trials; as did John Nauright (n.d.). These also build upon an extensive tradition of studies of Alex which Johannesburg intellectuals have developed. See, for example, Tourikis (1981), Sarakinsky (1984), and various publications and papers of the South African Institute of Race Relations and the Black Sash. This includes some non-academic work as well: a film called Dark City, a slide show made by Vicki Alhadeff for the History Workshop in 1983; a range of novels, short stories and poetry by such authors as Modikwe Dikobe, Wally Serote, memoirs and many others.

CHAPTER 2: PLACE, SPACE AND FRAME

1. The rich literature on township life conveys this – see for example Dikobe (1973); Lucas (1995); Wilson and Mafeje (1973); Pauw (1979); Brandel-Syrier (1971); Bozzoli (1979); Mayer (1961); Mphahlele (1959), and many others.
2. Pillay (1984) found the same, as did Morris et al (1999: 25) in the case of Soweto.
3. See, for a study of this phenomenon of spatial consciousness in a Pretoria township, Schoonraad (1995)
4. Adapted from Lamont et al. (n.d.: 16). The Carnegie survey found similar figures but it only analysed the employed: it found that unemployment of household heads was 11.3 per cent, and that most of these were under the age of 24. Employment categories were: Professional 3 per cent; Clerical 14.5 per cent; Sales 3.6 per cent; Service 23.5 (women were disproportionately represented here, presumably as domestic servants); Skilled 5.7 per cent; Semi-skilled 21.5 per cent; Labourer 28.2 per cent. See Pillay (1984)
5. Calteaux (1994), quoting Ntshangase (1993: 204). See also Izwi Lase Township, 5, April/May 1983. In fact many varieties of language fall under this umbrella name. Women did use it, but this meant men labelled them as depraved. See Calteaux (1994: 230) quoting Slabbert: 'We tend to classify her as a shebeen girl. If a lady speaks tsotsitaal you call her names and you don't respect her'.
6. Leading to an exhibition of solidarity by Alex residents when Coloureds were forced by the state to 'bus' their children to 'Coloured' schools far away, when apartheid reached its height.
7. See Glaser (1990a), in which he names many gangs that were active in

Alexandra in the period of his study, and whose influence upon the rebellion has not been explored, although it is extremely likely to have been powerful in shaping a culture of youth gang and mob behaviour which was certainly present in the 1980s.

8. Statement by Paul Tshabalala, a resident of Alexandra and of a long-standing Alexandran family; one of the accused in the treason trial on corruption by peri-urban police; given to Cheadle, Thompson and Haysom as background to the case.

9. Five boycotts had occurred before the eighties: in 1940, 1942, 1943, 1944 and 1957.

10. See Nauright (1998) for a discussion of earlier removals in Alex.

11. See Couzens (1979). They had their own magistrate, committee of justice and chief of police there. Alex's working-class poet, Modikwe Dikobe, had been the secretary. They also had a school committee, their own teachers, and schools; they wore their own lapel badges.

12. Run by the University of the Witwatersrand, the Alexandra Health and University Clinic has a long and proud history in the community, and played an important role during the rebellion.

13. See Ramagaga (1988), in which he describes the origins of the major schools in the townships as follows: Carter Memorial: Methodist; Pholosho Community: Anglican; Holy Cross: Catholic; Ikage Lower Primary: Apostolic Church in Zion (a black church); Ithute Community: African Methodist (black run); Eufundisweni: community-built; Zenzeleni Community: community-built; Gordon Memorial: Presbyterian; Skeen Memorial: Dutch Reformed; Bovet Community: Swiss Mission; M. C. Weiler: United Progressive Jewish Reform Congregation; Ekukhanyisweni Primary: Church of Assemblies of God; Dr Knak and Iphutheng: Lutheran; Alexandra High: Rev. Bishop Paulos Mabiletsa. By the seventies nearly all of these schools had been subjected to government control as part of the Bantu Education policy. The Holy Cross school moved to Soweto during and because of the removals of the 1963–79 period.

14. I use this concept to refer specifically to the matter of space; this, amongst other things, distinguishes this study from that of Carter (1991a) who is more concerned with political hegemony. See, for a 'contestation' version of hegemony, Hebdige (1979); Williams (1980); Hall et al. (1976).

CHAPTER 3: THE FAILURE OF THE STATE

1. See Bapela (n.d.); see also the 'Constitution of AYCO', pamphlet; both in Cheadle, Thompson and Haysom archives of the Mayekiso trial (hereafter CTH archive)

2. What exactly this metaphor means is not always clear. It is a phrase, together with words such as 'rumblings' or 'volcanic', which is often used *ex post facto*; but this does not necessarily mean that something crucial did not exist – perhaps the shaking up of moral certainties, or the interference with sedimented memories of what spaces should be about?

3. Here I take a very different analytical perspective from that of Jeremy Seekings, who seeks to understand the nature of quiescence, his assumption perhaps being that rebellion is 'normal'. I have operated from the opposite assumption – that quiescence was to be expected in so well-designed and authoritarian an oppressive system, and that it was rebellion which needed explanation. See Seekings (1990: 250).

4. Alexandra always was racially mixed, even up to the 1980s, when 5 per cent of the population was coloured.

5. Ralph Bunche, in Edgar (1992), describes Orlando vividly in his perceptive observations on his trip to South Africa in 1937.
6. Original visions for township designs are to be found in Floyd (1951), Connell et al. (1939), and Calderwood (1953).
7. For Alexandran examples of this, see Tourikis (1981). See, for examples of the types of 'better off' standholders in a variety of townships, Wells (1983), Bozzoli (1991), Mothibedi (n.d.), and Lebello (1987).
8. By 1943 there were 422 shops and 248 stores in the township, according to the Annual Report of the Medical Officer of Health in Alexandra, the well known Dr A. B. Xuma. (Tourikis 1981: 24) But not all the owners of these were African – there were also Indians and Coloureds. Later trial evidence suggests that by the 1980s, to these ethnic minorities had been added Portuguese and Chinese shopkeepers.
9. Lt. Col. O. J. P. Horak of the SAP said in October 1942 that 'there is a large number of respectable natives' in Alexandra. Goodhew (1991) gives the most detailed portrayal of this class.
10. This type of argument is developed to its fullest by Charney (1994); he cites Doreen Atkinson's portrayal (1991) of the philosophy of township administration as 'patriarchal', and, using the concept of the 'clientelist state' he examines numerous areas of rule in which the 'balance of authority favour(s) local patrons over a centralised, rule-governed bureaucracy'.
11. Bunche, for example, suggests that bribery was not uncommon – although he also claims that this lent the system of local rule flexibility and stability. See Edgar (1992: 205).
12. Indeed one observer, perhaps rather romantically, noted that the relationship between African township residents and municipal employees was a relatively good one: 'In general this relationship appears to be excellent, the superintendents of the location and their assistants having the trust of the residents and being held in high esteem' (Haggie 1994: 71) – although this was followed by a statement that the municipal police were not tolerated quite as much! Jenny Robinson (1992b) also explores the world of the township administrator and his craft.
13. Besides the Rand, where the part played by liberals has been relatively well documented, see also Robinson (n.d.). Maylam (1990) does not, however, give the impression that these kinds of connections were central in Durban.
14. The Alexandra Clinic, always run by liberals, is a prime example; but there are many others.
15. See, for example, Sapire (1988: 104) who points out that the American Board Mission and Berlin Mission ran the only schools in Brakpan; that the former raised funds for a creche; and ran boys and girls clubs, an adult night school and a debating society. Edgar (1992: 186) makes clear that it was the Bantu Men's Social Centre that was perhaps the most well-known of these institutions.
16. Jeffrey (1991) discusses this feature of township culture more extensively. The role of local 'big man' L. M. Taunyane in soccer in Alexandra would be a good example. The 'big men' of the townships were not always drawn from the economic and cultural elite, although they inevitably overlapped; they gained their power from his control over patronage networks rather than economic resources, such as access to positions of authority in governance over political or social institutions, access to the elite and so on.
17. This phrase was actually Modikwe Dikobe's. See Couzens (1979). An interesting insider's view of this may be found in the memoir by Modise (1996).
18. Bunche gives a wonderful portrayal of the staidly dignified wedding of an elite family in these times. (Edgar 1992: 104)

19. See Bunche on the ways in which the pass laws could be 'fiddled' and educated Africans could ensure they were treated 'leniently' (Edgar 1993: 173-4). Goodhew (1991) mentions someone who believed that as a member of the elite he should be exempt from pass laws.
20. See Sapire (1988: 133) in which she describes how a Springs Advisory Board member said the government was 'morally bound' to give East Rand elite Africans freehold status to 'make natives free citizens of the country'.
21. For example Sapire (1988) shows how in Brakpan township popular militancy in 1939 to 1944 represented an upsurge of claims to do with such matters as living conditions and harsh rules; and spatially shaped means of struggle were used to establish demands for homes, water, the reduction of bus fares, the right to home brewing and the relaxation of a harsh administrative system (which had been introduced to cope with a moral panic of earlier times).
22. Here, this chapter breaks away from conventional analyses of Nationalist modernisation, by locating the discussion in the city alone, and by developing a separate periodisation for the transition in the urban areas. I am indebted to Deborah Posel for providing a backdrop to this section. Posel (1996) gave rise to a lively debate about the modernity of the apartheid state. She takes a slightly different path from this study – although it may be that the differences are due to the fact that she is talking about the state as a whole, whereas this study discusses only urban governance or lack of it.
23. Although rents were supposed from the fifties onwards to be 'economic'.
24. Via the Bantu Housing Board, the National Housing Fund, and compulsory employer contributions.
25. To give a sense of the degree of overcrowding, the population was 236 people per morgen (approximately two acres), as opposed to sixty-one in Orlando, forty-three in Atteridgeville, seventy-seven in Brededorp. Even District Six, the notoriously crowded Cape Town 'coloured' suburb, was only at a level of 221.
26. 'If you had a pass but you were not working, you were arrested and charged for a charge which was well known as Section 29 or Lofer Skaap ... Some people were not given a chance to explain why they were not working. Some were looking for a job and could not find any and were arrested whilst looking for a job ... So people were even afraid to look for a job. Many people used to bribe the municipal police with money. I ... was also arrested at the age of 18 years in 1974 and slept in cells for a day, the following day I was taken to the magistrate at Wynberg and I was warned and discharged' (statement by Paul Tshabalala, CTH archives).
27. The argument here diverges strongly, therefore, from that made by Mamdani (1996). The implication of the argument made in this study is that there are more differences than parallels between the type of racism under apartheid and that in colonial and post-colonial regimes – and that the rebellions we are looking at here are of a very different species than those, say, elsewhere in Africa. Mamdani, by contrast, emphasises the similarities between them.
28. See Seekings (1990: 71ff), in which he argues that the first of the new councillors played a role involving 'elements of patronage, where the resources involved were very limited. Councillors provided services rather than goods, mediation and arbitration rather than jobs or contracts'. But he emphasises that the willingness and capacity to play the patronage role was uneven and extremely limited.
29. Seekings (n.d.) by contrast, suggests that Community Councils/Black Local Authorities 'retained significant support throughout the period' (1978–84) because 'residents only identified them as "sell-outs" when it became clear that

their functions had changed (i.e. that they were no longer just residents' representatives to the local administration, but that they were concerned with the divisive implementation of unpopular administrative decisions (especially rent increases and shack demolition))'. However local authorities could not survive without rent increases, and this placed them in structural opposition to their own constituents. For an overview see Urban Foundation (n.d.).

30. The Alexandra Standholders Protection and Vigilance Society was formed; in addition white liberals formed the Citizens Hostel Action Committee. Massive press campaigns were also run. See Black Sash (n.d.).

31. Some rights to remain in the city did survive the draconian apartheid laws. These were (usually very reluctantly) granted to those who could prove birth there and in many cases also required other housing and job guarantees.

32. A disproportionately high number of these were men: 17,960 adult males vs 8,870 adult females.

33. So said Piet Koornhof, Minister of Plural Relations and Development at the installation of the first Alexandra Liaison Committee, quoted in Sarakinsky (1984: 62).

34. Including removals of people to buses while alleged homes were being built for them. See Sebola (Z2689), for a vivid description.

35. Nicknamed the 'blackjacks' and 'green beans' – a force which was grossly under-funded. See *The Sowetan* (30 November 84).

CHAPTER 4: BOUNDED REVOLT

1. Two kinds of police were responsible for Alexandra – the Municipal Police, also called 'Peri-Urban' or 'West Rand Administration Board' police by residents; and the South African Police (SAP) themselves, the national police force. Municipal police tended to live in the township, and were sometimes regarded as greater enemies than the SAP because of their role in policing rent payments and other local matters, although the SAP, too, had a fearsome reputation.

2. Mayekiso trial, Exhibit XXX, mentioned in evidence by A. Zwane, M2144. See also Interview with Mr J. van Zyl, October 1992. This particular policeman had worked in Alexandra for twenty years, and his death was mentioned by one observer as a crucial point in the evolution of the war; see Colonel Dickinson (Z1807).

3. The homes of DConst. M. S. Mashile at 99 Thirteenth Avenue, DSgts. L. W. Monakali at 16 Sixth Avenue and J. Mothibi at 106 Phase 1 were reported to have been attacked (S56 Schedule 'A', CTH archives).

4. Councillors B. M. Nxumalo at 188 Phase 2; S. Mabiletsa at 53 Eleventh Avenue; and Z. Gasela at 37 Eleventh Avenue were also attacked it seems. See CTH archives Schedule B.

5. Samson Ndaba had already been burnt on 15 February. Then on 17 February his house was burnt down. He was suspected of being a spy because about thirteen members of AYCO had been arrested in the shack behind his house and he had not been arrested – the suspicion was that he had 'shopped' them. He possibly had also 'shopped' Vincent Tshabalala – or so it was thought. Rumours were strong that he was an informer after the Tshabalala death.

6. He said afterwards: 'I tried to talk to people because I helped a lot. Every year I had a Christmas party for the children and it look to me the same children and they came and damaged the place. I said, How can it happen? *A Christmas party for which children?* For the children, 1,500–2,000 children ... I used to give them presents and sweets and cold drinks and things, we give them some music. We

had some Swazi dances and at one time we had the Salvation Army and we give them a whole day of, at least, from about 11o'clock until 6 o'clock, like a party'.
7. They were: Alfred Mvandaba, Jacob Maruka, Steven Sithole, Mlungisi Mkhize and Amos Ramokhibitsane. See Mayekiso file on Six-Day War, list of Six-Day War deaths, CTH archives.
8. Photographs of the body are in the trial record, as Exhibits k and k1, CTH archives.
9. According to Mdakane: 'When we got there they were holding a bishops' conference. They allowed us to present the matter about Alexandra. We explained the problem we came about to them. They listened to it and the following bishops were then elected: Bishop Tutu, Reverend Stanley Makobe, Dr Beyers Naude, Dr Alan Boesak, and the president of the SACC, Bishop Manas Buthelezi, who agreed that they would personally go to Alexandra township to go and see for themselves, in order to talk to the people and the police, to stop the fighting that was taking place ... They would also talk about the problem of the police not accepting our problems' (Richard Mdakane, M2193).
10. Witch-burnings were much more common in the rural areas, but urban ones had occurred. See Ritchken (1987).
11. See Mayekiso file on Six-Day War, list of people shot, CTH archives. See also South African Press Association (SAPA) Report, 20 February 1986, CTH archives.
12. The rhythms of daily life are repetitive and relatively predictable – features which are reinforced by the ways in which modernity and industrial capitalism regulate and reify time. The capacity to control these rhythms is an aspect of power, and control thereof has been fought over historically. There are many occasions upon which this regulated and reified time is disrupted. Strata of the population – the 'uncaptured' peasantry in early capitalism, the unemployed, retired, homebound or insane –are not as subject to its rigours as those who are employed, at school or otherwise time-controlled. For them, the continuities and rhythms as experienced by those who live within the confines of 'normal' and 'reified' time are absent. They may experience this as an extension of their personal freedom – but it may also introduce a sense of unreality or abnormality into their lives.

CHAPTER 5: GENERATIONS, RESOURCES AND IDEAS

1. Carter says the call for 'ungovernability' had been made by the NEC of the ANC in January 1985, elaborated upon in a pamphlet entitled 'ANC call to the nation: the future is within our grasp' Lusaka, 25 April 1985, and distributed within SA shortly thereafter.
2. This pamphlet, which was issued by the National Executive Committee of the ANC, Lusaka, Zambia 25 April 1985, and also talked of as 'Oliver Tambo's Call to the Nation' was used extensively in the Zwane trial – see exhibit CCCC, PJ archives.
3. Thus in Eisenstadt's classic functionalist book, the majority of examples of types of generational cleavage are drawn from Africa (Eisenstadt 1956). The most recent study of traditionalist generational cleavage and their effects in contemporary African settings is Carton (2000).
4. Said by an elderly resident watching a group of teenagers erect a road block of burning tyres in Alexandra in April 1986, reported in Johnson (1988).
5. Johnson (1988: 43–4) quoting interviews with activists in Alexandra, April 1986.
6. See, for a subtle portrayal of the intended and unintended consequences of Bantu Education, Hyslop (1999).

7. One activist interviewed by Charles Carter said that male activists were all 'die hard chauvinists', and that they would do women a 'revolutionary favour' by encouraging them to participate. This contrasts strongly with Sitas's perhaps slightly optimistic claims of a 'new sisterhood' having emerged amongst comrades in Natal (Sitas 1992).
8. See Campbell (1994: 120–1) for Durban examples; and Morris et al. (1999: 33), which found that in the case of a Soweto survey, even given the reluctance of respondents to talk about such things 'approximately one in five of the women in the sample admitted to having been beaten by their spouse' and of these 'a little under half (i.e. one in ten overall, BB) reported being beaten regularly or severely'.
9. Ashwell Zwane's surreal progress towards this ambition included taking a leading position in a 'people's court'; experiencing a long trial for treason and sedition as chief accused, followed by several years in jail during which he studied law; being released early under the post-independence amnesty; studying law at the University of the Witwatersrand where he turned up in the author's class in Sociology! He finally obtained a law degree and practises as an attorney in Johannesburg.
10. Football names are common. Zwane talks of a speaker at the Diradeng funeral called 'Sparks': 'I only know him by his football name,' he said. Treason trial accused Patrick 'Terror' Lekota's nickname was also a football name.
11. Albert Sebola's admiration for Vincent Tshabalala, who had died in possession of a Scorpion and a bag of explosives, was patent (A. Sebola, Z2816).
12. '*Mama kutheni*' translates as: Mama, what is happening. Spelling in this and all other examples of comrade writings and literature is left as in the original, as an important indicator of the level of education of the grassroots comrades as opposed to those in more formal leadership positions.
13. Exhibit VV, poem found at 31 Seventh Avenue, Mayekiso trial, CTH archives.
14. This is mentioned in both Straker (1992); and Seekings (1990). For additional insight into comrade experience and motivation see Seekings (1993); Nkosi (n.d.); Marks (1994, 1995, 2001); Bundy (1987); and, for a portrayal of a much more war-like comrade culture, Sitas (1992).
15. Other words were used to mean 'comrade', for example *quabane* in Zulu/Xhosa. *Ngwenya* meant *comtsotsis*. The concept of *ngwenya* came, it was said, from the Eastern Cape Trade Union culture, where 'it was used to refer to rank and file members of organizations', i.e. 'ordinary people who were not intellectuals or ideologues well versed in organizational activity'. This implied that the grassroots comrades were in fact the comtsotsis as well and that only the leaders were true comrades. See Carter (1991a: 233).
16. Minutes of Zwane Youth Group meeting, 19 April 1986, exhibit E, Zwane trial, PJ archives.
17. For example, the names of those going on behalf of the Youth Group to a meeting at Thabisong were: Eddie Malatji, Andrew Maleka, Percy Shiburi, Mxolisi Zwane, Michael Yende, Arthur Msimango, Tsiki Khunou, Marry Modise, Elphus Mashego, Tsepo Makhene, Tommy Shibambu, Vusi Skosana, Edward Khubeka. Only one of these – Marry (Mary) Modise – was a woman. Minutes of Youth Group meeting, 30 May 1986, Exhibit H, Zwane trial, PJ archives.
18. Poem recorded in Zwane notebook found at 64 Fifteenth Avenue, exhibit G, Zwane trial, PJ archives.
19. *In camera* Witness 9, Z1153 – this was a witness for the prosecution, which adds weight to the testimony given in this particular respect.

20. Zwane Youth Group minutes, 19 April 1986, Zwane trial, exhibit E, PJ archives.
21. Zwane Youth Group minutes, 9 May 1986, discussing the handing out of the AYCO constitution to those present and what this meant. Exhibit E, Zwane trial, PJ archives.
22. A. Sebola's discussion of these minutes (Z2749–50); see actual minutes, exhibit D, Zwane trial, PJ archives. See this also typed out as 'Exhibit H, minutes of meeting of 30 May', Zwane trial, PJ archives.
23. Minutes of 'Zwane youth grouping', 19 April 1986, exhibit E, Zwane trial, PJ archives.
24. A. Sebola, discussing minutes of 23 April meeting (Z2647–8); see actual minutes, Exhibit D, Zwane trial, PJ archives.
25. Exhibit D, agenda for 23 May meeting of the Zwane Youth Group, Zwane trial, PJ archives. At the subsequent meeting, the issue was raised again.
26. Agenda, exhibit D, meeting around late May, Zwane Youth Group, Zwane trial, PJ archives.
27. They were worried about witchcraft. The agenda for an earlier meeting said 'Accusation of witches without back ground standing point'; Agenda, n.d. exhibit D, Zwane trial, PJ archives. See also A. Sebola (Z2662). This came up again at the 5 May meeting of the same 14–16 Avenue group of AYCO.
28. Soccer had existed for decades in Alexandra and had been substantially encouraged by charitable white individuals and liberal institutions. At one stage there had been about seventy-seven soccer teams and a powerful soccer league in Alexandra. There were also tennis leagues, 'Centres of Concern', and coaching in these sports, or training in the arts or typing. Some of the liberals concerned, such as treason trial witness for the defence, Ricky Valente, knew the key accused in the Mayekiso trial and often acted as intermediaries between those resisting, particularly adults, and the various arms of the state. They constituted part of the resource mobilising mechanisms used by adults in particular.
29. The ANC influence in the formation of AYCO was clear. Early leaders included Vincent Tshabalala and Neil Thobejane. The first executive consisted of Paul Mashatile (president), Constance Hlatshwayo (asst sec.); Jacob Mtshali (general secretary); Naomi River (publicity sec.); Nesto Kgope (treas.) and Patric Banda (organiser). See AYCO newsletter, 'Voice of Ayco', November/December 1983, and 1984, in possession of author. Later executive or centrally important members included Peter Makgoba, Obed Bapela, Immanuel Maike, Ernest Ndlovu and Aubrey Kitime.
30. Called *Ditshwantso tsa Rona*, this movement was suspicious of the 'charterists' potential for authoritarianism.
31. Document in possession of author.
32. Document in possession of author.
33. Including Paul Mashatile, Patrick Banda, Jacob Mtshali, Emmanuel Maake, Robert Mhlanbe and many other friends from school. Other organisations that participated included Thusong Youth Club; Thabisong Youth Club; Roman Catholic Youth Club; Methodist Youth; and Khanlezi Cultural Group.
34. Brief history of AYCO in documents relating to trial, Mayekiso trial, CTH archives.
35. See 'Fear of an Alex Councillor', *The Sowetan*, 28 December 1984, about how Albert Maphala, age 29, 'Councillor for Sports and Recreation' and the youngest to be elected in the December 1984 Council under Buti, was 'missed by three bullets on the night of December 6 while trying to arrange alternative overnight accommodation after he had had a heated argument with senior councillors in front of the council chambers during the day.

36. This version of events appears in *Izwi Lase Township*, the Trotskyist newsletter run by Ditshwantso tsa Rona, April 1982 – a paper which also played a part in publicising the Alexandra repertoire to its own residents.
37. Such intellectuals as Philip Bonner (now Professor of History at the University of the Witwatersrand), Bernie Fanaroff, (now a key figure in Safety and Security in the ANC government), Eddie Webster, (now Professor of Sociology at the University of the Witwatersrand), Alec Erwin (now Minister of Finance) and those involved in the Johannesburg-based, still very energetic History Workshop were active at the time. For a discussion of the role of intellectuals in South Africa during this period see Bozzoli (1990: 209–34). See also Moses Mayekiso (M2879).
38. Thus the unions and Mayekiso himself supported rent struggles in the Vaal Triangle because 'more than ten thousand of Mawu members are based in the Vaal Triangle' (Moses Mayekiso, M2771). He, too, was not averse to a little millenarianism, saying: 'We should refuse to pay rent until everyone is employed'.
39. When cross-examined he claimed he was not a pure 'workerist'. A workerist, he said, 'is a person who believed that the organised workers only, they are the people who can bring freedom. It is a person who does not believe that other sectors in the community such as youth organisations and students' organisations, women's organisations, he regards them as unimportant in the struggle, who believes in the pushing for the struggle on economic issues only' (Moses Mayekiso, M3113).
40. Mayekiso had links with non ANC sanctioned groups such as Salep, Socialist Worker, Militant and other Trotskyite British organisations.
41. He eventually completed a book, after the revolt, used considerably in this study. See Mayekiso (1996).
42. Manuscript found in Mayekiso home, Exhibit FF 25, unedited, Mayekiso trial, CTH archives.
43. The others tried were Richard Mdakane, and the young patriarch Paul Tshabalala, who was aged thirty at time of Six-Day War. A born and bred Alexandra resident, he went to Holy Cross School until Std 7. When his grandparents (who had owned land at 13 Fourteenth Avenue) were removed to Meadowlands, his mother – a domestic servant – stayed behind and was given a house in Fourteenth Avenue. He was variously a labourer, a machine operator, a packer, a clerk, a storeman, a delivery man, a caddy, and a casual labourer. He also became a professional football referee. He sometimes would act as a worker representative. He married five different women, had five children and cared for them as well as his sisters and his mother.

CHAPTER 6: COMMANDING THE TERRITORY

1. See Mayekiso and Zwane trials exhibit: 'Peoples' Court Minutes', CTH archives and PJ archives.
2. See also Exhibit FF22, annexure B9, 10, 11, 12, 13, Mayekiso trial, CTH archives.
3. The 'consolidation of youth groupings' was discussed extensively at the meeting on 2 June. Mentioned were the regions from: 1st–4th Avenues, 5th–7th Avenues, 8th–10th Avenues; 11th–13th Avenues, 14th–16th Avenues and 17th–22nd Avenues. Zwane trial Exhibit D, exhibits of 2 June meeting, PJ archives.
4. The owner of Goldie's Hairdressing Salon said her shop had closed for seven months after being boycotted, broken into, looted and damaged because her boyfriend's father had been the town clerk. The boyfriend himself, also a shop-

keeper, was forced to close down until his father had resigned later during the revolt, while Mayor Sam Buti's son had a similar experience. A shebeen-owner was boycotted because he worked for the Alexandra Council as a flat caretaker. He resigned from his job and reopened the shebeen.

5. See Exhibit Q, Zwane trial, PJ archives; and A. Sebola (Z2647).
6. *Alexandra Speak* Special Issue 'Forward to Peoples Power', 15 May 1986.
7. Mojalefa Moseki, article in *The Sowetan*, 14 April 1986. The article includes a picture of Theresa.
8. These statistics of burning, necklacing and destruction of buildings were given in evidence to the Mayekiso trial in a statement by state witness Brigadier Stadler. See file Ex 2. Exhibit AAAA, statement of Brig. Stadler, CTH archives.
9. Leepile Taunyane, chairman of the National Soccer League had resigned claiming it was for personal reasons; Percy Williams had been convicted of a criminal offence and was asked to leave; Councillor Koza's windscreen was shattered by 'so-called militants' on 30 June.
10. *The Star* saw Sam Buti's resignation as a 'failure of the Local Authorities Act' – as he had been a hopeful participant, wishing to make Alexandra an independent town. A former president of the widely accepted South African Council of Churches, he was well travelled and had started off as a popular and respected figure. See *The Star*, 6 April 1986.

CHAPTER 7: THE PRIVATE UTOPIA

1. Bodies lying in the street in the morning were not an uncommon sight in townships. See also Straker (1992).
2. 'When I first saw the anticrime campaign it was in 1985, in November. It were boys going into the shebeens requesting people to hand over their dangerous weapons, because there were many people dying during that time ... In December they were still doing it. We, the Alexandra residents, were very pleased about that, because they were not lashing any person.' (P. Tshabalala, M3855). See also A. Sebola (Z2679).
3. Exhibit D, minutes of the AYCO 14th–16th Avenue meeting, 30 May 1986, Zwane trial, PJ archives.
4. In the minutes of one of the AYCO 14th–16th Avenue meetings, the anti-crime camp is mentioned (early May); Zwane trial, PJ archives.
5. There were girls at *in camera* Witness 9's first anti-crime meeting, but they did not join the campaign. They went home. The prosecution found minutes of the meetings of the Zwane Youth Group for May and June. These were to provide a lot of the basis for the trial later. People signed up, at, for example, the one Friday meeting, to go on the campaign, choosing either to go on the Friday or the Saturday. The names were: **Friday** – Arthur Vilakazi, Jack Ngwenya, Tony Molepo, Mxolisi Zwane (i.e. Ashwell), Jabu Sithole, Lucky Makgale, Thabo Magagula, David Mafutha (one of the accused), Moses Ngobese, Mike, Fanyana, Phanuel, Thabo Nsundu, Bongani Hlatshwayo, Benson Mafiko, George Kumalo, Jabulani Nkosi, David Marallovu(?), Solomon Maluleka; and **Saturday** – Patrick Peterson, Joseph Makgalemele, Benson Mafiko (Matiko?) Anndeew Manuathela, Lucky Ngenge, Vusi Khubheka, Joel Chauke, Papi (unreadable), Mandla (unreadable), Philemon Phalogwane. Only Joseph Monunu signed up for the Sunday. (original spelling retained).
6. This witness gave evidence for the prosecution, but what he said is not inconsistent with the defence's evidence.
7. *In camera* Witness 9 (Z976ff), for the prosecution, confirms the anti-crime

campaign story given by Zwane and others. He was 'roped in' and went along on the Friday campaigns. His name appears on the list in Note 5.

8. Exhibit E, minutes of meeting of Youth Group 12/5/86, Zwane trial, PJ archives. Sebola explained what this meant:

'This referred to as a member who was present at the campaign said he saw that some of the members were not faithful, did not search some of their friends. And so such members will be punished by the whole youth group irrespective of position in the youth group, that the punishment will be by means of expulsion from the group, or suspension if I recall.' This version contrasted with that of the witnesses for the prosecution. A. Sebola (Z2685–6).

9. See also Suttner (1986). Discussions such as these do not always give sufficient consideration to the absence of thorough procedures for obtaining evidence, and the resulting high possibilities of wrongful conviction, or the vulnerability of such institutions to rapid decay and abuse. Exceptions to this are provided by the more detailed study of Mamelodi by Hund and Kotu-Rammopo (1983), and the absolutely frank description of a people's court in Cape Town in Burman and Scharf (1990); as in some of the Alexandra courts, they say, over time, 'a very strong prosecutorial, even persecutorial, momentum was generated by a particularly militant clique within the court', and courts in general soon lost the popular support they had initially had in the community.

10. See also *Weekly Mail*, 6 March 1986. This also appears in the inquest into his death. Moses Mayekiso (M2948) describes how his intestines were hanging out before he died.

11. It was at her larger than usual two-roomed home that T-shirts were stored and from there that many were sold and quite a few stolen, much to the chagrin of the AAC.

12. Mayekiso said the AAC did not like her ambiguity (Moses Mayekiso, M2971).

13. The 11 Eighth Avenue court must have already existed as it is reported that the women complaining of assaults went to the police, who advised them to go there' (Moses Mayekiso, M2176). See also R. Mdakane (M2183).

14. See Bapela's evidence that as early as 6 March he attended a meeting at 53 Nineteenth Ave (either this was next door or the addresses have been transcribed incorrectly) at which youth gathered and received a lecture on how to move away from the *tsotsi* life and from gambling, and become educated comrades, and at which they asked him to train them in history and so on. This had been a gangster headquarters before. He says it definitely became known as Youth Headquarters (O. Bapela, M3931).

15. Exhibit D – minutes of 2 June meeting, Zwane trial, PJ archives.

16. After the vigilante attack, journalists were called in by police to see inside the people's court. Photographs of this and of one of the barricades that had been erected appeared in *The Sowetan* and *The Star*, 25 April 1986.

17. Zwelakhe Sisulu, from his speech, recorded in *Transformation 1*, 1986, 'Peoples' Education for People's Power', quoted in Seekings (1993: 57).

18. The defence for the Mayekiso trial was at pains to separate out the *makhukhu*, which was pretty open about the presence of lashing, from the main house.

19. Exhibit AA, found at Obed Bapela's mother's house, was a record of this people's court hearings (Mayekiso trial, CTH archives).

20. I have chosen not to use evidence for the prosecution here, vivid though it may be, because of the risk of bias.

21. See Mayekiso indictment, Annexure C. Evidence found at the 31 Seventh Avenue and Nineteenth Avenue people's court. This is a very imperfect table. It appears to have been compiled by the prosecution from hand-written notes, which are not in the record. It covers the dates 3 March to 22 June, but most of

the cases were held during April. Most were at the Nineteenth Avenue court.

22. Abbreviated from the minutes of 29 May, of the people's court at 64 Fifteenth Avenue – or at least, this was where the minutes were found; it is not clear if the court was or was not at this address. Other minutes say the actual headquarters were at a nearby address (Exhibit F, Zwane trial, PJ archives). See also Exhibit K, minutes of Youth Headquarters, found by police at 64 Fifteenth Avenue, Zwane trial, PJ archives.

23. Defence lawyers did not refute the case as a whole, but did argue that the child had been malnourished and retarded, and that the case could have arisen because neighbours had lodged a complaint with the comrades. They also suggested that the husband may well have been beating his wife regularly.

24. Statement by a young boy, possibly Isaac Makgalamele (Exhibit OO, Zwane trial, PJ archives).

25. No real names are used here except for those such as Ashwell Zwane who are being discussed in the book more generally.

26. In fact he had several, as many as eight, such books.

27. Albert Sebola arrived at this stage, and observed that the case had begun to take the form of a family feud. The discussion indicated 'that there was a feud between two families, that one family was accusing another family there that one of their family members had killed their brother'. He participated because 'the other family wanted to pay revenge upon the other family accused of being the killers of their brother. And so as I wanted to promote peace between the two families' (A Sebola, Z2762).

28. These are mainly Advocate D. Soggot's words, in his cross-examination of *in camera* Witness 13, a business owner who was boycotted. He goes on to say that the older people were grateful to the youth (M398).

CHAPTER 8: REALISM AND REVOLUTION

1. Buti's co-operation appears to have been strategic – he sought to accept municipal status so he could get access to finance to develop Alex. And indeed he had since the removals of the late 1970s opposed the brutalisation of Alexandra, rejected Community Councils, commissioned a survey, sought to restore freehold and build accommodation. However this was simply seen as collaboration. Buti felt he had been betrayed by his own people (interview with Buti, *The Sowetan*, 17 July 1986). It was claimed he had been in charge of a corrupt body (for example in the case of the allocation of trading licences) and the expansion of the hated Municipal Police Force.

2. Pamphlet, 'Alex Bus Boycott Continues' issued by the Alexandra Commuters Committee, 11 Eighth Avenue. In February a second mass meeting was held at which the Alexandra Commuters Committee issued another pamphlet, 'Our demands have not yet been met' (Mayekiso trial, CTH archives).

3. See Marks (2001), for a discussion of the instrumental, rather than idealistic, justifications given by youths for the violence in which they engaged.

4. Populists (in other words the ANC) believed in a 'two stage' theory of revolution – the national revolution first, to be followed by the socialist revolution. Workerists, on the other hand, believed it should all happen at once, in 'one stage'. Mayekiso believed: 'Our Black brothers will exploit and oppress us after liberation just as has happened elsewhere in the world, if we go for two stages.' The Freedom Charter must be changed. 'You can't all be given land,' he said. Later he was criticised in public for his view on the Freedom Charter – the central symbolic document of the ANC.

5. The concepts of structured answerability and grassroots democracy were, the adults thought, not really present in youth who adopted a vanguardist stance, as did those adhering to the Black Consciousness movement. In his evidence in court, Mayekiso called such approaches Leninist/vanguardist. See Moses Mayekiso (M 2798–9).
6. Minutes of the 'Volunteers Coordinating Committee', held at 31 Seventh Avenue, on 17 February 1986 (Mayekiso trial, CTH archives). Ten people attended.
7. Ibid.
8. It is important to note that these were FOSATU (later COSATU), unions which had a strong tradition of focusing on material reality/experience, and on institutionalising democratic structures with systems of accountability and answerability.
9. For elaborate details see the AAC document, exhibit EE, written in May–June, in which yard, block, and street committees were proposed, with the idea that they build up to an elected executive. The document gives specific details about areas in Alex that did not fit into this model – such as flats and hostels – and how they might be included. Mayekiso trial, CTH archives.
10. Handwritten document found in Moses Mayekiso's house. This was an agenda for a meeting. Exhibit FF22, Mayekiso trial, CTH archives.
11. For an idea of the immense range of such phenomena, see press clippings nos 109, 156, 52, 53, 189, 38, 180, 212–14, 217, 115, 180, Press File 1. Mayekiso trial, CTH archives.
12. See A. Sebola (Z2639): 'one of the residents is demanding rentals from those who stays with him in that particular yard.' His name was Phineas and he was the 'Standlord' at 70 Fifteenth Avenue. Phineas, explained Sebola, 'had many houses there and he was demanding high rentals for those houses'.
13. One comrade remembered that 'the people in our yard' had gathered together to elect their rep., who was an elder.
14. Refilwe Mashego also commented 'by yard committee members we referred to us who are the owners of the houses. The adults in our yard … the people who have a say in a particular house' (R. Mashego, M4266–7).
15. These were mentioned in places, though not frequently. In Sebola's evidence, for example, one set of minutes of the AYCO meeting at the 14th–16th Avenue youth headquarters does mention block committees. Sebola said: 'A block committee as in Alexandra I will take maybe in a street starting from Vasco da Gama to London Avenue … and so we have streets in between starting from Vasco to John Brand, of which that refers to a block, and John Brand to Hofmeyer refers to a block … A block committee is a committee formed by yard reps. Different yard reps of different yards come together and they form a block committee' (A. Sebola, Z2676).
16. Exhibit EE5, handwritten notes, seized from South African Youth Congress offices, probably written by Mayekiso himself. Clearly Mayekiso would have wanted to distance himself from violence in his trial for treason, but these notes, and his actions in attempting to construct 'disciplinary systems' do appear to illustrate that his notions of 'discipline' were indeed more restrained than those of the youths, and even of many of the adults (Mayekiso trial, CTH archives).
17. Richard Mdakane (M2523, M2613–4). Ricky Valente went to the police to ask them to begin taking cases again: 'the yard committees were trying to bring peace within the community. We were hoping that the community would start respecting and the killing would stop. *And the stealing?* Yes, we were hoping that anything that is crime was going to be reduced … it is the decision of the entire community that the people's court must be closed'.
18. Mdakane claimed in fact that 'the AAC never formed people's courts and it

never ran the people's courts as a committee ... People were referring to the committees (Yard, block and street) as the people's courts because those committees were committees falling under the Action Committee.' (Richard Mdakane, M2587).

19. See exhibit H, Mayekiso trial, CTH archives. Matambo Mthibe, the accused in this case, subsequently gave evidence for the prosecution in the Mayekiso case.

CHAPTER 9: NATIONALISM AND THEATRICALITY

1. This article claimed the 'Young Lions' of Alexandra as the vanguard of the ANC's armed wing, but made it clear that what it called 'the revolt of the townships' was something which did not quite fit with ANC MK strategy, which until then had depended on guerrilla warfare.

2. Meyers's brother said that he died of teargas; the doctor said later that he was so drunk he may not have died of teargas. He was looting at the time. One young man had died of peritonitis during this period, but according to his brother, the family was forced by threats of 'burning' to bury him at a mass funeral rather than in his rural home at Soekmekaar. 'The comrades said any person who has died during this period or that period he was a soldier so he had to be buried there.' The family attempted to defy this instruction at first by taking the body to their own undertakers, but the comrades went to the undertaker and cancelled the arrangements. Before the funeral, the comrades erected tents at their house, and a night vigil was held at their home, which 500 comrades attended. The comrade was then buried at the mass funeral on 5 March. His family went to the Alexandra stadium by taxi, while the comrades carried the coffin on their shoulders. There they saw the coffin, covered with the ANC flag and with his name spelt incorrectly on it. See also Sergeant Kemp (Z2012).

3. These ranged from AYCO, ASCO, the Alex Traders Association, the Alex Taxi Association, the Alex Funeral Undertakers Association, Neusa, AWO, the Alex Parents Crisis Committee, and the Alex 'Voice of Priests'.

4. Wilson Moses also saw T-shirts at this 5 March meeting. In fact, he bought one for 13 Rand at 31 Seventh Avenue. He went to that funeral because 'All the people were going to the funeral. Many people were already wearing these t-shirts and I was shown where to go to if I want one.' Money was collected for this funeral 'in the yards', so as he was a yard rep, he collected money in his yard and took it to 31 Seventh Avenue (Wilson Moses, M348).

5. This was consistent with the army's general strategy in controlling internal 'unrest', which was more one of 'winning hearts and minds' than of direct repression at this stage, leading to the situation where some Alexandrans said they preferred having the army's presence to that of the police who were much more brutal and direct.

6. The police and army were said to have 'hijacked the funeral of AYCO member Jacob Mabisela' (said to have been killed by Azapo) on 21 June 1986. (A. Zwane, Z3798, Z4419).

7. Obed Bapela put it this way: 'My attitude about the AAC was this, that they would not take part in the structures that promote apartheid because they would bring oppression to the people and the people at that time did not like it. If anyone takes part in them, like the AAC taking part in it, people would no longer talk to the AAC. They would then cast a bad eye towards it. The AAC attitude was that these structures must be well-founded and must be non-racial in order that all the people in Alexandra should accept them. If they should take part in it, it should be the will of the people that they must go and participate' (O. Bapela, M3972).

8. See Mayekiso trial, evidence of various witnesses (M2984, M3790, M2257).
9. Document found in Mayekiso's room, which is a record of the resolutions taken by the organisations attending the 13 April Workshop. Out of this came demands for short-term and long-term goals which ended up as a pamphlet. See Exhibits FF20, 21 and 22, handwritten notes from workshop, Mayekiso trial, CTH archives.

CHAPTER 10: FROM VICTORY TO DEFEAT

1. Later, they lowered this claim to 60 per cent. When the first elections were held in 1994, the ANC gained a staggering majority in Alexandra, implying that a similarly large majority of people sympathised with the AAC.
2. See Mayekiso trial, evidence of various witnesses (M3038, M3896, M3899, M3801, M4093). A month later, on 23 May, various organisations began to plan together to set up a liaison committee, which would seek to establish a democratically elected local government. In addition, on 8 June a meeting of a huge range of organisations was held to plan to form 'one civic' organisation, with the same purpose.
3. The concept of the 'true comrade' is an interesting one, which many participants in the period refer to. True comrades lived by their ideals, were extremely well educated politically (usually through self-education in their own study-groups) and deeply committed to the struggle.
4. One hundred and thirty-six cars had been hijacked in the vicinity of Alex since beginning of March, according to *The Citizen*, 30 April 1986; ninety-two in March, and forty-four in April. 'Unruly youth' regularly visited township shops, and extorted the shopkeepers for food. Hijackings of 'targets' – cars connected to nearby industries or those of whites who drove near Alexandra – proliferated. Seventy cars were stolen in one week alone in mid-March of 1986 and some company cars were burned. The police warned motorists 'if they see a large dangerous-looking crowd as he approaches an intersection I would advise him to drive through if it is safe to do so. People tend to panic, especially if stones hit them.'
5. Letter from Richard Mdakane to his mother, sometime during March 1986. Exhibit KKK, Mayekiso trial, CTH archives.
6. Carter quotes the transcript of the SABC programme 'Comment' on the issue of 'Police protection', on 19 February 1986: 'The ordinary black man or woman in the urban unrest areas is helpless against radical intimidation. He is paralysed by the violence of the revolutionary political onslaught, typified again by events at Alexandra: the murderous attacks on moderates, police and councillors, the destruction of their homes and possessions, the strong-armed methods by which they are prevented from going to work.' Without 'effective police protection', people would be left to the 'mercy of the revolutionary clique and its hooligan storm-troopers', abandoned 'to the protection of the mob and the justice of the kangaroo court and the "necklace"'. This kind of propaganda made it difficult for sympathisers with the ANC cause to agree that some intimidation had indeed existed! (Carter 1991a: 4).
7. Poem found in documents seized at Youth Group Headquarters (Zwane trial exhibit L, PJ archives).
8. Poem written by Mpho Walter Mojapelo, AYCO and ASCO member aged 21 who had spent the night of the vigilante attack hiding in a tree. Quoted in Carter (1991a: 178).
9. It was definitely with police consent. By 31 March, the 'police patrolled the

streets 24 hours a day' and the soldiers were already there. At the time of the vigilante attack Casspirs patrolled the whole township day and night. It would have been impossible for anyone to launch this kind of attack without police consent.

10. Other vigilante attacks were happening around the country. One, for example, took place in Krugersdorp just the previous month. See Jon Qwelane (*Sunday Star*, 27 April 1986).

11. *Business Day* (29 April 1986) reported it differently. They said the gun battle lasted 'almost an hour, after which all houses in the area ... were thoroughly searched by police' and that police threw a hand grenade into the house.

12. *City Press* (27 April 1986) reported that: 'Three more people died in Alexandra in the past three days – one of them soccer star Vusi Silango, shot dead by security forces on Thursday night ... [as well as] Thulani Mdluli and Thulani Ngubane. These three deaths bring this week's unofficial death toll in Alex – a battleground for the second time this year – to 17. Asked to comment on the shootings a police spokesman ... said she knew only of a youth who was burnt to death on Thursday and another who was shot dead "while holding a petrol bomb". A friend said he and Silango were sitting around a fire at 11 pm when two men in SADF uniforms fired at them. "We ran away and Silango followed me home. When I turned around I saw blood oozing from his chest."' *City Press* also reported that Mdluli was shot on Friday on his way home: 'According to a friend ... they saw a group of armed soldiers and cops through their window. "After they passed the house, Mdluli went home. There was gunfire and we locked the doors. When we woke up the next day we found him dead in the street."' SACC worker Beatrice Mampane told *City Press* that 'when she phoned the Wynberg police station to report the killing, a cop said they "weren't involved with Alexandra's affairs any more".' Ngubane said, before he died, that he had been shot by a well-known cop. Later the police took reporters to the places that had been attacked. They were trying to prove that the attack had been by unknown private vigilantes. 'They were trying to justify the attack to counter the anarchy that existed in the township, as well as countering ... certain actions of the comrades who were attacking things.' See also Wilson Moses (M3050–1).

13. On 25 April 1986, *The Weekly Mail* reported that 'Alexandra was in a virtual state of siege yesterday, as community leaders blamed this week's violence on policemen and rejected any suggestion of interracial rivalry in the township ... Yesterday hippos and Casspirs patrolled the streets of the beleaguered township. Buffels guarded the stadium, and youths still moved around amongst barricades littering all the main roads. Journalists saw at least one youth armed with a petrol bomb. The shells of burnt out cars lay all along Seventh Avenue outside the "people's court", the focus of Tuesday night's attack.'

CHAPTER 11: MEMORY AND FORGETTING

1. See Mzwanele Mayekiso (1996: ch. 6) for a moving description of his arrest, interrogation and the experience of prison. Particularly impressive is his account of the powerful role played by the nationally known leaders, by Alexandran and other adults and by younger leadership in keeping prison life orderly and productive and in negotiating the prison's moral economy.

2. Ashwell Zwane, aged 22, Vusi Ngwenya, aged 22, David Mafutha, aged 21 and Piet Mogano, aged 25, were sentenced to eight years' imprisonment, of which four years was conditionally suspended for five years. Andrew Mafutha, aged 24, Arthur Vilakazi, aged 22, and Albert Sebola, aged 24, each received six years

with three years suspended. Philemon 'Chicks' Phalongwane, who could not be named for most of the trial proceedings as he was under 18, was given a four-year sentence, wholly suspended. They were only released after the first amnesty granted to political prisoners after 1994.

3. Himself a member of the ANC Youth League, Lekalakala did his research for the hearing from a series of academic books, theses and articles on the events of the 1980s, and was to have given a major portrayal of the story of the revolt of 1986. He arrived late, and found that much of this had been covered by Bapela, a much more central participant in the events.

4. Further research is needed into the selection of witnesses, which appears itself to have involved important processes of community-construction and sanctioning of existing narratives.

5. Bapela had also prepared his evidence using published documents and dissertations (some of it also gleaned from academic theses borrowed from me, reinforcing the argument that academics played an important, if indirect, role in constructing the TRC's narratives) as well as his own experience in giving evidence in the treason trial, and his own memories.

6. 'Found' probably means 'saw' – translation was sometimes rather rough, it appears.

CHAPTER 12: EPILOGUE

1. In the decade after liberation, the ANC government built approximately 1 million new homes.

2. 'Land Claims court has paid dispossessed residents R50 000 each' (*The Star*, 31 July 2000).

3. RDP refers to the Reconstruction and Development Programme, the first, relatively redistributive, development plan put forward by the ANC soon after it had come to power. This was replaced, later, by a far more neo-liberal and market-based plan, with the acronym 'GEAR'.

BIBLIOGRAPHY

Abel, R. 1995. *Politics by Other Means: law in the struggle against apartheid, 1980–1994*. London and New York: Routledge.

Abrams, P. 1982. *Historical Sociology*. Somerset: Open Books.

Adam, B. 1990. *Time and Social Theory*. Cambridge: Polity Press.

Adam, H. 1971. *Modernizing Racial Domination*. Berkeley and Los Angeles: University of California Press.

Adler, G. and J. Steinberg (eds). 2000. *From Comrades to Citizens: the South African Civics Movement and the transition to democracy*. Basingstoke: Macmillan.

African National Congress. n.d. *Documents of the Second National Consultative Conference of the African National Congress, Zambia, 16–23 June 1985*. Lusaka: ANC.

Altbach, P. and R. Laufer (eds). 1972. *The New Pilgrims: youth protest in transition*. New York: McKay.

Aminzade, R., J. A. Goldstone, D. McAdam, E. J. Perry, W. H. Sewell, S. Tarrow and C. Tilly. 2001. *Silence and Voice in the Study of Contentious Politics*. Cambridge: Cambridge University Press.

Anderson, B. 1991. *Imagined Communities*. 2nd edn. London: Verso.

Atkinson, D. 1991. 'Cities and citizenship: towards a normative analysis of the urban order in South Africa, with special reference to East London, 1950–1986', PhD thesis, University of Natal.

AYCO (Alexandra Youth Congress), n.d. *Constitution of AYCO*, unpublished.

Badcock, B. 1984. *Unfairly Structured Cities*. Oxford: Blackwell.

Badenhorst, C. M. and C. M. Rogerson. 1986. 'Teach the native to play: social control and organised black sport on the Witwatersrand 1920–1939', *Geojournal* 12 (2).

Ball, J. 1994. *The Ritual of the Necklace*. Johannesburg: Centre for the Study of Violence and Reconciliation.

Bapela, O. n.d. *A Short History of AYCO*, unpublished.

Bapela, M. S. W. n.d 'The People's Courts in a customary law perspective', unpublished paper.

Barker, L., A. Swart and G. Warren. 1986. 'The effects of the unrest on the lives of workers living in Alexandra', unpublished third year Research Project, Department of Sociology University of the Witwatersrand.

Barrell, H. 1984. 'The United Democratic Front and National Forum: their emergence, composition and trends', *South African Review 2*. Johannesburg: Ravan Press.

Barrell, H. 1988. 'The outlawed South African resistance movements', in S. Johnson (ed.), *South Africa: no turning back*. Basingstoke: MacMillan.

Barrell, H. 1990. *MK: the ANC's armed struggle*. Johannesburg: Penguin.

Barrell, H. 1991. 'The turn to the masses: the African National Congress' Strategic Review of 1978–9', *Journal of Southern African Studies* 18 (1).

Bayart, J.-F. 1993. *The State in Africa: the politics of the belly.* London: Longman.
Bayart, J.-F., S. Ellis and B. Hibou. 1999. *The Criminalisation of the State in Africa.* Oxford: J. Currey.
Benford, R. D. and S. A. Hunt. 1992. 'Dramaturgy and social movements: the social construction and communication of power', *Sociological Inquiry* 62.
Biko, B. S. (ed.). 1972. *Black Viewpoint.* Durban: Black Community Programmes.
Black Lawyers' Association. 1986. *Dark City: report on unrest in Alexandra,* pamphlet, Johannesburg: Black Lawyers' Association
Black Sash Transvaal Housing Committee's preliminary report on Alexandra (by G. Glover and G. Webster), n.d., mimeo.
Bloch, R. 1982. 'All little sisters got to try on big sister's clothes: the community council system in South Africa', seminar paper presented to the African Studies Institute, University of the Witwatersrand.
Boggs, C. 1976. *Gramsci's Marxism.* London: Pluto Press.
Boloch, G. 2000. 'Learning from populism: narrative analysis and social movement consciousness', paper presented at the American Sociological Association.
Bonner, P. 1985. '*Siyawugubha, Siyawugebhula Umhlaba ka Maspala* (We are digging, we are seizing great chunks of the municipality's land): popular struggles in Benoni, 1944–52', seminar paper presented to the African Studies Institute Seminar, University of the Witwatersrand.
Bonner, P. 1988. 'Family, crime and political consciousness on the East Rand', *Journal of Southern African Studies* 14 (3).
Bonner, P. 1990. 'The politics of black squatter movements on the Rand 1944–1952', *Radical History Review* 46 (7).
Bonner, P., I. Hofmeyr, D. James and T. Lodge (eds). 1989. *Holding their Ground: class, locality and culture in 20th century South Africa.* Johannesburg: Ravan Press.
Bozzoli, B. (ed.). 1979. *Labour, Townships and Protest.* Johannesburg: Ravan Press.
Bozzoli, B. 1983a. 'Marxism, feminism and South African Studies', *Journal of Southern African Studies* 9 (2)
Bozzoli, B. (ed.). 1983b. *Town and Countryside in the Transvaal: capitalist penetration and popular response.* Johannesburg: Ravan Press.
Bozzoli, B. 1987a. 'Class, community and ideology in the evolution of South African society', in B. Bozzoli (ed.), *Class, Community and Conflict: South African Perspectives.* Johannesburg: Ravan Press.
Bozzoli, B. (ed.). 1987b. *Class, Community and Conflict: South African Perspectives.* Johannesburg: Ravan Press.
Bozzoli, B. 1990. 'Intellectuals, audiences and histories: South African experiences, 1978–88', *Radical History Review* 46–7 [Winter]: 237–63, republished in J. Brown et al. (eds). 1991. *History from South Africa: alternative visions and practices.* Philadelphia: Temple University Press.
Bozzoli, B. 1991. *Women of Phokeng.* New York: Heinemann.
Bozzoli, B. 1998. 'Public ritual and private transition: the Truth Commission in Alexandra Township South Africa 1996', *African Studies* 57 (2).
Bozzoli, B. 2000. 'Why were the 1980s "millenarian"?: style, repertoire, space and authority in South Africa's black cities', *Journal of Historical Sociology* 13 (1).
Bozzoli, B. and P. Delius. 1991. 'Radical history and South African society' in J. Brown et al. (eds). *History from South Africa: alternative visions and practices.* Philadelphia: Temple University Press.
Brandel-Syrier, M. 1971. *Reeftown Elite.* London: Routledge and Kegan Paul.
Brown, J., P. Manning, K. Shapiro, J. Wiener, B. Bozzoli and P. Delius (eds). 1991. *History from South Africa: alternative visions and practices.* Philadelphia: Temple University Press.

Bundy, C. 1987. 'Street sociology and pavement politics: aspects of youth and student resistance in Cape Town 1985', *Journal of Southern African Studies* 13 (3).

Burman, S. and W. Scharf. 1990. 'Creating people's justice: street committees and people's courts in a South African city', *Law and Society Review* 24 (3).

Calderwood, D. M. 1953. *Native Housing in South Africa*. Johannesburg: University of the Witwatersrand.

Calhoun, C. (ed.). 1974. *Social Theory and the Politics of Identity*. Oxford: Blackwell.

Calteaux, K. 1994. 'A sociolinguistic analysis of a multilingual community', DLitt et Phil thesis, Rand Afrikaans University.

Campbell, C. 1992. 'Learning to kill: masculinity, the family and violence in Natal', *Journal of Southern African Studies* 18 (3).

Campbell, C. 1994. *Township Families and Youth Identity*, Report HG/MF-11. Pretoria: Human Sciences Research Council.

Canetti, E. 1962. *Crowds and Power*. London: Victor Gollancz.

Carter, C. E. 1991a. 'Comrades and community: politics and the construction of hegemony in Alexandra Township, South Africa 1984–7', unpublished PhD thesis, Oxford University.

Carter, C. E. 1991b. 'Community and conflict: the Alexandra Rebellion of 1986', *Journal of Southern African Studies* 18.

Carter, C. E. 1991c. '"We are the progressives": Alexandra Youth Congress activists and the Freedom Charter, 1983–5', *Journal of Southern African Studies* 17.

Carton, B. 2000. *Blood from your Children: the colonial origins of generational conflict in Southern Africa*. Charlottesville and London: University Press of Virginia.

Castells, M. 1977. *The Urban Question*. London: Edward Arnold.

Castells, M. 1983. *The City and the Grassroots*. Berkeley: University of California Press.

Cell, J. 1982. *Segregation: the highest stage of white supremacy*. Cambridge: Cambridge University Press.

Charney, C. 1994. 'A world of networks: power, political culture, and collective action in black South African communities 1945–65', History Workshop conference 'Democracy: popular precedents, practice, culture', University of the Witwatersrand.

Christopher, A. J. 1994. *The Atlas of Apartheid*. London: Routledge.

Cobb, R. 1970. *The Police and the People: French popular protest 1789–1820*. Oxford: Oxford University Press.

Cobbett, W. and R. Cohen (eds). 1988. *Popular Struggles in South Africa*. London: James Currey.

Cobley, A. G. 1997. *The Rules of the Game: struggles in black recreation and social welfare policy in South Africa*. Westport, CT: Greenwood Press.

Cohen, A. 1985. *The Symbolic Construction of Community*. Chichester: E. Horwood.

Cohen, J. L. 1985. 'Strategy or identity: new theoretical paradigms and contemporary social movements', *Social Research* 52.

Cohen, R. 1980. 'Resistance and hidden forms of consciousness amongst African workers', *Review of African Political Economy* 19.

Connell, P. H., C. Irvine-Smith, K. Jones, R. Kantorovich and F. J. Wepener. 1939. 'Native housing: a collective thesis', Witwatersrand University Press, Johannesburg.

Cooper, F. 1983. *Struggle for the City: migrant labour, capital and the state in Africa*. Beverley Hills: Sage.

Couzens, T. 1979. Introduction to the stories of Modikwe Dikobe, in B. Bozzoli (ed.). *Labour, Townships and Protest*. Johannesburg: Ravan Press.

Couzens, T. 1983. 'An introduction to the history of football in South Africa', in B. Bozzoli (ed.), *Town and Countryside in the Transvaal*. Johannesburg: Ravan Press.

Crossley, N. 2000. 'Working Utopias and social movements: an investigation using case study materials from radical mental health movements in Britain', paper presented to the British Sociological Association Annual Conference.

Crush, J. 1993. 'Scripting the compound: power and space in the South African mining industry', *Society and Space* 12.

Cumbler, J. T. 1979. *Class and Community in Industrial America: work, leisure and struggle in two industrial cities 1880–1930*. Westport, CT: Greenwood Press.

Cutten, P. 1951. 'The planning of a native township', *Race Relations Journal* 18 (2).

Davidson, B. 1952. *Report on Southern Africa*. London: Jonathan Cape.

Damoyi, P. 1986. 'We must ensure houses for all', *Work in Progress*, 44, September/October.

Davies, R. J. 1981. 'The spatial formation of the South African city', *Geojournal*, supplementary issue 2.

Davis, S. 1987. *Apartheid's Rebels: inside South Africa's hidden war*. New Haven: Yale University Press.

Delius, P. 1996. *A Lion amongst the Cattle*. Johannesburg: Ravan Press.

Dennis, N., F. Henriques and C. Slaughter. 1956. *Coal is our Life*. London: Eyre and Spottiswoode.

Diani, M. 1996. 'Linking mobilization frames and political opportunities: insights from regional populism in Italy', *American Sociological Review* 61.

Dikobe, M. 1973. *The Marabi Dance*. Oxford: Heinemann.

Dikobe, M. 1979. 'We shall walk' and 'The people overflow: a tribute to Schreiner', in B. Bozzoli (ed.), *Labour, Townships and Protest*. Johannesburg: Ravan Press.

Dissel, A. 1999. 'Youth, gangsterism and violence', Johannesburg: Centre for the Study of Violence and Reconciliation.

Doherty, J., E. Graham and M. Malek. (eds). 1992. *Postmodernism and the Social Sciences*. Basingstoke: Macmillan.

Donham, D. 1993. 'A note on space in the Ethiopian revolution', *Africa* 63 (4).

Donzelot, J. 1979. *The Policing of Families*. New York: Pantheon.

Durkheim, E. 1915. *The Elementary Forms of the Religious Life: a study in religious sociology*, trans. J. W. Swain. New York: Macmillan.

Edgar, R. R. (ed.). 1992. *An African American in South Africa: the travel notes of Ralph J. Bunche, 28 September 1937–1 January 1938*. Athens, OH: Ohio University Press.

Eisenstadt, S. N. 1956. *From Generation to Generation: age groups and social structure*. Glencoe, NY: The Free Press.

Esherick, J. W. and J. N. Wasserstrom. 1990. 'Acting out democracy: political theatre in modern China', *Journal of Asian Studies* 49 (4), November.

Fanon, F. 1967. *Black Skin, White Masks*. New York: Grove Weidenfeld.

Fanon, F. 1968. *The Wretched of the Earth*. New York: Grove Press.

Fanon, F. 1970. *A Dying Colonialism*. Harmondsworth: Penguin.

Feldman, A. 1991. *Formations of Violence: the narrative of the body and political terror in Northern Ireland*. Chicago and London: University of Chicago Press.

Floyd, T. B. 1951. *Township Layout*. Pietermaritzburg: Shuter and Shooter.

Fortier, A.-M. 1999. 'Space, place and icons: the shaping and negotiation of belonging(s)'. http//www.Lancaster.ac.uk/sociology.soc018af.html. March.

Foster, J. 1974. *Class Struggle and the Industrial Revolution*. London: Weidenfeld and Nicolson.

Foucault, M. 1977. *Discipline and Punish*. Harmondsworth: Penguin.

Frankel, P., N. Pines and M. Swilling (eds). 1988. *State, Resistance and Change in South Africa*. Johannesburg: Southern Books.

Frankenberg, R. 1966. *Communities in Britain*. Harmondsworth: Penguin.

Frederickse, J. 1986. *South Africa: a different kind of war*. Johannesburg: Ravan Press.

French, K. 1983. 'James Mpanza and the Sofasonke Party in the development of local politics in Soweto', MA thesis, University of the Witwatersrand.

Genovese, E. D. 1976. *Roll, Jordan, Roll*. New York: Vintage Books.

Gerhart, G. 1978. *Black Power in South Africa*. Berkeley and Los Angeles: University of California Press.

Geschwender, J. A. (ed.). 1971. *The Black Revolt: the civil rights movement, ghetto uprisings and separatism*. Englewood Cliffs: Prentice Hall.

Giddens, A. 1987. *The Constitution of Society: outline of a theory of structuration*. Cambridge: Polity Press.

Glaser, C. 1990a. 'Anti-social bandits, juvenile delinquency and the tsotsis: youth gang subculture on the Witwatersrand 1935–1960', unpublished MA dissertation, University of the Witwatersrand.

Glaser, C. 1990b. 'Anti-social bandits: culture, resistance and the tsotsi subculture on the Witwatersrand during the 1940s and 1950s', African Studies Institute seminar paper, University of the Witwatersrand.

Glaser, C. 1994. 'Youth culture and politics in Soweto, 1958–76', PhD thesis, Darwin College, Cambridge.

Glaser, C. 2000. *Botsotsi: the Youth Gangs of Soweto, 1935–76*. Portsmouth, NH: Heinemann.

Gobey, E., L. Guslandi and T. Waspe. 1984. 'Tomorrow *Azikwelwa*: this is your struggle, let's work together: Alexandra bus boycott January–February 1984', unpublished third year research project, University of the Witwatersrand.

Goffman, E. 1959. *The Presentation of Self in Everyday Life*. New York: Doubleday.

Goffman, E. 1961. *Asylums*. Harmondsworth: Penguin.

Goodhew, D. 1991. 'A history of the western areas of Johannesburg *c*.1930–55', DPhil thesis, Oxford University.

Gould, R. V. 1995. *Insurgent Identities: class, community and protest in Paris from 1848 to the commune*. Chicago and London: University of Chicago Press.

Gregory, D. and J. Urry. 1985. *Social Relations and Spatial Structures*. Basingstoke: Macmillan.

Grinaker, D. 1986. *Inside Soweto*. Johannesburg: Eastern Enterprises.

Gutman, I. 1982. *The Jews of Warsaw, 1939–43: ghetto, underground, revolt*. Brighton: Harvester.

Habermas, J. 1989. *The Structural Transformation of the Public Sphere*. Cambridge, MA: MIT Press.

Haggie, D. 1994. *Madam Chair and the House at Large: the story of ASHA, the African Self-Help Association*. Johannesburg: ASHA.

Hall, S., J. Clarke, T. Jefferson and B. Roberts. 1976. 'Subcultures, cultures and class', in S. Hall and T. Jefferson (eds), *Resistance through Rituals*, London: Hutchinson.

Harvey, D. 1985. *Consciousness and the Urban Experience*. Oxford: Basil Blackwell.

Harvey, D. 1989. *The Condition of Postmodernity*. Oxford: Basil Blackwell.

Haysom, N. 1987. 'Licence to kill: the South African police and the use of deadly force', *South African Journal of Human Rights* 3 (1).

Hebdige, D. 1979. *Subculture: the Meaning of Style*. London: Methuen and Co.

Hellman, E. 1940. *Problems of Urban Bantu Youth*. Johannesburg: South African Institute of Race Relations.

Hellman, E. 1948: 'Rooiyard: a sociological survey of an urban native slumyard', *Rhodes Livingstone Institute papers*, 13. Cape Town: Oxford University Press.

Hellman, E. 1978. *Soweto: Johannesburg's African city.* Johannesburg: South African Institute of Race Relations.

Hill, C. 1972. *The World Turned Upside Down: traditional ideas during the English Revolution.* London: Temple Smith.

Hindson, D. 1987. *Pass Controls and the Urban African Proletariat.* Johannesburg: Ravan Press.

Hobsbawm, E. J. 1971. *Primitive Rebels: studies in archaic forms of social movement in the 19th and 20th centuries.* Manchester: Manchester University Press.

Hobsbawm, E. J. 1990. *Nations and Nationalism since 1780: programme, myth, reality.* Cambridge: Cambridge University Press.

Horrell, M. 1956. *The Group Areas' Act and its Effect on Human Beings.* Johannesburg: South African Institute of Race Relations.

Horrell, M. 1978. *Laws Affecting Race Relations in South Africa.* Johannesburg: South African Institute of Race Relations.

Horwitz, R. 1967. *The Political Economy of South Africa.* London: Weidenfeld and Nicolson.

Houghton, D. H. 1973. *The South African Economy.* Oxford: Oxford University Press.

Hund, J. and M. Kotu-Rammopo. 1983. 'Justice in a South African township: the sociology of Makgotla', *Comparative and International Law Journal of Southern Africa* 16.

Hunter, A. 1974. *Symbolic Communities.* Chicago: University of Chicago Press.

Hyslop, J. 1999. *The Classroom Struggle: policy and resistance in South Africa.* Pietermaritzburg: University of Natal Press.

Isserow, M. and D. Everatt. 1998. *Determining our own Development: a community-based socio-economic profile of Alexandra.* Johannesburg: Community Agency for Social Enquiry (CASE).

Jeffrey, I. 1985. 'Their will to survive: a socio-historical study of the Sharpetown swingsters', Honours thesis, University of the Witwatersrand.

Jeffrey, Ian 1991. 'Cultural trends and community formation in a South African township, Sharpeville, 1943–1985', MA thesis, University of the Witwatersrand.

Jochelson, K. 1988a. 'Urban crisis, state reform and popular reaction. a case study of Alexandra', BA Honours dissertation, Department of Sociology, University of the Witwatersrand.

Jochelson, K. 1988b. 'People's power and state reform in Alexandra', *Work in Progress*, 56–7.

Jochelson, K. 1990. 'Reform, repression and resistance in South Africa: a case study of Alexandra township 1979–89', *Journal of Southern African Studies* 16 (1).

Johnson, S. n.d. 'Soldiers of Luthuli: youth in the politics of resistance in South Africa', unpublished m: 33–4.

Johnson, S. 1988. *South Africa: no turning back.* London: Macmillan.

Jones, K. n.d. 'Contention and Cape Town civics in South Africa's transition', paper downloaded from http: //www.sociology.columbia.edu/

Kane-Berman, J. 1978. *Soweto: black revolt–white reaction.* Johannesburg: Ravan Press.

Katznelson, I. 1981. *City Trenches: urban politics and the patterning of class in the United States.* New York: Pantheon.

Keith, M. and S. Pile (eds). 1993. *Place and the Politics of Identity.* London and New York: Routledge.

Klandermans, B. 1997. *The Social Psychology of Protest.* Oxford: Blackwell.

Koch, E. 1983. 'Doornfontein and its African working class, 1914–1935', MA thesis, University of the Witwatersrand.

Kramer, J. n.d. 'Self-help in Soweto: mutual aid societies in a South African city', MA dissertation, University of Bergen, Norway.

Kuper, L. 1968. 'The political situation of non-whites in South Africa', in W. Hance (ed.), *Southern Africa and the United States*. New York: Columbia University Press.

Kynoch, G. 1999. 'From the Ninevites to the Hard Livings Gang: township gangsters and urban violence in twentieth century South Africa', *African Studies* 58 (1).

LACOM. 1989. *Comrade Moss*. Johannesburg: Learn and Teach Publications.

Lamont, T. M. with T. Augustyn and S. Marais. n.d. *Preliminary Report on a Socio-Economic Survey done in Alexandra*, unpublished.

Lash, S. and J. Urry. 1994. *Economies of Signs and Space*. London: Sage.

Lebello, S. 1987. 'The destruction of Sophiatown', Honours dissertation, University of the Witwatersrand.

Le Bon, G. 1977. *The Crowd: a study of the popular mind*. New York: Penguin.

Lefebvre, H. 1991. *The Production of Space*. Oxford: Blackwell.

Lemon, A. (ed.). 1991. *Homes apart: South Africa's segregated cities*. London: Paul Chapman.

Levi-Strauss, C. 1978. *Structural Anthropology*. Harmondsworth: Penguin.

Lewis, P. 1972. *Soweto: city within a city*. Johannesburg: South African Institute of Race Relations.

Lockwood, D. 1966. 'Sources of variation in working class images of society', *Sociological Review* 14 (2).

Lodge, T. 1983. *Black Politics in South Africa since 1945*. Johannesburg: Ravan Press.

Lodge, T. 1988. 'State of exile: the African National Congress of South Africa, 1976–86', in P. Frankel, N. Pines and M. Swilling (eds), *State, Resistance and Change in South Africa*. Johannesburg: Southern Books.

Lodge, T. and Nasson, B. 1991. *All, Here, and Now: black politics in South Africa in the 1980s*. New York: Ford Foundation and Foreign Policy Association.

Lucas, J. 1995. 'Space, society and culture: housing and local level politics in a section of Alexandra Township 1991–1992', unpublished MA thesis, University of the Witwatersrand.

Maasdorp, G. and R. Humphreys. 1975. *From Shantytown to Township*. Cape Town: Juta.

Mabin, A. 1989. 'Struggle for the city: urbanization and political strategies of the South African state', *Social Dynamics* 15.

Mabin, A. 1991. 'Origins of segregatory urban planning in South Africa, 1900–1940', *Planning History* 13.

Mabin, A. 1993. 'Bureaucracy, class and design; the planning of the townships from the forties to the nineties', paper presented to the 1993 History Workshop/Sociology of Work symposium, 'Work, Class and Culture', Johannesburg.

Mamdani, M. 1996. *Subject and Citizen: Contemporary Africa and the Legacy of Late Colonialism*. Princeton: Princeton University Press.

Manganyi, N. and A. du Toit (eds). 1990. *Political Violence and the Struggle in South Africa*. London: Macmillan.

Mangcu, X. 1993. 'Social movements and city planning', unpublished paper.

Mannheim, K. 1972. 'The problem of generations', in P. G. Altbach and R. S. Laufer (eds), *The New Pilgrims: Youth Protest in Transition*. New York: David McKay.

Manoim, I. 1983. 'The black press 1945–63', MA dissertation, University of the Witwatersrand.

Mannoni, O. 1956. *Prospero and Caliban: the psychology of colonization*. London: Methuen.

Marden, P. 1997. 'Geographies of dissent: globalisation, identity and the nation', *Political Geography* 16.

Marks, M. 1994. 'Organisation, identity and violence amongst activist Diepkloof youth 1985–1993', MA thesis, University of the Witwatersrand.

Marks, M. 1995. '"We are fighting for the liberation of our people": justifications of violence by activist youth in Diepkloof, Soweto', paper presented at the Institute for Advanced Social Research, University of the Witwatersrand.

Marks, M. 2001. *Young Warriors: youth politics, identity and violence in South Africa.* Johannesburg: Witwatersrand University Press.

Marks, S. and S. Trapido (eds). 1987. *The Politics of Race, Class and Nationalism in Twentieth-Century South Africa.* London: Longman.

Marks, S. and S. Trapido. 1991. 'Introduction', *Journal of Southern African Studies* 18 (1).

Marston, S. A. 1989. 'Public rituals and community power: St Patrick's Day parades in Lowell, Massachussets, 1841–1874', *Political Geography Quarterly* 8 (3).

Marx, K. 1963. *The Eighteenth Brumaire of Louis Bonaparte.* New York: International Publishers.

Marx, K. and F. Engels. 1972. 'The manifesto of the Communist Party', in R. Tucker (ed.), *The Marx-Engels Reader.* 2nd edn. New York: Norton.

Massey, D. 1994. *Space, Place and Gender.* Cambridge: Polity Press.

Mathabane, M. 1986. *Kaffir Boy: the true story of a black youth's coming of age in apartheid South Africa.* New York: Macmillan.

Mayekiso, Mzwanele. n.d. 'Civic struggles for a new South Africa: the making of a social movement in Alexandra Township', unpublished ms, unnumbered pages.

Mayekiso, Mzwanele. 1996. *Township Politics: civic struggles for a new South Africa,* Patrick Bond (ed.). New York: Monthly Review Press.

Mayer, P. 1961. *Townsmen or Tribesmen: conservatism and the process of urbanisation.* Cape Town: Oxford University Press.

Maylam, P. 1990. 'The local evolution of urban apartheid: influx control and segregation in Durban 1900–1951', paper presented to the History Workshop conference 'Structure and Experience in the Making of Apartheid', University of the Witwatersrand.

Memmi, A. 1965: *The Colonizer and the Colonized.* Boston: Beacon.

Meierhenrich, J. 2000. 'Agents, structure, exit, voice: apartheid's endgame and the state', paper presented to the Beofer Center for Science and International Affairs, John F. Kennedy School of Government, Harvard University, Boston.

McAdam, D., J. D. McCarthy and M. N. Zald (eds). 1996. *Comparative Perspectives on Social Movements: political opportunities, mobilizing structures and cultural framings.* New York: Cambridge University Press.

Modise, S. S. 1996. *Dark City: the origin and development of Alexandra Township,* author's publication.

Mogotsi, I. n.d. *The Alexandra Tales.* Johannesburg: Ravan Press.

Molteno, F. n.d. 'Reflections on Resistance: aspects of the 1980 students' boycott', unpublished paper.

Mothibedi, D. n.d. unpublished autobiography.

Modibedi, E. T. n.d. 'Justice in the People's Court in Mamelodi Township', mimeo.

Moore, J. and R. Barrington. 1978. *Injustice: the social bases of obedience and revolt.* New York: Macmillan.

Morris, A. D. 1984. *The Origins of the Civil Rights Movement: black communities organizing for change.* New York: Free Press.

Morris, A. et al. 1999. *Change and Continuity: a survey of Soweto in the late 1990s.* Johannesburg: Department of Sociology, University of the Witwatersrand.

Morris, P. 1981. *A History of Black Housing in South Africa.* Johannesburg: South Africa Foundation.

Motshekga, M. 1987. 'Alternative legal institutions in Southern Africa', paper read at a workshop on New Approaches in respect of the administration of justice, University of South Africa.

Mphahlele, E. 1959. *Down Second Avenue.* London: Faber and Faber.

Murray, M. 1987. *South Africa: Time of agony, time of destiny.* London: Verso.

Nauright, J. n.d. unpublished, untitled ms on the history of Alexandra township, 1912–1945.

Nauright, J. 1998. 'The Mecca of native scum and a running sore of evil: white Johannesburg and the Alexandra Township removal debate, 1935–1945', *Kleio.*

Ndletyana, M. 1998. 'Changing role of civic organisations from the apartheid to the post-apartheid era: a case study of the Alexandra Civic Organisation (ACO)', MA thesis, University of the Witwatersrand.

Nina, D. 1992. *Popular Justice in a 'New South Africa': from people's courts to community courts in Alexandra.* Johannesburg: University of the Witwatersrand, Centre for Applied Legal Studies.

Nkosi, T. n.d. *The Time of the Comrades.* Johannesburg: Skotaville Publishers.

Nolotshungu, S. 1982. *Changing South Africa: political considerations.* Manchester: Manchester University Press.

Ntshangase, K. D. 1993. 'The social history of Iscamtho', MA thesis, University of the Witwatersrand.

O'Dowd, M. C. 1991. *South Africa: the growth imperative.* Johannesburg: Jonathan Ball.

O'Dowd, M. C. 1996. *The O'Dowd Thesis and the Triumph of Liberal Capitalism.* Sandton: Free Market Foundation.

Omond, R. 1986. *The Apartheid Handbook.* Harmondsworth: Penguin.

Pauw, B. A. 1979. *The Second Generation.* Cape Town: Oxford University Press.

Pickering, W. S. F. 1984. *Durkheim's Sociology of Religion: themes and theories.* London: Routledge and Kegan Paul.

Pile, S. and M. Keith (eds). 1997. *Geographies of Resistance.* London and New York: Routledge.

Pillay, P. N. 1984. 'Alexandra: an analysis of socio-economic conditions in an urban ghetto', Carnegie Conference Paper 19. Cape Town: SALDRU.

Posel, D. 1984. 'Language, legitimation and control: the South African state after 1978', *Social Dynamics* 10 (1).

Posel, D. 1991. *The Making of Apartheid 1948–1961: conflict and compromise.* Oxford: Clarendon Press.

Posel, D. 1996. 'Modernity and measurement: further thoughts on the apartheid state', seminar paper, Institute for Advanced Social Research, University of the Witwatersrand.

Ramagaga, S. M. 1988. 'The contributions of the Holy Cross Sisters to black schooling in Alexandra, Johannesburg, with particular reference to the period 1950–1970', MEd research report, University of the Witwatersrand.

Ratcliffe, S. T. 1981. 'Alexandra Township: an alternative redevelopment', B.Arch thesis, University of the Witwatersrand.

Rauch, J. 1998. 'A survey of police commissioners' attitudes towards crime and violence', Johannesburg: Centre for the study of Violence and Reconciliation.

Rex, J. 1974. 'The compound, the reserve and the urban location: the essential institutions of Southern African labour exploitation', *South African Labour Bulletin* 1.

Ritchken, E. 1987. 'Burning the herbs: youth politics and witches in Lebowa', *Work in Progress*, 48, July.

Roberts, R. 1973. *The Classic Slum*. Harmondsworth: Penguin.

Robinson, J. n.d. 'Progressive Port Elizabeth: liberal politics, local economic development and the territorial basis of racial domination 1923–1935', unpublished paper.

Robinson, J. 1990. '"A perfect system of control"? Territory and administration in early South African locations', *Society and Space* 8.

Robinson, J. 1992a. 'Power, space and the city: historical reflections on apartheid and post-apartheid social orders', in D.M. Smith (ed.), *The Apartheid City and Beyond: urbanization and social change in South Africa*. London: Routledge.

Robinson, J. 1992b. 'Administrative strategies and political power in South Africa's black townships, 1930–1960', *Urban Forum* 2.

Robinson, J. 1996. *The Power of Apartheid: state, power and space in South African cities*. Oxford: Butterworth-Heinemann.

Rossi, P. H. (ed.). 1970. *Ghetto Revolts*. No place of publication, Aldine.

Rudé, G. 1959. *The Crowd in the French Revolution*. Oxford: Clarendon Press.

Rudé, G. 1964. *The Crowd in History: a study of popular disturbances in France and England, 1730–1848*. New York: J. Wiley.

Rudé, G. 1980. *Ideology and Popular Protest*. New York: Pantheon.

Ruiters, G. 1995. 'South African liberation politics: a case study of collective action and leadership in Katorus, 1980–1989', MA thesis, University of the Witwatersrand.

Sapire, H. J. 1987. 'The stay-away of the Brakpan location 1944' in B. Bozzoli (ed.), *Class, Community and Conflict*. Johannesburg: Ravan Press.

Sapire, H. J. 1988. 'African urbanisation and struggles against municipal control in Brakpan, 1920–1958', PhD thesis, University of the Witwatersrand

Sarakinsky, M. 1984. 'From freehold township to model township: a political history of Alexandra, 1905–1983', unpublished Honours dissertation, University of the Witwatersrand.

Saul, J. and S. Gelb. 1981. *The Crisis in South Africa: class defense, class revolution*. New York: Monthly Review Press.

Scharf, W. 1988. 'Images of punishment in the people's court of Cape Town', unpublished paper.

Scharf, W. and B. Ngcokoto. 1990. 'Images of punishment in the people's courts of Cape Town, 1985–7', in N. C. Manganyi and A. du Toit (eds), *Political Violence and the Struggle in South Africa*. Johannesburg: Southern Books.

Schlemmer, L. 1968. *The Negro Riots and South African Cities*. Johannesburg: South African Institute of Race Relations.

Schoonraad, M. 1995. 'Mamelodi: a culturally based analysis of the perception and usage of space by township dwellers', Masters thesis, University of the Witwatersrand.

Scott, J. 1976. *The Moral Economy of the Peasant: rebellion and subsistence in South East Asia*. New Haven: Yale University Press.

Scott, J. 1985. *Weapons of the Weak: everyday forms of peasant resistance*. New Haven: Yale University Press.

Scott, J. 1990. *Domination and the Arts of Resistance: hidden transcripts*. New Haven: Yale University Press.

Seekings, J. n.d. 'Summary thematic account of the East Rand 1978–1984', unpublished paper.

Seekings, J. 1988. 'Political mobilisation in the black townships of the Transvaal', in P. Frankel, N. Pines and M. Swilling (eds), *State, Resistance and Change in South Africa*. Johannesburg: Southern Books.

Seekings, J. 1989a. 'People's courts and popular politics', *South African Review* 5.

Johannesburg: Ravan Press.

Seekings, J. 1989b. 'People's courts in the PWV: an historical and sociological perspective', paper delivered to the Southern Africa History and Politics seminar, Oxford.

Seekings, J. 1990. 'Quiescence and the transition to confrontation: South African townships 1978–84', DPhil thesis, University of Oxford.

Seekings, J. 1991a. '"Trailing behind the masses": the United Democratic Front and township politics in the Pretoria–Witwatersrand–Vaal Region, 1983–4', *Journal of Southern African Studies* 18 (1).

Seekings, J. 1991b. 'Gender ideology and township politics in the 1980s', *Agenda*, 10.

Seekings, J. 1993. *Heroes or Villains? Youth politics in the 1980s*. Johannesburg: Ravan Press.

Seekings, J. 2000. *The UDF: a history of the United Democratic Front in South Africa, 1983–2001*. Cape Town: David Philip.

Serote, M. W. 1981a. 'Alexandra', in M. Chapman (ed.), *A Century of South African Poetry*. Johannesburg: Ad Donker.

Serote, M. W. 1981b. *To Every Birth its Blood*. Johannesburg: Ravan Press.

Sewell, W. H. 1996. 'Historical events as transformations of structures: inventing revolution at the Bastille', *Theory and Society* 25.

Shubane, K. n.d. 'The Soweto rent boycott', BA Honours dissertation, University of the Witwatersrand.

Sitas, A. 1992. 'The making of the comrades' movement in Natal 1985–91', *Journal of Southern African Studies* 18 (3).

Slabbert, S. 1994. 'A re-evaluation of the sociology of Tsotsitaal', *South African Journal of Linguistics* 12 (1).

Sluka, J. A. 1996. 'The writing's on the wall: peace process images, symbols and murals in Northern Ireland', *Critique of Anthropology* 16 (4).

Smith, D. M. (ed.). 1992. *The Apartheid City and Beyond: urbanization and social change in South Africa*. London: Routledge.

Snow, D. A., L. A. Zurcher and R. Peters. 1981. 'Victory celebrations as theater: a dramaturgical approach to crowd behaviour', *Symbolic Interaction*, vol. 4.

Snow, D. E. and R. Benford. 1992. 'Master frames and cycles of protest', in A. Morris and C. McC. Mueller (eds), *Frontiers in Social Movement Theory*. New Haven, CT: Yale University Press.

South African Institute of Race Relations. 1987. *Race Relations Survey, 1986*. Johannesburg: SAIRR.

Southern African Catholic Bishops' Conference. 1984. *Report on Police Conduct during Township Protests*. Johannesburg: SACBC.

Stadler, A. W. 1979. 'Birds in the cornfields: squatter movements in Johannesburg 1944–47', in B. Bozzoli (ed.), *Labour, Townships and Protest*. Johannesburg: Ravan Press.

Stavrou, P. n.d. *The Alexandra Community Crime Survey: a study of the perceptions and fear of crime of the residents in an area of Alexandra*. Johannesburg: Centre for the Study of Violence and Reconciliation.

Stedman-Jones, G. 1974. 'Working class culture and working class politics in London 1870–1900', *Journal of Social History* 7 (4).

Straker, G. 1992. *Faces in the Revolution*. Cape Town and Athens, OH: David Philip and Ohio University Press.

Suttles, G. D. 1968. *The Social Order of the Slum*. Chicago: Chicago University Press.

Suttles, G. D. 1972. *The Social Construction of Communities*. Chicago: Chicago University Press.

Suttner, R. 1986. 'Popular justice in South Africa today', paper presented to Socio-
    logy Department, University of the Witwatersrand.
Swanson, M. 1977. 'The sanitation syndrome: bubonic plague and urban native
    policy in the Cape Colony, 1900–1909', *Journal of African History* 18 (3).
Swilling, M. 1986. 'The United Democratic Front and township revolt', in W.
    Cobbett and R. Cohen (eds), *Popular Struggles in South Africa*. New Jersey:
    Africa World Press.
Swilling, M. 1994. 'Urban control and changing forms of political conflict in Uiten-
    hage, 1977–86', PhD thesis, University of Warwick.
Tarrow, S. 1996. 'The people's two rhythms: Charles Tilly and the study of conten-
    tious politics, a review article', *Comparative Studies in Society and History* 38
    (4).
Tarrow, S. 1998. *Power in Movement: social movements and contentious politics.*
    Cambridge: Cambridge University Press.
Thompson, E. P. 1967. 'Time, work discipline and industrial capitalism', *Past and
    Present* 36.
Thompson, E. P. 1968. *The Making of the English Working Class*. Harmondsworth:
    Penguin.
Thompson, E. P. 1971. 'The moral economy of the English crowd in the eighteenth
    century', *Past and Present* 50.
Thompson, L. M. 1966. *Politics in the Republic of South Africa*. Boston, MA: Little
    Brown.
Thrift, N. J. 1996. *Spatial Formations*. London: Sage.
Tilly, C., L. Tilly and R. Tilly. 1975. *The Rebellious Century, 1830–1930*. Cambridge,
    MA: Harvard University Press.
Tilly, C. 1978. *From Mobilization to Revolution*. Reading, MA: Addison-Wesley.
Tilly, C. 1995. *Popular Contention in Great Britain, 1758–1834*. Cambridge, MA:
    Harvard University Press.
Tilly, L. and C. Tilly (eds). 1981. *Class Conflict and Collective Action*. Beverley Hills,
    CA: Sage.
Tourikis, P. 1981. 'The political economy of Alexandra Township 1905–58', BA
    Honours dissertation, University of the Witwatersrand.
Traugott, M. 1995. 'Barricades as repertoire: continuities and discontinuities in the
    history of French contention', in M. Traugott (ed.), *Repertoires and Cycles of
    Collective Action*. Durham, NC: Duke University Press.
Truth and Reconciliation Commission. n.d. 'Truth: the road to reconciliation',
    pamphlet: TRC.
Truth and Reconciliation Commission. 1998. Report vols 1–5. Cape Town: TRC.
Turner, V. W. 1974. *Dramas, Fields, and Metaphors*. New York: Cornell University
    Press.
Turner, V. W. 1986. *The Anthropology of Performance*. New York: Paj Publications.
Urban Foundation. n.d. 'The black Town Councils: a study of their performance
    and reception in the urban black communities', unpublished paper.
Van den Berghe, P. L. 1965. *South Africa: a study in conflict*. Middletown, CT:
    Wesleyan University Press.
Van Onselen, C. 1976. *Chibaro: African mine labour in Southern Rhodesia, 1900–1933.*
    London: Pluto.
Wacquant, L. J. D. 1994. 'The new urban color line: the state and fate of the ghetto
    in post-Fordist America', in Craig Calhoun (ed.), *Social Theory and the Politics
    of Identity*. Cambridge, MA: Blackwell.
Webster, G. and G. Glover. 1984. *Alexandra*. November: The Black Sash.
Wells, J. 1983. '"The day the town stood still": women in resistance in Potchef-

stroom 1912–1930', in B. Bozzoli (ed.), *Town and Countryside in the Transvaal*. Johannesburg: Ravan Press.

Whyte, W. F. 1943. *Street Corner Society*. Chicago: University of Chicago Press.

Wieworka, M. 1991. *L'Espace du Racisme*. Paris: Editions du Seuil.

Williams, R. 1976. *Keywords*. London: Fontana.

Williams, R. 1980. 'Base and superstructure in Marxist cultural theory', in *Problems in Materialism and Culture*. London: Verso.

Wilson, M. and A. Mafeje. 1973. *Langa*. Cape Town: Oxford University Press.

Wilson, R. A. 2001. *The Politics of Truth and Reconciliation in South Africa: legitimising the post-apartheid state*, Cambridge: Cambridge University Press.

Wilson, W. J. 1978. *The Declining Significance of Race*. Chicago: Chicago University Press.

Wilson, W. J. 1987. *The Truly Disadvantaged: the inner city, the underclass and public policy*. Chicago: Chicago University Press.

Wilson, W. J. 1997. *When Work Disappears: the world of the new urban poor*. New York: A. A. Knopf.

Wolf, E. 1969. *Peasant Wars of the Twentieth Century*. New York: Harper and Row.

Wolpe, H. 1974. 'Capitalism and cheap labour power in South Africa: from segregation to apartheid', *Economy and Society* 1.

Woolcock, S. 1998. 'Social capital and economic development: toward a theoretical synthesis and policy framework', *Theory and Society* 27.

Wuthnow, R. (ed.). 1992. *Vocabularies of Public Life: empirical essays in symbolic structure*. London and New York: Routledge.

Young, M. and P. Willmott. 1962. *Family and Kinship in East London*. Harmondsworth: Penguin.

POLICE RECORDS

Wynberg Police Station, Johannesburg, Incident Book, February 1986.

Wynberg Police Station, Ops Book, February 1986.

INTERVIEWS AND DISCUSSIONS

Advocate D. Soggott and the legal team in the Mayekiso trial during the course of 1988.

The accused, Mayekiso trial, during the course of 1988.

Z. van Zyl, prosecutor in the Zwane trial, October 1992.

Advocate Norman Kades, November 1993.

Ashwell Zwane, December 1993.

N. Manoim, February 1994.

S. S. Modise, February 1994

PERIODICALS

The African Communist
The Alexandra Chronicle
Alexandra Speak
City Press
Financial Mail
Isizwe
Izwi Lase Township
Mayibuye
New Nation
Sechaba
The Sowetan

Speak
The Star
Sunday Star
Sunday Times
Voice of AYCO
Weekly Mail

TRIAL TRANSCRIPTS

Supreme Court of South Africa (Witwatersrand Local Division), 1987, *The State vs. Moses J. Mayekiso, Paul N. Tshabalala, Richard M. Mdakane, Obed K. Bapela and Mzwanele Mayekiso*, before the Honourable Mr Justice van der Walt (Case No 115/87) ('Mayekiso trial'). References to extracts from the transcript of this trial are referred to by the name of the witness whose testimony is being quoted, an 'M' to indicate that it is the Mayekiso trial that is being referred to, and a page number.

Supreme Court of South Africa (Witwatersrand Local Division), 1987, *The State vs. Ashwell M. Zwane, Vusi A. Ngwenya, Andrew Mafutha, David Mafutha, Arthur S. Vilakazi, Albert A. Sebola, Piet Mogano and Phillemon C. Phalongwane*, before the Honourable Mr Justice Grosskopf (Case No. 50/87) ('Zwane trial'). References to extracts from the transcript of this trial are referred to by the name of the witness whose testimony is being quoted, a 'Z' to indicate that it is the Zwane trial that is being referred to, and a page number.

ATTORNEYS' ARCHIVES

Archives of Mayekiso treason trial, Cheadle Thompson and Haysom Attorneys, Johannesburg (referred to in Notes as 'CTH archives').

Archives of Zwane treason trial, Priscilla Jana and Associates Attorneys, Johannesburg (referred to in Notes as 'PJ archives').

INDEX

Wuthnow, R., 223

Xuma, A. B., 47

yards, yard system, 15, 22, 23–4, 43–4,
  68, 99, 107, 189–97, 212; *see also*
  committees
'Young Americans', The, 28
youth, youths, 2, 14, 17, 26, 38, 39,
  62–3, 66, 73, 81, 84–5, 91–2,
  93–114, 198, 210, 234
  1976 generation, 88–9, 102, 115–16
  marginalisation of, 262
  misremembering of, 256–75
  role after apartheid, 262–83
  see also adults, comrades, generation
youth clubs, 110
  Thusong, 111, 119–20

youth groups, 39, 97, 98, 105, 120,
  126–31, 135, 140–2, 145–6, 149,
  154, 244
  3rd Avenue, 131
  7th Avenue, 131
  8th Avenue (Mdakane), 105, 129–
  30, 148, 154
  15th Avenue, 101, 131, 157–8
  19th Avenue, 120, 130–1, 156–7
  see also people's courts

Zeelie, Lieutenant, 69
Zulu-speakers, 27
Zwane, Ashwell, 68, 99–101, 106, 113,
  130–2, 147, 153, 158, 160, 171–
  5
  as 'Mugabe', 101, 148, 172–4